OXFORD THEOLOGICAL MONOGRAPHS

Editorial Committee

M. McC. ADAMS
P. M. JOYCE
O. M. T. O'DONOVAN

M. J. EDWARDS
D. N. J. MACCULLOCH
C. C. ROWLAND

OXFORD THEOLOGICAL MONOGRAPHS

EZEKIEL AND THE ETHICS OF EXILE
Andrew Mein (2001)

THEODORE THE STOUDITE
The Ordering of Holiness
Roman Cholij (2002)

HIPPOLYTUS BETWEEN EAST AND WEST
The Commentaries and the Provenance of the Corpus
J. A. Cerrato (2002)

FAITH, REASON, AND REVELATION IN THE THOUGHT OF
THEODORE BEZA
Jeffrey Mallinson (2003)

RICHARD HOOKER AND REFORMED THEOLOGY
A Study of Reason, Will, and Grace
Nigel Voak (2003)

THE COUNTESS OF HUNTINGDON'S CONNEXION
Alan Harding (2003)

THE APPROPRIATION OF DIVINE LIFE IN CYRIL OF ALEXANDRIA
Daniel A. Keating (2004)

THE MACARIAN LEGACY
The Place of Macarius-Symeon in the Eastern Christian Tradition
Marcus Plested (2004)

PSALMODY AND PRAYER IN THE WRITINGS OF
EVAGRIUS PONTICUS
Luke Dysinger, OSB (2004)

ORIGEN ON THE SONG OF SONGS AS THE SPIRIT OF SCRIPTURE
The Bridegroom's Perfect Marriage-Song
J. Christopher King (2004)

AN INTERPRETATION OF HANS URS VON BALTHASAR
Eschatology as Communion
Nicholas J. Healy (2005)

DURANDUS OF ST POURÇAIN
A Dominican Theologian in the Shadow of Aquinas
Isabel Iribarren (2005)

The Troubles of Templeless Judah

JILL MIDDLEMAS

OXFORD
UNIVERSITY PRESS

Great Clarendon Street, Oxford OX2 6DP

Oxford University Press is a department of the University of Oxford.
It furthers the University's objective of excellence in research, scholarship,
and education by publishing worldwide in

Oxford New York

Auckland Cape Town Dar es Salaam Hong Kong Karachi
Kuala Lumpur Madrid Melbourne Mexico City Nairobi
New Delhi Shanghai Taipei Toronto

With offices in

Argentina Austria Brazil Chile Czech Republic France Greece
Guatemala Hungary Italy Japan Poland Portugal Singapore
South Korea Switzerland Thailand Turkey Ukraine Vietnam

Oxford is a registered trade mark of Oxford University Press
in the UK and in certain other countries

Published in the United States
by Oxford University Press Inc., New York

© Jill Middlemas 2005

The moral rights of the author have been asserted
Database right Oxford University Press (maker)

First published 2005

All rights reserved. No part of this publication may be reproduced,
stored in a retrieval system, or transmitted, in any form or by any means,
without the prior permission in writing of Oxford University Press,
or as expressly permitted by law, or under terms agreed with the appropriate
reprographics rights organization. Enquiries concerning reproduction
outside the scope of the above should be sent to the Rights Department,
Oxford University Press, at the address above

You must not circulate this book in any other binding or cover
and you must impose the same condition on any acquirer

British Library Cataloguing in Publication Data
Data available

Library of Congress Cataloging-in-Publication Data

Middlemas, Jill Anne, 1971–
The troubles of templeless Judah/Jill Middlemas.
p.cm.—(Oxford theological monographs)
Revision of the author's thesis (doctoral)—University of Oxford, 2003.
Includes Bibliographical references (p.   )and index.
ISBN 0-19-928386-9 (alk. paper)
1. Judaism—History—Post-exilic period 586 B.C–210 A.D. 2. Jews—History—586 B.C–
70 A.D. 3. Palestine—History—To 70 A.D. 4. Bible. O.T—Criticism, interpretation, etc.
I. Title. II. Series.
BM176. M53 2005
296'. 09' 04—dc22
2005018655

Typeset by SPI Publisher Services, Pondicherry, India
Printed in Great Britain on acid-free paper by
Biddles Ltd., King's Lynn

ISBN 0-19-928386-9   978-0-19-928386-6

1 3 5 7 9 10 8 6 4 2

Dedicated in memory of my mother
Kaye Clements Middlemas
1939–2000

Acknowledgements

Since being introduced to the period known conventionally in Old Testament studies as the exile by Professor Jim Newsome in 1994, I have been captivated by the events that surrounded the destruction of Jerusalem and the heroic efforts made by a community to maintain identity and faith in the face of disaster. Reflecting on the still important contribution to our knowledge of the exile and its literature by Peter Ackroyd—whose death early this year has saddened his colleagues—led me to recognize the need for a current study of the period, especially from the perspective of the population that was left behind in Judah after the collapse of Jerusalem in 587 BCE. In 1998, I set out to determine what could be known of this period from biblical literature and from critical scholarship. This publication represents the culmination of my efforts to recapture a voice lost in the biblical worldview and in the modern academic discussion. I would like to acknowledge with gratitude all those who contributed their time and support to the fulfilment of my endeavours.

At Oxford University, I owe a significant debt to Hugh Williamson, Regius Professor of Hebrew, who supervised my doctoral studies. I am grateful also to John Barton, The Oriel and Laing Professor of the Interpretation of Holy Scripture, who served as my Oxford University Press *Doktorvater*. Their advice and support have contributed significantly to my accomplishments. It is now my pleasure to call them colleagues.

Equally, I remember those who encouraged me to begin this process in the first place—Professors Walter Brueggemann, David Moessner, Jim Newsome, and Kathleen O'Connor. Many others deserve thanks for their willingness to share their expertise with me along the way. They include Professors Joe Blenkinsopp, Hans Barstad, and John Day, and Drs Stephanie Dalley and Diana Edelman. Worthy of special mention are Drs David Reimer who acted as the external examiner at the defence of my doctoral thesis on 15 December 2003 and Paul Joyce who serves as one of the editors of the

Oxford Theological Monograph series. Both provided helpful suggestions for the revision of my thesis into a book.

I am aware of how much the presence and encouragement of friends has prompted me to continue working even when events proved frustrating or prohibitive. In Oxford, I am particularly grateful to Drs Niels Dechow, Francesca Stavrakopoulou, and Alison Salvesen. In my hometown of Tallahassee, Florida, there is a cloud of witnesses at Christ Presbyterian Church who along with a dear friend, Rosa Lee Knight, are like an extended family to me.

Finally and most importantly, I recall the wisdom, love, and support I received from my parents—Robert and Kaye Middlemas—which have proved invaluable to me. They oversaw the pursuit of my career with interest—gently guiding and advising. It is my deepest sorrow that my mother was unable to see the accomplishment of my graduate work. Her joy in life could not be eclipsed by the suffering that accompanied her death. It is my hope that this book conveys a measure of my respect for her.

Jill Middlemas Dechow

April 2005

Contents

List of Abbreviations	x
Introduction	1
1. The Social and Historical Situation in Templeless Judah	24
2. Conceptions of Judah, I: Idolatrous Cults	72
3. Conceptions of Judah, II: Yahwistic Worship	122
4. The Voice of the Land: Lamentations	171
Conclusion	229
Bibliography	236
Index of Biblical References	273
Subject Index	284

Abbreviations

AASOR	Annual of the American Schools of Oriental Research
AB	Anchor Bible
ABC	A. K. Grayson, *Assyrian and Babylonian Chronicles* (TCS, 5; Locust Valley: J. J. Augustin, 1975)
ABD	D. N. Freedman *et al.* (eds.), *The Anchor Bible Dictionary*, 6 vols. (New York: Doubleday, 1992)
ABRL	Anchor Bible Reference Library
AJSLL	American Journal of Semitic Languages and Literatures
ALASP	Abhandlungen zur Literatur Alt-Syrien-Palestinas
AnBib	Analecta biblica
ANE	Ancient Near East
ANET[3]	J. B. Pritchard (ed.), *Ancient Near Eastern Texts Relating to the Old Testament* (Princeton: Princeton University Press, 3rd edn. 1969)
AOAT	Alter Orient und Altes Testament
AOS	American Oriental Series
AS	*Anatolian Studies*
ATD	Das Alte Testament Deutsch
AUS	American University Studies
AUSS	*Andrews University Seminary Studies*
BA	Biblical Archaeologist
BAR	Biblical Archaeology Review
BASOR	*Bulletin of the American Schools of Oriental Research*
BAIAS	*Bulletin of the Anglo-Israel Archaeological Society*
BBB	Bonner biblische Beiträge
BCR	Bibliotheca di Cultura Religiosa
BDB	F. Brown, S. R. Driver, and C. Briggs, *The New Brown-Driver-Briggs-Gesenius Hebrew and English Lexicon with an Appendix Containing the Biblical Aramaic* (Peabody: Hendrickson, 1979)
BE	Biblische Enzyklopädie

BEATAJ	Beiträge zur Erforschung des Alten Testaments und des antiken Judentums
BEHS	Bibliothèque de l'Ecole des Hautes Etudes: Section des Sciences religieuses
BETL	Bibliotheca ephemeridum theologicarum lovaniensium
BHS	*Biblia Hebraica Stuttgartensia* (ed. K. Elliger, W. Rudolph, *et al.*; Stuttgart: Deutsche Bibelgesellschaft, 4th edn. 1990)
Bib	*Biblica*
BibInt	*Biblical Interpretation*
BIS	Biblical Interpretation Series
BJS	Biblical and Judaic Studies
BKAT	Biblischer Kommentar. Altes Testament
BN	*Biblische Notizen*
BO	Biblica et Orientalia
BRev	*Bible Review*
BS	Biblical Seminar
BZ	*Biblische Zeitschrift*
BZAW	Beihefte zur Zeitschrift für die alttestamentliche Wissenschaft
CBET	Contributions to Biblical Exegesis and Theology
CBOT	Coniectanea biblica, Old Testament Series
CBQ	*Catholic Biblical Quarterly*
CHJ, i	W. D. Davies and L. Finkelstein (eds.), *Cambridge History of Judaism*, i: *Introduction: The Persian Period* (Cambridge: Cambridge University Press, 1984)
CR	Colloquium Rauricum
CTM	Calwer Theologische Monographien
COP	Cambridge Oriental Publications
DMOA	Documenta et Monumenta Orientis antiqui
EAEHL	M. Avi-Yonah (ed.), *Encyclopedia of Archaeology: Excavations in the Holy Land*, iii (Englewood Cliffs: Prentice-Hall, 1975)
EB	Etudes Bibliques
EF	Erträge der Forschung
EI	*Eretz Israel*
ESHM	European Seminar in Historical Methodology

ET	English translation
ET	*Evangelische Theologie*
ExpT	*Expository Times*
FAT	Forschungen zum Alten Testament
FOTL	Forms of the Old Testament Literature
FRLANT	Forschungen zur Religion und Literatur des Alten und Neuen Testaments
GKC	*Gesenius' Hebrew Grammar* (ed. and enlarged by E. Kautzsch, 2nd edn. by A. E. Cowley; Oxford: Clarendon Press, 1910)
GN	Geographical name
GTA	Göttinger theologische Arbeiten
HAT	Handbuch zum Alten Testament
HAW	Handbuch der Altertumswissenschaft
HB	Hebrew Bible
HBT	*Horizons in Biblical Theology*
HCOT	Historical Commentary on the Old Testament
HeyJ	*Heythrop Journal*
HKAT	Handkommentar zum Alten Testament
HR	*History of Religions*
HSM	Harvard Semitic Monograph
HSS	Harvard Semitic Studies
HTR	*Harvard Theological Review*
HUCA	*Hebrew Union College Annual*
IAOP	Institute of Archaeology Occasional Publication
IB	G. A. Buttrick *et al.* (eds.), *Interpreter's Bible*, 12 vols. (New York: Abingdon Press, 1956)
ICC	International Critical Commentary
IEJ	*Israel Exploration Journal*
Int	*Interpretation*
ISK	Instituttet for Sammenlignende kulturforskning
JANES	*Journal of Ancient Near Eastern Studies*
JAOS	*Journal of the American Oriental Society*
JARCE	*Journal of the American Research Center in Egypt*

JBL	*Journal of Biblical Literature*
JCS	*Journal of Cuneiform Studies*
JEA	*Journal of Egyptian Archaeology*
JJS	*Journal of Jewish Studies*
JNES	*Journal of Near Eastern Studies*
JQR	*Jewish Quarterly Review*
JR	*Journal of Religion*
JSJSup	Supplements to the Journal for the Study of Judaism
JSOT	*Journal for the Study of the Old Testament*
JSOTSup	Journal for the Study of the Old Testament Supplement Series
JSS	*Journal of Semitic Studies*
JSSM	Journal of Semitic Studies Monograph
JTS	*Journal of Theological Studies*
KAT	Kommentar zum Alten Testament
KHAT	Kürzer Hand-kommentar zum Alten Testament
LAI	Library of Ancient Israel
LBS	Library of Biblical Studies
LD	Lectio divina
LXX	Septuagint
MT	Masoretic Text
NABU	*Nouvelles assyriologiques brèves et utilitaires*
NCB	New Century Bible Commentary
NCBOT	New Century Bible Old Testament
NEAEHL	E. Stern *et al.* (eds.), *New Encyclopedia of Archaeological Excavations in the Holy Land* (New York: Simon & Schuster, 1993)
NRSV	New Revised Standard Version of the Bible
OBO	Orbis biblicus et orientalis
OBT	Overtures to Biblical Theology
OLP	*Orientalia lovaniensia periodica*
OTG	Old Testament Guides
OTL	Old Testament Library
OTS	Oudtestamentische Studiën
PEQ	*Palestine Exploration Quarterly*

POS	Pretoria Oriental Series
PTMS	Pittsburgh Theological Monograph Series
QD	Quaestiones disputatae
QGS	Quaderni di geografia storica
RB	*Revue Biblique*
RHPR	*Revue d'histoire et de philosophie religieuses*
SAK	*Studien zur Altägyptischen Kultur*
SBLDS	Society of Biblical Literature Dissertation Series
SBLMS	Society of Biblical Literature Monograph Series
SBT	Studies in Biblical Theology
SBTS	Sources for Biblical and Theological Study
SEÅ	*Svensk exegetisk årsbok*
SH	Scripta Hierosolymitana
SHANE	Studies in the History of the Ancient Near East
SJOT	*Scandinavian Journal of Old Testament*
SO	Symbolae osloenses
ST	Studies and Texts
STL	Studia Theologica Lundensia
SVT	Supplements to Vetus Testamentum
TA	*Tel Aviv*
TB	Theologische Bücherei
TCS	Texts from Cuneiform Sources
TR	Theology and Religion
TS	Theologica Studien
TTS	Trierer Theologische Studien
TynB	*Tyndale Bulletin*
UF	*Ugarit Forschungen*
UBL	Ugaritisch-biblische Literatur
VT	*Vetus Testamentum*
WBC	Word Bible Commentary
WMANT	Wissenschaftliche Monographien zum Alten und Neuen Testament

WVDOG	Wissenschaftliche Veröffentlichung der Deutschen Orient Gesellschaft
ZA	*Zeitschrift für Assyriologie*
ZAW	*Zeitschrift für die alttestamentliche Wissenschaft*
ZBK	Zürcher Bibelkommentar
ZTK	*Zeitschrift für Theologie und Kirche*

Introduction

THE EXILIC PERIOD

The sixth century BCE represents a decisive period in ancient Israel as it is within these 100 years that interpreters isolate a watershed in the history, literature, and theology of the Old Testament. The turning point coincides with a period of time between 587[1] and 539 BCE known as the exilic age. For Judah, disaster, defeat, destruction, and disruption define the beginning of this period. Indeed, the assimilation of Judah into the Neo-Babylonian empire had severe repercussions for all spheres of Judahite existence including political, religious, and social. A decline begun already through a previous invasion in 597 climaxed in 587 when Neo-Babylonian forces captured and humiliated the king, burned Jerusalem, the seat of his power, to the ground, dismantled and desecrated the temple, and deported members of the royal family, priests, and other elites to Babylon. Every facet of what had been the kingdom of Judah lay in disarray and a state of collapse. With the demolition of the city of Jerusalem and its temple, the Neo-Babylonians struck a blow at the heart of Judah by shattering the tenets of its faith. Zion theology, the predominant ideology of the pre-exilic Jerusalem temple cult which

---

[1] There continues to be some dispute over the date of the second attack of Nebuchadnezzar on Jerusalem. A preference for 587 stems from general agreement with the results of a thorough study of this issue provided by J. Hughes, *Secrets of the Times: Myth and History in Biblical Chronology* (JSOTSup, 66; Sheffield: JSOT Press, 1990), 159–82, 229–32. Recent discussions include, G. Galil, 'The Babylonian Calendar and the Chronology of the Last Kings of Judah', *Bib* 72 (1991), 367–78; O. Edwards, 'The Year of Jerusalem's Destruction', *ZAW* 104 (1992), 101–6; G. Galil, *The Chronology of the Last Kings of Israel and Judah* (SHANE, 9; Leiden: Brill, 1996), 108–26.

rested on the dual foundation of the inviolability of the city and the eternal covenant with David, was called forcibly into question. In spite of so great a crisis, sometime after the subjugation of Babylon by the Persian ruler Cyrus, the descendants of exiled Jerusalemites and Judahites returned to Judah and rebuilt the temple in Jerusalem. In the interim, the situation for the communities in Judah, Egypt, and Babylon remains obscure. Nevertheless, this time period is taken to be a significant epoch during which great thinkers and theologians grappled with reformulating the concepts of Yahwistic community, faith, and politics.[2]

The importance ascribed to this period cannot be overestimated. The downfall of the kingdom of Judah set about a series of events which, in the estimation of the Hebrew Bible and biblical scholars, resulted in the greatest watershed in the history of ancient Israel, that is, a rift of such magnitude that it provides a turning point in every facet of the pre-exilic state including the political, religious, and social organization of the state of Judah. On the political front never again would Judah be ruled by a Davidic king and never again would Judah be a state independent of foreign control (except for a brief period under the Maccabees). After the return from exile, the leadership of Judah, or Yehud as it was to be called, fell to the priesthood and to those repatriated through the policies of the Persians. On the religious front the temple cult after the exilic age looked very different in terms of leadership, operation, and regulation. Before the fall of Jerusalem, religion in Judah can be characterized as Yahwistic. Although a variety of forms of the worship of Yahweh existed, the form beginning to dominate was monotheistic, aniconic, and oriented on one central sanctuary.[3] From the middle of

---

[2] Historical surveys of this time period can be found in two main types of literature, historical and theological. Recent historical works include, B. Oded, 'Judah and the Exile', in J. H. Hayes and J. M. Miller (eds.), *Israelite and Judaean History* (OTL; London: SCM Press, repr. 1990), 469–80; T. C. Mitchell, 'The Babylonian Exile and the Restoration of the Jews in Palestine (586–c.500 B.C.)', in J. Boardman *et al.* (eds.), *The Cambridge Ancient History*, III/2 (Cambridge: Cambridge University Press, 2nd edn. 1991), 410–40; H. M. Barstad, *The Myth of the Empty Land: A Study in the History and Archaeology of Judah during the 'Exilic' Period* (SO, 28; Oslo: Scandinavian University Press, 1996).

[3] O. Keel and C. Uehlinger, *Göttinnen, Götter, und Gottessymbole: Neue Erkenntnisse zur Religionsgeschichte Kanaans und Israels aufgrund bislang unerschlossener

the fourth century BCE onwards, a different form of religion emerged as Judaism. Traditionally, the exile is understood to be the decisive break between the two.[4] Moreover, it was a germinating period during which many posit great movements in the conceptual understanding of Israel's deity. For instance, located here are the first formulations of exclusive monotheism, the rise in individual responsibility, and the growth in the application of the concept of universal sovereignty, and the availability of the worship of Yahweh to foreigners. Moreover the community was maintained through the influence and authority of the elders who filled a necessary social vacuum. The importance ascribed to the events of 587 can be seen especially in the number of books which examine the exilic age from the perspective of 'biblical theology'.[5] Indeed, the exile is considered the defining period during which religious practice and theological interpretation were reassessed and reformulated.[6]

ikonographischer Quellen (QD, 134; Freiburg: Herder, 1992); ET *Gods, Goddesses, and Images of God in ancient Israel* (Minneapolis, Minn.: Fortress Press, 1998); D. V. Edelman (ed.), *The Triumph of Elohim: From Yahwisms to Judaisms* (Contributions to Biblical Exegesis and Theology, 13; Kampen: Kok Pharos, 1995).

[4] J. Wellhausen, *Prolegomena zur Geschichte Israels* (Berlin: de Gruyter, 1878, 6th edn. 1927). On Wellhausen's contribution to the study of the Old Testament, see various articles in *Semeia* 25 (1983) and J. Barton, 'Wellhausen's Prolegomena to the History of Israel: Influence and Effects', in D. L. Smith-Christopher (ed.), *Text and Experience: Toward a Cultural Exegesis of the Bible* (BS, 35; Sheffield: Sheffield Academic Press, 1995), 316–29.

[5] e.g. E. Janssen, *Juda in der Exilszeit: Ein Beitrag zur Entstehung des Judentums* (Göttingen: Vandenhoeck & Ruprecht, 1956); P. R. Ackroyd, *Exile and Restoration: A Study of Hebrew Thought of the Sixth Century BC* (London: SCM Press, repr. 1994); R. W. Klein, *Israel in Exile: A Theological Interpretation* (Philadelphia, Pa.: Fortress Press, 1979; repr. Mifflintown, Pa.: Sigler Press, 2000); J. D. Newsome, *By the Waters of Babylon: An Introduction to the History and Theology of Exile* (Edinburgh: T & T Clark, 1979); R. Albertz, *Die Exilszeit* (BE, 7; Stuttgart: W. Kohlhammer, 2002), ET *Israel in Exile: The History and Literature of the Sixth Century B.C.E.* (Studies in Biblical Literature; Atlanta, Ga.: Scholars Press, 2003).

[6] D. W. Thomas, 'The Sixth Century B.C.: A Creative Epoch in the History of Israel', *JSS* 6 (1961), 33–46; W. Brueggemann, 'A Shattered Transcendence? Exile and Restoration', in S. Kraftchick and B. Ollenburger (eds.), *Biblical Theology: Problems and Prospects* (Nashville: Abingdon Press, 1995), 169–82, repr. in *idem, Old Testament Theology: Essays on Structure, Theme, and Text* (Minneapolis, Minn.: Fortress Press, 1992), 183–203; B. Becking, 'Continuity and Discontinuity after the Exile: Some Introductory Remarks', in B. Becking and M. C. A. Korpel (eds.), *The Crisis of Israelite Religion: Transformation of Religious Tradition in Exilic and Post-Exilic Times* (OTS, 42; Leiden: Brill, 1999), 1–8.

Although the significance of this period is beyond dispute, the designation commonly used for it raises issues of its own. In the case of terminology, in both a descriptive and a conceptual sense, 'exile' or 'exilic' is a misnomer. The period can only be spoken of as 'exilic' when the perspective is taken from that of a community which experienced a forced existence outside the land of Judah.[7] Furthermore, it is not entirely appropriate to use the singular in conjunction with the disaster in the sixth century BCE because the Babylonians deported people in three separate instances in 598, 587, and 582. Moreover, 'exile' does not adequately represent the fact that some people chose to flee from Judah. After 587 a group reportedly settled in the neighbouring nation-states of Ammon, Moab, and Edom (Jer. 40: 11) and, following the assassination of Gedaliah, another group fled to Egypt with Jeremiah in tow (Jer. 41). In their case the identification of the period would be labelled more suitably the 'expatriate' or the 'refugee' period. Ascertaining a term inclusive of the various populations that continued to identify themselves with the worship of Yahweh and with the land following the events which led to the collapse of Judah as an independent state remains troublesome. An additional problematic point stems from the fact that from its inception Jewish history can be viewed as a series of exiles and restorations and that the situation of the exile *par excellence* never actually ceased to exist.[8] A series of deportations occurred in conjunction with the collapse of the northern kingdom in the eighth century BCE. In spite of this, the period has never been referred to as 'the exile'. From textual evidence it is clear that communities in Egypt and Babylon continued to flourish well into the Hellenistic period and beyond.[9] Nevertheless, the traditional and generally accepted

---

[7] P. R. Davies, 'Exile? What Exile? Whose Exile?', in Grabbe, *Leading Captivity Captive*, 128–38.

[8] M. A. Knibb, 'The Exile in the Literature of the Intertestamental Period', *HeyJ* 17 (1976), 253–72; R. Carroll, 'Israel, History of (Post-monarchic period)', *The Anchor Bible Dictionary*, iii (New York and London: Doubleday, 1992), 567–76. In the modern period the Zionist movement continues to refer to Jews displaced from Israel as 'in exile'. An introduction to this discussion with a view to the use of exile in the Old Testament, apocryphal books, and in Jewish tradition can be found in J. M. Scott (ed.), *Exile: Old Testament, Jewish, and Christian Conceptions* (JSJSup, 56; Leiden: Brill, 1997).

[9] On the question of when the exile is better understood as the Diaspora, see R. J. Coggins, 'The Origins of the Jewish Diaspora', in R. E. Clements (ed.), *The World*

terminology for the period of time between the destruction of the temple in 587 and the rise of Cyrus in 539 is the 'exile'. A perspective from that of the land, those people who remained behind following the series of deportations, demands a rethinking of our terminology for this period as does the growing unease in some circles over the terms 'exile' and 'return'.[10] A term more in keeping with the focal point of this thesis would be the Templeless period, understood to be the time sandwiched between the ruination of the sanctuary in Jerusalem in 587 (in other words, that crucial moment when communities whether in the land or in Diaspora had to reassess Yahwistic religion in the light of the loss of the central sanctuary whether through its desecration or by displacement) and 515, when temple construction was completed according to the biblical account.

The Templeless period—or that time during which worship at the central sanctuary in Jerusalem ceased or was altered to a significant degree and during which portions of the people of Judah had to grapple with religious existence without the traditional symbol of the temple—thus forms a significant era in which the entire social, political, and religious spheres of Judah were adapted and reformulated. The period of time between 587 and 515 forms the backdrop against which much of the interpretation and even the move towards the canonization of scripture took place. It represents a seminal period for discussion even among those scholars who choose to posit the locus of the production of the literature of the Hebrew Bible in the Persian and Hellenistic periods. Any understanding of this era, in fact, impacts several different discussions currently raging in Old Testament scholarship. What was the situation in the land? Where was the primary location in which reflection on theological concerns and observance of religious practices took place? Does the social situation in Judah in the early Persian period support the view

of Ancient Israel: Sociological, Anthropological, and Political Perspectives (Cambridge: Cambridge University Press, 1989), 163–81.

[10] R. Carroll, 'Exile! What Exile? Deportation and the Discourses of Diaspora', in Grabbe, *Leading Captivity Captive*, 62–79, too, grapples with this terminology with more pessimistic results. Note his alternative understanding of the perspective of exile: 'from the position of modern readers of the Bible there can really only be a sense of exile as something propounded by a Jerusalem—or Palestinian—orientated point of view' (67). See also the notes on this by L. L. Grabbe, 'Reflections on the Discussion', in Grabbe, *Leading Captivity Captive*, 146–56.

that the events which took place at the beginning of the sixth century BCE created an insurmountable rupture between the communities who remained behind in Judah and those who were deported to Babylon? It is not the purpose of the present study to answer all of these questions; rather, it is to provide a basis for the resolution of some of these issues by contributing a much needed study of the situation in Judah with a concentration on what was happening in the land and what, if any, distinctive interpretation took place there.

THE PRE-EMINENCE OF THE *GOLAH*

Research on this period has undergone a series of slight adjustments over the years. In one area in particular, that of the situation in the land after the assassination of Gedaliah, the consensus view has moved away from the concept of a completely depopulated Judah as reflected for the most part in nineteenth-century scholarship[11] to a slightly more generous twentieth-century perspective which acknowledges that the majority of the population remained in Judah, but, nevertheless, denies it much creative significance.[12] In the latter point of view, the generation of theological reformulation and writing attributable to this period took place among the exiles in Babylonia (the *Golah*). In distinction to their counterparts in the homeland, the *Golah* group is regarded as 'fruitful' either because they are thought to be the more socially adept community[13] or because subsistence level conditions in Judah made intense reflection and interpretation unlikely.[14] A representative opinion of the second of the two perspectives is that of

---

[11] A twentieth-century representative of this point of view is Y. Kaufman, *The Religion of Israel: From its Beginnings to the Babylonian Exile* (New York: Schocken Books, 1972), who follows the biblical representation of the empty land.

[12] A point similarly noted in T. Willi, *Juda-Jehud-Israel: Studien zum Selbstverständnis des Judentums in persischer Zeit* (FAT, 12; Tübingen: Mohr (Paul Siebeck), 1995), 22; Barstad, *The Myth of the Empty Land*, 13–23.

[13] Thomas, 'The Sixth Century B.C.', 33, and Ackroyd, *Exile and Restoration*, 44. An idea traceable perhaps to Jeremiah's analogy of the good figs who were deported versus the bad figs who remained behind in the land (Jer. 24).

[14] Oded, 'Judah and the Exile', 476–80; Mitchell, 'The Babylonian Exile', 415.

S. S. Weinberg in his very useful, but now dated, study of the archaeology of this period:

> It is highly unlikely that a material culture of any degree of sophistication could have been maintained during these centuries in Jerusalem without leaving more substantial remains than have been found so far; we must think more in terms first of squatters and then of people able to maintain only a mere subsistence level.[15]

The view commonly held of a Judah crippled until Persian imperial rule is exacerbated to some extent by the biblical texts themselves. In the first place, as a survey of literature on this period shows, a great number of texts are thought to stem from the portion of the population taken to Babylonia. More importantly, an intentional ideological interpretation sought literarily to remove the Judahites who did not experience the judgement of exile from the scene through two distinct, but nevertheless related, manoeuvres. These two find expression in the belief that the judgement of Yahweh results in the sentence of complete destruction for the people who remained in the land after 587, along with the concept of the empty land. The aptly termed 'myth of the empty land' propounds the belief that the 'day of Yahweh' resulted in the cessation of life in Judah. The great prophets of the exile, Jeremiah and Ezekiel, for instance, insisted that Yahweh's judgement for past and ongoing sin necessitated a complete break with the past. Their thought is undergirded with the idea that the population deported to Babylonia alone experienced Yahweh's redeeming punishment. Thus, they alone inherit the promises of restoration and blessing. This concept, though never expressly stated in Deutero-Isaiah, nevertheless, appears to inform its theological perspective within which the renewal of Judah comes about solely with the returnees.

A related endeavour—succinctly termed 'the myth of the empty land' by interpreters—contributes to the impression that the Babylonian exiles maintained and sustained an ideology of judgement and punishment by literary strategies that portrayed a Judah emptied of its inhabitants.[16] The land of Judah devoid of its population

---

[15] S. S. Weinberg, 'Post-Exilic Palestine: An Archaeological Report', in *Proceedings of the Israel Academy of Sciences and Humanities* (Jerusalem: Israel Academy of Sciences and Humanities, 1969–70), 81.

[16] H. M. Barstad, 'On the History and Archaeology of Judah During the Exilic Period', *OLP* 19 (1988), 25–36; R. Carroll, 'The Myth of the Empty Land', in D. Jobling

culminated in the Chronicler's assertion, found also in Leviticus, that the land lay fallow for a sabbath rest of 70 years (2 Chr. 36: 20–1 and Lev. 26: 34–5).[17] At least a century later, the effort to gloss over the community remaining in Templeless Judah found its staunchest defender in Ezra (and to a lesser extent Nehemiah) whose literature promoted the belief that the landed population were foreigners. Consequently, the repatriated Babylonian exiles became the only community to inherit legitimately the religion of pre-exilic Israel.[18] Even without the later corruption of details to discredit sixth-century Judah, the biblical material contemporaneous with the events themselves gives the impression that only a very small and insignificant portion of the population remained in Judah. Prophetic announcement of irrevocable and comprehensive doom coupled with repeated biblical asides that 'Jerusalem' (2 Kgs. 24: 14), 'Judah' (2 Kgs. 25: 21; Jer. 52: 27), 'all the rest of the city and the deserters... all the rest of the population' (2 Kgs. 25: 11), and 'all the people, young and old set out and went to Egypt' (2 Kgs. 25: 26) contribute to the belief that following the decline of Judah begun already in 597, the population decreases to all but 'the poorest people of the land' who were left to be 'vine-dressers and tillers of the soil' (2 Kgs. 25: 12).

The likelihood of a land completely bereft of its inhabitants is not only improbable, but also not entirely consistent with the biblical portrait of this time. Embedded within the prophecies of Jeremiah several texts predict hope and blessing for the Judahite population remaining in the land.[19] Twice in Jeremiah, the inhabitants in the

and T. Pippin (eds.), *Ideological Criticism of Biblical Texts Semeia* 59 (1992), 79–93; Barstad, *The Myth of the Empty Land*, 13–23; R. Carroll, 'Clio and Canons: In Search of a Cultural Poetics of the Hebrew Bible', *BibInt* 5 (1997), 308–15; idem, 'Exile! What Exile?', 65–6; R. J. Coggins, 'The Exile: History and Ideology', *ExpT* 110 (1999), 389–93.

[17] More on the ideology of the Chronicler in this respect can be found in Willi, *Juda-Jehud-Israel*, 21–4; S. Japhet, *The Ideology of the Book of Chronicles and its Place in Biblical Thought* (BEATAJ, 9; Frankfurt: Lang, 2nd rev. edn. 1997), 364–73, and idem, 'Exile and Restoration in the Book of Chronicles', in Becking and Korpel, *The Crisis of Israelite Religion*, 33–44; J. Blenkinsopp, 'The Bible, Archaeology and Politics; or The Empty Land', *JSOT* 27 (2002), 175–87.

[18] P. R. Davies, *In Search of 'ancient Israel'* (JSOTSup, 148; Sheffield: Sheffield Academic Press, 2nd edn. 1995); L. L. Grabbe, 'Israel's Historical Reality after the Exile', in Becking and Korpel, *The Crisis of Israelite Religion*, 22.

[19] Noted already by Janssen, *Juda in der Exilszeit*, 47; J. Bright, *Jeremiah* (AB, 21; Garden City, NY: Doubleday, 2nd edn. 1965), LIII–LIV; Ackroyd, *Exile and Restoration*,

homeland are called שאר׳ת 'the remnant', in Jeremiah 40: 11 and 42: 15. The term is later co-opted for the exiles, as in Jeremiah 23: 3 and Micah 2: 12, when it becomes associated with the theologically loaded concept of a righteous remnant.[20] During Gedaliah's short period as governor, Jeremiah describes the first harvest in terms that connote divine blessing: 'and they gathered wine and summer fruits in great abundance' (Jer. 40: 12). This brief glimpse of a Judahite community returning to normal activities, even blessed by the deity for their trouble, is further expanded by several hopeful prophetic oracles made to them. In a careful study of points of tension within the book of Jeremiah, Seitz finds prophecies of a more positive nature directed to the community in Judah.[21] In one instance, Ishmael and his fellow conspirators approach the prophet for an indication of what to do after their assassination of Gedaliah. Jeremiah prophesies with words echoing what he had said to the exiles previously in Jeremiah 29: 5: 'If you will only remain in this land, then I will build you up and not pull you down; I will plant you, and not pluck you up; for I am sorry for the disaster that I have brought upon you' (Jer. 42: 10–12). The prophetic oracle insists that a future is made available to those who will remain in the land and submit to Babylonian rule. The promises of blessing are overshadowed by an intentional process of refraction and reinterpretation by the community exiled to Babylon, the '*Golah* redactors' of Seitz.[22] Although never positive about the population in Judah, Ezekiel is at least aware of them. In two places, he criticizes an attitude prevalent there in which the people perceive themselves as the righteous remnant to whom possession of the land was bequeathed (Ezek. 11: 17; 33: 24).[23]

56–8, and *idem*, 'Historians and Prophets,' SEÅ 33 (1968), 18–54, 52 n. 44, but developed more fully in C. R. Seitz, 'The Crisis of Interpretation over the Meaning and Purpose of the Exile', *VT* 35 (1985), 78–97, and *idem, Theology in Conflict: Reactions to the Exile in the Book of Jeremiah* (BZAW, 176; Berlin: de Gruyter, 1989), 274–9.

[20] Janssen, *Juda in der Exilszeit*, 40.

[21] Seitz, 'Crisis of Interpretation' and *Theology in Conflict.*

[22] Seitz, 'Crisis of Interpretation', and *idem, Theology in Conflict.* Cf. E. W. Nicholson, *Preaching to the Exiles: A Study in the Prose Tradition in the Book of Jeremiah* (Oxford: Blackwell, 1970); K. F. Pohlmann, *Studien zum Jeremiabuch: Ein Beitrag zur Frage nach die Enstehung des Jeremiabuches* (FRLANT, 118; Göttingen: Vandenhoeck & Ruprecht, 1978).

[23] W. Brownlee, 'The Aftermath of the Fall of Judah According to Ezekiel', *JBL* 89 (1970), 393–404; S. Japhet, 'People and Land in the Restoration Period', in G. Strecker

Silence on the situation in Judah after the assassination of Gedaliah in the literature of the *Golah* need not equate to inactivity. Indeed, in all likelihood, it indicates self-interest and even censure.

Even whilst reading against the biblical rhetoric, it is still possible to maintain three reasons to place the locus for creative literary activity following the disaster of 587 with the Babylonian exiles rather than with those who remained behind in the land. The majority of scholars attribute significant portions of the Old Testament such as Isaiah 40–55, Ezekiel, the final form of Jeremiah, the Priestly work, and the Deuteronomistic History to the *Golah*. In addition, the promulgation of the theological concepts of individual responsibility and universalism, along with the increased significance ascribed to purity and holiness, can be attributed to the *Golah*. Finally, the exiled leaders appear to be the ones who upon return to Judah after the advent of Persian rule steer the province of Yehud along the course of its political and religious future.

IMPORTANT WORKS ON THE SITUATION IN 'EXILIC' JUDAH

Reacting against the concentration on Babylon as the provenance for the continuation of the traditions of pre-exilic Israel that dominated the scholarship of his time, C. C. Torrey asserted with ever-increasing conviction that the exile and return was a myth created by a segment of the population to provide ideological backing for its political and religious reformation.[24] Although the level of Torrey's scepticism has not been matched regarding the deportation of a number of people

---

(ed.), *Das Land Israel in biblischer Zeit: Jerusalem Symposium 1981* (GTA, 25; Göttingen: Vandenhoeck & Ruprecht, 1983), 106–8.

[24] C. C. Torrey, *The Composition and Historical Value of Ezra–Nehemiah* (BZAW, 2; Giessen: J. Ricker, 1896), 53–4, 62–5; *idem, Ezra Studies* (Chicago: University of Chicago Press, 1910), 285–9; *idem, Pseudo-Ezekiel and the Original Prophecy* (New Haven: Yale University Press, 1930), 31–3; *idem, The Chronicler's History of Israel: Chronicles-Ezra-Nehemia Restored to its Original Form* (Port Washington, NY: Kennikat, repr. 1973), pp. xxvii–xxviii.

from Judah in the sixth century except perhaps by Carroll,[25] his instinct that the majority of the population remained in Judah and contributed to the theological interpretation of the Old Testament has found confirmation in several important works which, too, have sought to redress the balance by focusing on the contribution of the Judahite population to the literature of the Old Testament. Although never producing a monograph on the exile, the contribution of Noth to the question of the provenance of the theological literature of this period should be acknowledged. In his *History of Israel* he concluded: '[the Judahites] continued to be the centre of Israelite life and history. For them the events of 587 B.C. did not in any way signify the end. The links with Israel's past were preserved here, just as was the worship in the holy place in Jerusalem'[26] and again: 'Palestine was and remained the central arena of Israel's history, and the descendants of the old tribes who remained in the land, with the holy place of Jerusalem, constituted not only numerically the great mass but also the real nucleus of Israel.'[27] The real contribution to this argument came about through Noth's work on the Deuteronomistic History[28] In his view, the great work which encompassed Joshua to 2 Kings introduced by a form of Deuteronomy was written in its entirety from source documents during the exile by an historian in Judah. Noth provides two main arguments in favour of locating the creation of the Deuteronomistic History in Judah rather than among the Babylonian exiles: (1) the sources for the construction of the history included local traditions centred around Bethel and Mizpah which

---

[25] Carroll, 'The Myth of the Empty Land'; *idem.*, 'Clio and Canons'; *idem.*, 'Exile! What Exile?'. Also of note in this regard is Davies, *In Search*, 41–4, 57–9, 75–93. See C. E. Carter, *The Emergence of Yehud in the Persian Period: A Social and Demographic Study* (JSOTSup, 294; Sheffield: Sheffield Academic Press, 1999), 309–16, for a balanced critique of this perspective.

[26] M. Noth, *Geschichte Israels* (Göttingen: Vandenhoeck & Ruprecht, 2nd edn. 1954), 264; ET *The History of Israel* (London: SCM Press, 2nd edn. 1983), 292; and *idem*, 'Die Katastrophe von Jerusalem im Jahre 587 v. CHR. und ihre Bedeutung für Israel', in *Gesammelte Studien zum Alten Testament* (Munich: Chr. Kaiser, 1960), 346–71; ET 'The Jerusalem Catastrophe of 587 B.C. and its Significance for Israel', in *The Laws of the Pentateuch and Other Essays* (Edinburgh: Oliver & Boyd, 1966), 260–80.

[27] Noth, *Geschichte Israels*, 267 = *History of Israel*, 296.

[28] M. Noth, *Überlieferungsgeschichtliche Studien* (Halle: Königsberger, 1943); ET *The Deuteronomistic History* (JSOTSup, 15; Sheffield: JSOT Press, 1981).

would have been more readily available in Judah; and (2) it recounted history, in Noth's view, from a more pessimistic perspective which elicited no hope for a return from exile by those who remained in the land. Noth's bold assertion that there was writing on the scale of the Deuteronomistic History by those who remained behind in the land of Judah, although challenged by the dual redaction hypothesis of Cross,[29] provides the basis for a re-examination of the situation of the population left behind in the land and the possibility of a contribution from this people to the literary activity of this period.

Building on Noth's preference for sixth-century Judah as the locus of creative writing after 587, Janssen produced a monograph on the significant number and wide variety of works attributable to Templeless Judah by those who remained faithful to the old traditions. Janssen adds two additional arguments in support of Noth's reasons for the placement of the Deuteronomistic History and uses them in conjunction with the redaction of Jeremiah in Judah. First, he highlights the concern of both works with the law and the lure of idolatrous Canaanite practice as being particularly relevant to the situation in Judah. Secondly, he argues that Solomon's temple depicted as a place of prayer in 1 Kings 8 fits the situation of Judah well since following its desecration it could no longer be used legitimately for sacrifice.[30] Janssen ascribes literature to these people on the basis of references to historical details and a fit with the time period after the destruction of the temple, the dissolution of the state, and the abolition of the Davidic king. Among texts from a Judahite provenance, Janssen includes Lamentations (excluding ch. 5), Isaiah 21, Obadiah, and Psalms 44, 74, 79, 89, and 102. If Janssen is correct, there are good reasons for considering that among those who remained behind there was a prolific group of writers and more importantly, a zealous group of faithful worshippers of Yahweh.

---

[29] See e.g. F. M. Cross, *Canaanite Myth and Hebrew Epic: Essays in the History of the Religion of Israel* (Cambridge, Mass.: Harvard University Press, 1973), 274–89; R. E. Friedman, *The Exile and Biblical Narrative: The Formation of the Deuteronomistic and Priestly Works* (HSM, 22; Chico, Calif.: Scholars Press, 1981); R. D. Nelson, *The Double Redaction of the Deuteronomistic History* (JSOTSup, 18; Sheffield: JSOT Press, 1981); G. Knoppers, *Two Nations under God: The Deuteronomistic History of Solomon and the Dual Monarchies*, 2 vols. (HSM, 52; Atlanta, Ga.: Scholars Press, 1993).

[30] Janssen, *Juda in der Exilszeit*, 26–31.

In recent times the situation of the people left behind in the land forms a natural enquiry in Willi's study which focuses more directly on the community in the Persian period.[31] Addressing the issue stemming from the Chronicler, that of the land of Judah as a *tabula rasa*, Willi highlights three sources that contradict this picture: (1) Old Testament literature like that of Haggai, Zechariah (1–8), parts of the books of Jeremiah (chs. 37–44; 52), Ezekiel, Lamentations, Deutero-Isaiah, and the Deuteronomistic History; (2) the archaeological and historical details; and (3) a re-examination of 2 Chronicles 36: 20–1. In his examination, he follows in the main the lines drawn already by Noth and Janssen, but his observation that the literature of the early Second Temple period, namely, the prophetic books of Haggai and Zechariah (1–8) along with archaeological finds, reveals continuity with the pre-exilic period is new. The overlap between the late monarchical period and the early Persian period suggests the existence of a viable community continuing its traditions in the land of Judah after the destruction of the temple.[32]

Though Noth and Janssen were perhaps over-zealous with their positioning of significant creative activity within Judah,[33] their studies highlight a type of argument that has not been followed for the most part in recent times with regard to Judah. Both were concerned with determining a distinctive Judahite perspective on the disaster of 587 relevant for the population that remained in the land. The shift in research over the last several decades to the Babylonian population and its setting has overshadowed the equally important issue of what and how the circumstances of the land inform its literary reflection and interpretation.

One of the most important works on the contribution of the Judahite population to the theology of the Old Testament remains that of Ackroyd, who endeavours to associate the historical situation with the theological. Ackroyd published his *Exile and Restoration* in

---

[31] Willi, *Juda-Jehud-Israel*, 21–6.

[32] R. Bedford, *Temple Restoration in Early Achaemenid Judah* (JSJSup, 65; Leiden: Brill, 2001). In his concern to ascertain the reliability of views that the early postexilic period was a time of societal tension centred on the control of and access to the Jerusalem temple, Bedford, too, finds much in common between the ideological concerns of the late monarchical period and the early Persian period.

[33] See the criticisms made by Ackroyd, *Exile and Restoration*, 65–8 and Nicholson, *Preaching to the Exiles*, 117–18.

1968 on the basis of his Hulsean lectures on the period of the restoration.³⁴ The main purpose of the book is to examine the underlying belief that resulted from the events of the 'exilic' period and its significance for the thought of later periods of time, as in the early post-exilic period and beyond. In accumulating a variety of texts stemming from the sixth century, Ackroyd provides a crucial study of the thought of the 'exilic age', especially with regard to the types of theological manoeuvres required to assess the effects of the sweeping devastations that accompanied the advent of Neo-Babylonian rule. In general he lists four major reactions to the events of 587: (1) a return to older cults, (2) the acceptance of the religion of the conquerors, (3) the recognition of divine judgement, and (4) the day of Yahweh as equivalent to prophetic predictions of divine punishment for sin.³⁵

Ackroyd's stated aim is to associate the theological reactions with the events of 587. This he accomplishes through the inclusion of a separate section on the situations of the populations of this period in their disparate locations³⁶ and by introducing his discussion of the theological contribution of specific biblical texts with historical details. Throughout he seeks to associate the historical reality with the types of reflection taking place. In his view, then, 'The understanding of the development of thought cannot be undertaken without an appreciation of the situation in which it grew.'³⁷ Unfortunately, in his analysis he tends to avoid overtly associating ongoing societal change with reflection and adaptation. On the one hand, he speculates on literary production in the homeland: 'there must have been present a large proportion of those who were educated and used to positions of

---

³⁴ Other works by Ackroyd that disclose his thinking on this period include 'Historians and Prophets'; *idem*, *Israel under Babylon*, 1–34; *idem*, 'The Temple Vessels: A Continuity Theme', in *Studies in the Religion of ancient Israel* (SVT, 23; Leiden: Brill, 1972), 166–81, repr. in P. R. Ackroyd, *Studies in the Religious Tradition of the Old Testament* (London: SCM Press, 1987), 46–60; 'The History of Israel in the Exilic and Post-Exilic Periods', in G. W. Anderson (ed.), *Tradition and Interpretation: Essays by Members of the Society for Old Testament Study* (Oxford: Oxford University Press, 1979), 320–50.

³⁵ Ackroyd, *Exile and Restoration*, 39–49. For a similar outline of responses to disaster of the sort that transpired in Jerusalem in 587 BCE, see Becking, 'Continuity and Discontinuity'.

³⁶ Ackroyd, *Exile and Restoration*, 17–38.

³⁷ Ibid., 13.

responsibility or the changed social conditions must have made it possible for the abilities of some of the less favoured groups to be revealed...Probably both of these happened'.[38] On the other hand, he attributes the adaptation of 'social conditions' with the historical events with which the exile is most often associated, such as, the fall of Jerusalem, the end of the state and the monarchy, the destruction of the temple, and the large-scale political changes which followed the rise to power of Cyrus and the fall of the Neo-Babylonian empire.[39] From one perspective it was the events of 587 that caused the need to reassess the inherited traditions of monarchical Judah. However, the significance of the day-to-day events for the construction of theological interpretation by the community in Judah remains obscure. A question-mark, therefore, exists over how the community in the land understood its relationship to its deity in the aftermath of those events in a possible period of reconstruction and renewal. New information about Templeless Judah has been brought forward in recent years that needs to be associated with the creation and generation of reflection in the homeland.

Interestingly a balance has been struck with regard to the association of the historical events of exile with their literature at least in terms of the community forcibly deported to Babylonia. Without going too far afield, it is helpful to mention two important contributions. The first represents a classic study of the Jeremianic prose narrative and sermons by Nicholson, who endeavours throughout to show that the material was developed within a circle of traditionists who refracted the prophecies of Jeremiah to address a particular historical context and religio-sociological situation.[40] It is his contention that the maintenance of the Jeremiah traditions served homiletic purposes by addressing concerns raised by the community in exile:

To put it another way, serious consideration must be given to the possibility that the book represents substantially the final literary expression and deposit of a tradition which grew and developed at the hands of a body of people who sought not only to transmit the prophet's sayings but to present an interpretation of his prophetic ministry and preaching on the basis of

[38] Ibid., 30.   [39] Ibid., 13–14.   [40] Nicholson, *Preaching to the Exiles*.

theological concerns and interests which were of vital importance for them in the age in which they lived.⁴¹

In his view, the group to which the traditionists belong is that of the exiled community in Babylon. Nicholson adduces four arguments in support of the placement of the formulation of the Jeremianic tradition among the deportees: (1) the emphasis on the law and ritual practices such as sabbath observance and circumcision, (2) the foregrounding of the issue of false prophecy, (3) the exilic attitude dismissing the community which remained in Judah, and (4) the promises of a restored Israel and return to the land. In associating these four features particular to the community forcibly deported and resettled in a foreign environment, Nicholson shows how prophecy directed at one group is updated and reinterpreted to meet the circumstances of another.

The concerted effort by Smith-Christopher is likewise of note in this regard.⁴² Smith-Christopher, too, acknowledges the need to associate the development of theological concepts with the day-to-day experience of relocation. In an article on the topic he reveals:

It is the intention of this essay to argue... that the assessment of the impact of the Babylonian Exile must make far more use of non-biblical documents, archaeological reports, and imaginative use of biblical texts that report on the crisis and its aftermath in order to construct a more realistic picture of the trauma of the Babylonian Exile in both its 'human' (that is, psychological and physical) and theological impact on the Hebrew people of the sixth and fifth centuries BCE.⁴³

The impact of displacement in a foreign environment on social organization forms a major area of his research. Through it he reveals that the context of the *Golah* community, dissociated from its symbolic universe, resulted in situation-specific interpretative moves to cope with contemporary circumstances. Various experiences distinctive to the *Golah* group such as displacement, an exhausting

---

⁴¹ Nicholson, *Preaching to the Exiles*, 4 (see, in fact, all of chs. 1 and 4).

⁴² Smith, *The Religion of the Landless*; D. L. Smith-Christopher, 'Reassessing the Historical and Sociological Impact of the Babylonian Exile (597/587–539 BCE)', in Scott, *Exile*, 7–36, and to some extent in ch. 6 of *idem*, *A Biblical Theology of Exile* (OBT; Minneapolis, Minn.: Fortress Press, 2002), 137–62. Because D. L. Smith now publishes as Smith-Christopher, I refer to him as such.

⁴³ Smith-Christopher, 'Impact of the Babylonian Exile', 10.

Introduction 17

journey, and resettlement in a foreign land in enclaves in the midst of foreigners, along with the loss of the religious and political symbols of the homeland, necessitated the implementation of strategies to maintain identity and ethnicity.[44] In his estimation, the social setting of exile led to two complementary shifts necessary for the community in exile: (1) the recognition of a strong social identity distinct from that of neighbouring peoples and (2) the creation of internal structures to maintain that identity.

By using modern-day experiences of deportation and relocation to illuminate an experience in the ancient world, Smith-Christopher sheds more light on the social situation of exile and its effects on social identity. His consideration of the impact of a sociological situation on the creation and maintenance of community identity has been followed to a lesser degree by Berquist, who sought to understand the reconstitution of Yehud as a province impacted by the policies of the Persian empire.[45] The insights of both further contribute to McNutt's use of sociological data in her reconstruction of ancient Israel.[46] In spite of the fact that neither Berquist nor McNutt contributes in any significant way to an understanding of Templeless Judah, their insights in this regard are worthy of mention. Everyday life impacts theological understanding and reflection.

In recent years, three major studies provide models for approaching the situation of the exile and that in Judah, in particular. The work of three scholars, Carter, Albertz, and Barstad, is distinguished by the intention of each to bring evidence other than documentary and biblical to bear on the question of the situation of Templeless Judah. Although dealing primarily with the question of the size and population of the province of Yehud in the Persian period, Carter includes evidence from excavation sites and geographical surveys for

---

[44] The maintenance of a Judaean persona is not unique to the exiles deported to Babylonia, as is shown by the extant letters of the Jewish military colony in Elephantine, modern-day Aswan. B. Porten, *Archives from Elephantine: The Life of an Ancient Jewish Military Colony* (Berkeley: University of California Press, 1968); B. Porten, 'The Jews in Egypt', in W. D. Davies and L. Finkelstein (eds.), *Cambridge History of Judaism*, i (hereafter *CHJ*, i), (Cambridge: Cambridge University Press, 1984), 372–400; M. Smith, 'Jewish Religious Life in the Persian Period', in *CHJ*, i. 219–78.

[45] J. L. Berquist, *Judaism in Persia's Shadow: A Social and Historical Approach* (Minneapolis, Minn.: Fortress Press, 1995).

[46] McNutt, *Reconstructing the Society of Ancient Israel* (LAI; London: SPCK, 1999).

Neo-Babylonian Judah. A more detailed picture of Neo-Babylonian Judah establishes boundaries within which a reasonable assessment of the potential for social and literary activity can take place. From an alternative perspective, Albertz concentrates on religious issues whilst considering sociological and historical data in his study of the various communities of the exilic period and their literature.[47] In contrast, Barstad deals exclusively with Judah through concrete evidence including historical details, archaeological evidence, and the role of imperial governance as a means to re-examine the potential of sixth-century Judah as a locus for creative literary activity.[48] Though having different starting-points, the three succeed in establishing essential areas of enquiry for any future investigation and discussion of the potential of sixth-century Judah.

Conscientiously not resorting to the use of biblical material, Carter has undertaken the painstakingly tedious task of tackling various reports on the material culture of Neo-Babylonian and Persian Judah. For him archaeological excavation reports and general surveys provide the foundation on which to build a probable model for the population, sociology, and socio-economic status primarily of Yehud in the Persian period, but with some attention to Judah in the Templeless period.[49] Carter's study is an important contribution to the field in that it cautiously analyses information to construct a realistic portrait of the situation of Judah and Yehud. He shows, for example, that certain reconstructions, like that attempted by Weinberg, are unrealistic when considered in the light of the material evidence.[50] A better understanding of the make-up of the community curtails speculations that would simply not be feasible under the conditions of the province. Sociology, socio-economic data, and the impact of imperial rule, therefore, figure in the factors determining

---

[47] Albertz, *Religionsgeschichte Israels* = *A History of Israelite Religion* and *idem, Die Exilszeit* = *Israel in Exile*.

[48] Barstad, *The Myth of the Empty Land* and *idem*, 'After the "Myth of the Empty Land": Major Challenges in the Study of Neo-Babylonian Judah', in O. Lipschits and J. Blenkinsopp (eds.), *Judah and the Judeans in the Neo-Babylonian Period* (Winona Lake, Ind.: Eisenbrauns, 2003), 3–20.

[49] Carter, *The Emergence of Yehud*, 31–74, 296; cf. J. Weinberg, *The Citizen-Temple Community* (JSOTSup, 151; Sheffield: Sheffield Academic Press, 1992).

[50] Bedford, *Temple Restoration*, shows this from the perspective of the textual evidence.

social identity in the sixth century BCE and beyond. Information of a more material nature is imperative in any study of this period so that a proper understanding of the structures which impact the communities in Judah and Babylon can be adduced.

Through a rather different approach, Albertz produced an analysis of Israelite religion as a long-awaited follow-up to his study on family piety and state religion.[51] In the two volumes of *A History of Israelite Religion in the Old Testament Period*, he deliberately combines an interest in the change of religious belief and practice over time with developments drawn especially from the insights of sociological enquiry. Albertz belongs to a group of the relatively few who endeavour to differentiate the impact of situations on the different communities of the exilic period. At one point he comments: 'The Israel of the exilic period consisted of at least three major groups in separate territories which were exposed to different historical developments, had different interests, and in part came into conflict over them.'[52] Three sociological situations and the developments that occurred as a result include that: (1) the loss of statehood led to the splintering of the groups of Judahites in their various territories, (2) the model of an older form of decentralized governance based on kinship lines came to fill the vacuum left by the loss of a central political authority, and (3) each group was impacted by close proximity to foreigners. In the case of Judah, the population was confronted by the encroachment of neighbouring peoples on territory once within its borders.[53] Notably, the ongoing nature of life in exilic Judah comes to the foreground in his discussion.

In *Die Exilszeit*, a new contribution to the study of the exilic period and its literature, Albertz provides a summary of the conclusions he reached in his earlier works. With reference to the situation in Judah, he includes specific details which impacted the community that remained behind in the land.[54] Beyond describing in greater detail the situation of Judah by using biblical literature outside the historiographical account, such as Jeremiah or Lamentations,

---

[51] R. Albertz, *Persönliche Frömmigkeit und offizielle Religion: Religionsinterner Pluralismus in Israel und Babylon* (CTM, 9; Stuttgart: Calwer, 1978).
[52] Albertz, *Religionsgeschichte Israels*, ii. 382 = *History of Israelite Religion*, ii. 374.
[53] Albertz, *Religionsgeschichte Israels*, ii. 382 = *History of Israelite Religion*, ii. 374–5.
[54] Albertz, *Die Exilszeit*, 81–5 = *Israel in Exile*, 90–6.

he helpfully addresses questions about population numbers and the impact of deportation on the situation in the homeland. Albertz's concern to link the ongoing events of the situation in the land with interpretation highlights the need for more consideration of the impact of social conditions on the development of religious thought.

Finally, the seminal contribution of Barstad in his *The Myth of the Empty Land* deserves mention here.[55] Seemingly as part of his wider desire to locate Deutero-Isaiah in Judah rather than Babylon, Barstad sought to redeem Judah from the wasteland to which it had been relegated by historians. In so doing, he provided an introduction to the evidence which ought to be used in conjunction with any discussion of this period. An historical reconstruction based on the biblical account supplemented with documentation from the ancient Near East, archaeological data, and the evidence of imperial administration indicate social conditions conducive for stable community life and the continuation of the normal activities of a state after the catastrophic events of 587. His study lays a firm foundation for a positive assessment of the population in Judah and its ability to participate in theological reflection.

One of the most helpful examples of the utilization of socio-historical factors as a means to illuminate the development of biblical conceptions is that of Seitz. His analysis of the continuation of the prophecies of Jeremiah provides a natural complement to the studies made by Carter, Albertz, and Barstad.[56] Importantly, Seitz attends to pre-exilic historiography in order to ascertain social factors that would continue after the fall of the nation and contribute to the development of the Jeremianic tradition. By so doing he draws attention to the differences between parts of the book of Jeremiah which exhibit a positive assessment on the homeland post-587 and those that do not. He carefully examines two recensions of the prophetic oracles, one which took place in Judah and the other in Babylon where they were redirected in line with the outlook of 2 Kings and Ezekiel. In addition to increased awareness of post-587 Judah, his study shows the correspondence between community and

---

[55] Barstad, 'On the History and Archaeology of Judah'; idem, *The Myth of the Empty Land*; idem, 'After the "Myth of the Empty Land" '.
[56] Seitz, 'Crisis of Interpretation' and *Theology in Conflict.*

literary development. It further highlights the need for more attention to Templeless Judah as a distinctive setting for literary development in its own right.

It is clear from recent studies that work on the Templeless period has to move in a new direction. A holistic picture made available through various types of evidence—imperial administration, archaeological, biblical, and sociological—must be used in conjunction in order to provide probable models. From the discussion of the concept of the 'myth of the empty land' it becomes clear that biblical evidence cannot be used alone; not only does the Bible provide disparate portraits, but some texts even attempt to discredit certain communities during this period. What is equally of concern is that a current study of Judah during this period is desperately needed to correlate new insights with theological interpretation. Such a study must incorporate current data from many fields in a reconstruction of Templeless Judah as a means of ascertaining whether or not it would have been a community in which serious theological reflection could and would have taken place. Once the former has been settled satisfactorily, it is also equally important to determine what type of thought might be pertinent to the community that remained in the land. Such would provide a bench-mark of sorts to assist in the assignment of additional pieces of biblical literature to Templeless Judah.

THE TASK AT HAND

From the above survey it is possible to note areas in which more thought needs to occur. In the first place, the still prevalent view that the only viable provenance for the production of significant Templeless literature is from the exiles in Babylonia must be reconsidered. The first chapter presents the biblical representation of history along with three portraits expanded on the basis of non-historiographical biblical material. The biblical representation of Templeless Judah is then laid alongside the evidence of archaeological endeavours and comparative imperial data in order to establish a more well-rounded framework with which to understand the nature of continued existence in the land. In so doing, it highlights features that would make future stability likely. It was in this milieu that religion and religious conceptualizations continued in the land.

Subsequent chapters turn to the interesting possibility of the types of religious practices that continued among the populace. It is apparent from the vast amount of material on the Templeless period that a significant degree of consensus reigns regarding the likelihood of some type of worship taking place in Judah. The second chapter provides an introduction to the perspective outside the land which portrayed Judah as participating in what it considered to be idolatrous and foreign religious practices. Subsequently, the third chapter considers what some circles would regard as Yahwistic worship and some of the literature associated by interpreters with ongoing rituals.

It becomes especially apparent in the discussion of the religiosity of the land that in many respects its conceptualization arose from perspectives not of the community in Judah. It will be shown in the second chapter that *Golah* perceptions influence the association of aberrant religious observance with the homeland, and in the third chapter that biblical scholars haphazardly attribute laments from the Psalter and elsewhere in the OT to religious observances held at the temple site. Since each interpretation of the Judahite response to 587 stems from material not clearly attributable to Judah of the time, the fourth chapter focuses on the literature most widely regarded in tradition and scholarship to stem from Templeless Judah—the book of Lamentations. An analysis of Lamentations provides a means to access Judahite thought in order to ascertain themes and concepts pertinent to the situation in the land in the aftermath of the catastrophe of 587. It is hoped that the delineation of motifs distinctive to Templeless Judah will enable a measuring line of sorts with which to designate other literature from this setting in the future.

The purpose of this thesis is not to deal exclusively with the social setting of the population left behind in Judah, because this has been effectively provided in Janssen's *Juda in der Exilszeit*, Barstad's *Myth of the Empty Land*, Seitz's *Theology in Conflict*, and Albertz's *Die Exilszeit*. It is, rather, to focus on one aspect of the discussion which has elicited a great deal of interest in the literature of Judah of this period. The issue of cultic worship represents one area in which there is wide disagreement over the particulars, but general agreement about its existence. Liturgy rather than history or prophecy provides an entry-point for the examination of the theological insights which stem from the community that remained behind in Judah. Since social conditions effect theological reflection, Judahite literature should differ from that relevant to the exiles in a Babylonian setting. Is there a distinctive contribution from the population in the land to the theology of the Old Testament? It is to this question we now turn.

1

The Social and Historical Situation in Templeless Judah

INTRODUCTION

The preceding chapter has shown that for anyone who desires to attend to either the people or the literature of Judah during the Templeless period a pressing concern lies with the need for more clarity about the situation in the homeland in the aftermath of the events of 587. It is imperative not only to give an account of recent models and contributions about sixth-century Judah but, more importantly, to associate the construction of religious belief with the events from which it arose. This is no easy task. Any attempt to reconstruct the historical situation of the Templeless period is fraught with difficulty. There is a real dearth of material attributable to this period and the primary source of information for the people of Judah in the Late Iron Age is the Hebrew Bible, whose use for historical reconstruction is debated. Moreover, the Hebrew Bible contains a gap in the historical presentation for the period under question.

This chapter provides the backdrop against which the literature from and about Judah in the Neo-Babylonian period took place. Traditionally, biblical historians have reconstructed this timeframe on the basis of the biblical portrait supplemented where applicable with extra-biblical ancient Near Eastern documentation and archaeological evidence. One of the major difficulties with this approach is that for the period subsequent to the fall of Jerusalem there is a complete gap in the historical information available in the historiographical record. The biblical historical account ceases after 587 only to resume fifty years later, thus yielding an almost insurmountable missing link in our knowledge of the period so crucial for the present study. In a recent article comparing the presentation of the Neo-Babylonian period in the historiographical books of Kings, Chronicles, Ezra–Nehemiah, and 1 Esdras, Japhet has shown the level of disinterest in events which took place therein.[1] The Kings account briefly relates the destructive events that coincided with the Jerusalem war of 587. Although it mentions the remaining poor people of the land, and the appointment and assassination of Gedaliah, it concludes with a glimpse of life outside the land with almost a postscript about the release of King Jehoiachin from prison in Babylon c.562. The record is not resumed until the period of the first return recounted in Ezra 1–6. If one were to reconstruct the history of Judah during the Neo-Babylonian period based on biblical historiography alone, very little would be written.

In addition to the incomplete portrait of the situation in Judah during this period, there is another factor to take into consideration, that is, increased concerns about the use of the Bible as a source of historical information.[2] There have been two extreme perspectives: on the one hand, those that regard the Hebrew Bible as an accurate window into history, and on the other, those who view its portrayal as too tendentious and stylized to be of any use.[3] Most interpreters lie

---

[1] S. Japhet, 'Periodization: Between History and Ideology: The Neo-Babylonian Period in Biblical Historiography', in Lipschits and Blenkinsopp, *Judah and the Judeans*, 75–89.

[2] For an introduction to the issues, see D. V. Edelman (ed.), *The Fabric of History: Text, Artifact and Israel's Past* (JSOTSup, 127; Sheffield: Sheffield Academic Press, 1991); L. L. Grabbe (ed.), *Can a 'History of Israel' be Written?* (JSOTSup, 245; Sheffield: Sheffield Academic Press, 1997); L. L. Grabbe (ed.), *Leading Captivity Captive: 'The Exile' as History and Ideology* (JSOTSup, 278 and ESHM 2; Sheffield: Sheffield Academic Press, 1998); V. Long (ed.), *Israel's Past in Present Research: Essays on Ancient Israelite Historiography* (SBTS, 7; Winona Lake, Ind.: Eisenbrauns, 1999).

[3] G. Garbini, *History and Ideology in ancient Israel* (London: SCM Press, 1988); P. R. Davies, *In Search of 'Ancient Israel'* (JSOTSup, 148; Sheffield: JSOT Press, 2nd edn. 1995) and *idem*, 'The Society of Biblical Israel', in T. C. Eskenazi and K. H. Richards (eds.), *Second Temple Studies*, ii: *Temple and Community in the Persian Period* (JSOTSup, 175; Sheffield: JSOT Press, 1994), 22–33; N. Lemche, *Die Vorgeschichte Israels: Von den Anfängen bis zum Ausgang des 13. Jahrhunderts v. Chr* (BE, 1; Stuttgart: Kohlhammer, 1996); ET *Prelude to Israel's Past: Background and Beginnings of Israelite History and Identity* (Peabody, Mass.: Hendrickson, 1998); K. W. Whitelam, *The Invention of Ancient Israel: The Silencing of Palestinian History* (London: Routledge, 1996); T. L. Thompson, *The Bible in History: How Writers Create a Past* (London: Pimlico, repr. 2000).

along a spectrum somewhere between the two and would be likely to agree with Barstad's conclusions that ' "Factual historical truth" must be replaced with "narrative historical truth", which is related to "factual truth", but not identical with it.'[4]

The problems encountered in the historical presentation are compounded by the means that conveyed it. The small amount of literature that could be attributed to the sixth century is not primarily historical in nature but prophetic, as in the case of Jeremiah, Ezekiel, and Deutero-Isaiah, or liturgical, as with Lamentations and certain psalms. On the latter, lament literature is not historical per se, but liturgical recital replete with formulaic language and abstract details which enable poems to be used more readily in the cult over time. It is, thus, less helpful in reconstructing an accurate portrait of this time period than historical narrative would be. Although references in poetry are elusive, they often correspond to actual events. It would be churlish, for instance, to deny the graphic portrayal of post-war conditions depicted in the poems of Lamentations a real-life setting.[5] But the association with specific events is quite another thing than the accurate depiction of those events. Liturgy, therefore, contributes more fruitfully towards a discussion of theological interpretation than to historical reconstruction.

Prophecy fares slightly better in this regard. Although prophetic literature is usually oracular and poetic, the redactors of Jeremiah and the editor(s) of Ezekiel provide more structured narrative. Even so, the redactors of Jeremiah refracted the prophetic message to the community in Babylon. Nonetheless, the prose passages found in the section commonly attributed to Baruch have been used by interpreters to provide more details of life in the homeland after 587. The book of Ezekiel, too, appears to relate to the exiles in Babylon even

---

[4] H. M. Barstad, 'The Strange Fear of the Bible: Some Reflections on the "Bibliophobia" in Recent ancient Israel Historiography', in Grabbe, *Leading Captivity Captive*, 126.

[5] J. Krecher, 'Klagelied', in D. O. Edzard (ed.), *Reallexikon der Assyriologie und Vorderasiatischen Archäologie*, vi (Berlin: de Gruyter, 1980–3), 1–6; W. W. Hallo, 'Lamentations and Prayers in Sumer and Akkad', in J. M. Sasson (ed.), *Civilizations of the Ancient Near East*, iii (London and New York: Simon & Schuster, 1995), 1872. Hallo notes, in conjunction with his helpful introduction to the range of Mesopotamian lament literature, that the city laments which share many similarities with the biblical Lamentations contain descriptions associated with particular events.

though in the first half of the book the prophet issues a clear and unequivocal declaration of the impending irrevocable punishment about to befall Jerusalem and Judah. In both accounts, some literature represents the situation in Judah, but the concern of the material with the Babylonian community makes any case tentative. In contrast, Deutero-Isaiah considers matters of a more historical nature in the first half of the collection, chapters 40–8, and even clearly forecasts Cyrus, for example, to release the community from exile in Babylon. The fact that Cyrus is named in the collection and ascribed the role of delivering Israel on Yahweh's behalf suggests that the historical figure has entered the political scene in the ancient world. Nevertheless, Isaiah 40–55 as poetry is notoriously difficult to ascribe to specific events with precision and it moves from more historical and political concerns in chapters 40–8 to ahistorical concerns in 49–55. Since veiled allusions can by nature refer to a variety of situations, it is not good scholarship to make a one-to-one correspondence between metaphor and actual historical details. Several possible allusions to Cyrus in Deutero-Isaiah, for example, could very easily refer to the prophet or another figure.[6] The difficulty in using prophetic literature because of its literary form is exacerbated by its concern to convey Yahweh's intentions and words to the *Golah* community in Babylon.

An additional difficulty lies with the time in which a biblical book is set: no text should be uncritically associated with the period with which it overtly deals. Take the case of the book of Daniel, for instance.[7] The biblical account of Daniel sets the activity of the visionary among Diaspora Jews during the Babylonian exile and the early Persian period. It is well known and almost universally

---

[6] Deutero-Isaiah names Cyrus in 44: 28 and in 45: 1 and alludes to him elsewhere in chs. 40–8. S. Smith, *Isaiah XL–LV: Literary Criticism and History* (Schweich Lectures; London: Oxford University Press, 1944), is one example of the tendency to understand Cyrus in much of the figurative language of Isa. 40–55.

[7] The literature on Daniel is vast. For a history of scholarship, see K. Koch, *Das Buch Daniel* (EF, 144; Darmstadt: Wissenschaftliche Buchgesellschaft, 1980), 55–77 and H. H. Rowley, 'The Unity of the Book of Daniel', in *The Servant of the Lord and Other Essays on the Old Testament* (Oxford: Blackwell, 2nd edn. 1965), 249–60. Otherwise, helpful introductions to the composition, setting, and text of the book can be found in the commentaries and in the various essays in J. J. Collins and W. Flint (eds.), *The Book of Daniel: Composition and Reception*, 2 vols. (SVT, 93; Leiden, Brill, 2001).

accepted that the prophetic account stems from the Maccabean period when Jewish identity was threatened by Antioches IV Epiphanes. The collection functions to encourage Jews outside the homeland by presenting them with a Jewish hero who triumphs through his faith in the God of Judaea over foreign oppression.[8] Certain historical details of the story alert scholars to the pseudepigraphic nature of Daniel so its provenance is rarely placed in the time with which it purports to deal.

In order to avoid a facile acceptance of the biblical portrait of Neo-Babylonian Judah (such as it is) and to avoid having to choose between material that accurately represents the sixth century BCE and that which does not, while at the same time acknowledging that the main source of information for certain details about Late Iron Age Judah is the Hebrew Bible, it seems appropriate to provide a synopsis of the situation as many biblical historians understand it mainly on the basis of the account in 2 Kings (supplemented where applicable with Jeremiah). The rather truncated picture of Neo-Babylonian Judah will be supplemented with the reconstructions of three interpreters who have used other biblical data to flesh out the situation in the homeland. The section which summarizes the biblical data reveals how the biblical writers understood Neo-Babylonian Judah, while the reconstructions made by Lipschits, Albertz, and Seitz exhibit scholarly conceptions of the period. After that discussion, the archaeological evidence and the ruling strategies of the Neo-Babylonian empire will be discussed to shed additional light. The evidence of both provides a means to evaluate the accuracy of the presentation of Neo-Babylonian Judah found within the conceptions of the biblical writers and the biblical historians.

JUDAH IN THE SIXTH CENTURY BCE

The situation within the land of Judah during the sixth century BCE is demarcated by two significant events within the biblical portrait:

[8] On the rise of hero literature, see D. L. Smith, *The Religion of the Landless: The Social Context of the Babylonian Exile* (Bloomington, Ind.: Meyer-Stone, 1989). Because D. L. Smith now publishes as Smith-Christopher, I refer to him as such.

(1) the fall of Jerusalem in 587 and (2) the rise of Cyrus in 539 and the subsequent return of the exiles to rebuild Jerusalem. The fall of Jerusalem actually represented the second and more disastrous incursion made by the Neo-Babylonians against Judah. The first occurred in 598 when Nebuchadnezzar led an army against Jerusalem (2 Kgs. 24: 2; Jer. 35: 11). During the battle the Neo-Babylonian troops besieged, captured, and looted Jerusalem (2 Kgs. 24: 10–11), exiled members of the royal household, prominent citizens including priests, and artisans to Babylon (2 Kgs. 24: 12–17), and replaced the young king Jehoiachin with his uncle, Mattaniah-Zedekiah[9] (2 Kgs. 24: 17).[10] Significantly for the biblical writers the Neo-Babylonians forcibly deported a number of citizens at that time. They summarized the event by 'Judah went into exile from its land' and recorded a conflicting series of numbers; 10,000 people according to 2 Kings 24: 14 but 8,000 according to 2 Kings 24: 16, and also 3,034 according to Jeremiah 52: 28. Whatever the real number, the biblical writers summarize the event '[Nebuchadnezzar] carried away all Jerusalem... no-one remained except the poorest people of the land' (2 Kgs. 24: 14) and explain it by 'Indeed, Jerusalem and Judah so angered the Lord that he expelled them from his presence' (2 Kgs. 24: 20).

The declining years of the relative independence of Judah witnessed another and final attempt at political sovereignty.[11] Zedekiah sought unwisely to throw off the Babylonian yoke in 588 by forging an alliance with neighbouring states (Jer. 27–28; cf. 2 Kgs. 24: 20),[12]

---

[9] Reading with Kings because 2 Chr. 36: 11 represents an alternative version in which Zedekiah is the elder brother of Jehoiachin.

[10] The event is recorded in the Babylonian Chronicles thus: 'The seventh year, in the month Kislev the king of Akkad assembled his troops and marched to Ḫatti and established his camps against the city of Yaḫudu [Judah]. In the month of Addar, the 2nd day, he took the city and seized the king. He installed a king of his choice. He took vast tribute and returned to Babylon.' Translated from the French. J-. J. Glassner, *Chroniques Mésopotamiennes* (La Roue à Livres; Paris: Les Belles Lettres, 1993), 200; cf. A. K. Grayson, *Assyrian and Babylonian Chronicles* (TCS, 5; Locust Valley: J. J. Augustin, 1975), hereafter *ABC*, 102.

[11] Regrettably, the Babylonian Chronicles break off after the eleventh year of Nebuchadnezzar (594/3).

[12] The Lachish ostraca support some type of coalition formed to rebel during this time. J. B. Pritchard (ed.), *Ancient Near Eastern Texts Relating to the Old Testament* (Princeton, NJ: Princeton University Press, 3rd edn. 1969), hereafter *ANET*³, 322.

probably encouraged by the stand-off which resulted from the military engagement of Egypt and Babylon in 601/600.[13] A swift and unmerciful Neo-Babylonian response ensued during which the invaders completely eradicated all of the meaningful symbols of the political, social, and religious spheres of Judah (2 Kgs. 25: 1; Jer. 52: 4). In the eighteenth (Jer. 52: 29) or nineteenth (2 Kgs. 25: 8) year of the reign of Nebuchadnezzar, the city of Jerusalem was captured, sacked, looted, and razed to the ground along with its temple, palace, and city walls, the inhabitants were put to death or taken into exile, and Zedekiah was forced to watch the murder of his sons before being blinded and taken to Babylon (2 Kgs. 25: 6–7 // Jer. 39: 5–7; 52: 9–11).[14] According to Jeremiah 34: 7, the Neo-Babylonians attacked all of the cities of Judah, especially the fortified towns of Lachish and Azekah. Once again the biblical account insists that 'the remnant of the people that was left in the city, the defectors who had gone over to the king of Babylon, and the remnant of the population were taken into exile' (2 Kgs. 25: 11) and 'Judah went into exile from its land' (2 Kgs. 25: 21; Jer. 52: 27) whilst at the same time admitting the presence of some people: 'But some of the poorest in the land were left ... to be vinedressers and field hands' (2 Kgs. 25: 12; Jer. 52: 16). The Kings account does not include any numerical data for the amount of deportees relocated after the second incursion, but Jeremiah estimates the number at 832 (Jer. 52: 29).

A few details are forthcoming concerning life in Judah after the collapse of Jerusalem in 587. According to the account in 2 Kings the Neo-Babylonians appointed Gedaliah, a nobleman with no connection to the Davidic line, as governor.[15] Gedaliah established his seat

---

See the qualification of this theory by B. Otzen, 'Israel Under the Assyrians', in M. T. Larsen (ed.), *Power and Propaganda: A Symposium on Ancient Empires* (Mesopotamia, 7; Copenhagen; Akademisck, 1979), 251–61.

[13] Glassner, *Chroniques Mésopotamiennes*, 200, cf. *ABC*, 101.

[14] A. Malamat, 'The Last Kings of Judah and the Fall of Jerusalem', *IEJ* 18 (1968), 137–56.

[15] The word for governor is not in the Hebrew, but the Hebrew verb of Gedaliah's reign implies governance at the very least. The verb is the hiphil of פקד 'to appoint, set over' (Jer. 40: 5, 7). There is not enough evidence to support his role as that of king, contra J. M. Miller and J. H. Hayes, *A History of Ancient Israel and Judah* (London: SCM Press, 1986), 421–5; F. Bianchi, 'Zerobabel re di Giuda', *Henoch* 13 (1991), 133–56; F. Bianchi, 'Le rôle de Zerobabel et de la dynastie davidique en Judée du VIe siècle au IIe siècle av. J.-C.', *Transeuphratène* 7 (1994), 153–65; A. Lemaire,

of governance in Mizpah located about 12 kilometres north of Jerusalem (2 Kgs. 25: 23, 25; Jer. 40: 6, 10, 12, 13, 15; 41: 1, 3) and set about to re-establish life in Judah. A group of royalists influenced perhaps by the king of Ammon in Jeremiah's account of Gedaliah's rule (Jer. 40: 14–15, cf. 41: 10) assassinated Gedaliah (2 Kgs. 25: 25; Jer. 41: 1–2, 18) and fled with 'all the people, young and old, and the officers of the troops' to Egypt (2 Kgs. 25: 26). After the rise and fall of Gedaliah, the Kings account ends among the exiles in Babylon (2 Kgs. 25: 27–30, cf. Jeremiah 52: 31–4). For the final time, the biblical writers depict the land emptied of its inhabitants. According to the implications of biblical historiography, conditions in Judah would have worsened after the death of Gedaliah.

For the situation in Judah, Kings presents a rather straightforward account of the fall of Jerusalem and the rapid installation and assassination of Gedaliah, only to end with an oddly appended postscript about the release of Jehoiachin from prison in Babylon. Although Jeremiah provides slightly more details about life in the homeland in the material traditionally associated with Baruch, the historical presentation actually resumes with an account about the period of the early return in Ezra 1–6. Written closer to the time of Ezra and Nehemiah in the fifth century BCE, Ezra 1–6 reconstructs the period surrounding the rebuilding of the temple in Jerusalem. The retrospective account of the early Second Temple period clearly serves ideological purposes and even appears to include a certain *Tendenz* within its historical account based on the prophetic material of Haggai and Zechariah 1–8 as well as source documents.[16] The

'Zerobabel et la Judée à la lumière de l'épigraphie (fin du VIe s. av. J.-C.)', *RB* 103 (1996), 48–57; J. Blenkinsopp, 'The Age of Exile', in J. Barton (ed.), *The Biblical World* (London and New York: Routledge, 2002), 416–39. Cf. Albertz, *Die Exilszeit*, 82 n. 153 = *Israel in Exile*, 92–3 n. 166.

[16] H. G. M. Williamson, 'The Composition of Ezra i–vi', *JTS* NS 34 (1983), 1–30; B. Halpern, 'A Historiographic Commentary on Ezra 1–6: Achronological Narrative and Dual Chronology in Israelite Historiography', in W. H. Propp, B. Halpern, and D. N. Freedman (eds.), *The Hebrew Bible and Its Interpreters* (Winona Lake, Ind.: Eisenbrauns, 1990), 81–142; L. L. Grabbe, *Judaism from Cyrus to Hadrian* (London: SCM Press, 1994), 30–6; L. L. Grabbe, *Ezra–Nehemiah* (OTR; London: Routledge, 1998), 125–32; P. R. Bedford, *Temple Restoration in Early Achaemenid Judah* (JSJSup, 65; Leiden: Brill, 2001), 85–181; C. Karrer, *Ringen um die Verfassung Judas: Eine Studie zu den theologisch-politischen Vorstellungen im Esra–Nehemia-Buch* (BZAW, 308; Berlin: de Gruyter, 2001), 215–21.

historical presentation skips from the decline of Judah to its rebirth. Significantly, the biblical writers associate the period of regeneration and renewal at the time of the rebuilding of the temple. It is clear that for the biblical writers the period of Neo-Babylonian Judah is defined by a period of inactivity which took place between the existence of the two temples.

What becomes clear in the above short historical survey is the absence of direct evidence for the situation in the homeland as well as the vague, even conflicting, nature of the sources. For instance, there is tension between the various accounts of deportation. Not only can the numbers of deportees not be reconciled with any ease, the threefold insistence that the land was uninhabited only to be contradicted by the existence of additional people to take into captivity is anomalous. Regrettably, very little can be confirmed from extra-biblical material. From the extant extra-biblical literature what can be known relates to Judahites outside the homeland, especially those in Babylonia[17] and Egypt.[18] The biblical writers present reconstructions of activity during the period prior to 587 and subsequent to 539, but there is a serious lack of an ongoing historical account for the time between those events. The biblical focus itself seems uninterested in the fate of Judah after Gedaliah's murder. The presentation of the period certainly justifies Oded's assessment that 'the Jewish population which remained in the country was in a state of depression, lack of confidence, economic poverty, and political and national inactivity'.[19]

---

[17] W. F. Albright, 'King Jehoiachin in Exile', *BA* 5 (1942), 49–55; M. D. Coogan, 'Life in the Diaspora: Jews at Nippur in the Fifth Century B.C.', *BA* 37 (1974), 6–12; R. Zadok, *The Jews in Babylonia during the Chaldean and Achaemenid Periods* (Haifa: University of Haifa Press, 1979); M. W. Stolper, *Entrepreneurs and Empire: The Murašû Archive, the Murašû Firm, and Persian Rule in Babylonia* (Uitgaven van het Nederlands Historisch-Archaeologisch Instituut te Istanbul, 54; Istanbul: Nederlands Historisch-Archaeologisch Instituut, 1985); F. Joannès and A. Lemaire, 'Trois tablettes cunéiformes à onomastique ouestsémitique (collection Sh. Moussaieff) (Pls. I–II)', *Transeuphratène* 17 (1996), 17–34.

[18] B. Porten, *Archives from Elephantine: The Life of an Ancient Jewish Military Colony* (Berkeley: University of California Press, 1968); B. Porten, 'The Jews in Egypt' in W. D. Davies and L. Finkelstein (eds.), *Cambridge History of Judaism*, i (hereafter *CHJ*, i) *Introduction: The Persian Period* (Cambridge: Cambridge University Press, 1984), 372–400; M. Smith, 'Jewish Religious Life in the Persian Period', in *CHJ*, i. 219–78; B. Porten and A. Yardeni, *Textbook of Aramaic Documents from Ancient Egypt: Texts and Studies for Students*, i: *Letters* (Winona Lake, Ind.: Eisenbrauns, 1986).

[19] Oded, 'Judah', 479.

The gap in the historical presentation for the period between 587 and 539 raises concerns about what transpired in the homeland. The biblical material provides a conception of Neo-Babylonian Judah emptied of inhabitants except for the relatively minor population of 'the poor people of the land' without a capital city and without the infrastructure or political authority to have any form of meaningful existence. Because of the nature of the biblical presentation it is important first of all to understand it as the historical circumstances conceptualized by the biblical writers and not to use it to provide the definitive historical portrait of the period. Nevertheless, in spite of the overall ideological portrait there are details embedded within the narrative which indicate factors that would contribute to a positive assessment of life in the homeland. There have been several recent attempts to utilize certain biblical texts in an indicative way as a means to flesh out the situation that transpired around the collapse of Jerusalem and thereafter. In spite of the attempts of the biblical writers to obfuscate the situation in the homeland, Lipschits, Albertz, and Seitz, among others, have contributed to the knowledge of life in Neo-Babylonian Judah.

In the first place, Lipschits considers the evidence located within the biography of Jeremiah (chs. 37–44) in order to ascertain Neo-Babylonian imperial policy in the region.[20] According to his analysis, the Neo-Babylonians were in the process of establishing Mizpah as an administrative centre prior to the destruction of Jerusalem in 587. Lipschits observes that an organized group of pro-Babylonian Judahites (Jer. 38: 18) were associated with the territory of Benjamin. Instructive for him is the incident where the townspeople accuse Jeremiah of 'deserting to the Chaldeans' (Jer. 37: 13) when they attempt to impede him from going to the land of Benjamin towards the end of the siege of Jerusalem in 587 and before its fall (Jer. 37: 11–15). Significantly, certain texts allude to the establishment of Gedaliah as a political figurehead before the collapse of Jerusalem. Importantly, the Babylonians were able to exercise authority immediately following the destruction of Jerusalem (Jer. 39: 14). In addition, Mizpah served as the locale towards which the prophet

---

[20] Lipschits, 'Nebuchadrezzar's Policy', 476–82 and *idem*, 'The History of the Benjamin Region', 159–61.

Jeremiah encouraged the people to return after the destruction (40: 5; cf. 2 Kgs. 25: 23; Jer. 40: 7, 11–12) and towards which he himself gravitated (40: 6) after Jerusalem's fall. This analysis certainly suggests the possibility that the Neo-Babylonians played an active role in converting Judah from a vassal kingdom to an imperial province with a newly established administrative centre in Mizpah north of the destroyed Jerusalem, perhaps even prior to the defeat of the state.

Concentrating on material he believes to represent Judahite existence in the period following the events of 587, Albertz reconstructs a plausible scenario for ongoing life in the homeland. He considers two portraits of Judah that are at variance with each other: Jeremiah 40: 7 to 43: 3, which indicates improvement and co-operation with the Babylonians, and Lamentations 1–2, 4–5, which suggests the suffering which would occur within an occupied territory.[21] Importantly, Albertz regards the opposing pictures as representing the period prior to and just after the assassination of Gedaliah and the military reprisals that would have taken place in conjunction with that event. After 582 (when he dates Gedaliah's murder), conditions would have worsened considerably in the land. This is an important distinction in the period, but is difficult to assess in conjunction with the biblical data alone. The lack of data has resulted therefore in uncertainty about the type of policy that existed after the assassination of Gedaliah. Albertz speculates, therefore, that Judah may have fallen under the political authority of a Babylonian governor or within the administration of Samaria, but notes that at least Lamentations 5: 14 indicates the possible leadership of the elders.[22] Although the rural population would have been largely unaffected by a change in leadership, foreign encroachment into the territory of Judah by neighbouring nation-states like Edom, Phoenicia and Philistia, and Ammon would have contributed to a sense of insecurity and instability.[23]

---

[21] Albertz, *Die Exilszeit*, 81–5 = *Israel in Exile*, 90–6.

[22] Albertz, *A History of Israelite Religion in the Old Testament Period*, ii: *From the Exile to the Maccabees* (London: SCM Press, 1994), 372; and *idem*, *Die Exilszeit*, 84 = *Israel in Exile*, 96. Note, however, that the text occurs within a lament about the lack of leadership, and see Lam. 5: 12.

[23] This argument is not unique to Albertz, but his understanding of it as a crucial social factor for the identity of the inhabitants of the homeland is an important insight. For a list of texts adduced in support of this point, see Albertz, *Die Exilszeit*, 84–5 = *Israel in Exile*, 96. cf. J. R. Bartlett, 'Edomites and Idumaeans', *PEQ* 131 (1999), 102–14, for an alternative perspective.

Finally, in an assessment of the historical, social, and theological background of the book of Jeremiah, Seitz highlights internal factors that would suggest the renewal of stability and quality of life after 587 and the assassination of Gedaliah. In particular, he raises to the foreground the leadership of the 'people of the land' during times of crises and evidence for scribal activity. Seitz noted that during periods when the succession of the throne was threatened in the Kings narrative, 'the people of the land' assured the smooth transition of leadership (2 Kgs. 11: 13–20; 21: 24; 23: 30).[24] The identity of the 'people of the land' remains in dispute, but widespread opinion agrees that they represent a class of land-owners who are distinct from the wider population of Judah and the elites of Jerusalem[25] and who functioned on occasion in an authoritative way in Jerusalem.[26] They appear to have rejected entanglements with Egypt and after the death of Josiah favoured co-operation with the Babylonians.[27] The 'people of the land' exercised authority in cases when the security of the nation was threatened, but not necessarily out of allegiance to the Davidic line, rather out of acceptance of the current system of rule. On this point, Seitz helpfully notes, 'It would overstep the evidence to claim that the "people of the land" had any special or historically significant allegiance to Davidic kingship *as such*. Rather, they accept the dynastic premise as it finds force in Jerusalem and work within it in ways open to them'[28] (italics his). Another group who acted similarly on at least one occasion were termed the 'people of Judah', that is, those who represent the wider population of the homeland (2 Kgs. 14: 19–22).[29] The appearance of 'the people of the land' or 'the people of Judah' during periods of political upheaval in times past suggests that the vacuum in leadership left by the assassination of Gedaliah would have been quickly filled in order to stabilize the situation.

---

[24] Seitz, *Theology in Conflict*, 7–102.

[25] Ibid., 46. The 'people of the land' are to be distinguished from the ambiguous 'people of Judah', princes, mighty men of valour, craftsmen and smiths, kings, priests, princes of Judah, princes of Jerusalem, and eunuchs (2 Kgs. 24: 14; Jer. 1: 18; 34: 19; 37: 2; 44: 21).

[26] For a discussion with references to other views, see Seitz, *Theology in Conflict*, 42–51, 55–71; T. Willi, *Juda-Jehud-Israel: Studien zum Selbstverständnis des Judentums in persischer Zeit* (FAT, 12; Tübingen: Mohr (Paul Siebeck), 1995), 11–17.

[27] Seitz, *Theology in Conflict*, 68–9.

[28] Ibid., 66–7.

[29] Ibid., 47, 49.

After asserting reasons to believe in the likelihood of the establishment of political authority after the untimely death of Gedaliah, the Neo-Babylonian appointed governor, Seitz further makes the case for ongoing literary activity in Judah. He argues for the existence of a scribal class with Deuteronomic leanings who held out hope for the community in Judah after the events of 598 and 587 in a scribal chronicle. The scribal chronicle in Seitz's view is the rough equivalent of the material in Jeremiah that scholars have attributed to Baruch. Of this material, Seitz finds Jeremianic prophecies updated after the events of 587 for the community in exile *and* that in the homeland. The author would have been among those scribal families that survived the deportations of 598 and who remained in Judah with Jeremiah before and after 587, but was relocated after the death of Gedaliah.[30] Seitz further suggests that the author of the scribal chronicle because of his sympathetic treatment of Gedaliah is likely to have stemmed from the Shaphan family.[31] Even though the scribal chronicle and the book of Jeremiah eventually reached Babylon where the prophecies would be updated again, this time through *Golah* redactors, it is possible that scribes remained in Judah after the Babylonian repercussions for the death of Gedaliah.[32]

Using the biblical material to arrive at the socio-historical situation of Neo-Babylonian Judah is clearly possible, but the biblical portrait itself does not encourage any positive assessment of the homeland during this time. It is clear from the reconstructions made by Lipschits, Albertz, and Seitz that the texts can be gleaned for clues about life in the land, but those details have to be read against the ideological portrait of the period. The last biblical details relevant to the population in Judah indicate an imperial policy aimed at the reconstitution of the province under a Babylonian appointed governor. Although nothing further is disclosed on this point after the death of Gedaliah, the silence of the biblical witness does not

---

[30] Seitz, *Theology in Conflict*, 241, 282–7.
[31] Ibid., 285; Albertz, *Die Exilszeit*, 81–2 = *Israel in Exile*, 91–2.
[32] D. W. Jamieson-Drake, *Scribes and Schools in Monarchic Judah: A Socio-Archaeological Approach* (JSOTSup, 109; Sheffield: Almond, 1991), argues for little scribal activity in sixth-century Judah based on the archaeological evidence. See the critique by Albertz, *Die Exilszeit*, 82–3 = *Israel in Exile*, 93.

demand the view that all normal life in Judah ceased.[33] In the first place, the biblical account locates vinedressers and ploughmen in Judah. Secondly, the Neo-Babylonian intention to encourage stability through the appointment of a governor did not necessarily change after the death of Gedaliah. The mention of governors in early Second Temple texts attests that from the beginning of Persian rule certain leaders of the community functioned in a capacity similar to that of Gedaliah. Haggai speaks of Zerubbabel as a governor (Hag. 1: 1, 14; 2: 2, 21) whilst the historical account of Ezra 1–6 reserves the title of governor for Sheshbazzar (Ezra 5: 14).[34] Given the nature of the material and uncertainty surrounding its facticity, a consideration of extra-biblical evidence is in order. In particular a consideration of the archaeological evidence and the Neo-Babylonian imperial strategies should confirm or disallow reconstructions of sixth-century Judah based on the biblical record alone.

ARCHAEOLOGICAL EVIDENCE OF THE HOMELAND

Given that the biblical evidence alone leaves certain questions about the nature and quality of life in the homeland unanswered, the social setting of Judah under Neo-Babylonian rule can be understood more completely through an assessment of archaeological evidence from excavations and surveys. At the forefront it should be acknowledged that as with other means of approaching this period the archaeological evidence does not provide a complete or entirely incontrovertible picture. In fact, the evidence provided by the material culture is itself fragmentary and difficult to assess. It is particularly difficult to isolate post-587 settlement layers, due to the fact that remains dating to after 587 look very similar to those of the late monarchical period or Iron Age II. Pottery, for instance, resembles previous forms,

---

[33] Lipschits, 'Nebuchadrezzar's Policy', 478–82, and *idem*, 'The History of the Benjamin Region', 161–5.

[34] H. G. M. Williamson, 'The Governors of Judah under the Persians', *TynB* 39 (1988), 59–82. Tattenai is given his full title as the 'governor of the province Beyond the River' (Ezra 5: 3, 6; 6: 6, 13), but he is not included here since he did not function in this capacity in Judah.

but with a decline in quality, thus, resulting in the ascription of 'Iron II degenerate'.[35] The real question, then, turns to where to date the transition between Iron Age II and Iron Age III, either in 587 or in 539. Traditionally, a break has been established after 587, which means that material evidence thought to stem from this time period was posited to the early part of the sixth century. It is now clear, however, that sixth-century remains show a decline—thus the so-called 'degenerate' forms—but no discontinuity until the end of the sixth or the beginning of the fifth century. Our parameters of the period must be realigned accordingly.[36] In addition, a tendency to excavate the most important biblical sites, the privileging of certain periods over others which has left damage to layers of interest in this study, and the poor execution and maintenance of records for site excavations, especially among work carried out in the early twentieth century, exacerbate the problem.[37] Nevertheless, the results of archaeological endeavours assist in filling in gaps in our knowledge.

Surveys and excavations contribute to our knowledge of sixth-century Judah by enabling the construction of the situation in Templeless Judah through locating settlements during the period. A question of vital concern is: What were the repercussions for Judah under Neo-Babylonian rule? Two very different pictures of Templeless Judah emerge in the literature. They are illustrated in a poignant way by the debate between Blenkinsopp and Stern that

[35] L. A. Sinclair, 'Bethel Pottery of the Sixth Century B.C.', *AASOR* 39 (1968), 70–6; S. S. Weinberg, 'Post-Exilic Palestine: An Archaeological Report', in *Proceedings of the Israel Academy of Sciences and Humanities* (Jerusalem: Israel Academy of Sciences and Humanities, 1969–70), 84, 88; R. Amiran, 'A Note on the "Gibeon Jar" ', *PEQ* 110 (1975), 129; E. Stern, *Material Culture of the Land of the Bible in the Persian Period, 538–332 B.C.* (Jerusalem: Israel Exploration Society, 1982), 229.

[36] G. Barkay, 'The Iron Age IIIb—The Sixth Century BCE', in A. Ben-Tor (ed.), *The Archaeology of ancient Israel* (New Haven, Conn.: Yale University Press, 1992), 372–3, and idem, 'The Redefining of Archaeological Periods: Does the Date 588/586 B.C.E. Indeed Mark the End of Iron Age Culture?', in A. Biran and J. Aviram (eds.), *Biblical Archaeology Today: Proceedings of the Second International Congress on Biblical Archaeology* (Jerusalem: Israel Exploration Society, 1993), 106–9; C. E. Carter, 'The Province of Yehud in the Post-Exilic Period: Soundings in Site Distribution and Demography', in Eskenazi and Richards, *Second Temple Studies*, ii. 120–2.

[37] C. E. Carter, *The Emergence of Yehud in the Persian Period: A Social and Demographic Study* (JSOTSup, 294; Sheffield: Sheffield Academic Press, 1999), 53; J. Blenkinsopp, 'The Bible, Archaeology and Politics; or The Empty Land Revisited', *JSOT* 27 (2002), 178–9.

occurred in a recent issue of *Biblical Archaeology Review* entitled 'The Babylonian Gap Revisited: There Was No Gap... Yes There Was'.[38] The issue rests on whether the focus should be on the devastating effects of the Neo-Babylonian military incursions that accompanied the early years of Nebuchadnezzar's reign or on the areas that were spared. Blenkinsopp takes the latter point of view. In contrast, Stern focuses on the devastation surrounding Jerusalem and the southern part of the former kingdom of Judah and argues for an almost completely incapacitated state. In some respects the debate presents an example of cross-communication. Blenkinsopp would not deny the sweeping destruction wrought by the Babylonians, but he carefully notes the sites where the archaeological evidence indicates activity continued during the sixth century. In response, although in agreement with some key facts, Stern presents evidence of the total destruction that took place in the south of Judah. In point of fact, none of the sites he lists in the Southern kingdom is located north of Jerusalem. What Stern does not consider is that which Blenkinsopp insists upon; that is, the Benjamin region north of Jerusalem shows signs of continuity.[39] Evidence supports the arguments of both, but that does not necessitate agreement with Stern's rhetorical question: 'But what political or other significance can a defeated population have when it has no significant urban centers, when its religious center has been burned down, when its primary trade routes no longer exist, and when it no longer has its own government?'[40] The purpose of this section is to engage with and answer these questions put forward by Stern.

The archaeological evidence indeed supports the general picture of devastation and ruin discerned from the biblical portrait.[41]

---

[38] J. Blenkinsopp, 'There Was No Gap', *BAR* 28/3 (2002), 36–8, 59; E. Stern, 'Yes There Was', *BAR* 28/3 (2002), 39, 55, and *idem*, 'The Babylonian Gap: The Archaeological Reality', *JSOT* 28 (2004), 273–7; cf. Blenkinsopp, 'The Age of Exile', 416–39, and *idem*, 'The Bible, Archaeology and Politics'.

[39] To be fair, Stern, *Material Culture*, 229, mentions as a notable feature of the Babylonian period that remains were uncovered in the Negev, Judaean Hills, and the area of Benjamin, but he does not develop the implication of this either here or in his later work.

[40] Stern, 'Yes There Was', 39; cf. E. Stern, 'The Babylonian Gap', *BAR* 26/6 (2000), 45–51, 76, and *idem*, *Archaeology in the Land of the Bible*, ii: *The Assyrian, Babylonian and Persian Periods 732–332 B.C.E.* (New York: Doubleday, 2001), 304–31.

[41] Weinberg, *Post-Exilic Palestine*; Barstad, *The Myth of the Empty Land*, 47–55; L. E. Stager, 'The Fury of Babylon: The Archaeology of Destruction', *BAR* 22/1 (1996),

Twenty-two sites contain destruction layers that can be attributed to this period. Included among them are Jerusalem, En-Gedi, Jericho, Lachish, Ramat Rahel, Tell Beit Mirsim, Beth-Shemesh, and settlements in the Judaean hill country and the Shephelah. The Babylonians thoroughly attacked Judah. The severe repercussions of the battle, siege, and subsequent deportations on the city of Jerusalem reveal the intensity and thoroughness of the Babylonian campaign.[42] Moreover, large areas of the territory of Judah were devastated and not resettled, leaving the main urban centres abandoned. Most areas remained uninhabited and in ruins until well into the Persian period. If one concentrates on the amount of widespread devastation that coincided with the Babylonian invasions of 598 and 587, the picture is indeed a grim one. Widespread destruction lends some credence to the view that Judah during the Templeless period was in a state of social, political, and economic depression, with little ability to recover from the disaster. From this point of view the impression given is a rudimentary one in which the Judahite inhabitants were barely able to eke out an existence.

Although numerous sites were almost completely annihilated, these are concentrated mostly in southern Judah.[43] It has long been recognized that the Benjamin region slightly to the north of Jerusalem suffered little at the hands of the Babylonians.[44] In fact, very little in terms of destruction was found and several sites show

---

56–69, 76–7; Carter, *The Emergence of Yehud*, 114–71; Lipschits, 'The History of the Benjamin Region', 165–84; H. M. Barstad, 'After the "Myth of the Empty Land": Major Challenges in the Study of Neo-Babylonian Judah', in O. Lipschits and J. Blenkinsopp (eds.), *Judah and the Judeans in the Neo-Babylonian Period* (Winona Lake, Ind.: Eisenbrauns, 2003), 3–20.

[42] O. Lipschits, 'Judah, Jerusalem and the Temple 586–539 B.C.', *Transeuphratène* 22 (2001), 129–42.

[43] Our knowledge of the material culture and settlement patterns of Neo-Babylonian Judah has been significantly increased due to the work of O. Lipschits. The brief overview of the period that follows is due in a large part to the excellent summaries of the evidence in his articles, but note his recent Ph.D. dissertation in Hebrew, 'The "Yehud" Province under Babylonian Rule (586–539 B.C.E.): Historic Reality and Historiographic Conceptions' (Ph.D. dissertation, Tel-Aviv University, 1997). The field will be greatly enhanced with the publication of his thesis in English under the title, *The Fall and Rise of Jerusalem: The History of Judah under Babylonian Rule* (Winona Lake, Ind.: Eisenbrauns, forthcoming).

[44] A. Malamat, 'The Last Wars of the Kingdom of Judah', *JNES* 9 (1950), 227; Graham, *Palestine during the Period of the Exile*, 24; Stern, *Material Culture*, 229;

improvement during the period.⁴⁵ Four sites which reveal continuous settlement well into the late sixth century are Mizpah (Tell en-Nasbeh),⁴⁶ Gibeah (Tell el-Fûl),⁴⁷ Gibeon (El-Jîb),⁴⁸ and Bethel, which are located towards the north of Jerusalem.⁴⁹ After the destruction wrought by the Babylonians, En-Gedi, for instance, appears to have been reoccupied.⁵⁰ Other sites that were the location of resettlement in this period include Azor, Beth-Shemesh, Mozah, Tell Negilah, and Ramat Rahel. To this list, Carter adds two sections of Jerusalem—Horvat Zimri (Pizgat Ze'ev 'D') and Khirbet er-Ras.⁵¹ Although burial caves on the outskirts of Jerusalem remained in use during the sixth century, they attest to only minimal habitation.⁵²

Barstad, *The Myth of the Empty Land*, 47–55; Lipschits, 'The History of the Benjamin Region', 165. A general survey of the region can be found in Y. Magen and I. Finkelstein (eds.), *Archaeological Survey of the Hill Country of Benjamin* (Jerusalem: Israel Antiquities Authority, 1993) (Hebrew).

⁴⁵ Two very important recent studies that examine the data and include comprehensive details for consideration are C. E. Carter, 'Ideology and Archaeology in the Neo-Babylonian Period: Excavating Text and Tell', in Lipschits and Blenkinsopp, *Judah and the Judeans*, 301–22, and O. Lipschits, 'Demographic Changes in Judah between the Seventh and the Fifth Centuries B.C.E.', in ibid., 323–76.

⁴⁶ J. R. Zorn, 'Nasbeh, Tell en-', in E. Stern, *et al.* (eds.), *New Encyclopedia of Archaeological Excavations in the Holy Land* (New York: Simon & Schuster, 1993) (hereafter *NEAEHL*), iii. 1098–1102; idem, 'Mizpah: Newly Discovered Stratum Reveals Judah's Other Capital', *BAR* 23/5 (1997), 29–38, 66; idem, 'Tell en-Nasbeh and the Problem of the Material Culture of the Sixth Century', in Lipschits and Blenkinsopp, *Judah and the Judeans*, 413–47.

⁴⁷ W. Lapp, 'Tell el-Fûl', *BA* 28 (1965), 2–10; P. M. Arnold, *Gibeah: The Search for a Biblical City* (JSOTSup, 79, Sheffield: JSOT Press, 1990). The early conclusions of Lapp have been reassessed; cf. the articles in N. L. Lapp (ed.), *The Third Campaign at Tell el-Fûl: The Excavations of 1964*, AASOR 45 (1981), and N. L. Lapp, 'Fûl, Tell el-', *NEAEHL*, ii. 444–8.

⁴⁸ There is quite a debate surrounding the dating of this site. Pritchard argued against the resettlement of the site after the Babylonian invasion; cf. J. B. Pritchard, 'El Jib', *NEAEHL*, ii. 511–14. However, tombs were in use; cf. H. Eshel, 'The Late Iron Age Cemetery of Gibeon', *IEJ* 37 (1987), 1–17, and D. V. Edelman, 'Gibeon and the Gibeonites Revisited', in Lipschits and Blenkinsopp, *Judah and the Judeans*, 153–67.

⁴⁹ J. L. Kelso, 'Bethel', *NEAEHL*, i. 191–4. Overviews of the results of archaeological excavations on these cities can be found in e.g. Barstad, *The Myth of the Empty Land*, 47–51; Carter, *The Emergence of Yehud*, 119–32; Lipschits, 'The History of the Benjamin Region', 165–84; Barstad, 'After the "Myth of the Empty Land" '.

⁵⁰ Weinberg, *Post-Exilic Palestine*, 83.

⁵¹ Carter, *The Emergence of Yehud*, 132–4.

⁵² G. Barkay, *Ketef Hinnom: A Treasure Facing Jerusalem's Walls* (Jerusalem: Israel Museum, 1986), 31. Lipschits, 'Nebuchadrezzar's Policy', 474 n. 11, notes that this

Jerusalem would not regain anywhere near its former settlement numbers until well into the Persian period. Finally, the Northern hill country around Bethlehem to the south of Jerusalem exhibits settlement continuity.[53]

Of the sites that evidence continuous habitation and prosperity, the most important is Mizpah (Tell en-Nasbeh). Excavations that took place at Mizpah reveal that it contained houses varying from more elaborate to less sophisticated and what appear to be storehouses or wine vats.[54] The destruction wrought by the Neo-Babylonians was limited in scope and focus—affecting mainly the fortified cities in the southern territory of Judah (cf. Jer. 34: 7). Since no destruction layers have been found in Benjamin, this region, in distinction to Jerusalem and its environs, survived the disaster of 587 relatively unscathed and became the arena in which life continued in the land. A second important location of habitation during the Babylonian period is Bethlehem around Ramat Rahel in the Judaean hill country where sites continued into the Persian period.[55] Its lack of major buildings suggests that unlike Mizpah it did not function in any administrative capacity although its status apparently changed under the Persians.[56]

The location of settled sites in Judah during the Templeless period provides initial confirmation that there was a remnant of the population in the land. How many people were left and what were their circumstances? Although it is very difficult to come to a consensus regarding the population of Judah at any time, it is especially difficult for the sixth century BCE because of the scarcity and nature of the sources. To overcome the problems provided by the divergent

evidence 'is exceptional and must not be considered as proof for the continuation of life in Jerusalem in the time of the exile'. With the appearance of potsherds showing transitional forms at Horvat Zimri and a storehouse with sixteen winepresses apparently in use during the sixth century, it appears that there was some degree of regeneration of life in Jerusalem, however minimal it may have been.

[53] A. Ofer, 'The Judean Hill Country: From Nomadism to a National Monarchy', in N. Na'aman and I. Finkelstein (eds.), *From Nomadism to Monarchy: Archaeological and Historical Aspects of Early Israel* (Jerusalem: Israel Exploration Society, 1994), 92–121; Carter, *The Emergence of Yehud*, 133–4; Lipschits, 'Nebuchadrezzar's Policy', 475.

[54] Zorn, 'Mizpah'; Lipschits, 'The History of the Benjamin Region', 165–70, 179.

[55] Lipschits, 'The History of Benjamin Region'; 'Demographic Changes in Judah', 330–1.

[56] Lipschits, 'Demographic Changes in Judah', 330–1.

numbers of the biblical accounts, two recent demographic studies by Carter and Lipschits incorporate archaeological evidence of this period in their assessments of the numbers of inhabitants in Judah. However, even given the fact that over the course of time new excavations and site surveys will alter figures, both specialists diverge significantly in their estimated population numbers. In addition, their conclusions actually differ quite remarkably from Weinberg's recent attempt to reconstruct the numbers of inhabitants.[57]

The figures in Table 1.1 lie uneasily alongside estimates of the number of people deported by the Babylonians. In different analyses, the percentage of the population taken into exile equals roughly 10 per cent.[58] Such a figure cannot work in conjunction with the results of Carter and Lipschits since the figure of Babylonian Judah should be smaller than that of Persian Judah and the estimated number of deportees would be much larger than 10 per cent. To bolster the

Table 1.1

	Estimated population, end of monarchical period	Estimated population, Persian Period
Carter[1]	60,000	20,650
Lipschits[2]	108,000	30,125
Weinberg[3]	220,000–250,000	211,800 (42,360 × 5)

[1] Carter, *The Emergence of Yehud*, 246–8.
[2] Lipschits, 'Demographic Changes in Judah', 363–4.
[3] Weinberg, *The Citizen-Temple Community*, 34–7, 41–8. The figure used for the population in the Persian period is based on Weinberg's observation that the number of members of his hypothetical citizen-temple-community equals 42,360 (Ezra 2: 64 = Neh. 7: 66) which made up roughly 20% of the population.

[57] J. Weinberg, *The Citizen-Temple Community* (JSOTSup, 151; Sheffield: Sheffield Academic Press, 1992), 34–48.
[58] R. A. Horsley, 'Empire, Temple and Community—but no Bourgeoisie! A Response to Blenkinsopp and Petersen', in Davies, *Second Temple Studies*, i. 163–74; Weinberg, *The Citizen-Temple Community*, 37; Blenkinsopp, 'The Age of Exile', 419–20. Interestingly, Weinberg and Blenkinsopp arrive at the figure after having estimated the amount of population being taken into exile while Horsley suggests this figure based on the fact that in ancient societies the ruling apparatus equalled 8 to 10 per cent, and it is just this part of the population that is taken into exile according to the biblical record.

percentage of lost population with an estimated figure that accounts for voluntary flight and death still cannot explain the fact that the habitation of Persian Yehud is roughly one-quarter or one-third that of the late monarchical period. This is not to mention the fact that the biblical figure of 42,360 (Ezra 2 // Neh. 7) for the amount of returnees is higher than the population of Yehud estimated by Carter and Lipschits. Weinberg's figure is surely too high,[59] but are the others too low or are some of the figures faulty; and if so, which ones? The estimation of even approximate figures for the population of the Neo-Babylonian period cannot be calculated with any degree of certainty.[60] It is fortunate that a determination of the number of people remaining in the homeland is not the crucial factor for this chapter. What is important is that a significant number of the population remained in Judah and that certain regions were settled. An important recent attempt to ascertain the population figure of Judah and the number of deportees made by Albertz includes the important observation: 'Such an estimate yields a highly realistic ratio of about two to one for the number of people remaining in Judah and the number in the Babylonian *golah*. Given the higher proportion of educated individuals in the golah, the two major population elements of the exilic period were of roughly equal importance.'[61]

What was the nature of life for those who remained behind? Two different portraits, striking in their divergence, emerge. The archaeological evidence is used in conjunction with the imperial ruling strategy of the Babylonians to support the view of, on the one hand, a neglected periphery and, on the other, a resilient community that contributed to imperial coffers. For those who concentrate on the widespread devastation that accompanied the Neo-Babylonian military incursions in the Levant, the Babylonians are understood to have operated on the basis of a policy which devastated peripheral regions and then neglected them.[62] This reconstruction is supported

---

[59] As is the figure 12,000 for the population of Jerusalem during the Babylonian period. E.-M. Laperrousaz, 'Jérusalem à l'époque perse (étendu et statut)', *Transeuphratène* 1 (1989), 56.

[60] I. Milevski, 'Settlement Patterns in Northern Judah During the Achaemenid Period', *BAIAS* 15 (1996–7), 7–29, at 18; Blenkinsopp, 'The Age of Exile', 418–20.

[61] Albertz, *Die Exilszeit*, 80 = *Israel in Exile*, 90.

[62] E. Stern, *Archaeology of the Land of the Bible*, ii: *The Assyrian, Babylonian, and Persian Periods (732–332 B.C.E.)* (ABRL; New York and London: Doubleday, 2001),

to some extent by the complete annihilation and lasting depopulation of Philistine cities including Ashkelon and Ashdod.[63] Moreover, according to a recent examination of rural sites in Judah made by Faust there is hardly any continuity between the Iron Age and the Persian period.[64] For him, the break between the settlements exhibits the drastic demographic decline in Judah that accompanied the 587 war. This view, then, contributes to the belief that Nebuchadnezzar's policy in Judah intentionally left a depopulated and devastated buffer zone in the southern Levant.

For a number of scholars, among them Barkay, Barstad, Blenkinsopp, Graham, and Lipschits, the lack of destruction in the Benjamin region and the remains of production centres for exportable products exemplifies a regenerated Judah able to contribute more than financially to the empire. Zorn observes that Mizpah contains remains consistent with the transformation of a border fortress into a provincial administrative centre.[65] In addition, the presence of Babylonian officials may be confirmed by Mesopotamian artefacts and the appearance of Mesopotamian-style coffins at the site.[66] Since Mizpah continued to be occupied and even improved in the Templeless period, it is highly likely that it continued to function as an administrative capital throughout this time. Blenkinsopp, in fact, argues that the administration facilitated the resurgence of cultic activity at nearby Bethel.[67] Although the Bible refrains from further details about Judah and its system of governance after the death of Gedaliah, its silence does not necessitate the conclusion that the Babylonians

---

307–11; so also, N. Na'aman, 'Province System and Settlement Pattern in Southern Syria and Palestine in the Neo-Assyrian Period', in M. Liverani (ed.), *Neo Assyrian Geography* (QGS, 5; Rome: Università di Roma, 1995), 114–15; Na'aman, 'Royal Vassals or Governors?', 42–4.

[63] Stager, 'The Fury of Babylon', and *idem*, 'Ashkelon and the Archaeology of Destruction: Kislev 604 B.C.E.', *EI* 25 (1996), 61*–74*; Stern, 'The Babylonian Gap'.

[64] A. Faust, 'Judah in the Sixth Century B.C.E.: A Rural Perspective', *PEQ* 135 (2003), 37–53.

[65] Zorn, 'Mizpah'.

[66] J. R. Zorn, 'Mesopotamian-Style Ceramic "Bathtub" Coffins from Tell en-Nasbeh', *TA* 20 (1993), 216–24.

[67] J. Blenkinsopp, 'The Judaean Priesthood during the Neo-Babylonian and Achaemenid Periods: A Hypothetical Reconstruction', *CBQ* 60 (1998), 25–43, and *idem*, 'Bethel in the Neo-Babylonian Period', in Lipschits and Blenkinsopp, *Judah and the Judeans*, 93–107.

did not simply appoint another governor or that the people of the land intervened to establish another ruler.[68] A local administrative presence would facilitate the collection and distribution of regional produce. Many of the sites in the Benjamin region show that the production of goods beyond Judah's consumption took place.[69] To these it might be possible to add the stamped wine jar handles found in Gibeon and Mozah as indicative of localized trade during this time.[70]

A sizeable population remained in the former kingdom of Judah, but for the most part it occupied areas to the north and south of Jerusalem. The production of wine and oil to be taken as tribute for the empire and the remains of silos in which to house them show that Babylonian Judah, although not prosperous, continued a degree of normal life. Even as the community was roughly continuous with that of the late monarchical period, from excavations it is clear that their material culture was as well.[71] Indeed, a cultural break does not begin until around the last third of the sixth century BCE, which coincides with layers of destruction at several sites.

The later part of the sixth century in Judah is unclear. What is known is that certain sites, such as Bethel, Gibeon, and Gibeah, show destruction layers dating to the last third of the century. In addition, there was a striking decline in the number of sites in Benjamin between Iron Age II and the Persian period.[72] Elsewhere, in conjunction with the steady decline of settlements that continued well into the Persian period in the Benjamin area, the Judaean hill country around Khirbet Tubeiqah south of Jerusalem shows an unprecedented increase in new sites, while the habitation of Jerusalem itself

---

[68] Also, Lipschits, 'Nebuchadrezzar's Policy', 483.

[69] J. N. Graham, ' "Vinedressers and Plowmen": 2 Kings 25: 12 and Jeremiah 52: 16', *BA* 47 (1984), 55–8; Barstad, 'After the "Myth of the Empty Land" ', 9–13.

[70] J. B. Pritchard, *Hebrew Inscriptions and Stamps from Gibeon* (Museum Monographs; Philadelphia, Pa.: University of Philadelphia, 1959), 15; N. Avigad, 'Two Hebrew Inscriptions on Wine Jars', *IEJ* 22 (1972), 1–9; Amiran, 'A Note on the "Gibeon Jar" '; Graham, ' "Vinedressers and Plowmen" ', 56; J. Zorn, J. Yellin, and J. Hayes, 'The m(w)sh Stamp Impressions and the Neo-Babylonian Period', *IEJ* 44 (1994), 161–83.

[71] Barkay, 'The Iron Age IIIb', and *idem*, 'The Redefining of Archaeological Periods'; Carter, 'The Province of Yehud in the Post-Exilic Period', 120–2.

[72] Lipschits, 'The History of the Benjamin Region', 180–4.

gradually increased.⁷³ Even though Mizpah continued to be settled, its population gradually decreased as its status declined due to a shift in settlement to Jerusalem and its environs. However, it remained the location for gubernatorial visits in the mid-fifth century during the time of Nehemiah (Neh. 3: 7).⁷⁴ Lipschits, in fact, explains the reduction in settlement in the Benjamin region in the early Persian period to have resulted from 'the transfer of the regional centre to Jerusalem and the decline in the status of Mizpah'.⁷⁵ On the basis of a degree of discontinuity in the settlement pattern at the close of the sixth century and a fixed time period in which new sites sprang up, Hoglund surmised that the data reflects an intentional imperial policy of ruralization.⁷⁶ Along with the first wave of repatriation, the empire settled populations on estates and moved settled inhabitants to new sites. Against him, Faust has argued that rural sites ceased in conjunction with 587.⁷⁷ In his view, no model adequately explains their decline at a later date. Besides providing a more complete assessment of the observable data, Hoglund's assertion of the implementation of an imperial policy to relocate settled populations to the southern half of the former kingdom provides the burden of proof that Faust claims is necessary to date the decline of rural sites at the end of the sixth century rather than at its beginning.

From the archaeological data, a general portrait of Judah during the sixth century emerges. Templeless Judah represents an era of contrasts which confirms the biblical portrait of dramatic destruction. At the same time evidence emerges of ongoing occupation in the Benjamin region around a newly established capital at Mizpah. In the light of the archaeological contribution to our knowledge of the

⁷³ Hoglund, 'The Achaemenid Context', 57–60; Milevski, 'Settlement Patterns in Northern Judah'; Carter, *The Emergence of Yehud*, 235–38, 246–48; Lipschits, 'The History of the Benjamin Region', 179–85. Lipschits, 'Demographic Changes in Judah', 354–55, locates the renewal of activity south of Jerusalem around Tekoa and marks a decline around Beth Zur, thought to be Tell Tubeiqah.
⁷⁴ On the date of Nehemiah's mission, see E. J. Bickerman, 'En marge de l'Écriture, I: Le comput des années de règne des Achéménides (Néh. i, 2; ii,1 et Thuc., viii, 58)', *RB* 88 (1981), 19–23.
⁷⁵ Lipschits, 'The History of the Benjamin Region', 185.
⁷⁶ Hoglund, 'The Achaemenid Context', 54–72.
⁷⁷ Faust, 'Judah in the Sixth Century B.C.E.', 45. See the critique of this line of thought by O. Lipschits, 'The Rural Settlement of Judah in the Sixth Century B.C.E.: A Rejoinder', *PEQ* 136/2 (2004), 99–107.

period, it is no longer possible to maintain the view that Judah remained a backwater, incapable of sustenance until the return of the exiles and the regeneration initiated under the Persian administration. Areas of Judah were clearly able to resume a measure of normal life under imperial rule. The archaeological evidence, moreover, supports details in the prose tradition of Jeremiah that suggested improved conditions in the territory of Benjamin. Carter's assessment that the situation in the land is somewhere between the extremes of destruction and complete renewal seems the most plausible.[78]

IMPERIAL ADMINISTRATION AND ITS EFFECTS ON COLONIAL JUDAH

From the biblical and archaeological data, a tantalizingly incomplete picture of sixth-century Judah emerges. As the archaeological evidence has been used in conjunction with Babylonian ruling strategies in order to argue for the resumption of an improvement in societal conditions in the homeland, it is important to consider the evidence for Babylonian rule. In the years immediately preceding its demise, the kingdom of Judah was enmeshed in a power struggle between larger empires which sought dominance in the Levantine region.[79] In fact, since becoming a vassal of Assyria at the time of the Syro-Ephraimite war, Judah negotiated through an ever-increasingly volatile situation. The great Mesopotamian states of Assyria and Babylon vied with Egypt for control of the Levant. Correctly noting that the operating structure and policies of the Neo-Babylonian empire are rarely taken into account in the construction of plausible scenarios for the population of sixth-century Judah, Barstad acknowledges that any assessment cannot proceed in isolation from a consideration of the wider system of empire.[80] The present section considers data

---

[78] Carter, 'Ideology and Archaeology in the Neo-Babylonian Period', 311.

[79] For an informed and readable history of the regions during this time period see, A. Kuhrt, *The Ancient Near East c.3000–330 B.C.*, ii (Routledge History of the Ancient World; London: Routledge, 1995).

[80] Barstad, *The Myth of the Empty Land*, 61–76. The following are notable for interpretations of biblical material in light of imperial data, M. Cogan, *Imperialism*

relevant to the time when Judah was under Babylonian control along with the systems of governance of Assyria and Persia where they have a bearing on an assessment of Babylonian ruling strategies. The particular concern is with the administrative organization of the Babylonian empire and the situation of Judah within it.

Because of a lack of natural resources, the Mesopotamian states long sought to exploit the resources of regions within their grasp. They required especially those commodities necessary for civilization such as stone, hardwood timber, and metal ores. Over time Assyria and arguably Babylonia developed complex centralized structures to facilitate the flow of goods and resources into their heartlands. An empire thus operated an advanced administrative and military structure in order to retain control of subject peoples and hence their resources. Through policy, a show of military force, and propaganda, the imperial authority encouraged the compliance of subject states, thereby assuring its own commercial well-being. Under Tiglath-pileser III (745–727), in fact, the Assyrians constructed a well-organized and well-connected provincial administration that would provide the model for subsequent empires.[81]

Tiglath-pileser III ascended the throne after three unstable reigns. In response to the instability that preceded and accompanied the early part of his rule, Tiglath-pileser III created a centralized authority and military machine that subjugated and maintained control over a vast area. These elements of empire would define Assyrian rule until its decline, which began around 640 and reached its culmination in 612. Under him military might became an art-form, and the occupation of vassal states was regular practice.[82] Of particular

---

and Religion: Assyria, Judah, and Israel in the Eighth and Seventh Centuries B.C. (Missoula, Mo.: Scholars Press, 1974); D. Aberbach, *Imperialism and Biblical Prophecy 750–500 BCE* (London: Routledge, 1993); D. S. Vanderhooft, *The Neo-Babylonian Empire and Babylon in the Latter Prophets* (HSM, 59; Atlanta, Ga.: Scholars Press, 1999).

[81] E. Forrer, *Die Provinzeinteilung des Assyrischen Reiches* (Leipzig: Hinrichs, 1920); G. Roux, *Ancient Iraq* (London: Penguin, 3rd edn. 1992); H. W. F. Saggs, *The Might that was Assyria* (London: Sidgwick & Jackson, 1984); Garelli, 'The Achievement of Tiglath-pileser III: Novelty or Continuity', in Cogan and Eph'al, *Ah, Assyria...*, 46–51.

[82] On Assyrian military matters see Y. Yadin, *The Art of Warfare in Biblical Lands in the Light of Archaeological Discovery* (London: Weidenfeld & Nicolson, 1963), 291–328; Saggs, *The Might that was Assyria*.

interest is the series of initiatives which he developed for dealing with subjugated states. In its simplest form, states existed in roughly three types of relationship with the Assyrian overlords: as vassal, as a subject state under threat, and as a full province within the empire.[83] Through a highly sophisticated centralized government, Assyria administered dependent states but allowed a measure of semi-autonomous existence as long as regular tribute was forthcoming each year. If a kingdom withheld tribute or rebelled, it became subject to a series of escalating military reprisals. The first infraction resulted in a military incursion during which the recalcitrant ruler would be replaced with someone loyal to Assyria, the territory of the state would be reduced, and members of the upper-classes were deported to the Assyrian heartland in Mesopotamia. Any further disloyal action resulted in a severe military assault, after which the Assyrians replaced the ruler with an Assyrian official, assimilated the state into the empire as a province, and resettled significant portions of the population elsewhere in the empire. Tiglath-pileser III instigated a deportation policy whereby subject populations were exchanged between different territories and states within the empire.[84] The appointment of Assyrian officials in subjugated areas required a well-connected system of governance which facilitated constant communication between the capital and outlying regions. Tiglath-pileser III implemented a system of royal roads which connected the farthest reaches of the empire to the centre. A plethora of extant documents attest the copious amounts and diversity of the type of communication which transpired.

The decline of the Assyrian empire would eventually lead to Babylonian rule, but not before the removal of the threat of the

---

[83] Assyrian policy had serious consequences for Israel and Judah. Cogan, *Imperialism and Religion*, provides an interesting study of the different effects caused by vassaldom and provincial status on the religion of the northern and southern kingdoms.

[84] The impact of the Assyrian policy of exchanging populations can be seen clearly in the aftermath of the fall of the northern kingdom. Israel's decline which began under Shalmenessar V was completed under Sargon II in 722 with the capture of its capital. In the aftermath the Assyrians implemented their policy of exchanging native populations. Because its population was scattered and new people brought in, the northern kingdom of Israel would never be able to recover an independent identity. It represents one feature that distinguishes its fall from that of its southern neighbour Judah.

Egyptian presence in the Levantine region. Even before the subjugation of Assyria by Babylonia in 612–610[85] and coinciding with the accession of Nabopolassar of the Chaldeans in 626, the failing empire became the location for a bi-polar power struggle between the Neo-Babylonians and Egyptians.[86] After the fall of Nineveh in 612, the Egyptians became the dominant power in the Levant.[87] This shift in the balance of power presumably had repercussions for the internal governance of states. Unlike the Assyrians, Egyptian rule never had a differentiated political and economic system. Rather, it operated a tribute system in which a dependent nation entered into a vassal relationship with Egypt. The Egyptians rarely interfered in local affairs as long as the leader had sworn an oath of allegiance to Pharaoh followed by continued loyalty and tribute.[88] Egyptian policy is illuminated by the Letter of Adon, which is an urgent request by a Philistine king for Egyptian assistance against an advancing foe.[89] The language of the king towards the Egyptian Pharaoh suggests that he ruled a state that was in a vassal relationship with Egypt and expected help from its suzerain. That Egypt's policy was based on the tribute system finds some confirmation in the Hebrew Bible when in the late seventh century Pharaoh Necho replaced Jehoahaz, the pro-Babylonian king of Judah, with his elder brother, Jehoiakim and exacted tribute (2 Kgs. 23: 31–6). It is telling that instead of

---

[85] Nineveh fell in 612, but pockets of Assyrian resistance continued to trouble the Babylonians for a short period of time.

[86] A. Malamat has covered this in great detail over many years. Malamat, 'The Last Wars of the Kingdom of Judah'; idem, 'The Twilight of Judah: In the Egyptian-Babylonian maelstrom', in J. A. Emerton (ed.), *Congress Volume: Edinburgh 1974* (SVT, 28; Leiden: Brill, 1975), 123–45; idem, 'The Last Kings of Judah and the Fall of Jerusalem', *IEJ* 18 (1968), 137–56; and idem, 'Caught Between the Great Powers: Judah Chooses a Side...and Loses', *BAR* 25/4 (1999), 34–41.

[87] Egyptian presence began to reassert itself either in the form of political domination or as a trade partner. Malamat, 'The Twilight of Judah', 127–8 and n. 10, favours the former view, but the evidence is ambiguous. A degree of both appears likely. A current discussion appears in Vanderhooft, *The Neo-Babylonian Empire*, 69–81.

[88] A. Spalinger, 'Egypt and Babylonia: A Survey (c.620 B.C.–550 B.C.)', *Studien zur Altägyptischen Kultur* 5 (1977), 221–44; B. J. Kemp, 'Imperialism and Empire in New Kingdom Egypt', in D. A. Garnsey and C. R. Whittaker (eds.), *Imperialism in the Ancient World*, ii (Cambridge: Cambridge University Press, 1978), 43–56. Kemp provides a helpful study of parallel Egyptian policy in an earlier period.

[89] B. Porten, 'The Identity of King Adon', *BA* 44 (1981), 36–52.

responding militarily after Josiah's interference at Megiddo Egypt simply removed a likely future foe from power.[90] The Egyptian response reveals a fundamental break with Assyrian policy and likely allowed Judah to regain a measure of independence.[91]

After the decisive defeat of the Egyptians at Carchemish in 605,[92] the Chaldean Nebuchadnezzar solidified his power base and ascended the throne at his father's death.[93] In the early part of the sixth century BCE Babylonian policies, particularly those of Nebuchadnezzar, focused on annihilating the Egyptian threat to its control over the Levant.[94] The yearly marches which took place between the years 605–601 appear to have been calculated attempts to subjugate the Levant in preparation for a strike against Egypt. Sometime in the early years of the reign of Nebuchadnezzar during military penetration in the West, the Neo-Babylonians assimilated Judah into their vast empire.[95] The exact year of Judah's subjugation by Babylon is unknown because the Babylonian Chronicles recorded a series of western campaigns for the years 605–601 without specific place names.[96] During that time, Judah along with other minor states remained in the precarious position of having to ascertain whether Egypt or Babylon would ultimately gain control of the region. The last twenty years of monarchic Judah reveal a policy of appeasement that fluctuated between the support for one of the Mesopotamian empires and support for Egypt. An unsuccessful attack by the Chaldeans against Egypt in 601 probably encouraged states in the Levant, among them Judah, to rebel. Under Jehoiakim, Judah sided with Egypt against Babylonian vassalage in 601 to its detriment.[97]

---

[90] K. G. Hoglund, *Achaemenid Imperial Administration in Syria-Palestine and the Missions of Ezra and Nehemiah* (SBLDS, 125; Atlanta, Ga.: Scholars Press, 1992), 14–17.

[91] Hoglund, *Achaemenid Imperial Administration*, 15; cf. Kemp, 'Imperialism and Empire in New Kingdom Egypt', 43–5.

[92] *ABC*, 99–100; cf. Jer. 46: 2

[93] J. Oates, *Babylon* (Ancient People and Places, 94; London: Thames & Hudson, rev. edn. 1986), 126–38; H. W. F. Saggs, *The Greatness that was Babylon: A Survey of the Ancient Civilization of the Tigris-Euphrates Valley* (London: Sidgwick & Jackson, rev. and updated 1988), 215–27; S. Dalley, 'Occasions and Opportunities, 1, To the Persian Conquest', in S. Dalley *et al.*, *The Legacy of Mesopotamia* (Oxford: Oxford University Press, 1998), 9–33.

[94] Malamat, 'The Twilight of Judah'; Lipschits, 'Nebuchadrezzar's Policy'.

[95] Malamat, 'The Twilight of Judah', 129–32.

[96] *ABC*, 101.

[97] *ABC*, 102; cf. 2 Kgs. 24: 1.

In 598 Judah experienced a direct military assault which, according to Babylonian records, resulted in the capture of the city, the replacement of its king with an imperial appointee, and the seizure of booty.[98] The Babylonian reasons for this, in addition to being a punitive response, seem to have arisen from a concerted effort to formulate a decisive policy in this region as a means to generate stability and allegiance. Lipschits writes:

[O]ne can understand the destruction of Jerusalem as one of a series of more determined and dynamic measures by the Babylonians after they perceived the danger to their rule in the southern Levant from the Egyptian threat... The destruction of Jerusalem was no impulsive revenge or punishment for the rebellion. This was a calculated act with political goals: to remove the House of David from government after they had disloyal proven, and to destroy Jerusalem which had proven again and again to be the center of resistance to Babylonian rule.[99]

However, it was not until 587 when the capital city of Jerusalem was destroyed and an alternative administrative centre established in Mizpah that Judah potentially became fully integrated into the Babylonian system.[100] As a subjugated state, Judah existed under the imperial authority of a Babylonian king. How did integration into the Neo-Babylonian empire affect Judah? A determination of the nature of Babylonian imperial policies is crucial to assessing the status of Judah during this period. Would it have been possible under the Neo-Babylonians for sufficient infrastructure to have existed for a stable community during the sixth century? The exact nature of the imperial system adopted under Nebuchadnezzar for the rule of subjugated states outside Babylon remains a matter of dispute. The issue rests on whether Babylon adopted the model of provincial governance from its Assyrian predecessors or rejected it entirely in favour of another model. On the surface, Nebuchadnezzar's early treatment of Judah followed Assyrian imperial policy in that the rebellion by Judah's kings led to the escalating reprisals initiated under Tiglath-pileser III. How far does this extend in terms of later ruling strategies?

---

[98] *ABC*, 102. [99] Lipschits, 'Nebuchadrezzar's Policy', 473.
[100] Lipschits, 'Nebuchadrezzar's Policy', 476–82.

The sources for the bureaucratic policies of the Babylonians are few and ambiguous. Although there are copious documents relating to the economic and social structures of Babylon from the time of Nebuchadnezzar until the end of the reign of the third ruler of the Persian empire, Darius I (522–486), there are hardly any that bear on the relationship between the outlying states of the empire and the central authority in Babylon.[101] In fact, the large numbers of extant Assyrian documents are not matched by its successor. In reconstructions of the sixth century BCE, Stern[102] and Na'aman,[103] followed by Stager,[104] argue that Judah became a province of Babylon and thus suffered under the imperial system. Vanderhooft, in distinction, argues that Judah remained a vassal kingdom and thus suffered by not being part of an imperial system.[105] Barstad[106] and Graham[107] advance a surprising third option under which Judah became part of a provincial system. Within it certain sites improved during the sixth century BCE, particularly those where goods required by the empire were produced. It is apparent that three models exist to explain the setting of sixth-century Judah: (1) as a Babylonian province Judah deteriorated because of imperial obligations; (2) as a vassal kingdom, Judah was not sponsored by the empire and was left in a significantly impoverished state; and (3) certain locations within Judah prospered from its status as an imperial province. In all three theories, appeal has been made to the archaeological record to determine Judah's status. As it is unclear how Judah was affected by the empire in its day-to-day operation, a consideration of the evidence for Neo-Babylonian policy is in order. Did the Neo-Babylonians operate a provincial system like the Assyrians before them?

---

[101] On the documents relating to Nebuchadnezzar's reign, see M. Streck, 'Nebukadnezar II', in E. Ebeling and B. Meissner (eds.), *Reallexikon der Assyriologie und Vorderasiatischen Archäologie*, ix (Berlin and New York: de Gruyter, 1998–2001), 194–201.

[102] E. Stern, *The Material Culture of the Land of the Bible in the Persian Period (538–332 B.C.)* (Warminster: Aris & Phillips, 1982); Stern, *Archaeology*, ii. 307–11.

[103] Na'aman, 'Province System and Settlement Pattern', and *idem*, 'Royal Vassals or Governors?'.

[104] Stager, 'The Fury of Babylon', 69.

[105] Vanderhooft, *The Neo-Babylonian Empire*.

[106] Barstad, *The Myth of the Empty Land*, 61–76.

[107] Graham, ' "Vinedressers and Plowmen" '.

One side of the argument favours the view that the Neo-Babylonians adopted the provincial system of the Assyrians.[108] In a summary of this position, Hoglund explores the three main pieces of evidence which are brought to bear on the discussion: the letter of Adon, the Wadi Brisa inscription, and the so-called 'Court Calendar'.[109] The Letter of Adon is a letter extant in Aramaic from the king of Ekron to Pharaoh in dire need of military assistance against Babylonian forces which loom on the horizon.[110] Although the letter is fragmentary, its right-hand side is preserved. The end of the letter possibly refers to the replacement of local officials with a Babylonian governor. Although the text itself reads פחה במטא [...] ונדא זנה 'and this commander [...] a governor in the land', Ginsberg and Fitzmyer regard the line as an attestation of the Babylonian adoption of the Assyrian practice of the appointment of governors. In their reconstructions, they supply an intervening verb 'to set up'.[111] If this is correct, the letter provides some support that the Neo-Babylonian rulers were implementing Assyrian administrative policies by making the state a province.

A second piece of evidence is a royal inscription from the time of Nebuchadnezzar called the Wadi Brisa inscription. Originally thought to stem from about the same time as the fall of Judah, 587, the inscription more likely represents the time period when Nebuchadnezzar marched against Philistia in a series of campaigns at the end of the seventh century BCE. The inscription recounts that the king had found a foreign enemy ruling Lebanon who robbed it of its 'riches'. In response and in coalition with his gods, Nebuchadnezzar boasted that 'I made that country happy by eradicating its enemy

---

[108] Graham, *Palestine During the Period of the Exile*; Saggs, *The Greatness that was Babylon*, 261; T. C. Mitchell, 'The Babylonian Exile and the Restoration of the Jews in Palestine (586–c.500 B.C.)', in J. Boardman *et al.* (eds.), *Cambridge Ancient History*, iii/ii (Cambridge: Cambridge University Press, 2nd edn. 1991), 415; Machinist, 'Palestine, Administration of'; Kuhrt, *The Ancient Near East*, 603–10; Barstad, *The Myth of the Empty Land*; Lipschits, 'Nebuchadnezzar's Policy', 468–9.

[109] Hoglund, *Achaemenid Imperial Administration*, 16–17.

[110] On the identification with Ekron, see Porten, 'The Identity of King Adon', 43–5.

[111] Hoglund, *Achaemenid Imperial Administration*, 18–19. Cf. H. L. Ginsberg, 'An Aramaic Contemporary of the Lachish Letters', *BASOR* 111 (1948), 24–7; J. A. Fitzmyer, 'The Letter of Adon to the Pharaoh', in *A Wandering Aramean: Collected Aramaic Essays* (SBLMS, 25; Missoula, Mo.: Scholars Press, 1979), 231–42; Porten, 'The Identity of King Adon'.

everywhere (lit: below and above). All its scattered inhabitants I led back to their settlements (lit: collected and installed)...I made the inhabitants of Lebanon live in safety together and let nobody disturb them.'[112] After having secured the region and repatriated deported inhabitants, the king created overland and overseas routes to facilitate the transport of timber to the heartland of Babylon. Effectively, the Babylonians had no qualms in following Assyrian practice in the manipulation of subject populations.[113] Whilst doing so, they elicited a concern, albeit a self-interested one, in the well-being of subject nations. In this case, Nebuchadnezzar assimilated Lebanon into the empire in order to secure a steady supply of cedar for his multiple building projects. The Chaldean king showed his benevolence through the promotion of propaganda which portrayed the previous ruler as a robber of the people and concomitantly highlighted his role in restoring the people to Lebanon under imperial protection. The inscription indicates that the Babylonians acted in states of the empire to maintain the constant flow of goods into the heartland much like the Assyrians before them.

Another inscription bears on the type of imperial structure which the Babylonians operated. The 'Court Calendar' prism, more appropriately a building inscription of Nebuchadnezzar II, provides an extensive list of officials in the court. The list begins with a survey of the court hierarchy and continues with the governors of Babylonian districts and closes with a series of client kings including those of Tyre, Gaza, Sidon, Arvad, and Ashdod.[114] The inscription does not mention governors outside of Babylon; instead, it lists the kings of Philistia and Phoenicia with a broken reference to 'the king of mir[...]' followed by one further unknown reference. On the basis of Assyrian inscriptions which record Phoenician and Philistine kingdoms found in the palace of Sargon II, Na'aman provides a plausible reconstruction of *Mir-[ru-na]*, a shortened form of the Phoenician kingdom, Samsimuruna, and restores Byblos.[115] A list of the kings of Phoenicia and Philistia appears after a series of officials that includes those in the Babylonian court proper and governors in Babylon and elsewhere in Mesopotamia. The list

---

[112] *ANET*³, 307. [113] Hoglund, *Achaemenid Imperial Administration*, 19–20.
[114] *ANET*³, 307–8. [115] Na'aman, 'Royal Vassals or Governors?', 40–1.

provides no positive evidence to confirm the existence of governors in the far reaches of the empire.

To the above three pieces of evidence, the Letter of Adon and the two inscriptions, Kuhrt adds two more: the fragmentary lines of the fifth Babylonian Chronicle and a funerary inscription from the time of Nabonidus. The fifth Chronicle, which records events from the twenty-first year of Nabopolassar (605 BCE) and continues until the eleventh year of Nebuchadnezzar II, contains a poorly preserved section about another of Nebuchadnezzar's western campaigns in lines 23–4 on the reverse side: 'He marched to Ḫatti. [All] the kings of [Ḫatti ca]me [in]to [his presence. He received] their vast tribute [and] returned [to] Ba[bylon].'[116] Although there are gaps in the lines, it is clear that Nebuchadnezzar met with the kings of Ḫatti land, that is Syria–Palestine, in order to collect tribute as he had done previously.

Kuhrt cites one additional text that can be brought to bear in an attempt to understand the policies of the Babylonians in this period.[117] Before breaking off, the last column of a funerary inscription commemorating the death of the mother of Nabonidus (555–539) includes a list of governors from regions outside of Babylonia proper: 'He slaughtered fat rams and assembled into his presence [the inhabitants] of Babylon and Borsippa together with [kings] from far off regions, he [summoned kings, princes] and governors from the [borders] of Egypt on the Upper Sea, to the Lower Sea, for the mourning' (ll. 18–24).[118] The Chronicle has the word for governors *gìr. nitá. meš* and Gadd has restored *lugal. meš nun. meš* 'kings, princes'. All people of the empire, including the leaders of subject states, were required to participate in the official mourning of the deceased mother of the king. If the inscription represents the ceremony, it was also the case that the governors of imperial provinces and possibly vassal kings were required to attend the public event.

---

[116] Glassner, *Chroniques Mésopotamiennes*, 200.

[117] Kuhrt, *The Ancient Near East*, 607–8.

[118] *ANET*³, 561–2; C. J. Gadd, 'The Harran Inscriptions of Nabonidus', *AS* 8 (1958), 35–92; H. Schaudig, *Die Inschriften Nabonids von Babylon und Kyros' des Großen samt den in ihrem Umfeld entstandenen Tendenzschriften* (AOAT, 256; Münster: Ugarit-Verlag, 2001), 509.

By no means does this limited number of texts provide unambiguous evidence of Neo-Babylonian imperial administration. In fact, some of the examples could very easily be regarded as examples of a tributary system. Since the Neo-Babylonians departed from typical Assyrian practice in at least three instances, once with respect to Judah, it is possible that they differed in their administrative policies as well. For instance, although the Neo-Babylonians practised deportation as a martial tactic, they did not exchange populations as had their Assyrian forebears.[119] Furthermore, deported populations appear to have been kept together in ethnic enclaves[120] whilst arable land in Judah was distributed among the population that remained (Jer. 39: 10; 2 Kgs. 25: 12 // Jer. 52: 16; cf. Ezek. 33: 21–7).[121] Secondly, the Babylonians responded to rebellion by Tyre in a unique way.[122] Subsequent to rebellion, Nebuchadnezzar besieged the city, reportedly for thirteen years, deported its citizenry, and replaced the king with judges. During the reign of Nabonidus, a native king who had been trained in the Babylonian court was reinstated to the Tyrian throne rather than being deposed and replaced. A third major departure from Assyrian practice was in the response and treatment of cities in the coastal region. Contrary to Assyrian reluctance to penalize Philistia in the event of treaty infractions because of its economic potential and probably its strategic location, the Babylonians devastated the region and annihilated many of its principal city-states.[123] Since Babylon operated policies in certain instances that were at variance with their predecessors, it could be that their method of rule differed as well.

[119] B. Oded, *Mass Deportations and Deportees in the Neo-Assyrian Empire* (Wiesbaden: Reichert, 1979).

[120] E. J. Bickerman, 'The Babylonian Captivity', in *CHJ*, i. 342–58; Smith, *The Religion of the Landless*, 35–41; W. Röllig, 'Deportation und Integration: Das Schicksal von Fremden im assyrischen und babylonischen Staat', in M. Schuster (ed.), *Die Begegnung mit dem Fremden: Wertungen und Wirkungen in Hochkulturen vom Altertum bis zur Gegenwart* (CR, 4; Stuttgart-Leipzig: Teubner, 1996), 109–12.

[121] Janssen, *Juda in der Exilszeit*, 49–54; Hoglund, *Achaemenid Imperial Administration*, 20–1; Kuhrt, *The Ancient Near East*, ii. 605–7.

[122] M. Elat, 'Phoenician Overland Trade within the Mesopotamian Empires', in Cogan and Eph'al, *Ah, Assyria...*, 29–31.

[123] Vanderhooft, *The Neo-Babylonian Empire*, 82–3. For archaeological evidence of the totality of the devastation see Stager, 'The Fury of Babylon', and *idem*, 'Ashkelon and the Archaeology of Destruction'.

The Social and Historical Situation

Indeed, Vanderhooft recognizes the lack of clear evidence provided by interpreters for their arguments in favour of the operation of an imperial system by the Neo-Babylonians and constructs an alternative model. Upon a reconsideration of the evidence, he argues that the Babylonians did not administer a provincial system.[124] In his view, they maintained a policy of military incursions to exact tribute whilst allowing the peripheral states to wither. The evidence he examines points to his assessment:

> The remains from the first half of the sixth century are admittedly meagre for the entire region, but this is part of the point; there is simply too little material to argue for widespread or durative Babylonian intervention or presence. Babylonian involvement, we should conclude, was not aimed at colonization or systematic economic exploitation, but was rather focused on control of the region through periodic military appearances that insured delivery of tribute.[125]

Vanderhooft begins his analysis with an examination of the conceptual understanding of rule that the Neo-Babylonians conveyed on royal inscriptions. In doing so, he notices a disjunction between the imperial ideas of the Assyrians and that of the Babylonians.[126] He highlights the fact that until the reign of Nabonidus, the last king, the Neo-Babylonian rulers refrained from using Assyrian titles (with the exception of Nabopolassar, whose inscriptions exhibit their rare use) and Assyrian concepts of conquest and kingship. Secondly, Vanderhooft takes into consideration the evidence for administrative interaction in the region and economic activity. He is particularly interested in the evidence for Neo-Babylonian dealings with the western periphery.[127] On a conceptual level and from material evidence of administration and trade with states in the Levant, Vanderhooft concludes that the Neo-Babylonians departed from the system of Assyrian governance and opted for a strategy that secured monetary sources without the involvement of cumbersome and costly imperial rule.

---

[124] Vanderhooft, *The Neo-Babylonian Empire*, 61–114, and *idem*, 'Babylonian Strategies of Imperial Control in the West: Royal Practice and Rhetoric', in Lipschits and Blenkinsopp, *Judah and the Judeans*, 235–62.
[125] Vanderhooft, *The Neo-Babylonian Empire*, 109.
[126] Ibid., 9–59.
[127] Ibid., 89–114.

Among the pieces of evidence he considers in conjunction with the question of the administrative 'geography', to use Vanderhooft's language, is a comparison of the Court Calendar prism and the Etemenanki cylinder,[128] a building inscription with much in common with the prism. Listed on both are the same regional zones which presumably supply tribute to Babylon in the form of corvée labour and timber. Of the cities in Phoenicia and Philistia, he concludes that there is little to suggest the operation of a provincial system. Instead, it appears that the Phoenician and Philistine city-states existed in a vassal relationship with Babylon. Additional support in his argument against a provincial system operated by the Babylonians is that in distinction to the large amount of detailed communication between Nineveh and the outlying regions of the Assyrian empire, there is almost a complete lack of Neo-Babylonian correspondence between the heartland and states in the periphery.[129] The implication is that Babylon maintained control over what was the Assyrian empire, but it did not directly intervene in the governance of individual regions.

Vanderhooft utilizes the case of Judah to test his reconstruction. The appointment of Gedaliah in his view contradicts a provincial model because there is almost no precedent for the establishment of a local official in such a system. Even more problematic for him is the failure of the biblical traditions to mention any Babylonian intervention after the murder of Gedaliah. In addition, Vanderhooft adds that the portrait of a depressed economy clarified by the material culture is not indicative of a provincial model.[130] In his final analysis:

the Babylonians had no interest in supervising the local economies, or in potential benefits to be derived from direct management of them. They were interested in receiving tribute, but apparently periodic (initially annual) campaigning ensured this, not a systematic bureaucratic presence.[131]

For Vanderhooft, states under Babylonian control in the western periphery of the empire existed in a vassal relationship and, therefore, suffered from not being incorporated in a provincial model.

---

[128] F. H. Weissbach (ed.), *Babylonischen Miscellen* (WVDOG, 4; Leipzig: Hinrichs, 1903), 59.
[129] Vanderhooft, *The Neo-Babylonian Empire*, 90–112. Cf. Stager, 'The Fury of Babylon' and *idem*, 'Ashkelon and the Archaeology of Destruction'.
[130] Vanderhooft, *The Neo-Babylonian Empire*, 104–10.
[131] Ibid., 111.

Although Vanderhooft's analysis is detailed and precise at many points, it suffers from asserting too much from interpretations that are open to debate, which has resulted in conclusions that do not take full account of the evidence. In the first place, Vanderhooft concludes that the purposeful avoidance of Assyrian epithets by the Neo-Babylonian kings, with the exception of Nabonidus, was a literary means of rejecting the Assyrian model of kingship. This is simply an unprovable assumption. It could be the case that the Neo-Babylonian rulers failed to use Assyrian royal epithets because they rejected the military overtones of the language, not their style of rule. Interestingly, Dalley has utilized the same evidence as Vanderhooft, but reached the opposite conclusion.[132] In her view, the Neo-Babylonian empire exhibited a smooth transition of power from Nineveh to Babylon.[133] Not only did Nabopolassar, the sovereign who established the Chaldean dynasty, utilize the common Assyrian royal title of 'mighty king' *šarru dannu*, even more telling in her view is the fact that he affiliated himself with the Neo-Assyrians, not the rulers of the Old Babylonian empire.[134] Additionally problematic is Vanderhooft's view that the lack of evidence of administrative correspondence between Babylon and the periphery provides proof of the lack of a provincial system. By the time of the Neo-Babylonian empire, as with the Persians after them, imperial correspondence probably would have been written in Aramaic on perishable materials, as Vanderhooft himself notes.[135] In the case of the Persian empire, the lack of records of an imperial regime has certainly not ruled out a provincial model.[136] Finally, certain documents suggest administrative continuity between the Assyrians and the Neo-Babylonians. In Syria, in the western fringe of the empire, records were kept according to the Assyrian model during Neo-Babylonian rule.[137]

---

[132] S. Dalley, 'The Transition from Neo-Assyrians to Neo-Babylonians: Break or Continuity?' *EI* 27 (2003), 25*–28*
[133] Her view follows the opinion of many scholars as noted by Vanderfhooft, *The Neo-Babylonian Empire*, 90–1.
[134] Dalley, 'The Transition'.
[135] Vanderhooft, *The Neo-Babylonian Empire*, 62–3 n. 3.
[136] A point also made by Barstad, 'After the "Myth of the Empty Land" ', 4.
[137] K. Radner, *Die neuassyrischen Texte aus Tall ŠĒḤ ḤAMAD* (Berlin: Dietrich Reimer Verlag, 2002); Dalley, 'The Transition', 27*.

The interpretation Vanderhooft proposes for the evidence he has gathered together fails to take into account the possibility that Babylonian policies may have altered over time. In the early part of Nebuchadnezzar's reign, as Vanderhooft argues, the Babylonians sought to vanquish the Egyptian threat in the Levant.[138] After a failed attempt to assist a deposed Egyptian Pharaoh to regain his throne in 567, the Egyptians and Babylonians observed what appears to have been an unofficial truce.[139] Although Vanderhooft's theory fits well with the beginning period of the empire when Babylon sought repeatedly to subjugate Egypt, his proposal may not correspond with the latter part of Nebuchadnezzar's reign when Egypt ceased to be a threat in the Levantine region. This is exactly the point of Elat's article, which Vanderhooft mentions but appears to misunderstand.[140] Amid a wider concern with the evidence for overland trade between the Mesopotamian empires and the western territories, Elat turns to Neo-Babylonian practice. He argues that a noticeable shift occurred under Nebuchadnezzar after the termination of hostilities with Egypt and the siege of Tyre. According to his analysis, the scant evidence of overland trade in the early years of Nebuchadnezzar contrasts sharply with that of the commercial exchange of wares that followed the cessation of the Egyptian threat in the Levant. Although the documents deal mainly with Tyre and Syrian cities, they raise the possibility that a regional strategic shift took place within Nebuchadnezzar's reign. In support of this view is the work of Malamat and Lipschits, who have shown how Nebuchadnezzar's actions in the early years of his reign were defined by constant struggle with Egypt.[141] It would not be surprising to find a change in policy toward the territories west of the Euphrates after that threat had been quelled.

A change in policy would explain the confused picture provided by the evidence and also the mixed positions taken by interpreters. As even Vanderhooft concedes, the Etemenanki cylinder and the Ebabbar temple tablets both mention governors who existed outside

---

[138] Vanderhooft, *The Neo-Babylonian Empire*, 81–9.

[139] Kuhrt, *The Ancient Near East*, 593, 644–5. This type of unofficial 'truce' was also observed between the Assyrians and Egyptians, although it has not been noted by most interpreters. A. Spalinger, 'Assurbanipal and Egypt: A Source Study', *JAOS* 94 (1974), 316–28'; idem, 'Psammetichus, King of Egypt I', *JARCE* 13 (1976), 133–47; idem, 'Psammetichus, King of Egypt II', *JARCE* 15 (1978), 49–57.

[140] Elat, 'Phoenician Overland Trade'.

[141] Malamat, 'The Twilight of Judah'; Lipschits, 'Nebuchadrezzar's Policy'.

of Babylon.[142] In his view, these documents could be taken as evidence for a provincial system were it not for the fact that they suggest a system in the coastal plain and the upper-Euphrates valley rather than in the southern and inland Levant.[143] The Etemenanki cylinder referred to the kings of Eber-Nari and the governors (*pīhatā[tim]*) and viceroys (*šakkanakkātim*) of Ḫatti land. The two tablets mention the governor (*pīhatu*) of Arpad near Carchemish. The appointment of Gedaliah as governor of Judah in 587 supports the likelihood of the existence of governors during Babylonian rule.[144] In his objection to this line of argument, Vanderhooft notes that there are no parallels for the placement of a native governor during the Babylonian period. There is a loosely related precedent, however, from the ninth and eighth centuries BCE, when local notables were established in the Euphrates region under the Assyrian empire.[145] Furthermore, the Persians who ruled after the Babylonians appointed native rulers elsewhere in what appears to be a continuation of preceding imperial policies.[146] In Judah, a gubernatorial system was surely in effect before the defeat of Babylon in 539. Two governors are mentioned in conjunction with the early period of Persian rule, Sheshbazzar and Zerubbabel.[147] Zerubbabel is called a governor (Hag. 1: 1, 14; 2: 2, 21), is spoken of in language used of the Davidic kings ('my servant' and 'signet ring', Hag. 2: 23), and performs the task of a Davidic king through overseeing temple reconstruction (Zech. 4: 9–10).[148] In Ezra,

---

[142] Vanderhooft, *The Neo-Babylonian Empire*, 106, who discusses this point with a different conclusion; cf. F. Joannès, 'Une visite du gouverneur d'Arpad', *NABU* (1994), 21–2.

[143] Vanderhooft, *The Neo-Babylonian Empire*, 104.

[144] Gedaliah is never called a 'governor'. Instead his appointment is described with the hiphil of פקד (2 Kgs. 25: 22, 23; Jer. 40: 5, 7, 11; 41: 2, 18), which has been used elsewhere to refer to someone set in charge of a house or a group of labourers (Gen. 39: 4, 5; 1 Kgs. 11: 28).

[145] Lipschits, 'Nebuchadrezzar's Policy', 479.

[146] P. R. Ackroyd, 'The Jewish Community in Palestine in the Persian Period', in *CHJ*, i. 130–61; E. Stern, 'The Persian Empire and the Political and Social History of Palestine and the Persian Period', in ibid., 70–81; A. B. Lloyd, 'The Inscription of Udjahorresnet: A Collaborator's Testament', *JEA* 66 (1986), 166–80; J. Blenkinsopp, 'The Mission of Udjahorresnet and those of Ezra and Nehemiah', *JBL* 106 (1987), 409–21.

[147] F. M. Cross, 'Reconstruction of the Judean Restoration', *JBL* 94 (1975), 15.

[148] W. H. Rose, *Zemah and Zerubbabel: Messianic Expectations in the Early Postexilic Period* (JSOTSup, 304; Sheffield: Sheffield Academic Press, 2000), argues for the view that the Davidic overtones should be seen as messianic.

the Hebrew letter, in 1: 8 Sheshbazzar is called the prince of Judah, but in the Aramaic letter he is given the title of governor (Neh. 5: 14–16).[149]

At another point, Vanderhooft overstates Nebuchadnezzar's policy towards Philistia. He stresses that the actions of Nebuchadnezzar along the coastal plain were designed to wreak havoc through devastation rather than create viable economies: 'Nebuchadnezzar's systematic destruction of Ashkelon, Ekron, Ashdod, Tel Batash-Timnah and other cities in Philistia and adjacent regions, seems to indicate a different attitude: he considered the economic viability of the region secondary to the imperative of pushing the Egyptians out by razing their client cities.'[150] The Wadi Brisa inscription paints a different picture in that it exhibits Nebuchadnezzar's concern to safeguard the well-being of Lebanon as a means to secure the flow of timber into Babylon. Such a move would be vitally important to Nebuchadnezzar, under whom the glorification of Babylon reached its zenith. Elsewhere, Vanderhooft uses the building inscriptions of Etemenanki and the Court Calendar to illustrate a change in Nebuchadnezzar's understanding of his rule. Under him construction work became of paramount importance as a means to showcase the importance of Babylon.[151] If the building inscriptions point to foreign contributions of corvée labour and timber, a natural assumption would be that Nebuchadnezzar required the constant importation of both. Imports on such a massive scale would almost necessitate a well-constructed and integrated empire based on a system of trade rather than one that relied on smash-and-grab tactics to gather booty. The latter may have served the empire in its early years when Babylon fought to gain the upper hand in the Levant, but it would not serve over a period of many years. After the cessation of hostilities between Babylon and Egypt and as the construction of physical symbols of the might and power of Babylon rose to greater importance, it is possible that Neo-Babylonian policy altered in the region of the Levant to ensure the flow of natural resources and goods.

---

[149] S. Japhet, 'Sheshbazzar and Zerubbabel: Against the Background of the Historical and Religious Tendencies of Ezra–Nehemiah', *ZAW* 94 (1982), 66–98, and *ZAW* 95 (1983), 218–29.

[150] Vanderhooft, *The Neo-Babylonian Empire*, 82–3.

[151] Ibid., 38–41.

The Social and Historical Situation 65

In support of a provincial model is the amount of overland trade that transpired. On the basis of business transactions recorded on a few cuneiform tablets, Oppenheim surveys two types of trade that appear to have existed in the Neo-Babylonian period: (1) that within Babylon of goods from locations outside the heartland and (2) trade across many states, especially among the northern and western regions.[152] Trade routes reached from Egypt, the Mediterranean coast, and Asia Minor into southern Babylon with the final destination being Babylon itself, apparently supervised by Tyrian middlemen.[153] In general, the goods brought to Babylon include metals (copper, iron, and tin), chemicals like dyes, luxury foodstuffs (wine, honey, spices, and olive oil) but rarely basic staples, and material from plant and animal fibres (linen and wool). Judah provided some of these items for the markets of the ancient Near East.[154] In an attempt to cast a shadow over the population that remained in Judah, the editors of the accounts of Kings and Jeremiah, in their insistence that only the vinedressers and farmhands were left, provide a clue as to at least one type of labour required by the Neo-Babylonian overlords: the production of goods for trade.

In later years Babylon would exhibit a degree of concern for territories in the Levant. According to the sixth Babylonian Chronicle, which deals exclusively with a military campaign conducted by Neriglissar, in his third year (557) the Babylonian king marched out to suppress an attack on Syria by the Anatolian state, Pirandu.[155] Lines 1–4 of the Chronicle read with few lacunae 'The third year: [*On the Nth day of the month*...] Appuashu, the king of Pirindu, mustered his [large] army and set out to plunder and sack Syria (*e-bir nār*[*i*...]). Neriglissar mustered his army and marched to Hume to oppose him.'[156] The reasons for the counter-attack are

---

[152] A. L. Oppenheim, 'Essay on Overland Trade in the First Millennium B.C.', *JCS* 21 (1967), 236–54.

[153] Oppenheim, 'Essay on Overland Trade'.

[154] Graham, ' "Vinedressers and Plowmen" '; L. E. Stager, 'The Firstfruits of Civilization', in J. N. Tubb (ed.), *Palestine in the Bronze and Iron Ages: Papers in Honour of Olga Tufnell* (Institute of Archaeology Occasional Publication, 11; London: Institute of Archaeology, 1985), 172–87; J. Patrich and B. Arubas, 'A Juglet Containing Balsam Oil (?) from a Cave Near Qumran', *IEJ* 39 (1989), 43–59.

[155] *ABC*, 103–4.

[156] Glassner, *Chroniques Mésopotamiennes*, 201; cf. *ABC*, 103.

not mentioned. Neriglissar could have responded out of an obligation to a vassal state, to secure the loyalty of a territory with valuable resources, or to maintain security in the region. Whatever the reasons, Neriglissar's actions do not suggest those of an empire completely unconcerned with territories under its control.

A second problem lies in Vanderhooft's implication that the existence of certain city-states as vassals was incompatible with a provincial system. This is not the case. Vassal states were a well-known feature of the Assyrian empire. In return for relative independence, various territories swore allegiance to Assyria, paid an annual tribute, offered occasional gifts, and supplied troops when required. The model for Assyrian rule can be thought of in terms of the three stages of incorporation in the empire mentioned already above, that is, vassal, punished vassal, and province, but this does not represent all cases.[157] Assyria granted an intermediary status somewhere between vassal and full province to some states in the border and peripheral areas, particularly in the west, among which were Gaza, Ashdod, and Egypt. Based on this Assyrian model, the Babylonian system could have responded to subjugated states on a case-by-case basis. Vanderhooft's argument needs to take into consideration greater flexibility in the imperial system than he allows. In Assyria, which in some respects resembles the case of Judah, the capital and major cities were devastated by the Neo-Babylonians and showed no signs of rebuilding or government initiative (with the exception of Babylonian-sponsored temple restoration in Ashur). However, the former Assyrian provincial centre of Dur-Katlimmu exhibits no signs of decline.[158] In fact, cuneiform tablets found there provide evidence of the regular functioning of Assyrian officials who maintained records in a style consistent with Neo-Assyrian models. If Kuhne's suggestion is correct, that the sympathies of Dur-Katlimmu lay with the Babylonians during the decline of Assyria, it provides a parallel to Mizpah. Although the Babylonians did not sponsor regeneration in

---

[157] M. Cogan, 'Judah under Assyrian Hegemony: A Re-examination of *Imperialism and Religion*', *JBL* 112 (1993), 406–8.

[158] H. Kuhne, 'Thoughts about Assyria after 612 BC', in L. al-Gailani Werr *et al.* (eds.), *Of Pots and Plans: Papers on the Archaeology and History of Mesopotamia and Syria presented to David Oates in Honour of his 75th Birthday* (London: Nabu, 2002), 171–5.

devastated regions, they allowed a degree of self-governance and renewal in segments of conquered states that proved loyal. Moreover, the case of Dur-Katlimmu shows that business transactions continued to be recorded in the Assyrian style, which suggests again that Babylon had not completely rejected Assyrian administrative prototypes.

Judah's change of status from a vassal kingdom to what appears to be a province provides one example of a shift in Babylonian policy, even though it came before the cessation of hostilities between Babylon and Egypt.[159] According to Lipschits, among others, Judah's second rebellion resulted in the loss of its status as a vassal kingdom and its incorporation into the empire as a province. Even before the destruction of the city of Jerusalem, the Babylonians were creating a district centre in Mizpah. After the devastation:

> The settlement of the remaining Jews had a defined status within the administrative structure of the Babylonian empire. In the description of the time of Gedaliah a region is mentioned which is called 'the land of Judah' (2 Kgs. 25: 22; Jer. 40: 12) or 'the land' (2 Kgs. 25: 24). Mizpah was located in its center and around it were 'the cities' (Jer. 40: 10), among them Gibeon (41: 12, 16) and the settlements around Bethlehem (41: 17). Note that the distribution of the 42 '*m(w)sh*' Stamp Impressions was over an area similar to this region...[160]

Suggestive of a provincial model is the retinue of Babylonian soldiers left behind in Mizpah (2 Kgs. 25: 24–5; Jer. 41: 3).[161] If Nebuchadnezzar did not adopt a provincial policy elsewhere in the region as Vanderhooft asserts, why does evidence from Judah suggest the contrary? Could Judah be a special case? Like the Assyrians before them, the Babylonians may have dealt with territories individually rather than through a monolithic policy. Judah's location would make it an exceptional case as it was not located along the coastal plain along which Nebuchadnezzar's troops would march to engage Egypt, as were the Philistian cities devastated by Nebuchadnezzar. As Judah was more inland and well-known for certain commodities,

---

[159] Lipschits, 'Nebuchadrezzar's Policy'.
[160] Ibid., 480.
[161] This is analogous to the case of Samaria; cf. Cogan, *Imperialism and Religion*, 97–102.

Nebuchadnezzar destroyed its city of governance and created a new administrative centre in Mizpah, possibly to safeguard production. Even after Gedaliah's assassination, it is likely that a governor, but not necessarily a Babylonian official, continued to rule in the land.[162] Furthermore, the Assyrians and Babylonians recognized the regional boundaries of territories so that provincial Judah was not annexed to Samaria as suggested by Alt.[163]

The evidence points to a change in policy during the reign of Nebuchadnezzar that has not been accounted for within assessments of this period. During the first part of his reign, Nebuchadnezzar sought to contain the threat of rebellion in the west and to eliminate Egyptian influence in the region. The military might of Babylon swiftly and comprehensively retaliated for any rebellion by vassal states to encourage stability and discourage the lure of Egypt. In the early period of Nebuchadnezzar, all the states in the Levant were accepted as vassals under the rule of Babylon. During subsequent years, when they continued to chafe against the Babylonian yoke and fomented rebellion by aligning themselves with Egypt, Nebuchadnezzar responded mercilessly to dissuade any further regional instability. After the Egyptian threat was neutralized, Babylonian policy adapted a provincial model to secure goods required in the homeland.

When Babylon succumbed to Cyrus in 539 BCE, the newly established Persian empire simply assimilated states and provinces previously subject to the Chaldeans.[164] Since the interest of the early rulers of the Persian empire, Cyrus and Cambyses, focused almost exclu-

---

[162] Mitchell, 'The Babylonian Exile', 414, speculates that Nebuchadnezzar probably installed a Babylonian after the assassination of Gedaliah.

[163] The view that Judah became subject to Samarian provincial authority at this time is that of A. Alt, 'Die Rolle Samarias bei der Entstehung des Judentums', in *Festschrift Otto Procksch zum 60. Geburtstag* (Leipzig: A. Deihert and J. C. Hinrichs, 1934), 5–28 = *idem, Kleine Schriften zur Geschichte des Volkes Israel*, ii (Munich: Beck, 1953), 316–37, who is followed by many, including most recently, S. McEvenue, 'The Political Structure in Judah from Cyrus to Nehemiah', *CBQ* 43 (1981), 353–64. Reasons for subsuming Judah within the territory of Samaria are not cogent; cf. M. Smith, 'Appendix: Alt's Account of the Samaritans', in *Palestinian Parties and Politics that Shaped the Old Testament* (London: SCM Press, 2nd edn. 1987), 147–53; Williamson, 'The Governors of Judah'; Hoglund, *Achaemenid Imperial Administration*, 69–86; Carter, *The Emergence of Yehud*, 279–83.

[164] *ABC*, 109–11.

The Social and Historical Situation 69

sively on empire building, it is generally accepted that until the time of Darius, the administration of the territories remained unchanged.[165] Persian governance even after the institution of satrapies by Darius remained consistent with the previous regime. Like vassal states under Baybylon, the satrapies had a semi-autonomous existence with relative freedom in the organization of their social institutions and structures.[166] Persian imperial policy even allowed the completion of the second temple in Jerusalem in 515.

In sum, a variety of information supports the contention that the Neo-Babylonians ruled over a provincial system modelled on the Assyrian empire.[167] It is possible that Neo-Babylonian policy changed in the region of the Levant following the suppression of an Egyptian threat. Judah would have existed as a province within the empire. As such, the homeland was provided with a stable situation through imperial rule that guaranteed the acquirement of tribute and the supply of goods to its centre. It is likely, therefore, that Nebuchadnezzar's attempts to support a degree of self-rule in Judah by the appointment of Gedaliah as governor continued after the untimely death of his appointee. The evidence of empire fits the expanded

---

[165] R. N. Frye, *The History of Ancient Iran* (HAW, 3/7; Munich: Beck, 1984), 87–126; J. M. Cook, 'The Rise of the Achaemenids and the Establishment of their Empire', in I. Gershevitch (ed.), *Cambridge History of Iran*, ii (Cambridge: Cambridge University Press, 1985), 213–14; I. Eph'al, 'Syria–Palestine under Achaemenid Rule', in Boardman *et al.*, *Cambridge Ancient History*, iv. 147; M. A. Dandamaev, *A Political History of the Achaemenid Empire* (Leiden: Brill, 1989), 33; M. A. Dandamaev and V. G. Lukonin, *The Culture and Social Institutions of Ancient Iran* (Cambridge: Cambridge University Press, 1989), 97; A. Lemaire, 'Histoire et administration de la Palestine à l'époque perse', in E.-M. Laperrousaz and A. Lemaire (eds.), *La Palestine à l'époque perse: Etudes annexes de la Bible de Jérusalem* (Paris: Cerf, 1994), 11–53.

[166] S. Dalley, 'Occasions and Opportunities, 2, Persian, Greek, and Parthian Overlords', in Dalley *et al.*, *The Legacy of Mesopotamia*, 35–9. There are two important differences in Persian administration in contrast to the Neo-Babylonian, whose consideration would take us too far afield. Nevertheless, they deserve mention. In the first place, the Persians initially appointed governors from the exiles who returned from Babylon, which diverges from the Neo-Babylonian practice of the establishment of local rulers, like Gedaliah, for instance. In the second place, the Persians gradually returned the capital to Jerusalem by moving populations to its environs and to the city itself. How these two policies which diverged from Neo-Babylonian administrative policies affected the social situation should impact further study on the Persian period.

[167] For a similar conclusion from a rather different angle, see R. H. Sack, 'Nebuchadnezzar II and the Old Testament: History versus Ideology', in Lipschits and Blenkinsopp, *Judah and the Judeans*, 221–33.

portrait of Judah made available from details about the social and political situation in the homeland in Jeremiah and the improvement in conditions reflected within the material culture.

CONCLUSIONS

A study of the historical situation based on the biblical representation, the archaeological record, and the operation of an imperial province fleshes out the situation in Templeless Judah. Nevertheless, due to the type of data at our disposal it has left certain questions unanswered. In spite of these gaps and the relative lack of any biblical description of the homeland in the sixth century, there are certain indications of continuity. The biblical hints that political stability would have been fostered by certain segments of the Judahite population, perhaps the 'people of the land', find a measure of support from the archaeological record that exhibits continuity and even prosperity in the Benjaminite region. The concern of the Neo-Babylonians with securing trade provides an additional reason to believe that the death of Gedaliah would not have entailed the loss of the country's infrastructure. Furthermore, the existence of a scribal class who operated during Gedaliah's administration suggests that literary activity would have continued in the land following his murder. A provincially administered empire required scribes to facilitate communication between the regions of the empire. Finally, the biblical hints about communal life from remarks about the 'the poor of the land' and 'the vinedressers and ploughmen' left behind in Judah are supported to some degree by archaeological evidence of site continuity in the Benjamin region and Babylonian policies elsewhere. Three sources about Templeless Judah—biblical history, the material culture, and imperial administrative policies—together suggest a degree of infrastructure in the homeland.

The sources for the social and historical situation in Judah paint a probable portrait of life in Judah. Political stability, the existence of scribes, and social continuity reveal a distinctive milieu in which Judahite reflection on the events would have taken place. One of the key points of the analysis of Smith-Christopher in *Religion of the Landless* is that a historical reconstruction alone is insufficient for understanding the theological innovation of the Babylonian exiles.[168] In a discussion of the construct of reality and religious symbols, Smith-Christopher observes that the social reality of a people is co-determinative for the creation and interpretation of meaning. The understanding of socially determinative factors, then, becomes imperative in ascertaining the development of theological traditions or religious symbols. One of the benefits of his analysis is that it takes full consideration of the effect of relocation on communities. He finds that the situation of exile—distance from the homeland and national symbols, in particular—resulted in the reassessment, reformulation, and appropriation of traditions as a means to cope with the crisis of new circumstances. It follows, then, that the significance of the social setting of exile for evaluating interpretation holds true for the social setting of the homeland in that the latter situation raises its own criteria for the construction of reality and religious reflection. In terms of the population in Judah, continuous habitation and communal stability are determinative features. This survey provides the distinctive setting of the 'poor people of the land', but no glimpse of their thoughts on it. Since Judah conceived of and maintained traditions primarily of a theological nature, the next two chapters consider the religious circumstances of the homeland as a means to assess how they engender an interpretation of the period distinctive to the Judahite population.

---

[168] D. L. Smith, *The Religion of the Landless: The Social Context of the Babylonian Exile* (Bloomington, Ind.: Meyer Stone Books, 1989); *idem*, 'Reassessing the Historical and Sociological Impact of the Babylonian Exile (597/587–539 BCE)', in Scott, *Exile*, 7–36, and to some extent in ch. 6 of *idem*, *A Biblical Theology of Exile* (OBT; Minneapolis, Minn.: Fortress Press, 2002), 137–62.

2

Conceptions of Judah, I: Idolatrous Cults

INTRODUCTION

The period after the destruction of the temple was one of severe disruption to the political, social, and religious spheres of Judah. In spite of the discontinuity that ensued, interpreters have recently concentrated on issues of continuity between the monarchic period and Yehud of the Persian period.[1] One feature of commonality between the period preceding the destruction of the temple and the early Second Temple period would be the observance of religious practices thought by some biblical traditions to be incompatible with Yahwistic worship. Becking, in general agreement with Ackroyd, for example, lists four possible outcomes of the catastrophic events of 587:

1. Abandonment of traditional religion and the embrace of the world view of the conquering power;
2. Reinforcement of indigenous Canaanite elements in Yahwistic religion;
3. A concentration on Yahwism in an orthodox, exclusive monotheistic form;

---

[1] P. R. Ackroyd, 'The Temple Vessels: A Continuity Theme', in *Studies in the Religion of Ancient Israel* (SVT, 23; Leiden: Brill, 1972), 166–81, reprinted in P. R. Ackroyd, *Studies in the Religious Tradition of the Old Testament* (London: SCM Press, 1987), 46–60; L. L. Grabbe, 'Israel's Historical Reality after the Exile', in B. Becking and M. C. A. Korpel (eds.), *The Crisis of Israelite Religion: Transformation of Religious Tradition in Exilic and Post-Exilic Times* (OTS, 42; Leiden: Brill, 1999), 9–32; H. Niehr, 'Religio-Historical Aspects of the "Early Post Exilic" Period', in Becking and Korpel, *The Crisis of Israelite Religion*, 228–44.

4. The reformulation of Yahwism in an altered religious, political, and social context.[2]

From Becking's assessment it is clear that in literature associated with the community in exile in Babylon a high priority is given to associating the persistence of the veneration of other deities with the community that remained in Judah. Although the *Golah* literature provides few details about the actual situation of ongoing life in the homeland, they fervently comment on its religiosity.

The impression provided by the biblical writers certainly suggests that illicit worship took place in sixth-century Judah. In historiography and prophecy the issue of idolatry comes repeatedly to the fore. The Deuteronomistic History places a great deal of the blame for the loss of the kingdom and homeland on what it considers to be inappropriate religious practices. In some respects similar, at least with regard to the perspective on the centrality of worship, the prophetic literature attributable to the Templeless period focuses on religion and religious praxis. Like the Deuteronomistic History the prophets Jeremiah and Ezekiel condemn what they consider to be idolatrous cultic practices and use their existence in Judah, even on the temple mount, to explain the disaster. One of the necessary components of the restoration of Jerusalem in Ezekiel's vision (chs. 40–8) is the purification of the temple.[3] Another prophet of the exile, Deutero-Isaiah, attributes little blame for the disaster, but contains lengthy passages about the evils of false worship, and the inefficacy of idols themselves, in the polemical passages and trial speeches.[4] Prophetic angst at the unorthodox religious practice does not cease with the return of the exiles to the land. Towards the end of the Templeless period, the vision sequence of Zechariah 1–8 contains passages about purification with

---

[2] B. Becking, 'Continuity and Discontinuity after the Exile: Some Introductory Remarks', in Becking and Korpel, *The Crisis of Israelite Religion*, 1–8. Cf. E. Janssen, *Juda in der Exilszeit: Ein Beitrag zur Frage der Entstehung des Judentums* (Göttingen: Vandenhoeck & Ruprecht, 1956), 94–104; P. R. Ackroyd, *Exile and Restoration: A Study of Hebrew Thought of the Sixth Century* B.C. (London: SCM Press, 1968), 39–49.

[3] J. D. Levenson, *Theology of the Program of Restoration of Ezekiel 40–48* (HSM, 10; Cambridge, Mass.: Harvard University Press, 1976); M. Greenberg, 'The Design and Themes of Ezekiel's Program of Restoration', *Int* 38 (1984), 181–208.

[4] A. Schoors, *I am God your Saviour: A Form-Critical Study of the Main Genres in Is. XL–LV* (SVT, 24; Leiden: Brill, 1973); R. J. Clifford, 'The Function of the Idol Passages in Second Isaiah', *CBQ* 42 (1980), 450–64.

one having to do with the return of a goddess to Babylon (Zech. 5: 1–11). Some time after the reconstruction of the temple Trito-Isaiah attributes the failure of Deutero-Isaiah's predictions of divine salvation and restoration to materialize to the continuation of the worship of other deities (Isa. 57: 3–13; 65: 3–4, 11; 66: 3, 17). According to the biblical material of the period and immediately thereafter, one area of continuity, therefore, between the final years of the monarchy and the early Second Temple period, is the worship of other deities either in distinction to or in conjunction with the worship of Yahweh.

The criticism against the worship of other deities in literature during and just after the Templeless period indicates that the continuation of ritual observance for other deities may have actually occurred.[5] Ackerman in *Under Every Green Tree* provides the first major synthesis of literature that attests to the existence of popular religion[6] in sixth-century Judah.[7] In it, she utilizes four biblical texts thought to stem from the Babylonian and early Persian periods: Jeremiah 7 and 44 (grouped as one); Ezekiel 8; Isaiah 57: 3–13, and 65: 1–7, in order to substantiate the persistence of religious practices deemed foreign or syncretistic by the biblical writers after the disaster of 587 among the populace remaining in the land. In her view, the portrayal of the worship of other deities, rather than disclosing syncretistic or foreign influences, actually exhibits worship practices indigenous to the cult of Yahweh. Furthermore, she directly contradicts the belief espoused, for example, by Ackroyd, that the resurgence of these rituals was influenced by the disasters of 598 and 587. Rather, they represent a continuation of religious expression from the seventh century.[8]

---

[5] So, also, Niehr, 'Religio-Historical Aspects', 239.

[6] The terminology 'popular religion' will be avoided in this chapter. It tends to connote the worship of the masses in distinction to the worship of the temple or at least select groups within the temple. As Ackerman's study shows, the cults highlighted were often portrayed in biblical literature as those in which the people, the monarchy, and cultic personnel participated. It often carries with it a pejorative sense reminiscent of statements like that of Y. Kaufmann, *The Religion of Israel: From its Beginnings to the Babylonian Exile* (New York: Schocken Books, abridged edn. 1977), 408, who, whilst speaking of the cult of the Queen of Heaven, terms it 'of a piece with the vulgar superstitions of the ignorant that are found everywhere down to this day'.

[7] S. Ackerman, *Under Every Green Tree: Popular Religion in Sixth-Century Judah* (HSM, 46; Atlanta, Ga.: Scholars Press, repr. 2001).

[8] Ackerman, *Under Every Green Tree*, 214. cf., Ackroyd, *Exile and Restoration*, 40–1.

Conceptions of Judah, I: Idolatrous Cults

Whilst responding directly to claims to the contrary raised by Kaufmann,[9] Ackerman adduces several arguments in support of the view that during this period rituals considered aberrant by some were practised in the land even within the temple precincts. In the first place, the kings of Judah who succeeded Josiah are consistently and unanimously labelled among those who 'did evil in the eyes of Yahweh'. Without further elucidation it is difficult to determine the exact meaning of the phrase, but Ackerman suspects that it could imply that post-Josianic monarchs reinstated religious practices previously quelled. The stereotypical expression aligns Josiah's successors with other kings in Israel and Judah who were condemned for their association with the worship of other deities.[10] In addition, Ackerman cites biblical references in order to show that the prophet Jeremiah considered the temple to be defiled by illicit worship practices (Jer. 7: 30; 32: 34; cf. 7–8: 3) and that his contemporaries in Egypt deserved denunciation for the worship of the Queen of Heaven (Jer. 44: 17, 21).[11] The temple vision of Ezekiel 8, similarly, emphasizes the veneration of other deities within the temple precincts. The presence of false worship at the sanctuary repulses the deity to such an extent that the divine presence rises up from the holy of holies and abandons the temple to its fate. Finally, the appearance of what are considered to be unorthodox religious practices in the early Second Temple text of Isaiah 56–66 suggests the continuation of illicit practices throughout the sixth century. Ackerman uses this material in an historical task to reconstruct the type of worship that would have taken place in Templeless Judah.

Attestation of what is considered to be illicit religious expression prompts a consideration of those rituals condemned in the literature of this period. Ackerman's study has accomplished this already by considering the major biblical texts that speak of these practices

---

[9] Kaufmann, *The Religion of Israel*, 405–9.

[10] L. E. Toombs, 'When Religions Collide: The Yahweh/Baal Confrontation', in J. M. O'Brien and F. L. Horton (eds.), *The Yahweh/Baal Confrontation and Other Studies in Biblical Literature and Archaeology* (Studies in the Bible and Early Christianity, 35; Lewiston, NY: Mellen Biblical Press, 1995), 39, also takes this view in his comparative study of the religions of Baal and Yahweh. He labels the following kings of Judah outright Baalists: Ahaz (2 Kgs. 16: 34), Manasseh (2 Kgs. 21: 1–9), and Jehoiachin (2 Kgs. 24: 8–9).

[11] Ackerman, *Under Every Green Tree*, 48–51.

(Jer. 7, 44; Ezek. 8; Isa. 57, 65). Although a major contribution to an understanding of the religiosity, or more accurately the perceptions of religious life, in the land, Ackerman's study could be supplemented by a consideration of the material grouped according to the practices rather than the biblical texts that attest them. A broad consideration of the condemned rituals has the benefit of accounting for a greater variety of literature thought to convey and condemn other cultic rituals or deities. In addition, the approach advocated here highlights more clearly the inclusion of Baal and a few other idolatrous behaviours attributed to this period.

Grouping the material according to practices also raises awareness of the importance of literary strategies in the defamation of other deities and rituals. The texts that describe what are considered to be aberrant ritual practices actually stem in every case but one from outside Judah in the Templeless period. Texts from Jeremiah and Ezekiel may indeed reflect on the situation of the religious experience of the people in the land, but the motif of idol worship also functions within the wider rhetoric of the exilic community: (1) to contribute to the explicit expression of exclusive monotheism with its equally powerful insistence that other deities are merely stone or wood with no divine power, (2) to explain the disaster of 587 as a breach of covenant, and (3) to portray the only community worthy of the status of the righteous remnant as that which had experienced deportation to Babylon. Since the portrait of the communities in Judah and in Egypt participating in those activities that brought about the destruction of the state in the first place serves propagandistic purposes in *Golah* literature, it raises the question of whether these texts can be trusted to reveal the actual situation in the land at this time. Zechariah 1–8 represents a bridge text in that, like the book of Haggai, it stems from the late Templeless period, but reflects the situation after the repatriation of the exiles. As such, it shares themes in common with other literature from the close of the period like the Holiness Code (Lev. 17–26) and Ezekiel 40–8 which emphasize ways to live securely in the land. It may, therefore, reflect accommodation between the thoughts which arose among the community in the homeland and that which experienced exile to Babylonia, rather than actual rituals. In addition, the material thought by interpreters (not including Ackerman in this case) to indicate the veneration of a goddess

Conceptions of Judah, I: Idolatrous Cults

is highly metaphorical and could arguably represent the personification of behaviours undesirable during the restoration period. Of the four pieces of literature, Trito-Isaiah is the last and reflects growing anxiety about the failure of the accomplishment of Deutero-Isaiah's prophecies of renewal and restoration. In this collection attributed to a different setting and author than Isaiah 40–55,[12] a nucleus of material (chs. 60–2) similar in thought and style to the surrounded by various oracles that qualify its singularly positive message.[13] The qualification serves two purposes: (1) to explain the delay in the salvific intervention of Yahweh predicted by Deutero-Isaiah and the oracles of chapters 60–2 and (2) to proclaim that concomitant with the miraculous appearance of Yahweh, a portion of the community will experience salvation whilst those who continue to practise wrongful behaviour are doomed to destruction.

Because the literature in Jeremiah and Ezekiel in its final form stems from thought aligned with the exiles in Babylonia and because an actual reference to goddess worship in Zechariah 5 is debatable, the only more certain way to attribute the worship of other deities to Templeless Judah is through the isolation of references that assert the existence of such worship and their continuity in early Second Temple literature. The material in Trito-Isaiah provides at least some justification for the historical task which Ackerman set about

---

[12] B. Duhm, *Das Buch Jesaja* (HAT; Göttingen: Vandenhoeck & Ruprecht, 4th edn. 1922). J. A. Middlemas, 'Divine Reversal and the Role of the Temple in Trito-Isaiah', in J. Day (ed.), *Temple and Worship in Biblical Israel: Proceedings of the Oxford Old Testament Seminar* (London and New York: T & T Clark International, 2005), pp. 164–87 examines various factors having to do with the composition, themes, and dating of Trito-Isaiah in more detail. I refer the reader to the references there.

[13] C. Westermann, *Das Buch Jesaja: Kapitel 40–66* (ATD, 19; Göttingen: Vandenhoeck & Ruprecht, repr. 1986), 236–46. Westermann's understanding of the growth of Trito-Isaiah is followed by many, including K. Pauritsch, *Die neue Gemeinde: Gott sammelt Ausgestossene und Arme (Jesaja 56–6): Die Botschaft des Tritojesaia-Buches literatur-, form-, gattungskritisch und redaktionsgeschichtliche untersucht* (AnBib, 47; Rome: Biblical Institute Press, 1971); P. E. Bonnard, *Le Second Isaïe, son disciple et leurs éditeurs: Isaïe 40–66* (EB; Paris: J. Gabalda, 1972); R. H. O'Connell, *Concentricity and Continuity: The Literary Structure of Isaiah* (JSOTSup, 188; Sheffield: Sheffield Academic Press, 1994), 215–33; P. A. Smith, *Rhetoric and Redaction in Trito-Isaiah: The Structure, Growth and Authorship of Isaiah 56–66* (SVT, 62; Leiden: Brill, 1995), 26–44, extends the material of the nucleus to 63: 6.

and will be considered briefly here. The first text in Trito-Isaiah that exhibits the worship of other deities occurs in 57: 3–13. The extent of the oracle and its date feature in a great many discussions of the poem. On the former issue, the question lies on the relationship of the poem to the oracles that precede it in 56: 9–57: 2 and follow it in 57: 14–21. The best solution is that advanced by Polan and Smith, who consider 57: 3–13 part of a wider unit of 56: 9–57: 21 yet, nevertheless, a stanza in its own right.[14] It is a unified composition marked off from the larger composition by the 'But as for you' ואתם of verse 3, a regular 3 + 2 or *qinah* metre, the form of a trial speech, and the mixed judgement/salvation oracle of verse 13. The date of the poem as part of the unit has also been of interest. Westermann and Vermeylen, who break the poem down into originally independent units, understand verses 3–6 and 7–13a, and verses 6–13a, respectively, as of pre-exilic origin, primarily because of references to cultic practices considered to have ceased with the fall of the kingdom.[15] In addition to the fact that various features strongly suggest the unity of the poem which in themselves argue against any division into shorter units that might have an origin before the Second Temple period,[16] the commonality with denunciations typical of prophecy before the fall of the kingdom merely shows that the author attributed the same problems to his current situation. Around the time of the construction of the temple, the anonymous Trito-Isaiah castigated his contemporaries for participating in illicit worship practices.

The prophet utilizes the form of a trial speech or ריב demarcated by the invitation in verse 3, 'But as for you, come here' ואתם קרבו הנה, a series of questions that serve as a type of cross-

---

[14] G. J. Polan, *In the Ways of Justice Toward Salvation: A Rhetorical Analysis of Isaiah 56–59* (AUS, 13 and TR, 13; New York: Peter Lang, 1986), 91–172; Smith, *Rhetoric and Redaction*, 67–71. P. D. Hanson, *The Dawn of Apocalyptic* (Philadelphia, Pa.: Fortress Press, 1975), 77–9, 186–202, maintains the unity of 56: 9–57: 13, but attributes 57: 14–21 to an earlier period of time. O. H. Steck, 'Beobachtungen zu Jesaja 56–59', *BZ* 31 (1987), 228–46, considers it the first of two units of composition which forms part of the larger unit of 56: 1–57: 21.

[15] Westermann, *Das Buch Jesaja*, 256–9; J. Vermeylen, *Du Prophète Isaïe à l'apocalyptique: Isaïe I–XXXV, miroir d'un demi-millénaire d'expérience religieuse en Israël*, 2 vols. (EB; Paris: J. Gabalda, 1977–8), 458–61.

[16] Polan, *In the Ways of Justice*, 103–7; Smith, *Rhetoric and Redaction*, 78–80.

examination, and a series of indictments.[17] Yahweh stands as the prosecutor and judge of a group of people who are defined by illicit cultic practices. Adultery, sorcery, and sexual deviance figuratively illustrate the wantonness of the people's behaviour in their service of other deities. The poem stresses the persistence of the behaviour in verses 3–4 with the use of sons בני, seed זרע, and children ילדי as well as the pervasiveness of the problem through the extremes the accused is willing to go to in worshipping other gods—ascending a high mountain הר גבה ונשא (v. 7) and descending into the depths of the underworld itself עד שאול (v. 9).[18] The oracle functions to distinguish the idolaters set aside for judgement who will find no salvation in their pursuits (vv. 6, 13a) from the faithful who will possess the land (v. 13b).

The theme of diametrically opposed fates of those considered by the prophet to be engaged in illicit cultic practices and those who adhere to Yahweh alone comes to the fore in the concluding chapters of the collection—chapters 65–6. The presence of various cultic abuses in 65: 3–4, 7, 11; 66: 3–4, 17 once again reveals that the prophet regards practices engaged in by his contemporaries to be inconsistent with Yahwism. As with 57: 3–13, the extent of the unit and its date have caused some controversy. Although Hanson followed by many separates chapter 65 from 66,[19] several reasons advanced by Smith highlight the integrity of 65–66: 17.[20] Thematically the two chapters are alike in the constant contrast drawn between the righteous destined for salvation and the idolaters doomed to destruction. Moreover, 66: 17 forms a structural ring with 65: 1–7 by recapitulating the motif of idolatry there. It concludes with the assertion that the idolaters and their deeds will vanish, punctuated by the messenger formula 'oracle of Yahweh'

---

[17] Polan, *In the Ways of Justice*, 124–32.
[18] So, also, Hanson, *Dawn of Apocalyptic*, 197–98; Polan, *In the Ways of Justice*, 126, 138–9.
[19] Hanson, *Dawn of Apocalyptic*, 135, 161–3, followed by Ackerman, *Under Every Green Tree*, 165 n. 1; B. Schramm, *The Opponents of Third Isaiah: Reconstructing the Cultic History of the Restoration* (JSOTSup, 193; Sheffield: Sheffield Academic Press, 1995), 154.
[20] Smith, *Rhetoric and Redaction*, 128–32. Cf. O. H. Steck, 'Beobachtungen zur Anlage von Jes 65–66', *BN* 38/39 (1987), 103–16, and E. C. Webster, 'The Rhetoric of Isaiah 63–65', *JSOT* 47 (1990), 89–102.

נאם יהוה. Like Isaiah 57: 3–13, the cultic abuses denounced in chapters 65 and 66 belong to the period of the author. A completely symbolic rendering of the passage does not do justice to the argument sustained by the prophet throughout the collection.[21] In addition, the juxtaposed salvation and judgement oracles in 65–66: 17 respond to the communal lament of 63: 7–64: 11 by explaining the delay in the coming of Yahweh and the division in the community between the faithful and the unfaithful that will take place when that event occurs. The cultic practices considered by the prophet to be incompatible with Yahwistic practice are, therefore, ritual observances that take place in his day.

As with 57: 3–13, chapters 65–66 attribute the abuses to consistent behaviour and focus on various aspects of idolatrous ritual. According to explicit and implicit references, the oracles clearly associate the current behaviour with past generations. In verse 7, for example, the prophet in his statement of judgement ascribes the appropriateness of the sentence to the fact that illicit behaviours were the result of 'your sin and the sins of your fathers together' עונתיכם ועונת אבותיכם יחדו (Isa. 65: 7a). Furthermore, the language with which the prophet condemns the abuses is reminiscent of Deuteronomistic language which links illicit practice between generations.[22] The prophetic rebuke centres on three impure ritual activities: (1) the offering of sacrifices and incense to unspecified other gods (Isa. 65: 3b, 7; 66: 3, 17a), (2) necromancy and incubation rites (Isa. 65: 4a), and (3) cultic meals involving unclean food that may be related to either of the above (Isa. 65: 4b; 66: 17b).[23]

---

[21] Contra, Hanson, *Dawn of Apocalyptic*, 179–80; K. Koenen, *Ethik und Eschatologie im Tritojesajabuch: Eine literarkritische und redaktionsgeschichtliche Studie* (WMANT, 62; Neukirchen-Vluyn: Neukirchener Verlag, 1990), 190–2.

[22] Koenen, *Ethik und Eschatologie*, 166–7; Smith, *Rhetoric and Redaction*, 138–9.

[23] Cultic meals should not exclusively be considered a violation of Mosaic law as maintained by Hanson, *Dawn of Apocalyptic*, 147; Ackerman, *Under Every Green Tree*, 202–12; B. B. Schmidt, *Israel's Beneficent Dead: Ancestor Cult and Necromancy in Ancient Israelite Religion and Tradition* (FAT, 11; Tübingen: Mohr (Paul Siebeck), 1994), 262. Cultic meals can have chthonic overtones or relate to fertility rituals, cf. R. de Vaux, 'Les sacrifices de porcs en Palestine et dans l'ancien Orient', in *Bible et Orient* (Paris: Editions du Cerf, 1967), 499–516, and W. Houston, *Purity and Monotheism: Clean and Unclean Animals in Biblical Laws* (JSOTSup, 140; Sheffield: Sheffield Academic Press, 1993), 124–80.

The mention of the persistence of improper worship in the early Second Temple period provides some evidence in support of Ackerman's contention that a number of worship practices took place in sixth-century Judah. Ackerman's concern to shed more light on the religious background of Templeless Judah is not incorrect even though it is also the case that the texts she utilizes in her analysis also serve propagandistic purposes and clearly function to condemn the community in the homeland. Since they contribute to the *Tendenz* of the *Golah*, the plurality of unorthodox rituals provide a conception of Templeless Judah that has been uncritically followed by modern interpreters of the period.

VARIETIES OF ABERRANT PRACTICES

There are a variety of illicit practices attributed to Templeless Judah. Although it is possible that they represent actual religious practice engaged in by the inhabitants of post-587 Judah, the fact is that their description and, indeed, condemnation occurs in literature that stems from other settings (in either location or time) and reflects ideological intentions. In spite of this fact, it is important to understand external perceptions of the homeland. A survey of what are considered to be non-Yahwistic practices proceeds by discussing the evidence for the veneration of the more prevalent deities such as goddesses, Molek, and Baal and concludes with those deities and rituals that appear less frequently. In so doing, it catalogues the wide variety of worship associated with Templeless Judah while at the same time raising awareness of literary strategies utilized to dissuade people from the worship of other deities.

An Unidentifiable Goddess?

Among the archaeological discoveries of this period are a number of female figurines. Known as the Judaean or Judahite Pillar Figurines because they are located almost exclusively in Judah with especially large numbers in Jerusalem, these statues of women were distributed during the late monarchical period and continued into the sixth century, after which their production appears to have ceased.[24] The limited chronology of the existence of the figurines, their location in household sites and tombs, and the distinctive features which characterize them as a group provide some indication that they ought to be viewed together and that their role was more than that of a toy[25] or votive offering.[26] The most likely use of the figurines was as imitations of cult images for devotion and protection.[27] The accentuated features of the breasts encircled by the arms, and enlarged, carefully crafted heads (although some were pinched), with the pubic triangle of earlier forms replaced by the conical base, suggest that they represented a localized version of a fertility goddess or a mother goddess figure. Patai was among the first to bring the Judaean Pillar Figurines to bear on the discussion of the possibility of a goddess who functioned as a consort of Yahweh.[28] No consensus has emerged as yet from the various proposals on the identity of the goddess represented by the figurines.[29] However, among those who

---

[24] Some helpful summaries of the dates and distribution of the Judaean Pillar Figurines include E. Stern, 'What Happened to the Cult Figurines? Israelite Religion after the Exile', *BAR* 15/4 (1989), 22–9, 53–4; R. Kletter, 'Between Archaeology and Theology: The Pillar Figurines from Judah and the Asherah', in A. Mazar, *Studies in the Archaeology of the Iron Age in Israel and Jordan* (JSOTSup, 331; Sheffield: Sheffield Academic Press, 2001), 179–216; K. Prag, 'Figurines, Figures and Contexts in Jerusalem and Regions to the East in the Seventh and Sixth Centuries BCE', in Mazar, *Studies in the Archaeology of the Iron Age*, 218–20. The cessation of the production of the figurines is sometimes dated to the destruction of Jerusalem, but they are found in sites that continued into the sixth century BCE such as Tel en-Nasbeh, Gibeon, Ramat Rahel, and Jerusalem. It is impossible to attribute their decline to a precise date within the sixth century BCE.

[25] A. R. Millard, 'Review of *A Primer of Old Testament Archaeology*', *PEQ* 95 (1963), 139.

[26] J. H. Tigay, *You Shall Have No Other Gods: Israelite Religion in the Light of Hebrew Inscriptions* (HSS, 31; Atlanta, Ga.: Scholars Press, 1986), 91–2; R. Moorey, 'Terracotta Imagery in Israel and Judah under the Divided Monarchy (*c*.925–586 B.C.)', Schweich Lectures, 14 November 2001.

[27] K. van der Toorn, 'Israelite Figurines: A View from the Text', in B. M. Gittlen (ed.), *Sacred Time, Sacred Place: Archaeology and the Religion of Israel* (Winona Lake, Ind.: Eisenbrauns, 2002), 59.

[28] R. Patai, *The Hebrew Goddess* (Detroit, Mich.: Wayne State University Press, 3rd edn. 1990).

[29] J. B. Burns, 'Female Pillar Figurines of the Iron Age: A Study in Text and Artifact', *Andrews University Seminary Studies* 36 (1998), 30–5, provides a useful survey of scholarly opinions.

argue for the identification of the figurines with a specific goddess,[30] Asherah is by far the most commonly named.[31] Although the exact date of the cessation of the production of the figurines cannot be known with certainty (i.e. early or late sixth century BCE), their very existence suggests the worship of a goddess or goddesses in Judah.

Interestingly, the Judaean Pillar Figurines correspond to certain texts thought to attest the veneration of a female deity in post-587 Judah. According to different interpreters, in certain instances the mention of female figures raises the question of the veneration of a goddess during the sixth century, such as (1) the Queen of Heaven in Jeremiah 7: 16–20 and 44: 15–19, 25; (2) the statue of jealousy in Ezekiel 8: 3, 5; and (3) the woman in the ephah in Zechariah 5: 1–11. Otherwise, the worship of Asherah has been identified in the offerings made in the gardens in Isaiah 65: 3b. It will be shown that it is very difficult to ascertain the identity of a female goddess, if only one is intended in all these texts. In fact, only two of the references provide details that make a positive identification likely. Other passages should be considered with caution.

In Jeremiah 7: 16–20 and 44: 15–19, 25, a female deity known only as the Queen of Heaven functions as part of prophetic rhetoric to explain the condemnation of the temple in Judah before its destruction in 587 and the refugees in Egypt some time after the assassination of Gedaliah. During a series of denunciations appended to the temple sermon (7: 1–15)—dated, therefore, to just before the destruction of the temple and so either the late seventh or early sixth century BCE—Yahweh uses a description of the participation by all levels of society in preparation for the worship of another deity as a

[30] J. Pritchard, *Palestinian Figurines in Relation to Certain Goddesses Known through Literature* (New Haven, Conn.: American Oriental Society, 1943), 86–7, is hesitant to ascribe a specific identity.

[31] e.g. R. Kletter, *The Judean Pillar-Figurines and the Archaeology of Asherah* (British Archaeological Reports, International Series, 636; Oxford: Tempus Reparatum, 1996); Burns, 'Female Pillar Figurines', 35–6; K. van der Toorn, 'Goddesses in Early Israelite Religion', in L. Goodison and C. Morris (eds.), *Ancient Goddesses: The Myths and the Evidence* (London: British Museum Press, 1998), 91–5; and J. M. Hadley, *The Cult of Asherah in Ancient Israel and Judah: Evidence for a Hebrew Goddess* (COP, 57; Cambridge: Cambridge University Press, 2000), 196–205. A.-J. 'Amr, 'Ten Human Clay Figurines from Jerusalem', *Levant* 20 (1988), 185–96, associates them with Ištar.

means of justifying final judgement on the city of Jerusalem and the temple:

> 17 האינך ראה מה המה עשׂים בערי יהודה
> ובחצות ירושלם: 18 הבנים מלקטים עצים
> והאבות מבערים את־האשׁ והנשים לשות בצק
> לעשות כונים למלכת השמים והסך
> נסכים לאלהים אחרים למען הכעסני:

Do you not see what they are doing in the cities of Judah and in the streets of Jerusalem? The children gather wood, the fathers kindle fire, and the women knead dough, to make cakes for the Queen of Heaven; and they pour out drink offerings to other gods, to provoke me to anger. (Jer. 7: 17–18)

v. 18 כונים MT 'cakes' based on the Akk. loanword *kamānu*, but note that K. J. H. Vriezen, 'Cakes and Figurines: Related Women's Cultic Offerings in ancient Israel', in B. Becking and M. Dijkstra (eds.), *On Reading Prophetic Texts: Gender Specific and Related Studies in Memory of Fokkelien van Dijk-Hemmes* (BIS, 18; Leiden: Brill, 1996), 251–63, traces the etymology of the word to Hebrew כן, thereby suggesting a shape standing upright.

v. 18 לִמְלֶכֶת הַשָּׁמַיִם MT 'to the work of the heavens' intending the host of heaven. Supported by the G of 7: 18, Pesh., Targ., and many MSS in which an aleph is added (למלאכת). R. P. Gordon, 'Aleph Apologeticum', *JQR* NS 69 (1978–9), 112, regards the Masoretic pointing as an intentional obfuscation of the worship of the Queen of Heaven. Read לְמַלְכַּת 'to the Queen of' with the G of 44: 17, 18, 19, 25, supported by A, S, T, and V. This title is unknown elsewhere in the HB. Hermopolis Letter 4: 1 mentions a temple of the Queen of Heaven, cf. J. T. Milik, 'Les papyrus araméens d'Hermoupolis et les cultes syro-phéniciens en Egypte perse', *Bib* 48 (1967), 556–64.

In a parallel text traditionally attributed to exilic redaction (Jer. 44: 1–30),[32] the issue of the worship of this female deity is raised after the flight to Egypt. The worship of other deities and the Queen of Heaven appears in a type of appendix to the book of Jeremiah.[33] The speech divides into several segments: the report of a divine word that came to Jeremiah in Egypt (vv. 1–14), the response of the people (vv. 15–19), and Jeremiah's rebuttal (vv. 20–5).[34] The divine recital of the idolatrous history of the people, namely the burning of incense to

---

[32] Seitz, *Theology in Conflict*, 228–35, 287–9.
[33] Holladay, *Jeremiah*, ii. 283.
[34] Ibid., ii. 285–6, 303–4.

other nameless gods (vv. 3, 5), and its continued practice in Egypt (v. 8) leads to the pronouncement of judgement that this remnant like Judah will be cut off (vv. 7, 11–14). Though the deity fails to mention a particular god or goddess in his speech, the people respond by emphatically associating their current ritual observance with the Queen of Heaven (vv. 15, 17, 18, 19), only failing to mention her when they refuse to take notice of Jeremiah's prophecy in verse 16. As a type of rejoinder, Jeremiah reiterates that just as their burning incense to other gods brought down the wrath of Yahweh on Jerusalem, so shall their present behaviour (vv. 20–3). Condemning them to a like fate, he tells them to keep worshipping the Queen of Heaven (vv. 24–5). The sequence reveals that the people have an inverted type of logic in that they insist that it was the cessation of the veneration of the Queen of Heaven that brought about the disaster, not Yahweh's judgement for improper ritual practice as in Jeremiah's view. For them, blessing and security emanated from the goddess. Their perspective represents an alternative to the theological reflection of the disaster of 587 made by the *Golah* community in Babylon. Although attributed to the refugees in Egypt, Ackerman suggests that this heterodoxy might be indicative of a type of response which occurred in the homeland.

In Jeremiah's view the worship of this female deity brought about disaster and would result in the destruction of the refugees in Egypt. The recipient of such prophetic vitriol and condemnation deserves further investigation. Who exactly is this 'Queen of Heaven'? The 'Queen of Heaven', rather than being the name of an extant goddess of the ANE, clearly represents the title of a tantalizingly inexplicit deity. As with the Judaean Pillar Figurines, there is still no unanimity on the referent.[35] Opinions vacillate between the names of female

---

[35] Surveys of attempts to determine the exact identity of the goddess being referred to in Jeremiah include S. M. Olyan, 'Some Observations Concerning the Identity of the Queen of Heaven', *UF* 19 (1987), 161–74; Ackerman, *Under Every Green Tree*, 5–35; C. Frevel, *Aschera und der Ausschließlichkeitsanspruch YHWHs: Beiträge zu literarischen, religionsgeschichtlichen und ikonographischen Aspekten der Ascheradiskussion* (BBB, 94/1–2; Weinheim: Beltz Athenäum, 1995), 444–71; and most recently, J. Day, *Yahweh and the Gods and Goddesses of Canaan* (JSOTSup, 265; Sheffield: Sheffield Academic Press, 2000), 144–50. Cf. W. McKane, 'Worship of the Queen of Heaven (Jer 44)', in I. Kottsieper *et al.* (eds.), *'Wer is wie du, Herr, unter den Göttern?': Studien zur Theologie und Religionsgeschichte Israels* (Göttingen: Vandenhoeck & Ruprecht, 1994), 318–24, on the text.

deities known in the Hebrew Bible, Asherah,[36] Ashtoret,[37] and Anat,[38] various female deities of the ancient world including Ištar,[39] or a combination of two Semitic goddesses.[40] A minority opinion suggests that the lack of clear references to the characteristics of the deity and her cult makes any particular association inconclusive.[41] According to Ackerman, however, the biblical depictions provide four features which make a determination possible: (1) the title 'Queen of Heaven' along with a presumed association with astral

[36] The term asherah in the feminine singular and plural occurs 40 times in the Old Testament in nine books and mostly from the hand of the Deuteronomists (Exod. 34: 13; Deut. 7: 5; 12: 3; 16: 21; Judg. 3: 7; 6: 25, 26, 28, 30; 1 Kgs. 14: 15, 23; 15: 13; 16: 33; 18: 19; 2 Kgs. 13: 6; 17: 10, 16; 18: 4; 21: 3, 7; 23: 4, 6, 7, 14, 15; Isa. 17: 8; 27: 9; Jer. 17: 2; Mic. 5: 13 (ET 14); 2 Chr. 14: 2 (ET 3); 15: 16; 17: 6; 19: 3; 24: 18; 31: 1; 33: 3, 19; 34: 3, 4, 7). Only in six of the instances does it seem to denote a goddess rather than a cultic object: Judg. 3: 7; 1 Kgs. 15: 13 // 2 Chr. 15: 16; 1 Kgs. 18: 19; 2 Kgs. 21: 7; 23: 4, 7. P. R. Ackroyd, 'Goddesses, Women and Jezebel', in A. Cameron and A. Kuhrt (eds.), *Images of Women in Antiquity* (London: Routledge, rev. edn. 1993), 252; J. Day, 'Asherah in the Hebrew Bible and Northwest Semitic Literature', *JBL* 105 (1986), 385–408; K. Koch, 'Aschera als Himmelskönigin in Jerusalem', *UF* 20 (1988), 97–120; M. Dijkstra, 'Goddess, Gods, Men and Women in Ezekiel 8', in Becking and Dijkstra, *On Reading Prophetic Texts*, 92.

[37] Found as Aštaroth in Judg. 2: 13; 10: 6; 1 Sam. 7: 3, 4; 12: 10; 31: 10 and Aštoreth in 1 Kgs. 11: 5, 33; 2 Kgs. 23: 13. Olyan, 'Some Observations'; J. M. Hadley, 'The Fertility of the Flock? The De-Personalization of Astarte in the Old Testament', in Becking and Dijkstra, *On Reading Prophetic Texts*, 115–33, and idem, 'Chasing Shadows? The Quest for the Historical Goddess', in J. A. Emerton (ed.), *Congress Volume: Cambridge 1995* (SVT, 66; Leiden: Brill, 1997), 172–7.

[38] Anat does not occur as the name of the goddess but as a proper name of places (Jer. 1: 1) and people (Judg. 3: 31; 5: 6; 1 Chr. 7: 8; 8: 24; Neh. 10: 19). Van der Toorn, 'Goddesses in Early Israelite Religion'.

[39] M. Weinfeld, 'The Worship of Molech and of the Queen of Heaven and its Background', *UF* 4 (1972), 149–54.

[40] S. Ackerman, ' "And the Women Knead Dough": The Worship of the Queen of Heaven in Sixth-Century Judah', in P. L. Day (ed.), *Gender and Difference in Ancient Israel* (Minneapolis, Minn.: Fortress Press, 1989), 109–24, and idem, *Under Every Green Tree*, 8–35. Ackerman understands that the Queen of Heaven is a syncretistic deity whose character incorporates aspects of west Semitic Aštarte and east Semitic Ištar. Other views include those of M. S. Smith, *The Early History of God: Yahweh and the Other Deities in Ancient Israel* (Grand Rapids, Mich.: Eerdmans, 2nd edn. 2002), 127; O. Keel and C. Uehlinger, *Göttinnen, Götter, und Gottessymbole: Neue Erkenntnisse zur Religionsgeschichte Kanaans und Israels aufgrund bislang unerschlossener ikonographischer Quellen* (QD, 134; Freiburg: Herder, 1992), 388–9, ET *Gods, Goddesses, and Images of God in ancient Israel* (Minneapolis, Minn.: Fortress Press, 1998), 339–40; Day, *Yahweh and the Gods*, 146, 149.

[41] R. P. Carroll, *Jeremiah: A Commentary* (OTL; London: SCM Press, 1986), 213; J. M Hadley, 'Who Is She? The Identity of the Queen of Heaven', (forthcoming).

bodies, (2) the cultic practices which include the burning of incense, the pouring out of libations, and the making of cakes in the image of the goddess, (3) the association of the goddess with fertility and war, and (4) the special appeal of the cult to women.

The distinguishing features isolated by Ackerman are problematic. In the first case, the title 'Queen of Heaven' in and of itself does not connote an association with numinous phenomena. Placed within the speech of the people in Jeremiah 7 and 44, it represents a title by which she was known among the populace which could very well simply represent her exalted status as the consort of an unmentioned 'King of Heaven'. Secondly, the text is not clear on the exact procedure for making the cakes for the goddess in that it remains ambiguous on whether or not the cakes were fashioned in her image or had her likeness or symbol stamped upon them. Thirdly, Ackerman's association of the deity with fertility and war comes about only after a forced reading of the passages. Finally, the special significance of the cult for women does not do justice to the inclusion of men, women, and children in the indictment by Yahweh in 7: 18, and the extension to fathers, kings, and princes by the people in 44: 17, and by Jeremiah in 44: 21. In this instance, Ackerman contradicts herself in that she conceives of the special appeal to women as a means of ascertaining the identity of the goddess, while at the same time utilizing the wider appeal of the cult in order to suggest that the worship of the Queen of Heaven was intrinsic in Judah. This is especially apparent with Ackerman's conclusion that the veneration of the Queen of Heaven was not the religion of a minority, but one, potentially, of all Yahweh worshippers from royalty to the people. Of Ackerman's designating features, only the epithet 'Queen of Heaven' without astral overtones and the types of cultic activities associated with her worship can be used indicatively.

Any identification of the anonymous figure known only by the epithet 'Queen of Heaven' with a particular goddess is conjectural due to the nature of the sources. Indeed, certain difficulties confront the interpreter who seeks to ascertain her referent: (1) the biblical evidence of the worship of goddesses in ancient Israel and Judah is incomplete, (2) texts which convey the worship of female deities are polemical, and (3) the writers were at pains to portray the worship of other deities as foreign imports and not indigenous to Yahweh worship. The most defensible case can be made for the association of the Queen of Heaven with Asherah. Of the three ANE goddesses known from the Hebrew Bible, in terms of sheer numbers, Asherah, occurring forty times overall, is the most common by far.[42] However, contextual attestations of Asherah the goddess and asherah as some type of cultic symbol[43] obscure a precise understanding of this deity. Moreover, what appears to be a programmatic initiative to eradicate her worship appears in the Hebrew Bible in depictions of her cult as foreign[44] and through literary objectification and conflation.[45] Contrary to both, certain texts (Judg. 6; 2 Kgs. 13: 6) hint that her worship was considered at various times an integral part of Yahweh worship,[46] and in some places she appears as a goddess.[47]

In fact, mounting evidence provides some indication that Asherah was worshipped alongside Yahweh in the Jerusalem temple as his consort.[48] Such a notion is not as inconceivable as the biblical portrait attests. At the Jewish temple in Elephantine, Yahu, the head

---

[42] Koch, 'Aschera'.

[43] Opinions vary between asherah as a wooden pole, a stylized tree, or even a living tree. A current survey is available in S. A. Wiggins, *A Reassessment of 'Asherah': A Study According to the Textual Sources of the First Two Millennia* B.C.E. (AOAT, 235; Neukirchen-Vluyn: Neukirchener Verlag, 1993), 1–20; Hadley, *The Cult of Asherah*, 4–37.

[44] Ackroyd, 'Goddesses', 254–5.

[45] For instance, her name frequently occurs with the definite article, an almost unheard of phenomenon. T. Binger, *Asherah: Goddesses in Ugaritic, Israel and the Old Testament* (JSOTSup, 232; Sheffield: Sheffield Academic Press, 1997), 121–6; Hadley, 'The Fertility of the Flock?' Similarly, S. M. Olyan, *Asherah and the Cult of Yahweh in Israel* (Atlanta, Ga.: Scholars Press, 1988), 1–20, argues that a concerted effort was made to literarily demythologize Asherah the goddess by a wilful confusion of her with other goddesses and through an association with Baal. Cf. Day, *Yahweh and the Gods*, 48, 60–1.

[46] Ackroyd, 'Goddesses', 255–6; M. S. Smith, 'God Male and Female in the Old Testament: Yahweh and his "Asherah" ', *TS* 48 (1987), 335–7; Olyan, *Asherah*, 3. Especially on the contribution of Judg. 6, see Ackroyd, 'Goddessess', 255.

[47] Judg. 3: 7; 1 Kgs. 15: 13 // 2 Chr. 15: 16; 1 Kgs. 18: 19; 2 Kgs. 21: 7; 23: 4, 7. See the excellent surveys in Wiggins, *A Reassessment of 'Asherah'*.

[48] See the reservations by Tigay, *You Shall Have No Other Gods*, 93; J. H. Tigay, 'Israelite Religion: The Onomastic and Epigraphic Evidence', in P. D. Miller *et al.* (eds.), *Ancient Israelite Religion: Essays in Honor of Frank Moore Cross* (Philadelphia, Pa.: Fortress Press, 1987), 173–5; R. S. Hess, 'Yahweh and his Asherah? Epigraphic Evidence for Religious Pluralism in Old Testament Times', in A. D. Clarke and B. W. Winter (eds.), *One God, One Lord in a World of Religious Pluralism* (Cambridge: Tyndale House, 1991), 5–33.

of the pantheon, was worshipped alongside four other deities, two of whom, known only from the papyri, appear to have been female consorts, Anat-Yahu and Anat-Bethel.[49] In spite of the fact that the Elephantine texts provide strong evidence for an association of Yahweh's consort with a female deity other than Asherah, the Kuntillet 'Ajrud and Khirbet el-Qôm inscriptions along with internal biblical evidence suggest that in Judah the female deity most likely associated with Yahweh was Asherah. Extra-biblical inscriptions from Kuntillet 'Ajrud and Khirbet el-Qôm[50] pair Asherah with Yahweh. The inscriptions associate the two through a reference to Yahweh of GN and 'his asherah'.[51] A significant amount of discussion features whether or not the 'asherah' refers to the cult symbol or the goddess. Dever, for example, claims that the evidence from Kuntillet 'Ajrud clearly identifies Asherah as the consort of Yahweh, thus confirming the conclusion reached by some interpreters.[52] Because proper names do not appear in the Hebrew Bible with pronominal suffixes, it is more likely the case that the reference is to the cult symbol.[53] Nevertheless, the cult symbol represents the goddess so even though the inscriptions do not confirm the role of Asherah, they surely hint at it.[54]

Outside ancient Israel, Asherah equates to Athirat in Ugaritic mythological and liturgical texts dated between the fourteenth and

---

[49] K. van der Toorn, 'Anat-Yahu, some other Deities, and the Jews of Elephantine', *Numen* 39 (1992), 80–101. D. V. Edelman has pointed out in private communication that as a military colony, the Elephantine community may have been particularly attracted to the worship of Anat because of her association with war.

[50] With Emerton, I regard the picture of the figures as distinct from the inscription and shall not consider it here.

[51] Z. Meshel, 'Kuntillet 'Ajrûd: An Israelite Site from the Monarchical Period on the Sinai Border', *Qadmoniot* 9 (1976), 118–24; Lemaire, 'Les inscriptions'; Meshel, 'Did Yahweh Have a Consort?'; J. Naveh, 'Graffiti and Dedications', *BASOR* 235 (1979), 27–30; Z. Zevit, 'The Khirbet el-Qôm Inscription Mentioning a Goddess', *BASOR* 255 (1984), 39–47; J. M. Hadley, 'The Khirbet el-Qôm Inscription', *VT* 37 (1987), 50–62.

[52] W. G. Dever, 'Asherah, Consort of Yahweh? New Evidence from Kuntillet 'Ajrud', *BASOR* 255 (1984), 21–37.

[53] Emerton, 'New Light on Israelite Religion', and *idem*, ' "Yahweh and his Asherah": The Goddess or Her Symbol?', *VT* 49 (1999), 315–37; Keel and Uehlinger, *Göttinnen, Götter*, 237–82 = *Gods, Goddesses*, 210–48.

[54] Keel and Uehlinger, *Göttinnen, Götter*, 263–4 = *Gods, Goddesses*, 232–3; Day, *Yahweh and the Gods*, 60.

twelfth centuries BCE.⁵⁵ In them, she appears alongside the chief deity, El, as a consort and the mother of the gods. Various epithets attest her status, including, 'Great Athirat of the Sea', 'the Progenitress of the Gods', 'Elat' (the feminine of El), and 'Great Lady'. As Yahweh has assimilated many attributes associated with El it is not surprising that the worship of El's consort similarly was taken over.⁵⁶ Although Yahweh is not known in the Hebrew Bible by the epithet 'the King of Heaven' except in the Aramaic of Daniel (Dan. 4: 34), he is known as 'king',⁵⁷ his dwelling place is quite often spoken of as being in the heavens,⁵⁸ and he is termed 'the God of Heaven' (Ezra 1: 2),⁵⁹ all of which suggests that a Queen of Heaven as the consort of Yahweh is possible. It is clear from Egyptian and Canaanite sources that the manifestation of goddesses took on specificities peculiar to the regions in which they were found. In terms of Asherah, for example, elsewhere in Mesopotamia she was known as Ašratum, who was the 'Goddess of the Steppes', whereas the same goddess in Canaan known as Athirat in Ugarit, a coastal city, was conceived of as 'the Goddess of the Sea'.⁶⁰ Asherah could therefore have been known in ancient Israel by a regionalized expression not found of her elsewhere in the ANE.

⁵⁵ W. A. Maier, *'Ašerah: Extrabiblical Evidence* (HSM, 37; Atlanta, Ga.: Scholars Press, 1986); Hadley, *The Cult of Asherah*, 38–43.
⁵⁶ F. M. Cross, *Canaanite Myth and Hebrew Epic: Essays in the History of the Religion of Israel* (Cambridge, Mass.: Harvard University Press, 1973), 44–7; Olyan, *Asherah*, 38–61; Day, *Yahweh and the Gods*, 13–41. For a rather unconventional perspective, see M. Dijkstra, 'El, YHWH and their Asherah: On Continuity and Discontinuity in Canaanite and Ancient Israelite Religion', in M. Dietrich and O. Loretz (eds.), *Ugarit: Ein ostmediterranes Kulturzentrum im Alten Orient*, i: *Ugarit und seine altorientalische Umwelt* (Münster: Ugaritverlag, 1995), 43–73.
⁵⁷ Num. 23: 21; 1 Sam. 12: 12; Pss. 10: 16; 24: 8, 10; 29: 10; 47: 3; 84: 3; 93: 1; 95: 3; 96: 10; 97: 1; 98: 6; 99: 1; Isa. 6: 5; 33: 22; 41: 21, *et al.*
⁵⁸ H. Niehr, 'In Search of YHWH's Cult Statue in the First Temple', in K. van der Toorn (ed.), *The Image and the Book: Iconic Cults, Aniconism and the Rise of the Book Religion in Israel and the Ancient Near East* (CBET, 21; Leuven: Peeters, 1997), 73–95, however, argues that heaven became Yahweh's dwelling place only in the period after the exile as a reaction against the destruction of the temple. The concept of Yahweh in the heavens was emphasized after the 'exile', but does not necessarily originate in that time period.
⁵⁹ It is found most commonly in post-exilic texts. D. K. Andrews, 'Yahweh and the God of the Heavens', in W. S. McCullough (ed.), *The Seed of Wisdom: Essays in Honour of T. J. Meek* (Toronto: University of Toronto Press, 1964), 45–57, looks at the expression 'God of the Heavens' in the Old Testament and Aramaic papyri.
⁶⁰ Day, 'Asherah', 386.

A female deity, frequently thought of as Asherah, has been associated with other texts in the literature from this period and the early Second Temple period. Indeed, 'the statue of jealousy' in Ezekiel 8: 3, 5, the woman in the ephah in Zechariah 5, and the burning of incense in Isaiah 65: 3 have all been associated with Asherah.[61] In Ezekiel 8, which forms part of the temple vision of the prophet, Ezekiel is transported to Jerusalem in 592 between the two deportations of 598 and 587 and is shown among other abominations in the temple what appears to be a statue set up opposite the altar of Yahweh.[62] The approach followed here in conjunction with Ezekiel's temple vision is that advocated by most commentators, that is, to understand the four scenes as independent instances of idolatry within the environs of the temple.[63] In the first scene at the north gate of the temple (vv. 3b, 5), the prophet encounters a statue traditionally rendered the 'statue of jealousy that provokes jealousy'.[64] Again he looks about and sees 'at the north gate (was) the altar of[65] this statue of jealousy in the

---

[61] Her presence has also been noted among the fertility cult imagery of Isa. 57: 3–13, but I will argue below that only one cult is being referred to in this passage and it has nothing to do with the worship of Asherah.

[62] W. Zimmerli, *Ezechiel 1–24* (BKAT, 13; Neukirchen-Vluyn: Neukirchener Verlag, repr. 1969, 1979), 191–2, 211, and Ackerman, *Under Every Green Tree*, 39 n. 10, 53–5, based on a textual difficulty in v. 3, suggest that the image is located at the northern gate of the city and not of the temple. The text is difficult and convoluted, but the other scenes are at the temple.

[63] Attempts to argue for a single ritual throughout Ezek. 8: 1–18 have not been successful. Cf. H. G. May, 'The Departure of the Glory of Yahweh', *JBL* 56 (1937), 309–21; T. H. Gaster, 'Ezekiel and the Mysteries', *JBL* 60 (1941), 289–310.

[64] MT המקנה *hiphil* participle, thought to be a variant spelling of קנא 'to be jealous' (GKC 75qq), hence 'the one that provokes jealousy'. Yahweh is provoked to jealous anger by the people's idolatry (Ezek. 5: 13; 16: 38, 42; 23: 25). Interestingly, no other variant spelling of קנא is attested. It more naturally suggests the nominative use of the *hiphil* participle of קנה 'to acquire', but in some cases 'create', usually used of the deity (Gen. 14: 19, 22; Deut. 32: 6; Pss. 74: 2; 139: 13), but once of a human (Gen. 4: 1). The only other occurrence in the *hiphil* is dubious, but its rarity and application to human initiative may have overshadowed the meaning intended here. Used in conjunction with a statue of jealousy, if taken as a *hophal*, it might have the sense of 'the one that was fashioned'. Provocatively, the most frequent use of *qnh* 'to create' in Ugaritic texts is associated with Athirat. Cf. H. C. Lutzky, 'On "the Image of Jealousy" (Ezekiel VIII 3, 5)', *VT* 46 (1996), 121–4, but see Day, *Yahweh and the Gods*, 62–3.

[65] MT וְהִנֵּה מִצָּפוֹן לְשַׁעַר הַמִּזְבֵּחַ סֵמֶל הַקִּנְאָה הַזֶּה בַּבִּאָה 'There north of the altar gate was this image of jealousy in the entrance.' There is no mention of an altar gate elsewhere in the HB. A slight emendation suggested by W. Eichrodt, *Der Prophet*

entrance' (Ezek. 8: 5). Without any other information, the object is difficult to identify because it is only known as 'the image of jealousy, the one that causes jealousy' סמל הקנאה המקנה (v. 3) and 'this image of jealousy' סמל הקנאה הזה (v. 5). On the basis of inner-biblical interpretation and the worship of images that incites Yahweh to anger in Deuteronomy, it is held to refer to a cultic statue of Asherah. Established in the temple by King Manasseh according to 2 Kings 21: 7, the cult object was called 'the image of Asherah' פסל האשרה. In later biblical tradition (2 Chr. 33: 7, 15) the Chronicler renders it 'the image of the statue' פסל הסמל and clearly referring to the same symbol, Manasseh removed the 'foreign deities and the idol' אלהי הנכר ואת־הסמל from the temple (2 Chr. 33: 15).[66] In addition, the early traditions of Israel understand idols to provoke Yahweh's jealous rage.[67] For example, Deuteronomy 4: 23–4 states: 'Be wary lest you forget the covenant of Yahweh your God, which he made with you, and make a graven image פסל תמונת in the form of anything which Yahweh your God has forbidden you. For Yahweh your God is a devouring fire, a jealous God אל קנא.' The association in the biblical tradition between Ezekiel's סמל and Asherah is supported by Yahweh's depiction as a deity who was enraged by the creation and worship of other deities. Although biblical tradition clearly associates the statue at the temple with an image of Asherah, the identification of the image with any female deity remains speculative.

To some the Chronicler's view actually associates the vision with events that took place in the temple precincts before Josiah's reforms removed the statue set up by Manasseh (2 Kgs. 21: 7).[68] Should it

Hesekiel Kapital 1–18 (ATD, 22; Göttingen: Vandenhoeck & Ruprecht, 1959), 45, and followed by Zimmerli, *Ezechiel*, i. 192; Ackerman, *Under Every Green Tree*, 40–1, n. 14, yields: 'There north of the gate was the altar of this statue of jealousy.'

[66] Eichrodt, *Hesekiel*, 58–9; McKay, *Religion in Judah*, 22–3; R. Patai, 'The Goddess Asherah', *JNES* 24 (1965), 37–52; Greenberg, *Ezekiel 1–20*, 168; Koch, 'Aschera', 111–12; Ackerman, *Under Every Green Tree*, 56–7; Lutzky, 'On "the Image of Jealousy" '.

[67] Ackerman, *Under Every Green Tree*, 57–60.

[68] C. C. Torrey, *Pseudo-Ezekiel and the Original Prophecy* (Yale Oriental Series, 18; New Haven, Conn.: Yale University Press, 1930), 58–112; Kaufmann, *The Religion of Israel*, 407–8; Greenberg, *Ezekiel 1–20*, 168, 201–5, followed by R. W. Klein, *Ezekiel: The Prophet and His Message* (Studies on Personalities in the Old Testament; Columbia: University of South Carolina Press, 1988), 407–9. They are refuted by Ackerman, *Under Every Green Tree*, 47–51; Kutsko, *Between Heaven and Earth*, 47–53.

represent the statue set up by Manasseh and torn down by Josiah (2 Kgs. 23: 6), it would provide little assistance in ascertaining the religiosity of Jerusalem between the Babylonian incursions of 598 and 587. It is plausible that the statue was restored by a successor to Josiah.[69] Interestingly, Morton Smith argues that the reference to the cessation of the worship of the Queen of Heaven in Jeremiah 44: 18 implies that rituals in her honour continued until the siege of Jerusalem. Subsequently, during the siege, they were halted in order to direct all available sacrifices to Yahweh, the main deity of the city.[70] His analysis would fit well with the vision of Ezekiel which the chronology of the book places in the sixth month of 592. More significantly, the belief that the statue refers retrospectively to the time of Manasseh and seeks to explain the final judgement on the temple as accomplished already is not wholly satisfactory. Part of the rhetoric of the book of Ezekiel, particularly with regard to the temple vision of chapters 8–11, is to emphasize the judgement on the population that remains behind in Judah and the transfer of hope for the future restoration of all Israel exclusively to the exiles in Babylon.[71] Were the vision harking back to the time of Manasseh, the thrust of the polemic would be neutralized. The temple vision in its entirety, therefore, more naturally falls at a time contemporaneous with the prophet, on the eve of the destruction of the temple. Furthermore, along with other evidence it attributes the veneration of this goddess to the period after Josiah's reforms and up to the destruction of the temple. It may be the case as Ackerman suggests that the veneration of a goddess continued after the fall of the temple in 587, but there is no direct evidence to confirm it.

It would be attractive if the early Second Temple text about the woman in the Epha in Zechariah 5: 5–11 could be used to support the existence of a cult to a goddess during the Templeless period. The prophetic ministry of Zechariah as recorded in chapters 1–8 overlaps that of Haggai. It is associated with the years 520–518—the time of the reconstruction of the temple—by a precise chronological

---

[69] Eichrodt, *Hesekiel*, 58–9.
[70] M. Smith, 'The Veracity of Ezekiel, the Sins of Manasseh, and Jeremiah 44: 18', *ZAW* 87 (1975), 11–16.
[71] T. Renz, *The Rhetorical Function of the Book of Ezekiel* (SVT, 76; Leiden: Brill, 1999).

framework (Zech. 1: 1, 7; 7: 1). Even though the dating scheme and some other details are thought to stem from the hand of an editor, most scholars do not dissociate the prophecy from the early Second Temple period.[72] In the early period of the return, a woman is carted away from Judah en route to Babylon (vv. 6–11). Rather than understanding the woman as personified apostasy, the Meyers and Uehlinger identify her with a goddess.[73] Three references in the episode certainly imply that the woman is a female deity: (1) 'This one (fem.) represents their sin[74] throughout the land' (v. 6), (2) 'This one (fem.) is idolatry'[75] (v. 8), and (3) 'in the land of Shinar/Babylon a sanctuary will be built for her in its former place'[76] (v. 11). Associated with idolatry and wickedness, this is no ordinary woman. She embodies concepts considered to be incompatible with Yahwism and as the representation of idol worship likely represents a female deity. Notice, for example, that this is the only occasion when רשעה has the definite article. Two female deities known in the Hebrew Bible,

---

[72] P. R. Ackroyd, 'The Book of Haggai and Zechariah I–VIII', *JJS* 3 (1952), 151–7; W. A. M. Beuken, *Haggai–Sacharja 1–8: Studien zur Überlieferungsgeschichte der frühnachexilischen Prophetie* (Assen: Van Gorcum, 1967); C. L. Meyers and E. M. Meyers, *Haggai, Zechariah 1–8* (AB; New York: Doubleday, 1987), pp. xliv–xlviii, l–lxiii; R. Mason, *Preaching the Tradition* (Cambridge: Cambridge University Press, 1990), 197–234.

[73] Meyers and Meyers, *Zechariah 1–8*, 301–9, 313–16; C. Uehlinger, 'Die Frau im Efa (Sach 5, 5–11): eine Programmvision von der Abschiebung der Göttin', *Bibel und Kirche* 49 (1994), 93–103, and idem, 'Figurative Policy, Propaganda und Prophetie', in Emerton, *Congress Volume: Cambridge 1995*, 344–7.

[74] MT עינם LXX and S understand עון. With *BHS* and many commentators, I accept that the confusion of ו and י is a common scribal error (cf. the Dead Sea Scrolls) and emend to עונם in keeping with the thrust of the passage, against Meyers and Meyers, *Zechariah 1–8*, 297–8. See the commentaries.

[75] MT הרשעה 'the evil thing/wickedness'. As idolatry in LXX and V. The feminine noun occurs elsewhere Deut. 9: 4, 5; 25: 2; Isa. 9: 17; Ezek. 5: 6; 18: 20, 27; 33: 12, 19; Mal. 1: 14; 3: 15, 19; Prov. 11: 5; 13: 6. Whilst referring to general wicked behaviour in some places, in others it potentially represents the worship of idols by Jerusalem in Ezek. 5: 6 and idolatry as in Deut. 9: 4, 5, cf. Deut. 8: 19, 20, where the sin of the nations is equated to idolatry. Cf. Ackroyd, *Exile and Restoration*, 205; Meyers and Meyers, *Zechariah 1–8*, 302–3. This is the only case where it appears with the definite article.

[76] MT על־מכנתה Note the use of מכונה in Ezra 3: 3, where it represents the former place of the altar. Meyers and Meyers, *Zechariah 1–8*, 309. Were it not for the frequent use of כן in building contexts, it would be convenient if it could be associated with the same root associated with the cakes baked for the Queen of Heaven in Jer. 7: 18.

Asherah[77] and Ashtaroth,[78] appear with the definite article. Furthermore, her return to Babylon and the establishment of a temple in her honour in its former place suggest that she is a deity associated with Babylon. The leading goddess of the Babylonian pantheon was Ištar. Her Canaanite equivalent is Astarte, who was sometimes equated with Asherah in the Hebrew Bible, so either could be in view.[79] The Meyers suggest that רשעה could be a play on the name of either of the two Canaanite goddesses.[80] Uehlinger, in fact, regards this passage as the attempt to dissuade from the worship of Asherah. Without any further details about this woman, it is difficult to identify her with a particular goddess. However, clues in the text certainly suggest that she should be understood as a deity.[81]

Finally, Ackerman includes the ritual of burning incense in Isaiah 65: 3b among the worship of Asherah.[82] Such a firm designation of the cult is simply impossible given the nature of the worship delineated in the text. The people are only described as 'sacrificing in gardens, burning incense on bricks'. Although there is confirmation that the worship of Asherah coexisted with that of Yahweh at the *bamoth*, beyond a depiction of burning incense, there are simply no references either to how many deities may be in view or who that deity may be. Ackerman argues that the existence of fertility language provides a reference for Asherah, but the main fertility deity in the Old Testament is not depicted as Asherah, but as Baal. Further, as shall be argued below, Ackerman's other identification with Asherah in Isaiah 57 is faulty and cannot be used to suggest that the biblical writer is keen to address specifically the cult of Asherah among the condemned cultic abuses. The biblical writer is probably concerned

---

[77] When singular, Asherah more frequently appears with the ה of the definite article; Judg. 6: 25, 26, 28, 30; 1 Kgs. 15: 13; 16: 33; 18: 19; 2 Kgs. 13: 18; 18: 4; 21: 7; 23: 4, 6, 7.

[78] When Ashtaroth appears in the plural, in every case but one (1 Sam. 31: 10), the name appears with the definite article (Judg. 2: 13; 10: 6; 1 Sam. 7: 3, 4; 12: 10). In all cases when Ashtoreth is singular, she appears without the definite article (1 Kgs. 11: 5, 33; 2 Kgs. 23: 13).

[79] There appears to have been some confusion between the two, even deliberate polemicizing, cf. Smith, *The Early History of God*, 126–7, 130.

[80] Meyers and Meyers, *Zechariah 1–8*, 303, suggest that רשעה is an anagram of the names of the goddesses. It is close, however, but not exact.

[81] Contra, Niehr, 'Religio-Historical Aspects', 240.

[82] Ackerman, *Under Every Green Tree*, 165–94.

with religious practices dedicated to a multiplicity of deities other than Yahweh without particular reference to any one.[83] More importantly, the attribution of worship to other deities whatever their identity in Trito-Isaiah suggests this was an area of concern at the time of the reconstruction of the temple.

The material remains of female figurines that seem to represent a goddess resonate with certain texts from the Templeless period that support the existence of the worship of a goddess in Judah. The fact that the goddess is never named in texts of this period makes an exact identification of her speculative. In the case of Jeremiah's Queen of Heaven in chapters 7 and 44 as well as with the statue of jealousy in Ezekiel 8, a case for the association of the female deity with Asherah can be defended. Other attempts to find allusions to Asherah have been less successful, although a goddess in Zechariah 5: 5–11 seems to be in view. In any event, literature from the *Golah* and from the early Second Temple period attribute the veneration of a goddess to sixth-century Judahites in the land.

Even as the Judaean Pillar Figurines fell out of use in Judah in the early part of the fifth century, the worship of a goddess appears to have eventually ceased. The reasons for this are obscure, but there does seem to have been an active literary campaign to minimalize the worship of Asherah and her status as a deity. The veneration of other deities came under attack in Babylonian exilic literature which laid the blame for the destruction of Jerusalem in 587 on the judgement of Yahweh for religious malpractice. In the early Second Temple period, religious rituals on behalf of deities other than Yahweh resulted in the ongoing application of divine wrath whilst the allusion to a goddess who embodies apostasy in Zechariah 5 dissuaded from her worship. At the same time, the biblical writers downplayed the divine status of Asherah. In spite of being represented as a deity six times in the Hebrew Bible, Asherah is more commonly portrayed as some type of symbol. It may be the case that already during this period a variety of deities who had been worshipped in ancient Israel were subjected to a similar procedure to downplay or even to deny their existence.

[83] M. Dahood, 'Textual Problems in Isaia', *CBQ* 22 (1960), 406–8.

Child Sacrifice

Another cult found criticized during this time period concerns the practice of human sacrifice, particularly that of child immolation. Jeremiah (Jer. 7: 31; 19: 5; 32: 35, and alluded to in 2: 23; 3: 24) and Ezekiel (16: 20, 21, 36; 20: 26, 31; 23: 37) both mention child sacrifice as one of the reasons for the judgement of Judah and Jerusalem. The sacrifice of children is depicted in a variety of ways as either burning with fire שרף באש (Jer. 7: 31; 19: 5), passing over or through העביר (Jer. 32: 35; Ezek. 16: 21 + נתן; 20: 26, 31 + באש; 23: 37 + לאכלה), giving נתן (Ezek. 16: 21, 36), slaughtering שחט (Ezek. 16: 21), or sacrificing זבח (Ezek. 16: 20 + לאכלה). It has been argued that the actual sacrifice of children is not entailed, but their dedication to another deity, or that only children who had died from natural causes were offered.[84] The issue has been widely discussed,[85] but suffice it to say that העביר used with 'in the fire' (Ezek. 16: 20) corresponds to Jeremianic usage where children are burned by fire (Jer. 7: 31; 19: 5), but is less graphic. Moreover, sacrificing children for food (Ezek. 16: 20) elucidates the passage in 23: 37 where children are dedicated as food. Finally, the conflated reading of the slaughtering of children and offering them by passing them over (16: 21) clearly indicates that sacrificial offerings are in view. Provocatively, the threefold insistence by Yahweh that this type of ritual was neither commanded nor conceived by him (Jer. 19: 5; 32: 35), strengthened by 'not even commanded' in Jeremiah 19: 15, suggests that people engaged in

---

[84] M. Weinfeld, 'The Molech Cult in Israel and its Background', in P. Peli (ed.), *Proceedings of the Fifth World Congress of Jewish Studies* (Jerusalem: World Union of Jewish Studies, 1969), 37–61 (Hebrew) and 227–8 (English summary), and *idem*, 'Worship of Molech'; M. Cogan, *Imperialism and Religion: Assyria, Judah and Israel in the Eighth and Seventh Centuries B.C.E.* (SBLMS, 19; Missoula, Mo.: Scholars Press, 1974), 77–83; M. Weinfeld, 'Burning Babies in ancient Israel', *UF* 10 (1979), 411–13.

[85] O. Eissfeldt, *Molk als Opferbegriff im Punischen und Hebraishen und das Ende des Gottes Moloch* (Halle: Max Niemeyer Verlag, 1935); M. Smith, 'A Note on Burning Babies', *JAOS* 95 (1975), 477–9; G. C. Heider, *The Cult of Molek: A Reassessment* (JSOTSup, 43; Sheffield: JSOT Press, 1985), 66–81; J. Day, *Molech: A God of Human Sacrifice in the Old Testament* (COP, 41; Cambridge: Cambridge University Press, 1989), 15–22; and the recent discussion in F. Stavrakopoulou, *King Manasseh and Child Sacrifice: Biblical Distortions of Historical Realities* (BZAW, 338; Berlin and New York: Walter de Gruyter, 2004), chs. 4, 5, and 6.

this type of cultic activity considered it an acceptable Yahwistic practice.[86]

In spite of the denunciations of Jeremiah and Ezekiel, the practice continued into the early Second Temple period. Trito-Isaiah focuses on the continuation of the practice in order to explain why Yahweh had not returned as redeemer to Zion and, further, to insist categorically that upon the return of the deity, those who continue abominable practices will be excluded from the restoration community. The most famous passage where child sacrifice features is Isaiah 57: 3–13. Noted already as a unified oracle following a condemnatory passage about the improper social behaviour of the leaders, the concern throughout is with what the prophet considers an inappropriate religious practice. The poem breaks into four thematic units; verses 3–4 are the call to a trial and identify the indicted, verses 5–6 introduce the ritual practices considered to be incompatible with Yahwism, verses 7–10 describe the extent to which the accused is willing to go in the abandonment of Yahweh and further illustrate the aberrant ritual practice, and verses 11–13 describe how Yahweh issues his judgement for this behaviour, concluding that those who venerate other deities depend on them for a non-existent future whilst those who cling to Yahweh will inherit a future in the land.

The introduction features the call of the prophet to the children of a sexually promiscuous woman and their mother in verses 3–4. Because the woman is anonymous, her characterization as a practitioner of sorcery, an adulteress,[87] and a whore comes to the

---

[86] J. D. Levenson, *The Death and Resurrection of the Beloved Son: The Transformation of Child Sacrifice in Judaism and Christianity* (New Haven, Conn.: Yale University Press, 1993), 4–5. Cf. Ezek. 20: 26, where Yahweh commanded the people to sacrifice their firstborn. Day, *Molech*, 66–71, maintains a distinction between the cults of Yahweh and Molek.

[87] מְנָאֵף וַתִּזְנֶה MT 'an adulterer and she who plays the harlot'. The versions and 1QIsa^a support the MT. However, the relationship between the substantized participle 'adulterer' and the waw consecutive second person feminine imperfect of זנה suggests that there is something amiss. Ackerman, *Under Every Green Tree*, 102, suggests that מנאפת זנה was divided incorrectly as מנאף תזנה which resulted in the further corruption by metathesis of the ו and ת This is certainly possible and it explains the difficult ותזנה. Since the prophet only addresses a plural masculine group and a singular feminine person, and not a singular male figure, 'adulterer' does not fit in an introductory line which calls the mother and her children to account for their behaviour.

foreground. Moreover, the sons are listed as the children and seed of transgression פשע and deception שקר, terms associated elsewhere with idolatrous worship (v. 4).[88] The concept of adultery נאף is used alongside זנה in Jeremiah and Ezekiel as a means of condemning Jerusalem for idolatrous behaviour. Where the prophets utilize the metaphor of prostitution for idolatry, Israel or Samaria and Jerusalem are personified as whores and adulteresses (Jer. 3: 8, 9; Ezek. 16: 32, 38; 23: 37).[89] The term applies both to the behaviour of the people who worship other deities (Jer. 5: 7; 9: 2) and the land which is full of adultery (Jer. 29: 23). In addition to providing a parallel term for sexually promiscuous behaviour, נאף also appears in the context of child sacrifice in Ezek. 23: 37 (cf. 23: 39, 45). The noun for sorcery ענגה similarly occurs in contexts of child sacrifice (2 Kgs. 21: 6 // 2 Chr. 33: 6; Deut. 18: 10, 14).[90] Through his use of terms, the prophet introduces the objects of the indictment as those who engage in idolatry. In addition, the fact that the terms for adultery and sorcery occur with reference to child sacrifice elsewhere provides an initial hint that the idolatrous practice in view might be that of child sacrifice. The fertility language, so often interpreted as indicative of the worship of Asherah or another fertility deity, is used only metaphorically to suggest the behaviour of the accused.

Fertility language already used to identify the protagonists in the call to trial as idolaters introduces a series of accusations in verses 5–6. In spite of the change of person between a masculine plural and second feminine singular in verses 5–6, the two verses form a chiastic pattern and have a unity of thought.[91] The mother and the sons are thus aligned in the prophetic rebuke:

5 הנחמים באלים תחת כל־עץ רענן
שחטי הילדים בנחלים תחת סעפי הסלעים:
6 בחלקי־נחל חלקך הם הם גורלך
גם־להם שפכת נסך העלית מנחה
העל אלה אנחם:

[88] On the use of these terms in reference to pagan deities, see Westermann, *Jesaja 40–66*, 322; Day, *Molech*, 61.
[89] A. Fitzgerald, 'The Mythological Background for the Presentation of Jerusalem as Queen and False Worship as Adultery in the OT', *CBQ* 34 (1972), 404–16.
[90] Polan, *In the Ways of Justice*, 131.
[91] M. Weise, 'Jesaja 57,5f', *ZAW* 72 (1960), 25–32.

The ones who comfort themselves among the trees underneath every luxuriant tree; the ones who slaughter the children in the wadis underneath the clefts of the cliffs. Among the dead of the wadi is your portion, they, they are your lot. Even to them you have poured out a libation, you have offered a grain offering. Shall I be comforted on account of these things? (Isaiah 57: 5–6)

v. 5 הַנֵּחָמִים MT points as a *niphal* participle masc. pl from נחם 'to be sorry, consoled' supported by LXX. In an attempt to maintain the fertility cult language, many commentators understand a *niphal* ptc from חמם 'to be warm' and translate 'burning with lust'. In addition to the fact that this root does not occur in the niphal, where it does occur it never has the sense of 'burning with lust'. The Masoretic translation makes good sense in line with the contrast developed throughout the poem.

v. 5 אֵלִים MT 'gods' apparently supported by LXX, V, Targ. which translate 'idols'. But the similar structure of 5a and 5b with באלים תחת כל־עץ רענן parallel to בנחלים תחת סעפי הסלעים where 5b has two places 'wadis' and 'clefts of the cliffs' with parallel prepositions ב and תחת suggests that באלים is a place. In Isa. 1: 29, the אילים are the location of activities similar to here and 'oaks' is the only possible translation. On another rendering of the prepositions, see. J. C. Greenfield, 'The Prepositions B...TAHAT...in Jes 57: 5', *ZAW* 73 (1961), 226–8; cf. Day, *Molech*, 16 n. 2, for a critique of Greenfield's translation.

v. 5 רַעֲנָן MT 'green, luxuriant'. On the rendering luxuriant, cf. D. W. Thomas, 'Some Observations on the Hebrew Word רַעֲנָן', in B. Hartmann et al. (eds.), *Hebräische Wortforschung: Festschrift zum 80. Geburtstag von Walter Baumgartner* (SVT, 16; Leiden: Brill, 1967), 387–97.

v. 6 בְּחַלְּקֵי MT understood to be from חלק (I) 'smooth'. The odd *daghesh* in the *lamed* could be a *daghesh dirimens* (GKC 20h). Normally it is translated 'smooth stones', with reference to 1 Sam. 17: 40, and Targ. W. H. Irwin, '"The Smooth Stones of the Wady"? Isaiah 57,6', *CBQ* 29 (1967), 31–40, associates it with a common Ugaritic root חלק 'to die, perish' and understands it as a reference back to the slaughtered children in v. 5b. I follow him.

v. 6 מנחה MT 'grain offering'. B. Levine, 'Ritual as Symbol: Modes of Sacrifice in Israelite Religion', in Gittlen, *Sacred Time, Sacred Place*, 125–35, provides an accessible introduction to sacrifices and offerings.

On the basis of themes, the two verses form a chiastic pattern which highlights the central idea.[92]

---

[92] Unlike Weise, 'Jesaja 57,5f', 26, I do not relocate 6c with the editors of the *BHS*, hence the chiastic pattern proposed here is slightly different from the one he advocates.

a The ones who comfort themselves (הנחמים) among the trees, under every luxuriant tree (v. 5a)
  b (are) the ones who slaughter children in the wadis, under the clefts of the cliffs (v. 5b)
    c Among the dead of the wadi is your portion.
      They, they are your lot. (v. 6a)
  b′ Even to them you have poured out a libation,
      you have offered a grain offering. (v. 6b)
a′ Shall I be comforted (אנחם) on account of these things? (v. 6c)

The idea of comfort associates A and A′: the idolaters seek consolation through the worship of foreign deities and Yahweh enquires whether they think their behaviour is compatible with his own appeasement. The prophet utilizes the Deuteronomic phrase 'under every luxuriant tree' (v. 5a) without its counterpart 'on every high hill' as a stock phrase that functions metaphorically rather than indicatively.[93] Moreover, the trees as the location of ritual practice are not mentioned again in the poem. As such, verse 5a does not castigate the participation in fertility rituals as elsewhere in the Hebrew Bible, but introduces the concept of idolatry and points toward the worship that is the object of the prophetic rebuke. Here sexual imagery is a metaphor akin to Leviticus 20: 5–6, where the language of prostitution is applied to the worship of other deities: 'I...will cut off...both him and all who follow him in playing the harlot after Molek. And if any person turns to ghosts and spirits and plays the harlot after them, I will set my face against that person and cut him off from among his people.'[94] The prophet outlines the offences in B and B′ through the presentation of the veneration of other deities: children are ritually sacrificed and offerings are made to other gods. In 6a, the prophet oddly speaks of a plural 'they' in his exclamation 'they, they are your lot' הם הם גורלך without a referent. Lewis understands הם as a reference to the children being slaughtered and argues for an interpretation of a cult of the dead.[95] However, Lewis's argument cannot stand because in the second half of the line

[93] Holladay, 'On Every High Hill'.
[94] Day, *Molech*, 10–12, 82–83, followed by Schmidt, *Israel's Beneficent Dead*, 258–59.
[95] Lewis, *Cults of the Dead*, 143–55.

sacrifices are being poured out and brought 'to them' להם. In this case, the referent for the suffixed preposition is the הם of verse 6a and it is surely not the sacrificed children to whom offerings are being made. In Ezekiel 16: 20, 21—part of the oracle denouncing Jerusalem personified as a harlot which has much in common with this oracle—with reference to children being offered as sacrifices, the prophet relates that they are sacrificed 'to them' with no referent.[96] Though ambiguous, the text certainly implies that other deities are the recipients of the offerings. Presumably, in a passage about the harlotry of a woman depicting her idolatry as here, the exact referent can be implied rather than explicitly stated. The highlighted centre of the section is C with an indictment that anticipates the thrust of the following section (vv. 7–10) and its conclusion in verse 13. Those who venerate other deities will find that the idols, not Yahweh, are their refuge and that is slim comfort, indeed, as they are without efficacy.

Three important issues have been raised in conjunction with the first part of the indictment: (1) the prophet uses the image of ritual activity among the trees as metaphorical language drawn from other prophetic literature to demonstrate that throughout the oracle idolatrous worship is the focus, (2) the practice especially worthy of the prophetic rebuke in this poem is child sacrifice, and (3) these rituals are not consistent with Yahwism. In the third section of the poem (vv. 7–10), these three themes intermingle to show the extent to which the woman is willing to go, to a high mountain and to the depths of Sheol, in her abandonment of Yahweh (cf. v. 10). The image of the woman who sets up her bed (v. 7a), widens it (v. 8b), and loves it (8c) is used as a metaphor like that of the harlot in Ezekiel 16 and 23, where adulteress Jerusalem entertains many paramours. As in the preceding verses, the prophet does not use fertility language to castigate fertility rituals, but to show the pervasiveness and persistence of the idolatry. Heider,[97] Lewis,[98] and Schmidt,[99] too, recognize

---

[96] Ezek. 16: 20 'You sacrificed them to them to be eaten' ותזבחים להם לאכול, similarly v. 21 'And you slaughtered my children and gave them by passing them through the fire to them' ותשחטי את־בני ותתנים בהעביר אותם להם. Elsewhere, the ambiguous להם is used in the context of the idols גלולים and should be understood with reference to them (Ezek. 16: 36; 23: 37).

[97] Heider, *The Cult of Molek*, 381.

[98] Lewis, *Cults of the Dead*, 158.

[99] Schmidt, *Israel's Beneficent Dead*, 258–9.

Conceptions of Judah, I: Idolatrous Cults 103

that the sexual behaviour of the woman in this section functions metaphorically, in order to clarify idolatrous worship as the object of the prophetic rebuke. The allusion to Molek in verse 9a obscured by the Masoretic pointing suggests that this is the only cult in view. In verse 9, the Masoretic text has 'You journeyed to the king with oil' וַתָּשֻׁרִי לַמֶּלֶךְ בַּשֶּׁמֶן. The prophet maintains a unified condemnation of child sacrifice through the accusation of verse 5b and an allusion to Molek in 9a.[100] The emphasis in verses 7–10 is the extent to which the harlot is willing to go in her veneration of other deities, therefore, the proposal of שׁור as 'lavish oil on'[101] is not possible.[102] In the prophet's view, the ultimate rejection of Yahweh is the worship of another deity through the ritual of child sacrifice.

In spite of what appears to be a sustained attack on a cult of child sacrifice, the mortuary language in the poem has led to the association of the aberrant practices with the cult of the dead—a ritual venerating dead ancestors widely practised in the ancient world.[103] Lewis envisions the attack on a single cult, but he associates the mortuary language with the ritual worship of deceased ancestors.[104] He notes for example the mention of child sacrifice in verses 5b, 9a, the journey to Sheol in 9b, and other language evocative of death. Although he utilizes אלים, translated by him as 'gods' to support his

---

[100] Heider, *The Cult of Molek*, 379–80; Day, *Molech*, 50–2; Schmidt, *Israel's Beneficent Dead*, 254–9. Ackerman, *Under Every Green Tree*, 107, 126–39, understands the intention is to castigate child sacrifice, but renders as a type of offering, *mulk*, following Eissfeldt, *Molk als Opfervegriff*.

[101] G. R. Driver, 'Difficult Words in the Hebrew Prophets', in H. H. Rowley (ed.), *Studies in Old Testament Prophecy Presented to Prof. Theodore H. Robinson by the Society for Old Testament Study on his Sixty-Fifth Birthday, August 9th, 1946* (Edinburgh: T & T Clark, 1957), 58–9; Wernberg-Møller, 'Two Notes', *VT* 8 (1958), 307–8, followed by Ackerman, *Under Every Green Tree*, 107–8 n. 16.

[102] Day, *Molech*, 51–2, followed by, Schmidt, *Israel's Beneficent Dead*, 259 n. 537.

[103] L. Y. Rahmani, 'Ancient Jerusalem's Funerary Customs and Tombs. Part One', *BA* 44 (1981), 171–7; Lewis, *Cults of the Dead*; E. Bloch-Smith, *Judahite Burial Practices and Beliefs about the Dead* (JSOTSup, 123; Sheffield: Sheffield Academic Press, 1992). See most recently Schmidt, *Israel's Beneficent Dead*, who argues against the existence of such a cult until the post-exilic period. E. Bloch-Smith, 'Death in the Life of Israel', in Gittlen, *Sacred Time, Sacred Place*, 140, and T. J. Lewis, 'How Far Can the Texts Take us', in Gittlen, *Sacred Time, Sacred Place*, 189–202, point out weaknesses in Schmidt's analysis.

[104] Lewis, *Cults of the Dead*, 143–58, and idem, 'Death Cult Imagery in Isaiah 57', *HAR* 11 (1987), 267–84. Cf. Irwin, ' "The Smooth Stones of the Wady?" '.

contention, the above analysis has shown that this translation is not tenable. Similarly, his rendering of the two monuments יד and זכרון set up by the harlot in verse 8 as mortuary stelae cannot be sustained.[105] In the wider argument of Trito-Isaiah as here there is an emphasis on the inheritance of those who observe behaviour sanctioned by Yahweh (v. 13b). In Isaiah 56: 1–8, for example, the eunuchs who had been denied admittance into the congregation of Yahweh by Deuteronomic law are told that in the event that they follow the ordinances of Yahwism, they will be given a יד ושם 'a memorial and a name' (v. 5). Unlike the eunuchs who follow Yahweh, who are given an everlasting memorial better than sons and daughters, the harlot sets up a memorial and stares at it. The object of remembrance and the stele function symbolically to show that the woman establishes her own memorial by choosing to worship other deities. Her efforts are in keeping with the poet's accusation in Isaiah 56: 5a that idolaters seek their own comfort, namely by following their own desires rather than that which pleases their deity. In creating her own memorial the harlot brings about her own destruction by aligning herself with other deities who are inefficacious. Finally, Lewis argues that the 'gathered' קבוצים of verse 13 are dead ancestors, but the gathered things are more likely idols, as rendered by the translators of the Vulgate and Peshitta. Understanding them as idols contributes to the distinction of the passage between the inheritance of those who take refuge in Yahweh and the lack of a future for those who venerate other deities.[106]

Other arguments that build on the analysis by Lewis, like those by Kennedy and Ackerman,[107] for example, similarly fail in that benign terms are over-read in order to contribute to the ascription of a cult of the dead. The chthonic overtones of verses 3–13, so compelling for the isolation of rituals of the dead in Lewis's view, can be associated with the deity Molek, who has connections with the underworld.[108] The view thus advanced takes 57: 3–13 as a unified oracle condemning a single ritual practice in verses 5–6 and hinted at in verse 9, which is held by the prophet to be completely incompatible with

---

[105] So, too, Schmidt, *Israel's Beneficent Dead*, 257, but on other grounds.
[106] Schmidt, *Israel's Beneficent Dead*, 255–9.
[107] Kennedy, 'Isaiah 57:5–6'; Ackerman, *Under Every Green Tree*, 143–53.
[108] Heider, *The Cult of Molek*, 379–82.

Yahwism. The fertility language and mortuary terminology are not indicative of cultic practices, but function symbolically to denounce child sacrifice and Molek.[109]

Although there remains a significant degree of dispute regarding the exact referent of Molek, as a god[110] or as a type of sacrifice,[111] the biblical portrayal consistently depicts Molek as a deity. Seven places in the Hebrew Bible directly attest the existence of Molek (Lev. 18: 21; 20: 2, 3, 4, 5; 2 Kgs. 23: 10; Jer. 32: 35) whilst he appears at Isaiah 57: 9 (emending לַמֶּלֶךְ to לַמֹּלֶךְ). Elsewhere ample evidence of child sacrifice occurs across a variety of forms of biblical literature (Deut. 18: 10; 2 Kgs. 17: 17; 23: 10; Jer. 3: 24; 7: 31; 19: 5; 32: 35; Ezek. 16: 21, 36; 20: 26, 31; 23: 39; Ps. 106: 37–8). Unfortunately, the fact that the biblical writers do not portray the cult of child sacrifice in a consistent way or with standard terminology has led to a variety of proposals considering the practice of child sacrifice in ancient Israel. Biblical texts distinguish the occurrences of the practice between those held under exceptional circumstances (Judg. 11; 2 Kgs. 3: 27) and those ritually practised (Deut. 12: 31; Ezek. 16: 21; 23: 39; Ps. 106: 37–8), but provide little in terms of a concrete description. As we have seen, it appears as a ritual sacrifice in the condemnations of Jeremiah and Ezekiel. Child sacrifice existed in the ANE, where many interpreters understand it as a type of sacrifice—a *mulk* sacrifice.[112]

According to prophetic literature of the time the cult of child sacrifice continued during the Templeless Judah and into the Second Temple period. Rather than being in honour of Yahweh, the biblical writers portrayed it as a foreign practice imported from the Canaanites and for a god known by the epithet Molek. Its denunciation during this period provides another example of a corrupt ritual practice attributed to the population in Judah.

---

[109] Contra Ackerman, *Under Every Green Tree*, 101–63; Schramm, *The Opponents*, 127–32; C. Nihan, 'Trois cultes en Ésaïe 57,3–13 et leur signification dans le contexte religieux de la Judée à l'époque perse', *Transeuphratène* 22 (2001), 143–67; who identify fertility rituals, child sacrifice, and rituals for the dead as the objects of the prophetic rebuke.

[110] Heider, *The Cult of Molek*; Day, *Molech*; Levenson, *Death and Resurrection*.

[111] Eissfeldt, *Molk als Opfervegriff*.

[112] Eissfeldt, *Molk als Opfervegriff*, followed by L. E. Stager and S. R. Wolff, 'Child Sacrifice at Carthage: Religious Rite or Population Control?' *BAR* 10/1 (1984), 31–51; Ackerman, *Under Every Green Tree*, 119–39. Day, *Molech*, 9–13, critiques Eissfeldt's position.

Baal

Baal was the title of a fertility deity associated with natural phenomena in Ugaritic texts.[113] He had many local manifestations in the Levantine area. The worship of Baal reached its zenith in the northern kingdom during the rule of Ahab and Jezebel, where his veneration threatened to supersede that of Yahweh.[114] However, his cult was not eradicated, even after Elijah's efforts, and led to the fall of the northern kingdom according to Jeremiah 23: 13 (cf. 23: 27). Among the kings of Judah, Manasseh is especially associated with the rise of Baal worship (2 Kgs. 21: 1–9). In spite of Deuteronomic criticism it remained popular in the southern kingdom until its downfall.[115] That it was a contributing factor in the impending judgement of Judah is clear from Jeremiah.[116] Certain material suggests the worship of Baal continued at least up to 587 (Jer. 2: 8; 7: 9; 9: 13; 11: 13, 17; 12: 16; 23: 27 and in the plural 2: 23; 9: 14). Just as Ezekiel's ascription of idolatrous worship at the temple signalled its disaster, these texts in Jeremiah could function similarly. There is no direct attestation of Baal worship in the Second Temple period, probably signalling that his cult fell out of favour in Yehud.

An interesting innovation during the Templeless period correlates the sacrifice of children to Molek with the worship of Baal (Jer. 19: 5; 32: 35; cf. 7: 31). These three texts, each having to do with child sacrifice, show an interesting development:

7:31 ובנו במות התפת אשר בגיא בן־הנם
לשרף את־בניהם ואת־בנתיהם באש
אשר לא צויתי ולא עלתה על־לבי:

---

[113] A. S. Kapelrud, *Baal in the Ras Shamra Texts* (Copenhagen: Gad, 1952); N. C. Habel, *Yahweh Versus Baal: A Conflict of Religious Cultures* (Concordia Theological Seminary, 6; New York: Bookman Associates, 1964); J. van Zijl, *Baal: A Study of Texts in Connexion with Baal in Ugaritic Epics* (AOAT, 10; Neukirchen Vluyn: Neukirchener Verlag, 1972); Cross, *Canaanite Myth and Hebrew Epic*, 147–56, 190–4; Smith, *The Early History of God*, 65–101; Day, *Yahweh and the Gods*, 68–127.

[114] L. Bonner, *The Stories of Elijah and Elisha as Polemics Against Baal Worship* (POS, 6; Leiden: Brill, 1968); F. C. Fensham, 'A Few Observations on the Polarisation Between Yahweh and Baal in 1 Kings 17–19', *ZAW* 92 (1980), 227–36; R. B. Chisholm, 'The Polemic against Baalism in Israel's Early History and Literature', *BS* 150 (1994), 267–83; Toombs, 'When Religions Collide', 41–5.

[115] Smith, *The Early History of God*, 47.

[116] F. E. Eakin, 'Yahwism and Baalism before the Exile', *JBL* 84 (1965), 407–14.

And they built the high places of the Topheth which is in the valley of Ben Hinnom to burn their sons and their daughters by fire which I did not command or conceive.

19:5 ובנו את־במות הבעל לשׂרף את־
בניהם באשׁ עלות לבעל אשׁר לא־צויתי
ולא דברתי ולא עלתה על־לבי:

And they built the high places of Baal to burn their sons by fire as burnt offerings to Baal which I did not command nor declare nor conceive.

32:35 ויבנו את־במות הבעל אשׁר בגיא
בן־הנם להעביר את־בניהם ואת־בנותיהם
לַמֹּלֶךְ אשׁר לא־צויתים ולא עלתה
על־לבי לעשׂות התועבה הזאת
למען החטי את־יהודה:

They built the high places of Baal which is in the valley of Ben Hinnom to pass their sons and their daughters over to Molek which I did not command nor conceive to do this abominable thing by causing Judah to sin.

The three texts share the following features:

(1) each begins with a form of בנה;
(2) בנה is followed by what is built (the high places of the Topheth as 7: 31 or of Baal as 19: 5; 32: 35);
(3) the sequence continues with the means of sacrifice (7: 31 and 19: 5 have שׂרף באשׁ whilst 32: 35 has העביר);
(4) Yahweh's objection to the practice concludes the statement.

As one of the appendices to Jeremiah's first temple sermon, 7: 31 contains the simplest form of the three.[117] The later texts differ from 7: 31 in that there are additions in 19: 5 and 32: 35 and one divergence, whilst in 19: 5 there is one omission. Unlike 7: 31 and 32: 35, which locate the rituals in the Valley of Hinnom, 19: 5 omits a specific location. The divergence is in what is built. In 7: 31, the high places of the Topheth are built whilst in 19: 5 and 32: 35 the high places of Baal are built. The phrase 'the high places of the Topheth' is slightly odd as elsewhere it is a single place (Jer. 19: 13 כמקום התפת). There are four additions in 19: 5 and 32: 35, two of which need not

[117] G. J. Janzen, 'Double Readings in the Text of Jeremiah', *HTR* 60 (1967), 433–47; E. Tov, 'L'incidence de la critique textuelle sur la critique littéraire dans le livre Jérémie', *RB* 79 (1972), 189–99.

detain us: the addition in 19: 5 of Yahweh's objection that he did not declare it and that of 32: 35 with its declaration that the practice is an abomination whose establishment caused Judah to sin. The other two additions are more telling. As if the addition of the high places of Baal in 19: 5 were not enough to indicate the association of this practice with the fertility god, after the mention of the burning of children the text correlates it with the veneration of Baal by adding 'as burnt offerings to Baal' עלות לבעל Whilst in agreement with 19: 5 that the places of offering were the high places of Baal, after the mention of the dedication, 32: 35 designates Molek as the god to whom the children were offered לַמֹּלֶךְ.

The differences between the two later texts and the earlier one are significant as they disclose the conflation of Baal and Molek. It is likely that this was a literary means to stigmatize the cult of Baal in order to stimulate a decline in the popularity of the deity and practices in his honour. Outside these texts, nowhere is the veneration of Baal associated with child sacrifice. In what appears to be the simplest form of a condemnatory statement, 7: 31 oddly places the Topheth in conjunction with high places which is not found elsewhere with the root במה. According to 2 Kings 23: 10, the Topheth is the place where child sacrifice to Molek took place. The allusion in Jeremiah 7: 31 appears to be to Molek as elsewhere in Jeremiah, the offerings to Baal are in the form of incense (Jer. 7: 9; 11: 13, 17; 32: 29). Nevertheless, 19: 5 and 32: 35 associate the high places not with a location as in 7: 31, but with the deity Baal. In 19: 5, the addition clearly identifies Baal worship with child sacrifice. By aligning Baal with Molek, 32: 35 goes even further by explicitly naming Molek as the deity to whom the children are sacrificed at the high places of Baal.

The deliberate literary conflation of Molek and Baal in the above texts made in an explicit way may provide an indication of two other places where the strategy also occurred. In the general condemnation of sacrifice in Jeremiah 3: 24, the object who devours the sons and daughters is known only as הַבֹּשֶׁת 'the shameful one'. Although thought to represent Baal,[118] the vowels of Molek, the god of child sacrifice in the OT, seem to be those of Hebrew בֹּשֶׁת 'shame', which might provide an early indication of the way the foreign god was

---

[118] Day, *Yahweh and the Gods*, 81–83.

perceived by the biblical writers. If הבשת is an indirect reference to Molek, the deity appears in conjunction with Baal, apparently conflated again where, speaking of the threat of coming disaster, Jeremiah (11: 13) notes the prevalence of 'the altars to the shameful one, altars to burn incense to Baal' מזבחות לבשת מזבחות לקטר לבעל. Like Asherah, Baal, too, suffered from systematic literary downsizing. Biblical writers dissuaded the practice of his cult by polemically associating him with Molek and child sacrifice, a ritual practice unknown in his veneration elsewhere in the ANE.

Various Minor Cults

Other literature associates the population of Templeless Judah with the worship of a wide variety of other lesser known deities. Among the accusations levelled against Judah by Jeremiah is, 'their gods have become as many as their cities' (Jer. 11: 13), which serves to summarize the type of ritual behaviour condemned throughout the book; burning incense to other gods (Jer. 1: 16; 11: 12; 18: 15; 19: 4, 13), worshipping them (Jer. 1: 16), following after them (7: 6, 9 (+ בעל); 11: 10; 13: 10; 16: 11; 25: 6; 35: 15), and pouring out drink offerings (Jer. 32: 29).[119] Idolatry functions alongside social injustice in the prophecy of Jeremiah to explain the disasters of 598 and 587. In distinction, Ezekiel places a greater emphasis on cultic sin; as one commentator notes, 'more dramatically than either Jeremiah or Second Isaiah (indeed than any single book of the Hebrew Bible, including the Deuteronomic corpus), Ezekiel targets the sin of idolatry'.[120] Even more so than Jeremiah, Ezekiel in chapters where the issue of false worship dominates (chs. 6, 8, 14, 16, 18, 20, 22, 23) uses vague language that makes it difficult to identify specific deities with any certainty. The inexactitude of Jeremiah and Ezekiel resonates with Trito-Isaiah, which portrays members of the early Second Temple community observing a variety of practices (Isa. 65: 3, 7), one of which is very obscure (Isa. 66: 17). Among those posited to the time are cults with more definable features with which to ascertain the

---

[119] Kutsko, *Between Heaven and Earth*, 29, compares Jeremiah's language of idolatry with that of Deuteronomy, the Deuteronomistic History, and Ezekiel.
[120] Kutsko, *Between Heaven and Earth*, 25.

activities being condemned, but these appear rarely. In fact, the worship of two identifiable figures occurs in the final three cultic abominations visited by Ezekiel on his temple tour—the worship of Tammuz (the only deity apart from Yahweh named in Ezekiel), idols, and the sun. Trito-Isaiah in the early Second Temple period briefly mentions cultic rituals on behalf of the deities of fortune, Gad and Meni, and those associated with a cult of the dead.

Even more abominable than the worship of the statue of jealousy in the temple precincts is the second example of improper worship shown to Ezekiel in 8: 7–13. In a rather bizarre incident, the prophet is told to burrow into a secret hideaway to witness illicit activity. Surveying what he finds inside the room, Ezekiel recounts:

9 ויאמר אלי בא וראה את־התועבות
הרעות אשר הם עשים פה:
10 ואבוא ואראה והנה כל־תבנית רמש
ובהמה שקץ וכל־גלולי בית ישראל
מחקה על־הקיר סביב סביב:
11 ושבעים איש מזקני בית־ישראל ויאזניהו
בן־שפן עמד בתוכם עמדים לפניהם ואיש
מקטרתו בידו ועתר ענן־הקטרת עלה:
12 ויאמר אלי הראית בן־אדם אשר זקני
בית־ישראל עשים בחשך איש בחדרי
משכיתו כי אמרים אין יהוה ראה אתנו
עזב יהוה את־הארץ:

He said to me, 'Enter and See the evil abominations which they are doing there.' So, I entered and looked, there engraved on the wall all round were all the detestable objects and all the idols of the house of Israel. Before them stood seventy of the elders of the House of Israel, including Jaazaniah son of Shaphan, worshipping before them. Each had a censer in his hand, and the fragrant cloud of incense was ascending. He said to me; 'Do you see, O son of Man, what the elders of the House of Israel are doing in the dark, each in his chamber of carved images saying Yahweh does not see us, Yahweh has forsaken the land.' (Ezek. 8: 9–12)

v. 10 תבנית רמש ובהמה MT 'creeping things and beasts' is omitted in the LXX, syntactically difficult, and thought to be a gloss influenced by Deut. 4: 17–18. Cf. Zimmerli, *Ezechiel*, i. 193, 216–17; Greenberg, *Ezekiel 1–20*, 169; Ackerman, *Under Every Green Tree*, 43 n. 22, 69. It appears to explain the odd use of the term שקץ here. Elsewhere in Ezekiel, one of the three frequently occurring terms for idols is שקוץ 5: 11; 7: 20; 8: 9, 13; 11: 18,

21; 20: 7, 8, 30–1; 37: 23. The two other more frequent terms תועבה and גלולים occur in this section and suggest idol worship is the ritual condemned (vv. 9, 10). On the terms for idols in Ezekiel, see Kutsko, *Between Heaven and Earth*, 25–35. I delete the gloss, understanding a consistent oracle against idols as the intent of the passage and שֶׁקֶץ as a variant of שִׁקּוּץ with Targ. (שקוצים). Cf. J. L. McLaughlin, *The marzēaḥ in the Prophetic Literature: References and Allusions in Light of the Extra-Biblical Evidence* (SVT, 86; Leiden: Brill, 2001), 203.

v. 11 עמדים לפניהם MT lit. 'standing in their presence' is terminology used in the cult for worship and service. Cf. Zimmerli, *Ezechiel*, i. 194.

v. 12 בחדרי משכיתו MT 'in the chambers of his carved image'. Since the men are gathered together presumably in one room, the plural here is slightly odd. It may be influenced by אִישׁ 'each one'. I translate the singular with the versions.

v. 12 משכיתו MT 'his carved image'. Based on Lev. 26: 1 and Num. 33: 52, many translators favour 'figured stone'. But only in Lev. 26: 1 in the expression אבן משכית does it connote 'carved stone' whereas in Num. 33: 52 it appears only as כל משכיתם 'all their carved images' parallel to molten images. The versions are not helpful as LXX, S, and V understand 'secret' and the Targ. renders 'bed'. The 8th-century Aramaic inscription, Panammuwa II, has *mśky* as an 'image or statue'. Cf. H. Donner and W. Röllig, *Kanaanäische und aramäische Inschriften*, i (Wiesbaden: Harrassowitz, repr. 1966), 39–40, #215.18. Understanding stone reliefs is not necessary in this verse. These are idols, that is, carved images, set up or engraved in the walls (v. 10).

In distinction to the three other scenes that occur in Ezekiel 8, in which the accompanying spirit commands the prophet to witness intolerable activities taking place in the temple, in this one he is not shown sinful behaviour outright. Instead, he is told to dig into the wall in order to witness the rituals that take place in a private chamber located in the precincts of the sanctuary (vv. 7–8). The effort taken by Ezekiel highlights the secretive nature or the private location of the ritual. Once in the chamber described in verse 12 as the 'rooms of his idol', Ezekiel witnesses the worship of idols. By compiling language used for the veneration of objects such as 'abominations' (v. 9), 'idols' (v. 10, twice, v. 12), and burning incense (v. 11), elsewhere found used of the harlot offering incense intended for Yahweh to other deities as in Ezekiel 16: 18 and 23: 41, the passage emphasizes that the sinful behaviour that takes place in the room consists of idol worship.

In the past, even whilst deleting the gloss of verse 10, commentators, nevertheless, understood the animals to be instructive in ascertaining the ritual and suggested, for example, the worship of Egyptian animal totems,[121] influenced by the gloss of verse 10, or random, unidentifiable animal reliefs perhaps of Mesopotamian origin.[122] Influenced by the presence of false worship and understanding שֶׁקֶץ as a reference to unclean and impure food based on the prohibition against it in Leviticus 11, Ackerman argues for the depiction of a ritual feast in honour of other deities represented by the carved images.[123] Moreover, certain elements, such as regular ritual held in a room either owned or controlled by the participants, and the presence of Israel's aristocracy in a house amidst the palace complex, associate the feast in her view with a *bêt marzēaḥ*.[124] In her analysis, Ackerman understands a *bêt marzēaḥ* as:

> a religious and social institution. It is organized under the patronage of some god, and its primary activity is the worship of that god at a ritual banquet held periodically in the god's honor. This banquet is held at the *bêt marzēaḥ*, a house owned jointly by the members of the *marzēaḥ*... The *marzēaḥ* draws its membership from the upper classes of society... The purpose of the banquet, when specified, is funerary.[125]

Known throughout the ANE from the second millennium BCE up until the sixth century CE, a *bêt marzēaḥ*, thus, refers to an exclusive club of wealthy individuals or influential men who met on occasion to feast together to honour a deity or deities. Contrary to Ackerman, however, even in the Hebrew Bible the ritual banquet can, but does not have to, occur in a funerary context.[126] McLaughlin provides the most thorough discussion of the *marzēaḥ* in the ancient world and in the Hebrew Bible. He noted that despite its prevalence in the ancient

---

[121] Eichrodt, *Hesekiel*, 60; Zimmerli, *Ezechiel*, i. 216–17.
[122] Greenberg, *Ezekiel*, 169–70.
[123] Ackerman, *Under Every Green Tree*, 70–1.
[124] S. Ackerman, 'A MARZĒAḤ in Ezekiel 8: 7–13?', *HTR* 82 (1989), 267–81, revised in *idem*, *Under Every Green Tree*, 38, 41–4, 53–5, 67–79.
[125] Ackerman, *Under Every Green Tree*, 76.
[126] T. J. Lewis, 'The *Marzēaḥ*: A Death Cult Banquet?' in *Cults of the Dead*, 80–94; J. L. McLaughlin, 'The *marzēaḥ* at Ugarit: A Textual and Contextual Study', *UF* 23 (1991), 265–81; D. Pardee, 'Marzihu, Kispu and the Ugaritic Funerary Cult: A Minimalist View', in N. Wyatt *et al.* (eds.), *Ugarit: Religion and Culture* (UBL, 12; Münster: Ugarit Verlag, 1996), 273–87.

world the ritual is only mentioned twice in the Hebrew Bible (Amos 6: 7 and Jer. 16: 5).[127] Consequently, interpreters have associated a number of allusions in biblical texts with the *marzēaḥ* ritual. In order to ascertain the veracity of such ascriptions, McLaughlin isolates three criteria common to descriptions of this practice in ANE material: (1) the involvement of the leading citizens or the wealthy, (2) the presence of idols, and (3) excessive drinking and feasting. Of the biblical passages associated with the *marzēaḥ*, then, McLaughlin finds that only four meet his criteria (Amos 4: 1; Hos. 4: 16–19; Isa. 28: 7–8 (22); Ezek. 39: 17–20).[128] Ezekiel 8: 7–13 in his view does not contain all the elements necessary in a reference to a *marzēaḥ*.

In conjunction with McLaughlin's criteria, Ackerman's analysis contains two features of the feast which include eating in the presence of idols. Upon further consideration her argument for the actual consumption of food in the Ezekiel passage is tenuous. In a response to Ackerman, Dijkstra, for instance, points out that had Ezekiel had a *marzēaḥ* in mind, he would have been more explicit as elsewhere he overtly condemned unacceptable dining practices, as in Ezekiel 18: 6, 11, 15; 22: 9.[129] Even more damning is the absence of lounging and drinking commonly associated with the feast elsewhere. In agreement with Dijkstra on his second point, McLaughlin adds that there is likewise no reference to a meal because שׁקץ more commonly refers not to unclean food, but to animals forbidden for consumption.[130] Moreover, the secretive nature of the religious activity as presented in Ezekiel 8 is not in keeping with what is known about a *marzēaḥ* feast elsewhere. At times it was a private affair, even exclusive, but never secret as here.[131]

---

[127] C. Maier and E. M. Dörrfuß, ' "Um mit ihnen zu sitzen, zu essen und zu trinken" Am 6, 7; Jer 16, 5 und die Bedeutung von *marzēaḥ*', ZAW 111 (1999), 45–57.

[128] McLaughlin, *The marzēaḥ in the Prophetic Literature*, provides an accessible and well-argued study of the practice through an analysis of ANE and biblical material. J. J. Jackson, 'Style in Isaiah 28 and a Drinking Bout of the Gods (RS 24.258)', in J. J. Jackson and M. Kessler (eds.), *Rhetorical Criticism: Essays in Honor of James Muilenburg* (PTMS, 1; Pittsburgh: Pickwick, 1974), 85–98, associated Isa. 56: 2–57: 13 with a *bêt marzēaḥ*. McLaughlin, *The marzēaḥ in the Prophetic Literature*, 180–3, shows that Jackson's conclusion is untenable.

[129] Dijkstra, 'Goddess, Gods, Men and Women in Ezekiel 8', 94–7.

[130] McLaughlin, *The marzēaḥ in the Prophetic Literature*, 195–205.

[131] Ibid., 204–5.

Although not a *marzēaḥ*, the depiction of the ritual behaviour in Ezekiel's second vision of aberrant religious practice at the temple addresses the worship of other deities, specifically through the representation of idols. Following Eichrodt, Ackerman was correct in her proposal to understand שֶׁקֶץ apart from the gloss which associated it with the images of creeping things and animals. Against her and Eichrodt, however, שֶׁקֶץ should not be understood in the light of Levitical prohibitions against food, but rather within the context of Ezekiel itself. Along with other indicators of idol worship, it represents a general indictment as do the appearances of שִׁקּוּץ in other places in the book. With this in mind, the other significant features of the pericope—the secretive nature of the ritual and the presence of members of the aristocracy—make sense. The Babylonian incursion in 598 was understood by Ezekiel as a warning to an idolatrous nation. The ritual practice of other deities would have been forbidden in certain circles. The elders of the community clandestinely sought to hide their continued worship of other deities within the temple precincts, perhaps because they represented deities not sanctioned by the governing power as Eichrodt suggested.[132] Since they believed that Yahweh could not see because he had forsaken the land (v. 12), their concern was with their fellow Jerusalemites. As the other scenes in the temple vision relate to the worship of individual deities, such as the statue of jealousy and Tammuz, or a single object, like the sun, it is not surprising to have condemnation of general idol worship at the temple site in addition to Ezekiel's resounding criticisms elsewhere.

In Ezekiel 8: 14, the third greatest abomination that the prophet sees during his temple tour is women participating in a mourning ritual to the deity Tammuz. Within the vision sequence, Ezekiel recounts that '[Yahweh] brought me to the entrance of the gate of the house of Yahweh that is on the north, and there sat the women who were wailing for Tammuz'. Known as a fertility deity from the Babylonian pantheon whose death and resurrection marked seasonal transitions, his worship consisted of mourning rituals that coincided with the period of the deity's death and banqueting at the time of his rebirth.[133] Although never explicitly mentioned anywhere else in the

[132] Eichrodt, *Hesekiel*, 60.
[133] See the commentaries and S. Langdon, *Tammuz and Ishtar* (Oxford: Clarendon Press, 1914); J. Johns, 'The Worship of Tammuz', *JBL* 36 (1917), 100–11; A. Moortgat,

Hebrew Bible, Yamauchi proposes that Tammuz is alluded to in less explicit texts such as Isaiah 17: 10–11 and Daniel 11: 37, but these are less certain.[134] In the Ezekiel passage, the cult receives no more description than the mere fact that women who were the main practitioners were found lamenting on the temple site. Very little is know about the cult in Judah such as how it became known in the southern kingdom and whether or not it ought to be associated with the worship of Baal and the Queen of Heaven.[135] However its cult became known in Judah, Ezekiel certainly takes the existence of the worship of Tammuz seriously because this is the only instance where he specifically mentions the name of a deity other than Yahweh.

In the final vision of Ezekiel (8: 16–18) the prophet sees the greatest of the four abominations taking place inside the inner court of the temple between the portico and the altar. He finds twenty-five men facing away from the temple prostrated before the sun:

16 ויבא אתי אל־חצר בית־יהוה הפנימית
והנה־פתח היכל יהוה בין האולם ובין
המזבח כעשרים וחמשה איש אחריהם
אל־היכל יהוה ופניהם קדמה והמה
משתחויתם קדמה לשמש:
17 ויאמר אלי הראית בן־אדם הנקל
לבית יהודה מעשות את־התועבות
אשר עשו־פה [...]

And he brought me to the inner court of the house of Yahweh. It was at the entrance of the temple of Yahweh between the portico and the altar twenty-five men their backs to the temple of Yahweh and their faces towards the east were worshipping the sun towards the east. And he said to me, 'Do you see, Son of Man, is it such a slight thing that the house of Judah does the abominable things that they do here?'... (Ezek. 8: 16–17a)

v. 16 משתחויתם MT appears to be a scribal error for משתחוים (GKC 75kk).

Tammuz: Der Unsterblichkeitsglaube in der altorientalischen Bildkunst (Berlin: de Gruyter, 1949); O. R. Gurney, 'Tammuz Reconsidered: Some Recent Developments', *JSS* 12 (1962), 150–60; E. M. Yamauchi, 'Additional Notes on Tammuz', *JSS* 11 (1966), 10–15; T. Jacobsen, 'Toward the Image of Tammuz', *HR* 1 (1962), 189–213, reprinted in a collection of his essays, *Toward the Image of Tammuz and Other Essays on Mesopotamian History and Culture* (HSS, 21; Cambridge, Mass.: Harvard University Press, 1970), 73–103 (90–1 on Ezek. 8: 14); Ackerman, *Under Every Green Tree*, 79–93; M. S. Smith, 'The Death of "Dying and Rising Gods" in the Biblical World: An Update with Special Reference to Baal in the Baal Cycle', *SJOT* 12/2 (1998), 272–7.

[134] E. M. Yamauchi, 'Tammuz and the Bible', *JBL* 84 (1965), 283–90.
[135] Ackerman, *Under Every Green Tree*, 91–3; van der Toorn, 'Israelite Figurines', 56.

The passage condemning the worship of the sun extends from verse 16 to verse 18. The relationship of verses 16–17a to verses 17b–18 is difficult. In 17b–18, the oracle focuses on social sin that is abominable to Yahweh and concludes with a judgement that corresponds to the series of aberrant practices recounted.[136] As 17b–18 do not contribute to a discussion of the final and most grievous act of defiance against Yahweh, they will not be considered here. The final destination of his vision finds Ezekiel confronted by the most abhorrent practice, that of the worship of the sun in place of Yahweh. The location of the men between the vestibule and the altar may signify that the participants in this action are priests.[137] Although commentators appeal to Joel 2: 17—where the priests officiate in a comparable location, that is, between the inner court and the altar on fast days—its application to the first temple could be anachronistic.[138]

In spite of the condemnation of the veneration of natural phenomena,[139] archaeological evidence and place names and personal names in the Hebrew Bible attest that sun worship was widely practised in Israel and Judah.[140] In the last chapters of Kings, Manasseh is said to have bowed down to the host of heaven (2 Kgs. 21: 3, 5) and Josiah removed vessels for the sun and host of heaven from the temple in Jerusalem in his purification of the sanctuary (2 Kgs. 23: 4, 5). In Josiah's campaign to eradicate non-Yahwistic practices, the vestiges of the worship of the sun were removed from the temple (2 Kgs. 23: 5, 11). In spite of his efforts the cult reappears by the time of Ezekiel at the temple (Ezek. 8: 16). Similarly, Jeremiah[141] in two

---

[136] See the commentaries. J. G. Taylor, *Yahweh and the Sun: Biblical and Archaeological Evidence for Sun Worship in Ancient Israel* (JSOTSup, 111; Sheffield: JSOT Press, 1993), 148–58, follows the MT of vv. 17b–18. Whilst so doing, he argues that Yahweh was being worshipped as the sun. This may be the case, but it is not relevant to the purposes here.

[137] Originally suggested by A. Bertholet, *Das Buch Hesekiel* (KHAT, 12; Freiburg: Mohr (Paul Siebeck), 1897), 49–50, followed by Smith, *The Early History of God*, 150; Taylor, *Yahweh and the Sun*, 156 n. 4.

[138] Greenberg, *Ezekiel 1–20*, 172; Ackerman, *Under Every Green Tree*, 98–9, but note the reticence of Eichrodt, *Hesekiel*, 67.

[139] Taylor, *Yahweh and the Sun*, 105–7, 172–83, argues that the expression 'host of heaven' includes the sun in certain instances.

[140] Taylor, *Yahweh and the Sun*, 24–98; Day, *Yahweh and the Gods*, 152–4.

[141] H. G. May, 'Some Aspects of Solar Worship at Jerusalem', *ZAW* 55 (1937), 269–81.

Conceptions of Judah, I: Idolatrous Cults 117

oracles of judgement predicts that in 598 the Babylonians will eradicate people who worship the 'host of heaven' (Jer. 8: 2) along with the houses on which they venerated heavenly bodies (Jer. 19: 13). The inclusion of the veneration of the host of heaven that probably included the sun in Jeremiah shows another instance in which the Judahite population was conceived of as participating in heterodox religious praxis.[142] Although evidence has been advanced in favour of a solarized cult of Yahweh[143] or significant use of solar terminology for Yahweh,[144] Ezekiel represents the veneration of the sun as contrary to Yahwistic practice and resolutely condemns it here.[145] After all, the men have turned their backs to the temple during the ritual.

The appearance of repeated denunciations of other cultic infractions in Trito-Isaiah associates Judah of the early Second Temple period with the continuation of practices considered to be idolatrous in some circles. In Trito-Isaiah, for example, in contrast to the servants of Yahweh who will receive a blessed future (Isa. 65: 8–10), a group aligned with the idolaters of Isaiah 57: 3–13 and 65: 1–7 is singled out for destruction by ואתם in Isaiah 65: 11–12 (cf. the constant shift between blessing and curse in vv. 13–16). In verse 11, they are indicted for worshipping Gad and Meni—the gods of fortune and fate.[146] Another ritual criticized in this period is an

---

[142] A discussion of the origin of this practice in Judah is outside the scope of this analysis. Further information can be found in Ackerman, *Under Every Green Tree*, 93–8; Taylor, *Yahweh and the Sun*; Day, *Yahweh and the Gods*, 151–6.

[143] M. Smith, 'Helios in Palestine', *EI* 16 (1982), 204*–206*; Stähli, *Solare Elemente im Jahwegaluben des Alten Testaments* (OBO, 66; Göttingen: Vandenhoeck & Ruprecht, 1985); H. Niehr, *Der höchste Gott* (BZAW, 190; Berlin: de Gruyter, 1990), 141–63; Taylor, *Yahweh and the Sun*; O. Keel and C. Uehlinger, 'Jahwe und die Sonnengottheit von Jerusalem', in W. Dietrich and M. A. Klopfenstein (eds.), *Ein Gott Allein? JHWH-Verehrung und biblischer Monotheismus im Kontext der israelitischen und altorientalischen Religionsgeschichte* (OBO, 139; Freiburg: Universitätsverlag, 1994), 269–303.

[144] M. S. Smith, *Psalms: The Divine Journey* (Mahwah, NJ: Paulist Press, 1987), 52–62; idem, ' "Seeing God" in the Psalms: The Background to the Beatific Vision in the Hebrew Bible', *CBQ* 50 (1988), 171–83; idem, 'The Near Eastern Background of Solar Language for Yahweh', *JBL* 109 (1990), 29–39; and idem, *The Early History of God*, 148–53.

[145] Greenberg, *Ezekiel*, 171; Ackerman, *Under Every Green Tree*, 93–9; Dijkstra, 'Goddess, Gods, Men and Women in Ezekiel 8', 104–13. Cf. N. Sarna, 'Psalm xix and Northeast Sun-God Literature', *Fourth World Congress of Jewish Studies*, Papers 1 (Jerusalem: World Union of Jewish Studies, 1967), 171–5.

[146] Tigay, *You Shall Have No Other Gods*, 13, 66–7, 69.

aspect of the cult of the dead. In a series of denunciations, Isaiah 65: 4 most likely depicts the combination of incubation, the search for a divine answer through dreams, with necromancy, the consultation of the dead:

הישבים בקברים ובנצורים ילינו
האכלים בשר החזיר ופרק פגלים כליהם:

The ones who sit in the graves and spend the night in secret places, those who eat the flesh of pigs and polluted soup in their dishes.

ובנצורים MT From נצר 'to guard preserve'. The *qal* passive connotes the sense of something guarded, i.e. 'secret', as here and Isa. 48: 6; Prov. 7: 10. Dahood, 'Textual Problems in Isaia', pp. 408–9, followed by some, divides it בן צורים 'inside the rocks (or mountains)', understanding tombs hewn in the mountains. See the cogent objections by Lewis, *Cults of the Dead*, 159–60; Ackerman, *Under Every Green Tree*, 195 n. 112.

ופרק MT Reading ומרק 'a fragment of foul things' with the *Qere*, 1QIsa[a], LXX, Vulgate, and Targum.

Included within an oracle of judgement which climaxes in retribution in verses 6–7, verses 1–5 set forth a series of accusations of wrongful behaviour. Isaiah 65: 4 thus continues the thrust of verse 3 where people contravene what is acceptable Yahwistic practice by 'sacrificing in gardens and burning incense on bricks'.[147] The location of the practitioners 'in graves' and 'in secret places' along with the LXX interpretation 'for the sake of dreams' has led to the association of this passage with necromancy and incubation. Except for this passage, incubation receives no direct criticism in the Hebrew Bible, as elsewhere it appears as an acceptable means of obtaining information.[148] Thus, as Lewis, Ackerman, and Schmidt conclude, the prophet intends to deter the association with necromancy of gathering information from the deity in dreams. How does the consumption of impure foods fit within the rebuke? There is a great deal of discussion on whether the two activities are part of one idea or two. Ackerman argues for the latter so that the first part of verse 4 refers to people who are engaging in a mix of necromancy

---

[147] לבנים could be translated 'incense altars' or 'bricks' without any change in meaning. Cf. Dahood, 'Textual Problems', 406–8; Ackerman, *Under Every Green Tree*, 166 n. 3, 169–85.

[148] Lewis, *Cults of the Dead*, 158–60; Ackerman, *Under Every Green Tree*, 198–200; Schmidt, *Israel's Beneficent Dead*, 264.

and incubation rites while the second deals with the issue of purity/impurity.[149] However, the fact that impure food can be associated with cults of the dead suggests that the two acts depict a singular religious practice, thus forming a neat parallel with the religious practice portrayed in verse 3b, where sacrifices and burning incense take place in the gardens.[150] Moreover, condemned sources of food appear again in the context of ritual practices in the gardens in Isaiah 66: 17. The unclean food source can be seen either as a metaphor used to depict a defiled cult[151] or as food actually consumed at such rituals.[152] In either case, it corresponds to the necromancy and incubation rituals of the first part of the verse. According to the prophet, the consultation of the dead was an unacceptable practice in which the inhabitants of the early restoration period participated.

CONCLUSIONS

A variety of literature has been surveyed as a means of portraying the diversity of worship practices that the biblical writers, followed by modern interpreters, associated with sixth-century Judah. Some of these were included in Ackerman's description of 'popular religion' in sixth-century Judah as representing actual worship practices that took place in the homeland. A couple of features come to light beyond the delineation of the diversity of idolatrous practices that were attributed to the inhabitants of post-587 Judah. The first is that the veneration of other deities is resoundingly and resolutely condemned as incompatible with Yahwism. Further, it is associated directly with the fall of Jerusalem and Judah. Its occurrence in the Second Temple period continued to cause the consternation of the biblical writers. This perception of the events of the early sixth century and the people in the homeland is not a view that comes

---

[149] Lewis, *Cults of the Dead*, 159; Ackerman, *Under Every Green Tree*, 194–212; Schmidt, *Israel's Beneficent Dead*, 261–2; Schramm, *The Opponents*, 156–7.
[150] De Vaux, 'Les sacrifices de porcs'; Heider, *The Cult of Molek*; Houston, *Purity and Monotheism*, 165–8.
[151] Lewis, *Cults of the Dead*.
[152] Heider, *The Cult of Molek*; Houston, *Purity and Monotheism*.

from the people in Judah themselves. Rather, it is superimposed upon them from the community deported to Babylon. As such, it may or may not reflect their reality or even their perception of their reality. Was the worship of idols and other gods so trying for the community in Judah?

The second issue relates to the first in that it is clear that the exiles in Babylon programmatically sought to deny the divinity of other deities as a means to curtail their worship. This literary move fits well with the intention and emphasis of *Golah* literature as a whole. At least in terms of Judah, the response of the refugees in Egypt suggests that a degree of the population did not consider religious practices in honour of other deities to be incompatible with Yahwism. But again, the origin of this response and its application to the community in Egypt arises from the perspective of the exiles and is incorporated into Jeremiah by the *Golah* redactors. In the case of Jeremiah 44, it clearly serves the wider purpose of removing the community in Egypt from a blessed future in the land. In the examination of the heterodox religiosity of the period, it became clear that a diversity of literary strategies were at work to show the dangers and folly of unorthodox religious practices. Much biblical material clearly functions polemically in order to dissuade the worship of anything besides Yahweh. In many respects, the literature is equivalent to the masterful polemical passages of Deutero-Isaiah and the subtle use of language by Ezekiel who, for instance, denied divine status to other deities by never using אלהים when speaking of other deities as had his contemporaries the Deuteronomists. Awareness of the literary enterprise results in a degree of uncertainty over how much this material can be used indicatively to describe ongoing ritual practices actually taking place in post-587 Judah. Ackerman has provided a helpful study of the period which may correspond to actual events, but it is important to be more aware of the way the biblical texts function to dismiss the community that remained in Judah from promises of future blessing.

It is possible to reconstruct outside impressions of unorthodox religious praxis which may relate to real practice in sixth-century Judah, but it does not provide a Judahite perspective on their religiosity. In fact, biblical writers of the time were not overly concerned with Judahite reflection on the disaster, their situation, and their future. If the exiles desired to return to the land, what did the people in the land desire? If the exiles perceived the disaster of 587 as a direct result of idolatrous behaviour, as the judgement of Yahweh on recalcitrant Judah, what did the Judahites think? If the inhabitants of the homeland were worshipping other deities after 587, it was surely not because they considered that behaviour to have brought down the covenant curses predicted in Deuteronomy. They must have continued those practices thinking that they were behaving as good Yahwists. So what did they think? How is their perception different from that of their brethren in exile? With this religio-history in mind, the next chapter turns to important scholarly endeavours to reconstruct what might be considered acceptable Yahwistic practice located in Templeless Judah.

3

Conceptions of Judah, II: Yahwistic Worship

INTRODUCTION

The previous chapter revealed that one possible feature of continuity in the religio-historical situation of the land occurred in the observance of cults considered idolatrous in certain circles. Those practices were ascribed to the inhabitants of Judah, however, by literature not of their own hand. The amount of attention directed towards noting the presence of heterodox worship in Templeless Judah tends to obscure Yahwistic practices that may have taken place among the people. What of Yahwistic belief that would merit the approval of the exiled community in Babylon? This chapter considers the places where commentators associate the continuation of Yahwistic practice in Judah along with the type of worship generally attributed to that setting, that is, a cult of lamentation. Upon closer examination much of the lament literature thought to have taken place in public ritual in Judah exhibits themes and concepts of such diversity that a simple one-to-one correspondence with Judah is no longer tenable. This chapter will show that much of the liturgy associated with Yahwistic practice in Judah leaves us wanting with respect to Judahite belief and reflection.

WORSHIP IN THE LAND: CONTINUITY

After the tragic events of 587, the appointment of Gedaliah as governor over the province of Judah reinstated a sense of normality and provided a stable centre to which refugees gravitated. However, the resurgence that accompanied Gedaliah's governance took place in Mizpah. Tellingly, Jerusalem is not mentioned in the Gedaliah account in either Kings or Jeremiah. The city that had once functioned as the centre of the kingdom no longer served in this capacity in the aftermath of the Babylonian attack. Lamentations, for example, highlights the significant tragedy that accompanied the collapse of Jerusalem and even portrays it as emptied of people (Lam. 1: 1). The Babylonians thoroughly disrupted the ability of Jerusalem to function as a political and religious centre through their termination of the influence of the Davidic line and the priests of the temple.[1] With respect to religious practice the two main accounts of the time graphically portray the end of the functioning of the sanctuary through the murder of various high-ranking temple personnel by Nebuchadnezzar—the chief priest, Seraiah, the second priest, Zephaniah, and three keepers of the threshold (2 Kgs. 25: 18–21; Jer. 52: 24–7; cf. Lam. 2: 6c, 20). The removal of the priests and the destruction of the temple resulted in the cessation of its use as a cultic site at least for a time. In various places the poet of Lamentations includes the loss of ritual as one of the outcomes of the catastrophe: 'The paths of Zion are mourning, for those coming to appointed feasts are no more' (Lam. 1: 4), 'He has perpetrated violence against his booth like a garden, ruined his appointed feasts; Yahweh has caused feast and sabbath to be forgotten in Zion' (Lam. 2: 6ab), and 'Adonai has rejected his altar, scorned his sanctuary' (Lam. 2: 7a). The issue of the ruination of the temple continues to cause consternation in the period after the ascension of Cyrus. Between 520 and 518, the prophets Haggai and Zechariah (chs. 1–8) encouraged the people to rebuild the temple in accordance with Yahweh's will.[2] Their efforts highlight the issue of whether or not the temple provided a ritual centre during the time preceding their prophetic ministry.

Although the biblical literature vividly illustrates the ferocity and breadth of the Babylonian attack, most interpreters of this period,

---

[1] O. Lipschits, 'Judah, Jerusalem and the Temple 586–539 B.C.', *Transeuphratène* 22 (2001), 140.

[2] P. R. Bedford, *Temple Restoration in Early Achaemenid Judah* (JSJSup, 65; Leiden: Brill, 2001), provides a thorough study with references to the literature.

nevertheless, associate societal renewal with the resurgence of Yahwistic religious practices.[3] Based on analogies in the ancient world in which the destruction of a city and its sanctuary failed to stifle the expression of worship, the temple could continue to be the location for mourning rituals at the very least. For instance, in the autobiographical composition about the mother of Nabonidus who served as a priestess in the house of Sin, the moon-god, Adad-Guppi described her ongoing service in the sanctuary after its destruction and the mourning rituals she assumed.[4] Similarly, the Jews at Elephantine lamented the loss of their temple for roughly three years after its razing until its reconstruction.[5] A common reaction to the demolition of a temple was the institution of mourning rituals. In the biblical literature, although there is no direct evidence of the restitution of worship, certain texts (Jer. 41 from the Temple-less period and Zech. 7–8 from the early Second Temple period) hint at it.

When considering the question of the use of the temple, whatever its condition, as the locus for some type of religious observance, one must be cognizant in the first instance of the central role temple ideology played in the ancient world. It is unlikely that a functioning society could exist without regular ritual mediated through a cultic setting. In the ancient world the temple represented the place through which people experienced the divine. In particular, the temple in Jerusalem represented the royal palace of the deity Yahweh from which he exercised cosmic authority.[6] Realized in a programmatic

[3] E. Janssen, *Juda in der Exilszeit: Ein Beitrag zur Frage der Entstehung des Judentums* (FRLANT, 69; Göttingen: Vandenhoeck & Ruprecht, 1956), 101–4; P. R. Ackroyd, *Exile and Restoration: A Study of Hebrew Thought of the Sixth Century B.C.* (London: SCM Press, repr. 1990), 25–31.

[4] T. Longman, 'The Adad-Guppi Autobiography', in W. W. Hallo (ed.), *The Context of Scripture*, i. *Canonical Compositions from the Biblical World* (Leiden: Brill, 1997), 477–8.

[5] B. Porten, *Archives from Elephantine: The Life of a Jewish Military Colony* (Berkeley, Calif.: University of California Press, 1968), 289–93, and *idem*, *The Elephantine Papyri in English: Three Millennia of Cross-Cultural Continuity and Change* (DMOA, 22; Leiden: Brill, 1996), 139–47.

[6] The literature on this is vast. For an introduction to the conceptualization of temple ideology in Jerusalem and further references, see R. E. Clements, *God and Temple* (Oxford: Blackwell, 1965); R. J. Clifford, *The Cosmic Mountain in Canaan and the Old Testament* (HSM, 4; Cambridge, Mass.: Harvard University Press, 1972); T. N. D. Mettinger, *The Dethronement of Sabaoth: Studies in the Shem and Kabod Theologies* (CBOT, 18; Lund: Gleerup, 1982), 19–37; O. H. Steck, 'Zion als Gelände

way through worship, the sanctuary took on aspects of Zion theology which included the concept of the inviolability of the city and the covenant with the Davidic kings protected and constituted by the presence of the deity. The deity's presence symbolized divine order and favour through which the people and the land were blessed. Especially after the time of Josiah during which the Jerusalem temple became the only location sanctioned as the ritual centre, its loss would have been keenly felt. In the wider ancient Near East, this was certainly the case. The Sumerian city laments vividly describe the destruction of a temple in terminology suggestive of the reaction of eyewitnesses after the fact. They were created to be liturgical accompaniments to ceremonies which marked the reconstruction of the sanctuary[7] and attest anger, frustration, and loss as well as the desire for the deity's return and blessing.

In a segment of an historical tradition widely held to reflect the actual events of the Templeless period Jeremiah 41: 5 provides the earliest indication that ritual observance continued after the fall of Jerusalem.[8] Set during the governorship of Gedaliah, on the day of his murder but unbeknownst to them, a group of eighty men set out to observe the Feast of Weeks, one of the three great pilgrimages to the temple (Exod. 23: 14–16; 34: 23; Deut. 16: 13–17).[9] Bearing grain offerings מנחה and incense לבונה, they travelled to 'the house of Yahweh' בית יהוה to pay homage:

ויהי ביום השני להמית את גדליהו ואיש לא
ידע: ויבאו אנשים משכם משלו ומשמרון
שמנים איש מגלחי זקן וקרעי בגדים
ומתגדדים ומנחה ולבונה בידם להביא
בית יהוה:

On that day after the murder of Gedaliah when no-one knew, eighty men arrived from Shechem, Shiloh, and Samaria with their beards shaved, their

und Gestalt: Überlegungen zur Wahrnehmung Jerusalems als Stadt und Frau im Alten Testament', *ZTK* 86 (1989); Bedford, *Temple Restoration*, 2–4, 66–70.

[7] W. W. Hallo, 'Lamentations and Prayers in Sumer and Akkad', in J. M. Sasson (ed.), *Civilizations of the Ancient Near East*, iii (London and New York: Simon & Schuster, 1995), 1871–3.

[8] C. R. Seitz, *Theology in Conflict: Reactions to the Exile in the Book of Jeremiah* (BZAW, 176; Berlin: de Gruyter, 1989), 274–9.

[9] S. Japhet, 'People and the Land in the Restoration Period', in G. Strecker (ed.), *Das Land Israel in biblischer Zeit: Jerusalem Symposium 1981* (GTA, 25; Göttingen: Vandenhoeck & Ruprecht, 1983), 119 n. 12.

clothes cut, and their bodies gashed, with offerings and incense in their hands to bring to the house of Yahweh. (Jer. 41: 5)

The destination and their offerings are thought to be significant. Although the location of the sanctuary will be discussed further below, the expression בית יהוה generally refers to the temple in Jerusalem, though it is used to speak occasionally of other cultic sites (Exod. 23: 19; 34: 26; Josh. 6: 26) and of the sanctuary in Shiloh when it housed the Ark of the Covenant (1 Sam. 1: 24; 3: 15; 2 Sam. 12: 20). Whatever their final destination, in the aftermath of the catastrophe of 587 pilgrims from cities of the former northern kingdom of Israel journeyed to present grain offerings and incense in a ritual consistent with worship practices of the past. In this instance and contrary to practice typically associated with the Feast of Weeks, they adopted physical signs of mourning such as clean-shaven faces, clothing rent in despair, and bodies gashed.[10] The behaviour of the men is not consistent with organized public ritual, but with a voluntary religious response to disaster by isolated individuals. Although no other biblical picture substantiates the observance of such rituals after the death of Gedaliah, there is no reason to believe that individual religious reactions to the events of 587 ceased during this period.[11]

In fact, the period of lawlessness that inevitably ensued after the assassination of Gedaliah and the wanton murder of seventy of the eighty pilgrims must have been quickly quelled since the band of rebels eventually fled to Egypt (Jer. 41: 17–18; 43: 4–7) and according to the archaeological record many towns in the Benjamite region continued to be the locus of renewal until the close of the sixth century. In addition, certain texts in Zechariah 1–8—widely regarded as stemming from and relating to the early Second Temple period—point to the observance of public rituals which would be consistent with the restitution of normal communal activity and indicative of

---

[10] An introduction to mourning rituals can be found in E. Lipiński, *La liturgie pénitentielle dans la Bible* (LD, 52; Paris: Editions du Cerf, 1969), 11–25; G. A. Anderson, *A Time to Mourn, a Time to Dance: The Expression of Grief and Joy in Israelite Religion* (University Park, Pa.: Pennsylvania State University Press, 1991); X. H. T. Pham, *Mourning in the Ancient Near East and the Hebrew Bible* (JSOTSup, 302; Sheffield: Sheffield Academic Press, 1999), 16–35.

[11] Japhet, 'People and the Land', 105.

a functioning state. According to Zechariah 7–8, joined by a ring structure which opens (7: 1–6) and closes the oracle (8: 19) with a concentration on commemorative days of fasting,[12] certain days were set aside to observe the loss of the city, temple, king, and governor.[13] It may certainly be the case that the passage of time and the restitution of stability would be more conducive for the installation of public fast days following the catastrophe of 587 and the period of uncertainty surrounding the time of Gedaliah's death. Nevertheless, in 7: 5 a divine oracle about the necessity to observe a fast for the temple which was in the process of being rebuilt provides a rough estimate of seventy years in which commemorative rituals were observed:

אמר אל כל עם הארץ ואל הכהנים לאמר
כי צמתם וספוד בחמישי ובשביעי וזה
שבעים שנה הצום צמתני אני:

Say to all the people of the land and to the priests: When you fasted and mourned in the fifth and seventh month these seventy years, was it really for me that you fasted? (Zech. 7: 5)

The rhetorical question responds to a query raised in 7: 3 by a delegation who referred to the period of their mourning as 'these many years' זה כמה שנים.[14] The divine response in verse 5 reveals that fasts took place during some seventy years prior to the prophetic activity of Zechariah, which is roughly equivalent to the time between the destruction of the temple in 587 and the time of the prophecy in 518 (7: 1).[15] Equally, it corresponds to a round figure for the duration of the exile in the prophecy of Jeremiah.[16] The figure

---

[12] Zech. 8: 20–3 are a type of appendix separated off by the opening messenger formula of v. 20 and a difference in focus. C. L. Meyers and E. M. Meyers, *Haggai, Zechariah 1–8* (AB; New York: Doubleday, 1987), 442–3; Y. Hoffman, 'The Fasts in the Book of Zechariah and the Fashioning of National Remembrance', in O. Lipschits and J. Blenkinsopp (eds.), *Judah and the Judeans in the Neo-Babylonian Period* (Winona Lake, Ind.: Eisenbrauns, 2003), 169–70.

[13] Hoffman, 'The Fasts in the Book of Zechariah', 192–4.

[14] On this odd phrase and its referent, see the commentaries and especially Meyers and Meyers, *Zechariah 1–8*, 387; Hoffman, 'The Fasts in the Book of Zechariah', 187–8.

[15] Meyers and Meyers, *Zechariah 1–8*, 386–9.

[16] J. Applegate, 'Jeremiah and the Seventy Years in the Hebrew Bible: Inner-Biblical Reflections on the Prophet and His Prophecy', in A. H. W. Curtis and T. Römer (eds.), *The Book of Jeremiah and its Reception* (BETL, 128; Leuven: Leuven University Press, 1997), 91–110.

seventy probably serves a dual purpose—to refer to the actual time between the destruction of the temple and its reconstruction and to align the period with prophecy. Constructively, it establishes the observance of mourning rituals within the period prior to the prophetic activity of Zechariah, and thus, to the Templeless period.[17]

Moreover, the two passages relating to fasts indicate that there was some flexibility in public mourning rituals during the Templeless period and further suggest that observances of this nature were widespread among the various populations of Judah. Through the mention of an ever-increasing number of fasts (one in v. 3, two in v. 5, and four in 8: 19) and a variety of means to commemorate them (abstinence, fasting, mourning, and lamenting), the section discloses that there was some variation within the ritual observance and practices during the period. The initial question that sparks communication about fasting occurs in 7: 3 and cites only the fast in the fifth month. Through the prophet Zechariah, the deity responds twice to the query (7: 5; 8: 19). The first aligns the fast of the fifth month with the fast of the seventh, whilst the second adds two additional fasts, in the fourth and tenth months. The dates of the fasts correspond to the significant losses occasioned by the Neo-Babylonian military strikes. According to biblical and rabbinical tradition, in the fifth month mourning took place in remembrance of the destruction of the temple and the king's palace (2 Kgs. 25: 8) whilst that of the seventh month corresponded to the assassination of Gedaliah (2 Kgs. 25: 25; Jer. 41: 1–3). The fasts of the fourth and tenth months, respectively, are thought to correspond to the beginning of the siege (2 Kgs. 25: 1; Jer. 39: 1) and the capture of the city of Jerusalem (2 Kgs. 25: 3).

In a recent article, Hoffman has analysed the disparity between the questions in 7: 3 and the prophetic answers in 7: 5 and 8: 19 with particular attention to the fasts.[18] One of his arguments relates specifically to the escalating number of fasts, the addition of the

---

[17] A seventy-year period is applied to the period of suffering of Judah by the angelic messenger who liaises with Zechariah in 1–8. The use of עד מתי (Zech. 1: 12) and the association of the lament with the eleventh month are thought to connect it with the prayers on a fasting day. D. L. Petersen, *Haggai–Zechariah 1–8* (OTL; Philadelphia, Pa.: Westminster, 1984), 146–7. Cf. Tollington, *Tradition and Innovation*, 184–5, who considers this verse in conjunction with Psalm 79 in the context of fast days.

[18] Hoffman, 'The Fasts in the Book of Zechariah', 194–7.

seventh in the first response and that of the fourth and tenth months in the subsequent response. In his view, the inclusion of these narrative details reflects a situation at the time of the early return in which different fasts were being commemorated by different groups. For instance, the fast of the seventh month which would have been more pertinent to the community in the homeland or in Egypt was not likely to have been observed by the community in Babylonia.[19] Moreover, the correlation of the fast associated with the death of Gedaliah and the fasts that commemorated the siege of the city and breaching of the walls with ritual memorializing the destruction of the temple functions to equate all four in terms of significance. The inclusion of all four fasts in the divine oracle of 8: 19 provided a means of reconciliation for the community. It is equally significant that the target audience of the reply is greater than the delegation that brought the enquiry in the first place. It includes all the people of the land along with the priests (v. 5).[20] Hoffman's argument has the merit of explaining the juxtaposition of three fasts with the one fast that initially sparked the query in 7: 3. In his analysis of Zechariah, Hoffman finds that the fasts that commemorated the downfall of the political and religious edifices of Judah as well as the inclusion of social groups suggest a period of accommodation. Moreover, it shows that four fasts would have been available for ritual observance by the population that remained in the land of Judah prior to the prophetic ministry of Zechariah with one especially pertinent to them—that for Gedaliah.

One further detail in the narrative is important with regard to the situation in the homeland. It relates to the presence of priests at the temple before its completion, which provocatively begs the question of the role of the priesthood during the sixth century. The text while not clarifying the situation nevertheless suggests that priests could function as an authority without the Jerusalem temple. Zechariah 7: 3

---

[19] P. W. Ferris, *The Genre of Communal Lament in the Bible and Ancient Near East* (SBLDS; Atlanta, Ga.: Scholars Press, 1992), 81–3, too, suggests that fasting was a regular practice in Babylon. Cf. T. Veijola, 'Das Klagegebet in Literatur und Leben der Exilsgeneration am Beispiel einiger Prosatexte', in J. A. Emerton (ed.), *Congress Volume: Salamanca 1983* (SVT, 36; Leiden: Brill, 1985), 286–307.

[20] Bedford, *Temple Restoration*, 275–6; Hoffman, 'The Fasts in the Book of Zechariah', 197–9.

describes a scene in which a priestly ruling was sought to adjudicate a ritual matter before the temple was fully operative. A similar type of question posed to the priesthood occurs in Haggai (2: 10–14), likewise dated by a precise editorial framework to the period before the completion of the temple.[21] Zechariah 7: 3 within the overall message of chapters 1–8 reasserts the dominance of Jerusalem as the centre for cultic matters. In so doing it discloses that priests could have functioned in an authoritative capacity on the temple site before its reconstruction. Although set in the period of the early return, the behaviour of the priests points to the possibility that they could have adjudicated ritual matters in sixth-century Judah even whilst the temple lay in ruins.[22]

Pilgrimage and commemorative events allowed a devastated populace to ritually remember its loss. Indeed, the glimpses provided by Jeremiah 41 and Zechariah 7: 5; 8: 19 show that individually and collectively the people who remained in the land after the series of deportations that accompanied the destruction of Jerusalem mourned the loss of their nation, their leadership, and the symbol of their deity's presence in their midst. Their behaviour corresponds to both the spontaneous worship of individuals and more organized public ritual.

LOCATIONS OF WORSHIP

As seen already in the discussion of Jeremiah 41: 5, the ambiguity of the reference to the House of Yahweh has sparked interest in the destination of the travellers. Were they headed to the ruins of the sanctuary in Jerusalem or to another site? Commentators have proposed two locations of ritual observance: the first at the ruins of the Jerusalem temple and the second at a sanctuary in the Benjamin region.

---

[21] K. Koch, 'Haggais unreines Volk', *ZAW* 79 (1967), 52–66, has provided the most thorough discussion of the form of this unit and sets it alongside two similar passages. His arguments support the unity of the passage.

[22] J. Schaper, *Priester und Leviten im achämenidischen Juda: Studien zur Kult- und Sozialgeschichte Israels in persischer Zeit* (FAT, 31; Tübingen: Mohr Siebeck, 2000), has provided a useful current study of the priesthood with primary attention to the Persian period.

Jerusalem

On the basis of the episode recounted in Jeremiah 41: 5 in which mourners headed south bearing offerings, most modern interpreters envision the temple site as a place in which cultic activity continued.[23] The actual passage does not provide a clear destination, rather the pilgrims head towards the 'house of Yahweh'. The ambiguity begs the question of whether the entourage headed to the sanctuary in Jerusalem or somewhere else such as Mizpah or Bethel.[24] There are several reasons to believe that the sanctuary in Jerusalem is intended. In the accounts of the destruction wrought by the Babylonians, the temple is called בית יהוה (2 Kgs. 25: 9, 13 // Jer. 52: 13, 17). Appropriately, the designation is not used for any other cultic site after the intention is made in 1 Kings 3 to build the temple.

More importantly in Jeremiah, the expression occurs 29 times outside of this passage and always refers to the temple in Jerusalem (Jer. 7: 2; 17: 26; 19: 14; 20: 1, 2; 26: 2, 7, 9, 10; 27: 16, 18, 21; 28: 1, 3, 5, 6; 29: 26; 33: 11; 35: 2, 4, 5; 36: 6, 8, 10; 38: 14; 51: 51; 52: 13, 17, 20). Whereas the expression is found elsewhere in the Hebrew Bible to denote the sanctuary at Shiloh where the Ark of the Covenant was housed (1 Sam. 1: 24; 3: 15; 2 Sam. 12: 20), even in comparisons likening the fate of the temple in Jerusalem to that of Shiloh, neither Jeremiah nor the people in their rebuttal to him ever speak of a sanctuary there.[25] It is especially within Jeremiah's lengthy diatribes against the temple that this becomes a glaring omission. When utilizing a comparison with Shiloh to illustrate the expected fate of the temple should the people refuse to repent, the prophet mentions only the name of the town of Shiloh, tellingly without naming the

---

[23] See the list of references by Lipschits, 'Judah, Jerusalem, and the Temple', 137–8 n. 34.

[24] Lipschits, 'Judah, Jerusalem, and the Temple', 137–8 n. 34, following J. Blenkinsopp, 'The Judaean Priesthood during the Neo-Babylonian and Achaemenid Periods: A Hypothetical Reconstruction', *CBQ* 60 (1998) and now, most recently, *idem*, 'Bethel in the Neo-Babylonian Period', in Lipschits and Blenkinsopp, *Judah and the Judeans*.

[25] On the date of the destruction of Shiloh, see J. Day, 'The Destruction of the Shiloh Sanctuary and Jeremiah VII 12, 14', in J. A. Emerton (ed.), *Studies in the Historical Books of the Old Testament* (SVT, 30; Leiden: Brill, 1979).

temple that existed there.²⁶ In addition, when the people respond to Jeremiah, they, too, fail to mention the site of public worship that existed there.²⁷ Although the prophet might not be expected to mention a temple outside Jerusalem, surely the people felt no such constraints. In a comparison specifically relevant to the temple in Jerusalem, the equivalent edifice in Shiloh ought to have been mentioned. The omission of a location for worship outside of Jerusalem within a context where it would be expected is significant. Consistent with other literature that corresponds to a time after the construction of the sanctuary, the expression בית יהוה is used exclusively for the temple in Jeremiah. Because it is not used for another legitimate sanctuary the 'House of Yahweh' to which the pilgrims travel in Jeremiah 41: 5 can only be the Jerusalem sanctuary.

In spite of the fact that the temple had been targeted by the Babylonians, it could have been used as the location for certain rituals. In the ancient world, holy sites retained their sanctity long after they were destroyed. The type of worship that would have taken place there is closely related to its condition.²⁸ During the comprehensive military campaign of 587, the Babylonians burnt the temple with fire (2 Kgs. 25: 9 // 52: 13), smashed the bronze pillars, furniture, and 'sea' (2 Kgs. 25: 13 // Jer. 52: 17), and took the bronze and remaining vessels to Babylon as booty (2 Kgs. 25: 14–15 // Jer. 52: 18–19). Any additional information about the condition of the altar is not forthcoming. On this, Jones comments that 'It would have required a deliberate act of demolition, for it was as solid as the walls of the city,'²⁹ which were in fact pulled down.³⁰ If it was not pulled down, it was defiled (Lam. 2: 20). Since the mourners who journey to the temple carry cereal offerings מנחה and incense לבונה, but not burnt sacrifices עלה, it appears that they intended to make non-sacrificial offerings. The implication is that the altar could not

---

²⁶ Jer. 7: 14 'I will do to the house in which my name is called as I did to Shiloh'; Jer. 26: 6a 'Then I will make this house like Shiloh.'

²⁷ Jer. 26: 9 'Why have you prophesied in the name of Yahweh saying, "This house will be like Shiloh...?"'.

²⁸ Ackroyd, *Exile and Restoration*, 25–9.

²⁹ D. R. Jones, 'The Cessation of Sacrifice after the Destruction of the Temple in 586 B.C.', *JTS* NS 14 (1963), 12.

³⁰ Ackroyd, *Exile and Restoration*, 25.

be used.³¹ The Jerusalem temple depicted as the site of non-sacrificial offerings fits well with its depiction in 1 Kings 8 as a house of prayer (esp. vv. 44–51).³²

There nevertheless remains some speculation about whether or not all sacrifices at the temple site ceased. Certain texts in Ezra leave open the possibility that sacrifices continued during the Templeless period (Ezra 4: 2; 6: 3).³³ Janssen, for example, argued that the fear of the people of the lands, in those who erect the altar in Ezra 3: 3, arose because they were replacing a provisional altar established during this time.³⁴ However, it is difficult to follow Janssen's reasoning on this point as the entire episode in Ezra 3: 1–6 places a great deal of emphasis on the resumption of burnt sacrifices (vv. 3, 4, 5, 6). Furthermore, it is made clear that it is only after the building (v. 2) and setting up (v. 3) of the altar by Jeshua, the priests, and Zerubbabel and his entourage that sacrifices are made. The state of the temple and the small population of Jerusalem and its environs during the Neo-Babylonian period make regular use of the temple for ritual observance unlikely (Lam. 1: 4; 2: 6, 7). This is in agreement with the conclusions of Noth, who envisioned the continuation of a considerably reduced cult,³⁵ and of Lipschits, who comments on the limited amount of ritual activity that would have taken place there and on it being more spontaneous than organized.³⁶ Whilst the temple may have been used for sporadic ceremonies, it is unlikely that it was the location of regular cultic ritual.

Bethel

The condition of the temple in Jerusalem suggests it was the location of a considerably reduced cult. In the light of the fact that the

---

³¹ Jones, 'Cessation of Sacrifice'.

³² Janssen, *Juda in der Exilszeit*, 102, 104; Jones, 'Cessation of Sacrifice', 22–3; Ackroyd, *Exile and Restoration*, 26–8. 1 Kgs. 8: 31–2 refers to the altar, but is thought to reflect a time when the temple was still standing rather than in ruins.

³³ H. G. M. Williamson, *Ezra, Nehemiah* (WBC, 16; Waco, Tex.: Word Books, 1985), 46, 71.

³⁴ Janssen, *Juda in der Exilszeit*, 103.

³⁵ Noth, 'Die Katastrophe von Jerusalem', in *Gesammelte Studien*, 349–52, 368–9, = 'The Jerusalem Catastrophe', in *The Laws of the Pentateuch*, 263–4, 278.

³⁶ Lipschits, 'Judah, Jerusalem and the Temple', 139–41.

political, social, and religious spheres of ancient cultures intertwined, the resurgence of activity in the Benjamin area raises the possibility of the renewal of more regular ritual. In fact, the re-establishment of normative activity in the Benjamin region of Babylonian Judah would necessitate a fully operative sanctuary. A likely location for the existence of such a site would have been Mizpah or Bethel (just 6 km north of Mizpah)—long a holy site of the region—adjacent to the administrative centre of the province created by the Babylonians. Blenkinsopp has argued this position most forcefully.[37] In the first place, he understands the destination of the delegation of mourners in Jeremiah 41: 5 to be a possible reference to Bethel, as it was located just north of Mizpah. Moreover, the ambiguous reference in Zechariah 7: 2 allows the rendering of Bethel as the place to which the delegation led by Sar-ezer and Regem Melek journeyed, thereby suggesting Bethel as the site where ritual matters could be adjudicated. In conjunction with his argument, Blenkinsopp surveyed biblical stories about early Israelite history dated to the Neo-Babylonian period. In Judges 20–1; 1 Samuel 7: 5–6, 9–10; 10: 17, for instance, allusions are made to Mizpah as a key political and religious centre. The centrality of Mizpah and Bethel in biblical tradition, then, reinforces the likelihood that the two functioned in a significant way during the Templeless period.

Although I am in general agreement with the establishment of an alternative cultic centre at Bethel as proposed by Blenkinsopp, the references in Jeremiah 41: 5 and Zechariah 7: 2 do not contribute to his argument. In terms of Jeremiah 41: 5, as we have seen above, the referent for 'the House of Yahweh' is more properly understood within the context of Jeremiah as the temple in Jerusalem. It would be odd for the expression to mean Bethel here, especially given the prophet's reticence to speak of another cultic sanctuary in Shiloh when one would have been expected. Similarly with Zechariah 7: 2, as attractive as the suggestion is, the evidence for understanding Bethel as the city towards which Sar-ezer, Regem Melek, and his compan-

---

[37] Blenkinsopp, 'The Judaean Priesthood', 25–34; 'Bethel', 93–108; cf. *idem*, 'The Age of the Exile', in J. Barton (ed.), *The Biblical World*, i (London and New York: Routledge, 2002), 425–6. This is an older argument dating back to F. Giesebrecht, *Das Buch Jeremia* (Göttingen: Vandenhoeck & Ruprecht, 2nd edn. 1907); H. W. Hertzberg, 'Mizpa', *ZAW* 47 (1929).

ions head is difficult. The sentence structure, though ambiguous in certain respects, favours an interpretation of Bethel as the subject. The text is:

וישלח בית אל שר אצר ורגם מלך ואנשיו
לחלות את פני יהוה:

And Bethel sent Sar-ezer and Regem Melek and his men to entreat the favour of Yahweh.

The verse lacks certain indicators like the definite direct object marker to indicate what is being sent or other indicators of the place to which the men travelled. The Septuagint, Peshitta, and Targum understand Bethel as the destination,[38] but normal Hebrew syntax is verb, subject, and object even when prepositions or direct object markers are missing. When a location is implied rather than indicated by a preposition or the locative ה it tends to follow the subject of the sentence as an adverbial accusative. In several texts where Bethel appears as an adverbial accusative, it always takes this position as, for example, Judges 1: 22; 'And the house of Joseph went up also to Bethel' ויעלו בית־יוסף גם־הם בית־אל.[39] In Zechariah 7: 2 the position of Bethel directly after the verb implies that it functions as the subject of the sentence.[40] Most commentators accept this understanding, but fail to locate it within the context of the Second Temple period or the collection of Zechariah 1–8.[41]

Although Bethel functions as the subject, it does not invalidate Blenkinsopp's concern to locate a cultic sanctuary there. Within the context of the passage, Bethel sends a delegation to Jerusalem for

---

[38] Some Greek MSS and the Ethiopic version read 'from Bethel'.

[39] Bethel as the adverbial accusative occurs also in Judg. 20: 18, 26, 31; 21: 2; 2 Kgs. 2: 2, 23; 10: 29; 23: 4; Hos. 12: 5; Amos 4: 4. For a discussion, see *Genesius' Hebrew Grammar* (ed. and enlarged by E. Kautzsch, 2nd English edn. by A. E. Cowley; Oxford: Clarendon Press, 1910), 118d–g. There could be another explanation for the misplacement of the adverbial accusative, but the likelihood of its being misplaced is not very great. Furthermore, in the context of Zech. 1–8, the passage more appropriately illustrates the reinstatement of the authority of the temple of Jerusalem for religious matters.

[40] A place name can connote its inhabitants (Judg. 12: 5; Amos 5: 5). In addition, v. 3 suggests that the place is the temple (House of Yahweh) by referring to the priests operating there during the construction of the temple.

[41] Ackroyd, *Exile and Restoration*, 206–9; Meyers and Meyers, *Zechariah 1–8*, 382; Hoffman, 'The Fasts in the Book of Zechariah', 200–2.

a priestly ruling. Set within Zechariah 1–8, this narrative sequence contributes to the overall portrait of the centrality of Jerusalem as the place where Yahweh is to be sought by all nations (Zech. 8: 20–3).[42] Moreover, it strongly suggests that the scene functions to re-establish the religious authority of Jerusalem. Though not overt, Zechariah 7: 2 hints that Bethel functioned as a religious centre before the period of the early return. The inclusion of Bethel rather than Mizpah confirms this suggestion. During the Templeless period, Mizpah functioned as an administrative centre, yet the delegation did not depart from Mizpah, but Bethel. The inclusion of Bethel in a passage about a religious matter confirms a religious connection. Hence the delegation departs from Bethel, the location of religious authority during the Templeless period, to have a ritual matter adjudicated in Jerusalem. If correct, this interpretation supports Blenkinsopp's argument regarding the importance of Bethel as a cultic centre during this period. Though Jeremiah 41: 5 cannot be used to support Blenkinsopp's argument, several factors support the view that a sanctuary was established at Bethel to provide an avenue for religious observance: (1) the veiled association of Bethel with matters of a religious nature in Zechariah 7: 2, (2) Bethel featuring prominently as a sacred site in literature of the time, and (3) the likelihood that religious ritual would have accompanied the installation of a provincial administration.

A text that stems from the early Second Temple period potentially supports a ritual site at Bethel during the sixth century.[43] In the midst of an invective against an anonymous woman, the accusation is made in Isaiah 57: 7 that:

על הר גבה ונשא שמת משכבך
גם שם עלית לזבח זבח:

Upon a high and lofty mountain you (2fs) have made your bed. You (2fs) have even gone up there to offer a sacrifice.

---

[42] N. Allen, 'The Identity of the Jerusalem Priesthood During the Exile', *HeyJ* 23 (1982), 263–4.

[43] This passage is dealt with more fully in the context of an examination of the way in which the temple functions in Isaiah 56–66 in J. A. Middlemas, 'Divine Reversal and the Role of the Temple in Trito-Isaiah', in J. Day (ed.), *Temple and Worship in Biblical Israel: Proceedings of the Oxford Old Testament Seminar* (JSOTSup; London and New York: T & T Clark International, 2005).

מִשְׁכָּבֵךְ MT 'your bed'. In a passage in which one image used to portray idolatrous worship is that of a sexually deviant woman, *mškb* should have its normal meaning, contra T. J. Lewis, *Cults of the Dead in ancient Israel and Ugarit* (HSM, 39; Atlanta, Ga.: Scholars Press, 1989), 149–51, who relates it to a grave, and P. D. Hanson, *Dawn of Apocalyptic* (Philadelphia, Pa.: Fortress Press, 1975), 199–200, who understands a veiled allusion to the temple mount and thus reads *mškn*.

Although anonymous, the woman who climbs the mountain is one and the same as the unnamed mother of transgressing children in verse 3 who is characterized as sexually deviant. As noted already in Chapter 2, the description clearly associates her behaviour as well as that of her sons with idolatry. In the prophetic rhetoric, the poem denounces the observance of practices incompatible with Yahwism and includes in the condemnation the location of those practices at the wadis (Isa. 57: 5–6) and a vague allusion to a mountain referred to only as the one that is 'high and lifted up'.

Because the main concern with the poem has lain with issues of redaction and the underlying religious milieu, most commentators assume that the nameless woman as well as the mountain are Jerusalem. In distinction, Beuken and Ackerman, apparently independently, actually examine the identity of the woman. They provide arguments in favour of associating her and the mountain with Jerusalem and the temple mount.[44] It will be shown that the woman and the site in Isaiah 57 do not represent Zion and the temple but another location of ritual practice.

Beuken devotes considerable attention to supporting his contention that Zion is the referent here in an examination of the identity of the woman and the mountain. Through an association of passages aligned by the repetition of key words, he concludes that the woman is Jerusalem and the mountain is the temple mount. In his view, Isaiah 1: 21; 40: 9 and chapter 47 illuminate Isaiah 57: 7. In a scene similar to 57: 7, Jerusalem in 40: 9 is told to climb a high hill to declare that the

---

[44] W. A. M. Beuken, 'Isaiah 56.9–57.13: An Example of the Isaianic Legacy of Trito-Isaiah', in J. W. van Henten *et al.* (eds.), *Tradition and Re-Interpretation in Jewish and Early Christian Literature: Essays in Honor of Jürgen C. H. Lebram* (Studia post-Biblica, 36; Leiden: Brill, 1986). Ackerman, *Under Every Green Tree*, 113–16. Cf. Hanson, *Dawn of Apocalyptic*, 198–200; P. A. Smith, *Rhetoric and Redaction in Trito-Isaiah: The Structure, Growth and Authorship of Isaiah 56–66* (SVT, 62; Leiden: Brill, 1995), 85–6.

predicted divine intervention is about to take place. She is Jerusalem who climbs a mountain, but her attributes of sorcery, adultery, and harlotry associate her in Beuken's interpretation with the figure of Babylon personified as a woman condemned in chapter 47. Condemned to destruction like mother/daughter Babylon, the mountain climbed by the woman in Isaiah 57 becomes the antithesis of the holy mountain of Yahweh spoken of in 57: 13b. According to this analysis, the depravity of Jerusalem is confirmed by Isaiah 1: 21, where the prophet laments, 'How the faithful city has become a harlot.' When Beuken collates these texts, he concludes that the nation represented by the city personified as a harlot brings sacrifices and offerings to a mountain that in spite of being presented as a contrast to Mount Zion is nevertheless that which was at one time the holy mountain of the deity. He concludes: 'The woman addressed, the adulterous Zion, does not climb the mountain as a herald of good tidings to announce God's arrival (40: 9), but she climbs the holy mountain of YAHWEH in order to bring there to her lovers, the gods, offerings in adultery (57: 7).'[45]

Beuken's argument, though intricately crafted, is problematic at several key junctures. The fact that texts can be associated by the repetition of key words or expressions does not necessitate that they subsequently refer to the same situation.[46] In fact, his evidence actually implies the opposite of that which he concluded. The condemned woman who participates in a variety of unacceptable worship practices in verses 6–13 and the mountain of verses 7–8 are being consciously contrasted with Zion. In the first place, a contrast exists between Yahweh, who is described in a variety of terms having to do with height, and other things that are raised up against him to be brought low in the wider material of Trito-Isaiah and the book of Isaiah. For instance, in the same chapter, the prophet distinguishes between the mountain described as high and lifted up גבה ונשׂא in 57: 7 and the Lord who is high and lofty רם ונשׂא 57: 15 (cf. 6: 1; 33: 10; 49: 22).[47] The mountain in verse 7 must be a mountain that

[45] Beuken, 'Isaiah 56.9–57.13', 53.

[46] Polan, *In the Ways of Justice*, 162–3, discusses the use of word play. His summary is helpful, 'This style of paronomasia creates a sense of ambiguity, *for a single word either carries more than one connotation or its uses display contrasting situations*, yet by their common root, these words stand in relationship with one another.' (Italics added.)

[47] Smith, *Rhetoric and Redaction*, 68–71, and Polan, *In the Ways of Justice*, argue well for the extension of the poetic unit through v. 21.

takes the place of the true worship of Yahweh, thus eliciting the divine protest in 57: 11, 'Whom did you dread and fear that you lied and did not remember me?' Furthermore, the woman and her transgressing children in verses 3–13a have no part in the redemption offered in 57: 13b. In 13b, the prophet speaks only of a singular male figure, clearly excluding the woman and the plural male addressees of verses 3–4; 'The one who takes refuge in me will possess the land, so that he may inherit my holy mountain.'[48] The prophet clearly distinguishes between a condemned group and a righteous remnant in 65: 11, where he singles out for denunciation a separate group participating in unacceptable religious practices, by turning to them with ואתם. There the prophet chastises them for having abandoned Yahweh and having forgotten his holy mountain, that is, Mount Zion.

Just as the mountain cannot be the temple mount, the woman cannot be Zion who ascends the mountain to sing praises about her deity as in 40: 9. Not only is there no salvation for this woman (note the change in person back to third masculine singular between 13a and 13b where the salvation oracle is pronounced), the mountain which she ascends is unparalleled anywhere else in the Isaianic material! The fact that the text most similar to 57: 6–13 is the one in which Babylon as a wife, mother, and sorceress is condemned for her haughty mockery of God (ch. 47) is surely telling. Beuken's analysis of 56: 9–57: 13 logically leads to the opposite conclusion from the one he draws. The contrast between Zion and the unnamed woman can be further substantiated. In two other oracles in which a feminine person is directly addressed, she is called Zion (60: 14; 62: 11; // Jerusalem 62: 1). Elsewhere the prophet refers to Zion on four occasions *always* in the context of salvation (59: 20; 61: 3; 66: 7–8, 10–13), although once the sorry state of Jerusalem is used in a lament to encourage the deity to intervene (64: 9). Furthermore, it is exactly the anonymous status of the woman that discourages any association with Zion. The emphasis in the prophetic oracles lies with the renaming of the city of Jerusalem in Yahweh's restoration (62: 3, 12). Because an anonymous figure cannot be renamed, it is unlikely that she represents the city. Finally, Trito-Isaiah stresses the rapidly approaching glorification of

---

[48] Schramm, *The Opponents of Third Isaiah*, 132, understands the passage similarly.

Jerusalem. It would certainly be unusual for the prophet to denigrate and condemn to judgement the woman and mountain of Isaiah 57: 3–13 if they represented Jerusalem. Instead, the anonymous woman, her sons, and the mountain represent all those things destined for condemnation and destruction when Yahweh intervenes to bring about the salvation predicted by Deutero-Isaiah and Isaiah 60–2. At that time, the deity shall glorify Jerusalem.

Just as the practitioners of illicit cultic rituals in Trito-Isaiah are contrasted with the deity and that which meets his approval in Isaiah 57, in the wider tradition of Isaiah, the theme of the eminence of Yahweh contrasts with that of earthly things raised up. In chapter 2, which introduces concepts important throughout the collection, for example, the editor portrays the period of restoration as one of conflicting fates—between renewal for selected individuals and doom for the other.[49] Isaiah predicts that concomitant with the exaltation of the deity, the prestige of the temple mount will be elevated (2: 2). In conjunction with the exaltation of Yahweh and his holy mountain all things raised up in distinction or defiance of the deity will be brought low. Included among those things destined for decline are the haughty eyes of humankind עיני גבהות אדם, the pride of humankind רום אנשים (2: 11), all that is proud, haughty and lofty כל גאה ורם ועל כל נשא (2: 12), even the high and lofty cedars of Lebanon כל ארזי הלבנון הרמים והנשאים (2: 13), all the high mountains כל ההרים הרמים, lofty hills הגבעות הנשאות (2: 14), every high tower כל מגדל גבה (2: 15), and finally concluding with that with which the contrasting invective began, the haughtiness and pride of humankind גבהות האדם and רום אנשים (2: 17). The thrust of Isaiah 57: 3–13 set within the context of oracles dated to the early Second Temple period and within the collection of Isaianic oracles as a whole insists that everything raised up in distinction to Yahweh and in opposition to the deity's holy mountain will be brought low. The high and lofty mountain of 57: 7 where the observance of condemned rituals takes place cannot be the holy mountain of Yahweh. It is more likely that it represents another cultic site where religious rituals took place.

---

[49] H. G. M. Williamson, *The Book Called Isaiah: Deutero-Isaiah's Role in Composition and Redaction* (Oxford: Clarendon Press, 1994), 143–54; M. A. Sweeney, *Isaiah 1–4 and the Post-Exilic Understanding of the Isaianic Tradition* (BZAW, 171; Berlin: de Gruyter, 1988).

Through a slightly different approach, Ackerman advances two points in favour of an association between Jerusalem and the woman and the temple mount. With Hanson,[50] she regards the bed משכב as a veiled reference to a sanctuary משכן. She supports this association because a door and doorpost (Isa. 57: 8a) are features more consistent with a shrine than a bed. Additionally, she highlights three expressions that lend support to her contention: (1) הר גבה elsewhere always refers to the temple mount, (2) the use of נשא in conjunction with the high hill/mountain, and (3) the appearance of the holy mountain of Yahweh הר קדשי in 57: 13. In response to Ackerman, the association of the mountain with the temple mount is not clear even from her analysis. Even if verse 7 alludes to the משכן, it more commonly refers to the tabernacle in use before the temple was built, but it is also used of the sanctuary in Shiloh (Ps. 78: 60) and of general habitation (Isa. 22: 16).[51] A sanctuary may be in view, but it does not have to be the temple mount. Furthermore, although הר גבה may refer to the temple mount elsewhere, the הר גבה ונשא never does. Since the prophetic indictment of verses 7–10 highlights the extent to which the woman is willing to go in her abandonment of Yahweh, the mountain more naturally refers to a cultic site established in distinction to the holy mountain of verse 13. The identification of the high and lofty mountain of 57: 7 has obscured the polemical intention of the passage.

The association of the mountain with sacrifices considered by some to be incompatible with the proper worship of Yahweh features in a section about the extent to which a woman is willing to go in her abandonment of acceptable Yahweh worship (Isa. 57: 7–10). The high and lofty mountain she climbs functions within this segment of the poem to show that she even makes sacrifices at a cultic place that is not the temple mount. Although the site remains anonymous, its description as a place where sacrifices were made and as a mountain raised up in distinction to Mount Zion suggests that it is the location of regular ritual. It is not surprising that the name of an alternative place of regular religious practice was obscured by the

---

[50] Hanson, *Dawn of Apocalyptic*, 199–200.
[51] M. Haran, *Temples and Temple Service in ancient Israel: An Inquiry into the Character of Cult Phenomena and the Historical Setting of the Priestly School* (Oxford: Clarendon Press, 1978), 14 n. 3.

biblical writers. A similar obfuscation occurred in the Zecharaiah 7: 2 passage. It was not in the interest of a community which believed the only legitimate sanctuary to be that of Jerusalem to refer specifically to another location of religious ritual. The ambiguous reference to a condemned cultic site by part of the early return community could be a direct assault on a sanctuary at Bethel operative during the Templeless period. The likelihood is increased by the fact that the mountain in 57: 7 is not Mount Zion. A measure of support for this comes from the description of Bethel on two occasions as Mount Bethel הר בית אל (Josh. 16: 1; 1 Sam. 13: 2). Just as the mountain cannot be the temple mount, the woman is not Jerusalem. Instead, she represents only that part of the community that continues to participate in worship not considered Yahwistic in some circles.

The preceding argument has shown that a plausible referent for the anonymous mountain in Isaiah 57: 7 is Bethel. Lest it be confused with a previous argument on Isaiah 57: 5–6, it is important to understand the role played by 57: 7–10 in its larger unit (Isa. 57: 3–13). An anonymous woman climbed an unspecified mountain established as an alternative to Yahweh's holy mountain in order to offer sacrifices. The passage in which this occurs is focused on the extent the accused is willing to go in the abandonment of Yahweh. The reference to child sacrifice occurs in a separate stanza (vv. 5–6) and locates those practices in the wadis and under the clefts of the cliffs. The emphasis in verses 7–10 is on the length of the journey (cf. v. 10) and that the way chosen by the woman leads to an end that is not sanctioned nor blessed by the deity. Considering the belief in some circles of the centrality of the Jerusalem temple, the establishment of another site for worship during the Templeless period would be considered wrongful behaviour, akin to that which brought about the catastrophe of 587 in the first place. The worship of a deity of child sacrifice, condemned in verses 5–6, is being associated with other foul deeds, such as worship at another cultic sanctuary (vv. 7–8), but not necessarily located there. It would not be tenable to hold, therefore, that child sacrifice took place at Bethel. The stanzas of verses 5–6 and 7–10 refer to two separate instances of wrongful cultic behaviour, but have been placed together to highlight the future destruction of certain members of society. This interpretation is akin to Leviticus 20: 2–5 especially verse 3: 'I myself will set my face against them, and will cut them off from the people, because they have given of their offspring to Molek, defiling my sanctuary and profaning my holy name.' On this McKay's understanding is instructive: 'The immediate implication of this text is that the cult was practised at a Yahweh-shrine, but it could also be that the expression is little more than a pietistic description of the perversion of Yahwism by those who remained worshippers of the god of Israel and also took part in the Molech cult.'[52] McKay understands that either a site of Yahweh worship is being condemned as the place of child sacrifice or the practitioners of such a cult are doomed. With reference to Isaiah 57, it is possible to suggest that a site of worship is being denounced rather than the people. The conjoining of child sacrifice to a sanctuary at Bethel would represent a literary strategy that has no basis in reality.

The joining of verses 5–6 with its denunciation of child sacrifice to 7–10 with its condemnation of a cultic site, probably Bethel, heightens the invective against an operative sanctuary outside of Jerusalem. Child sacrifice was considered the most abominable ritual practice by the biblical writers. Its placement in a passage castigating the abandonment of Yahweh through ritual practice at another site functions like the conflation of Baal and Molek, to dissuade the use of the site. To those who offered sacrifices at Bethel during the Templeless period, their offerings represented acceptable Yahwistic practice. During the period of the reconstruction of the second temple, that sanctuary would be condemned in the strongest language possible. This explains the utilization of fertility language which does not signify the actual practice of fertility rituals and also why there are veiled allusions to journeying to Molek and Sheol in verse 9. The Judahites during the period without a temple would have considered the veneration of their deity at another sanctuary appropriate. During the rebuilding of the temple or soon thereafter, such an attitude was not possible. Just as the prophets of the early Second Temple period reasserted the centrality of Jerusalem, Trito-Isaiah in Isaiah 57: 3–13 reasserts the authority of the Jerusalem temple, the 'holy mountain' of verse 13, by showing that those who worship elsewhere choose their own end which leads to death.

---

[52] J. W. McKay, *Religion in Judah under the Assyrians 732–609 BC* (SBT 2/26; London: SCM Press, 1976), 106 n. 104.

It seems likely that Bethel functioned as a centre of regular religious activity during the years of the Mizpah administration.[53] A cultic institution at Bethel would require the presence of priests to officiate over the rituals. The Neo-Babylonians primarily deported temple personnel from Jerusalem. It is plausible that among the poor people of the land, the vinedressers and ploughmen, rural priests were also left to provide religious guidance in the Templeless period. These rural priests would be of Levitical descent who were made redundant during Josiah's reforms and the centralization of cultic practices in Jerusalem.[54] During the sixth century, they would have the opportunity to participate in, if not lead, ritual practices among the temple ruins. The priesthood that officiated at the shrine could be identified with the Aaronites long associated with the sacred site at Bethel.[55] Whereas the ruins of the Jerusalem temple were probably used for sporadic observances, a sanctuary at Bethel would have had a fully operative altar complete with temple personnel. This context potentially clarifies the sincere proposal to aid temple construction by the northern delegation in Ezra 4, who say that they had been sacrificing continually to Yahweh since the time of their arrival under Esar-haddon in the eighth century (Ezra 4: 2).

The examination of a number of biblical clues about worship at the Jerusalem temple and another site in the Benjamin region reveals that it is possible to locate the observance of spontaneous and regular mourning rituals at the site of the temple ruins and at a sanctuary at Bethel.

JUDAHITE NATIONAL LAMENTS?

General scholarly consensus associates the implementation of national public fasts with worship during the Templeless period. Indeed, certain lament psalms and the book of Lamentations are

[53] The location of Bethel as the site of regular ritual observance need not preclude the existence of sanctuaries at other sites in the Benjamin region.
[54] Allen, 'The Identity of the Jerusalem Priesthood'.
[55] T. J. Meek, 'Aaronites and Zadokites', *AJSLL* 45 (1929); F. S. North, 'Aaron's Rise in Prestige', *ZAW* 66 (1954); H. G. Judge, 'Aaron, Zadok and Abiathar', *JTS* ns 7 (1956); Blenkinsopp, 'The Judaean Priesthood'; *idem*, 'Bethel'.

thought to have their *Sitz im Leben* in communal fasts called to commemorate the events that took place around the collapse of Jerusalem. Traditionally in ancient Israel, public fasts were called in conjunction with political or natural disasters.[56] Ferris, for instance, has considered the second part of Solomon's temple dedication prayer in 1 Kings 8 indicatively as a way to ascertain services which accompanied national disasters in ancient Israel. He found that situations in which such prayer might be appropriate include a defeat in battle (vv. 33–4), a drought (vv. 35–6) or other natural disasters (vv. 37–45), and forced deportation (vv. 46–50).[57]

Because public mourning ritual is thought to have evolved in the land some time after the catastrophe of 587, many commentators regard certain communal laments to have taken place at the Jerusalem temple. Laments of the individual or the community traceable to this setting are found in the Psalter and the book of Lamentations. Laments commonly associated with sixth-century Judah include Psalms 44, 74, 79, 89, 102, 106,[58] the book of Lamentations (although not always in its entirety), Isaiah 63: 7–64: 11, and Nehemiah 9.[59]

---

[56] H. Gunkel and J. Begrich, *Einleitung in die Psalmen: Die Gattungen der religiösen Lyrik Israels* (Göttingen: Vandenhoeck & Ruprecht, 1933), 177–89. The German has never been translated into English, but an accessible version exists in H. Gunkel, *The Psalms: A Form-Critical Introduction* (BS, 19; Philadelphia, Pa.: Fortress Press, 1967). Cf. S. Mowinckel, *The Psalms in Israel's Worship*, i (Sheffield: JSOT Press, repr. 1992), 193–5; Ferris, *The Genre of Communal Lament*, 78–84, 105–6.

[57] Ferris, *The Genre of Communal Lament*, 106–8. Cf. Joel.

[58] Psalm 106 does not contain the three elements of a lament form: lament, profession of trust, and petition. Instead, it contains a lengthy historical recital that showcases the saving deeds of Yahweh on behalf of his covenant people and their repeated failures. It is a completely different genre more akin to a penitential prayer, and though it may belong to this period, it deserves separate treatment. It is thought to stem from the *Golah* because of references to the exile in v. 41, the captivity in v. 46, and the ingathering from the nations (v. 47). It has, however, been associated with communal laments that might have their *Sitz im Leben* at the ruins of the temple in Jerusalem by H. G. M. Williamson, 'Laments at the Destroyed Temple', *BRev* 4/4 (1990), 12–17, 44.

[59] H. G. M. Williamson, 'Structure and Historiography in Nehemiah 9', *Proceedings of the Ninth World Congress of Jewish Studies* (Jerusalem: Magnes Press, 1985), 117–31, includes the penitential prayer in Neh. 9 among literature of the Templeless period. M. J. Boda, *Praying the Tradition: The Origin and Use of Tradition in Nehemiah 9* (BZAW, 277; Berlin: de Gruyter, 1999), argues for a Second Temple date. There are certain aspects of the Psalm that suggest it might be placed in Templeless Judah, but a better understanding of the themes typical of Judah would provide a means to adjudicate the discrepancy.

Only the laments most commonly associated with the Templeless period will be considered here, Psalms 74, 79, 89, 102,[60] and Isaiah 63: 7–64: 11. The differences of Psalm 106 and Nehemiah 9 in form and function as well as the imprecise historical references of Psalm 44 exclude them from this analysis.[61] The book of Lamentations will be discussed in the next chapter. In form, all, except Psalm 102, deserve to be included among the communal laments even though Psalm 89 arguably represents a mixed form.[62] In terms of historical referents, communal laments describe a situation in a less stylized way than their individual counterparts and are more clearly associated with national disasters. The prayers of complaint included here refer to the desecration of the temple (Pss. 74, 79), the desolation of Judah (Isa. 63: 7–64: 11), the loss of the Davidic king (Ps. 89), and the ruination of Jerusalem (Ps. 102).

By and large, the laments attributed to Templeless Judah correspond to complaints of the people. The laments have a fairly consistent form. Gunkel's original three characteristic formal components of this genre[63]—the lament, the prayer of petition, and the certainty of a hearing—were expanded into five by Westermann, who included an address to God, lament, turning towards God, a petition, and a vow of praise.[64] By attributing more explicit purpose to the various lines, Ferris further delineates eight characteristic features: an invocation, hymn of praise, expression of confidence and trust, lament, appeal, and motivation for divine response, protest of innocence, expression of confidence and hope, and vow of praise.[65] The laments typically located in Templeless Judah have in common three basic formal components that correspond to those outlined by Gunkel: the lament, the confession of trust, and an appeal.[66] The

---

[60] Janssen, *Juda in der Exilszeit*, 19–20.

[61] It could very well respond to any military defeat of a king in the monarchic period. So, also, P. C. Craigie, *Psalms 1–50* (WBC, 19; Waco, Tex.: Word Books, 1983), 332–3.

[62] Gunkel and Begrich, *Einleitung in die Psalmen*, 117, 125–9, 140–71.

[63] Ibid., i. 35–6.

[64] C. Westermann, *Praise and Lament in the Psalms* (Atlanta, Ga.: John Knox Press, 1981), 52–81.

[65] Ferris, *The Genre of Communal Lament*, 91–2.

[66] Ferris, *The Genre of Communal Lament*, 93, 110–36. As his chart on p. 93 shows the communal laments attributed to the Templeless period do not evidence all these

lament section describes at variable length an event that has had dire consequences for the nation such as a military defeat, the death of a king, or the destruction of the temple. The confession of trust provides reasons for the deity to intervene in the present distress by focusing especially on divine power exhibited in mythical or historical actions in the past. This section corresponds loosely to Gunkel's 'confidence of being heard' in that it serves as the axis of the poem by indicating reasons to believe that the lament will be answered and in so doing provides the grounds for the appeal. The appeal corresponds to what is lamented. Through it the community petitions the deity to come to the nation's rescue. Because in many respects the lament and appeal are aligned, it is within the confessions of trust that the community attributes its understanding of the deity. As we will see the traditions used in this section show a remarkable amount of diversity that makes an attribution to a single setting difficult.

The formal elements of a lament relate to its function. In the Psalms, there is a 'formfulness' in the expression of grief such that it moves through orientation from disorientation to reorientation.[67] The lament itself corresponds to disorientation, that situation that disrupted the present Yahweh-run world order. The confession or profession of trust orients the community through an understanding of its deity and the power evidenced in his past actions throughout the cosmos and human sphere. Finally, reorientation corresponds to an appeal which believes fundamentally that Yahweh will hear the distress and act imminently. The lament and the appeal are often closely aligned. The real heart of the psalm occurs in the situation of orientation, that is, in the confession of trust. Westermann's understanding of the confession of trust as the re-presentation of history has been enriched by the studies of Clifford and Broyles. As part of a larger study on Psalm 89, Clifford examines the use of certain

elements. Only three occur in all of the communal laments: (1) direct address to the deity, (2) the complaint/lament, and (3) an appeal for divine assistance.

[67] I have borrowed this terminology from W. Brueggemann, 'Psalms in the Life of Faith: A Suggested Typology of Function', *JSOT* 17 (1980); *idem*, 'From Hurt to Joy, From Death to Life', *Int* 28 (1974); *idem*, 'The Formfulness of Grief', *Int* 31 (1977). All articles are reprinted in W. Brueggemann, *The Psalms and the Life of Faith* (Minneapolis, Minn.: Fortress Press, 1995).

themes in psalms of the same genre (Pss. 44, 74, 77, 80).[68] He makes two significant observations relating to themes found in the confessions of trust. The first is that the psalmist chooses certain myths of the deity's past actions appropriate to the problem of the present crisis. In his view, Psalm 74 with its lamentation over the desecration of the temple appeals to traditions about creation and the procession to the shrine in a hymnic recital. Secondly, he shows how the placement of the re-presentation of history varies between the psalms. Similarly, Broyles, after an extensive study on the form categories of the lament genre, concludes that specific motifs are utilized in relation to certain situations.[69] In his estimation, when the lament focuses on the inactivity of the deity, a recital answers with an emphasis on the activity of Yahweh in the past. For Broyles, too, there is a correspondence between what is lamented and the tradition appealed to in the confession of trust. The contribution of certain constituent themes especially come to light in the confessions of trust which invoke mythological and historical motifs in order to claim the power of Yahweh in the past as a means to recall it in the present in order to invite divine restoration in the future.

It is not the purpose of this thesis to argue for the historical setting of certain laments that have been attributed to Templeless Judah. Rather, I simply follow the majority opinion in the association of these psalms to sixth-century Judah.[70] It is significant that apart from the analyses of Klein and Williamson, there has been no concerted study of what thought is pertinent to Judah or how it would be developed in a different way than that of the Babylonian community. In his study of Psalms from the 'exilic' period, Klein understood that the idea of kingship divorced from the Exodus motif indicated a Judahite provenance because the concept of the new Exodus was so prevalent in *Golah* literature of the time.[71] By way of contrast,

---

[68] R. J. Clifford, 'Psalm 89: A Lament over the Davidic Ruler's Continued Failure', *HTR* 73 (1980), 37–40.

[69] C. C. Broyles, *The Conflict of Faith and Experience in the Psalms: A Form-Critical and Theological Study* (JSOTSup, 52; Sheffield: JSOT Press, 1989).

[70] R. S. Watson, 'The Theme of "Chaos" in the Psalter: A Reassessment' (D.Phil. thesis, University of Oxford, 2001), 130–71, has recently argued for the dating of several of the psalms to this period, including 74 and 89. I refer the reader to her thorough discussion.

[71] R. W. Klein, 'A Theology for Exiles: The Kingship of Yahweh', *Dialog* 17 (1978), 128–34.

Williamson has devoted a number of short studies to thought pertinent to lament liturgy from Judah.[72] In his attribution of a distinct category of laments in which an historical recital is combined with a confession of sin, he finds three elements indicative of a Judahite provenance: (1) the Babylonian conquest is considered one of many disasters to have taken place in the land with rare or no mention of the deportation of citizenry, (2) the appearance of concerns with situations especially pertinent to a setting in the land such as the destruction of the temple and the loss of sovereignty over the land and its produce, and (3) the lack of a request for specific future divine intervention.

The lament literature normally associated with Judah exhibits a wide variety of ideas, sometimes complementary and sometimes not. Since the confession of trust responds directly to the lament, the most accessible means of analysing lament literature is through the statements about orientation—to what does the community appeal in its movement from despair to petition? An analysis of the lament psalms attributed to the period reveals a significant amount of divergence in terms of language.

THE PSALMS: THEOLOGICAL MOTIFS

The laments associated with this time period show a great deal of variety in the types of images utilized in the confession of trust. Following a close study of a psalm associated with the Templeless period that elicits no true confession of trust (Ps. 79), the laments have been divided into sections based on the types of material present in an assertion of confidence. These sections ground the speaker's faith in past actions of Yahweh either in myth (Ps. 74) or in history (Isa. 63: 7–64: 11) or in a combination of the two elements (Pss. 89, 102) and provide a basis for the belief in future assistance from the deity.[73]

[72] Williamson, 'Structure and Historiography in Nehemiah 9'; *idem*, 'Laments at the Destroyed Temple'; *idem*, 'Isaiah 63,7–64,11: Exilic Lament or Post-Exilic Protest?', *ZAW* 102 (1990).

[73] In all the laments, the verse numbers in the analysis correspond to the Masoretic text, which in certain cases diverges from that of translations of the Bible.

No Confession of Trust: Psalm 79—A Lament for the People Despised by the Nations

On the basis of historical references alone Psalm 79, along with Psalm 74, has the greatest claim to belong to this period. It contains a short lament (vv. 1–5) followed by a series of petitions entreating the deity to vindicate the distressed community (vv. 6–13).[74] During the lament, the people agonize over the invasion of the land by foreigners, the defilement, if not the destruction of the temple,[75] the ruination of Jerusalem (v. 1), the slaughter of its inhabitants (vv. 2–3), and their subsequent disgrace (v. 4). Usually discussed in conjunction with Psalm 74, 79 deserves separate treatment because of the differences in the formulaic elements utilized between the two. Psalm 79 lacks a confession of trust which sets it apart from all the other national laments attributed to this time period with the exception of Psalm 137.[76] The lament of verses 1–5 moves directly into an appeal for divine assistance (vv. 6–12) and concludes with a vow of praise (v. 13) without a separate recital of Yahweh's past actions on behalf of the people. The series of petitions respond directly to the

---

[74] C. A. Briggs, *A Critical and Exegetical Commentary on the Book of Psalms*, ii (ICC; Edinburgh: T & T Clark, repr. 1951), 150–1; H.-J. Kraus, *Die Psalmen*, ii (BKAT, 15; Neukirchen-Vluyn: Neukirchener Verlag, 3rd edn. 1966), 97; A. A. Anderson, *Psalms*, ii (NCB; London: Oliphants, 1972), 538; A. Weiser, *Die Psalmen*, ii (ATD, 15; Göttingen: Vandenhoeck & Ruprecht, 1950), 518; M. E. Tate, *Psalms 51–100* (WBC, 20: Dallas: Word Books, 1990), 298–9. Later dates are not generally accepted, e.g. M. Buttenwieser, *The Psalms* (Chicago, Ill.: University of Chicago Press, 1938), 609–12; J. Morgenstern, 'Jerusalem—485 B.C.', *HUCA* 27 (1956), 126–30; W. O. E. Oesterley, 'Question of Maccabaean Psalms', in *Psalms* (London: SPCK, 1939), i. 67–73; idem, *Psalms*, ii. 364. On the difficulty with positing psalms to the Maccabean period after the discovery of the Dead Sea scrolls, see P. R. Ackroyd, 'Criteria for the Maccabean Dating of Old Testament Literature', *VT* 3 (1953).

[75] טמאו את־היכל קדשך 'They defiled your holy temple' is often not thought to include the destruction of the temple. However, the three images in v. 1 of the enemies entering the land, desecrating the temple, then destroying Jerusalem, shows an escalation in the violence which concludes with the complete annihilation of the city which would naturally include the temple. So, also, B. Weber, 'Zur Datierung der Asaph Psalms 74 und 79', *Bib* 81 (2000), 529.

[76] Ferris, *The Genre of Communal Lament*, 93, aligns Ps. 79 with Pss. 69 and 109, which have a vow of praise, cf. 80, 83, 142, which contain only the elements lament and appeal.

cries of complaint in verses 1–5.⁷⁷ Because the nations have disgraced Israel (v. 1), the people cry out for divine vengeance on the nations. Their appeal to the deity has three main sections,

- A call for vengeance on the nations גוים because of what they have done (vv. 6–7)
- A prayer that Yahweh not hold the sins of ancestors against the people, but save them (vv. 8–9 in an a–b–b'–a' structure)
- A prayer that Yahweh requite the nations/neighbours משכנים/גוים for their mockery (vv. 10, 12) and redeem his own people (v. 11, the heart of an a–b–a' structure corresponding to the verses)

The appeal correlates to the prayer of distress that focuses on the supremacy of the nations. What is missing in the lament is a separate focus on some aspect of the deity.

The lack of a clear confession of trust does not preclude communal belief in the power of Yahweh to act, because throughout the lament the poet correlates the honour of the deity to that of the people. Expressions like Jacob (v. 7), servants (vv. 2, 10), holy ones (v. 2), your people (v. 13), and the sheep of your pasture (v. 13) found within the psalm identify the lamenters as the chosen ones of Yahweh.⁷⁸ In addition, the repetition of 'your' attributing to Yahweh all the things destroyed including the inheritance of the land, the temple, servants, and faithful ones (vv. 1–2), emphasizes the concept of election, one of the themes associated with the Zion traditions.⁷⁹ The fundamental belief in a close relationship with the deity, even in election, explains to some degree the odd turn to praise in verse 13. Moreover, the fate of the community is linked to the divine reputation. The divine name (v. 9, twice) and reputation (v. 12) have been compromised through the derision (v. 4) and abuse (v. 2, 3, 11) of the chosen people. In verses 10 and 12 the two come together as one idea, as an intertwined unit whereby the nations question the power and might of Yahweh because of the bloodshed of his people, his servants, 'Why should the nations say, "Where is their God?" Let the

---

77. R. L. Cole, The *Shape and Message of Book III (Psalms 73–89)* (JSOTSup, 307; Sheffield: Sheffield Academic Press, 2000), 78–9.
78. W. M. Schniedewind, 'Are We His People or Not? Biblical Interpretation During Crisis', *Bib* 76 (1995), 545–56.
79. Broyles, *The Conflict of Faith and Experience*, 114.

vindication of the bloodshed of your servants be known among the nations before our eyes,' and 'Return sevenfold into the bosom of our neighbours the taunts with which they have taunted you, Adonai.' The conjoining of the circumstances of the people and the reputation of their deity finds its theological basis in the name-theology prevalent in the Deuteronomic formulation[80] or the emphasis on the vindication of the divine reputation in Ezekiel—both of which find their surest expression in literature of the *Golah*.[81]

The desecration of the holy temple, the loss of the land, and the consequent fate of the people of Judah became a problem for the honour of Yahweh. The appeal, thus, erupts spontaneously to indicate the reasons why the community believes that their deity will intervene. The lack of a separate prayer to delineate the basis for belief in the sure intervention of the deity suggests something about either the dating of the psalm or its intention. Like Psalm 137 with its immediate shift from lament to a cry for revenge, Psalm 79 moves from lament to appeal. The blunt, at times caustic, expression of grief and anger perhaps indicates that psalms of this time period without a confession of trust originated soon after the disaster of 587 before a concerted effort was taken to develop a theological interpretation of that event. Or the lack of an explicit section describing the portrayal of divine power in the past could also imply that the people were so certain of an answer to prayer that motivations or reminders to the deity were not felt to be necessary. In any event, a variety of traditions informs the language of the psalm and thus the belief in divine salvation, such as election from Zion theology, the efficacy of the name from Deuteronomic theology, and the vindication of the divine reputation as in Ezekiel, but they do not do so in isolation from the lament and appeal.

Mythological Recital: Psalm 74—A Lament for the Destroyed Temple

Alongside Psalm 79, Psalm 74 gains the most support for a placement in the Templeless period. Psalm 74 contains a lengthy section of

[80] So, also, Weber, 'Zur Datierung', 528–30, 531–2.
[81] Morgenstern, 'Jerusalem', 120–7, already noted that the emphasis on Yahweh's reputation aligned the thought of this psalm with that of Ezekiel.

lament (vv. 1–11) that includes various details that are suggestive of the destruction of Jerusalem, the temple, and its environs in 587.[82] That the psalm contains an almost singular concern with the ruined temple has been especially noted. Indeed, references to 'Mount Zion' (v. 2) and 'the perpetual ruins'[83] (v. 3a) are specifically related to the temple which is referred to with poetic licence as (1) a holy place מעד (v. 4), (2) a sanctuary מקדש (v. 7a), and (3) the dwelling place of your name משכן שמך (v. 7b). In the lament the people assert that the enemy has destroyed everything within the sanctuary (v. 3b), stood triumphant within it (v. 4), hacked at its edifice (vv. 5–6), burned it to the ground (v. 7a), and profaned it (v. 7b). The invaders did not desist with the destruction of the temple, they also burned all the meeting places of God מועדי אל in the land (v. 8).[84]

The emphasis on the length of time in which the present distress continued is a less often noted secondary focus of the psalm. Cole, in particular, raises awareness of the prevalence of time as a motif throughout the psalm.[85] He notes that the beginning and the end of the lament are connected by questions about the length of time the present situation will continue (למה and נצח in vv. 1, 10–11). Various terms and expressions reinforce the emphasis on time, including the fourfold use of perpetuity נצח (vv. 1, 3, 10, 19), the recurrence of questions about the length of the distress: how long? עד־מתי (vv. 9–10), and the appearance of other temporal terms: of old קדם (v. 2), from of old מקדם (v. 12), all day כל־היום (v. 22), and continually

---

[82] Commonly related to 587, Briggs, *Psalms*, ii. 150–1; Weiser, *Die Psalmen*, ii. 518; Kraus, *Die Psalmen*, ii. 97; Anderson, *Psalms*, ii. 538; K. Seybold, *Die Psalmen* (HAT, 1/15; Tübingen: Mohr (Paul Siebeck), 1996), 287.

[83] למשאות נצח MT 'perpetual ruins'. Whether or not the 'perpetual ruins' includes the temple has long been an interpretive crux. It is more likely that it is concerned with the loss of the national shrine because it follows v. 2b where Mt. Zion as the dwelling place is mentioned and it stands in a parallel relationship with קדש which is apparently another name for the temple in v. 3.

[84] The 'meeting places or appointed times of God' has been thought to refer to synagogues and used to champion a Maccabean date favoured by older commentators; e.g. H. Gunkel, *Die Psalmen* (HAT, 2; Göttingen: Vandenhoeck & Ruprecht, 4th edn. 1925–6), 322. Weber, 'Zur Datierung', 523–8, 530–1, has argued more recently that it refers to the sanctuaries of the northern kingdom. However, it is used of appointed times of festivals in Lam. 1: 4 (cf. 1: 15; 2: 7, 22) and of the place where such festivals were held (Lam. 2:6). On the translation, see A. Gelston, 'A Note on Psalm LXXIV 8', *VT* 34 (1984).

[85] Cole, *Shape and Message*, 31–4, 36.

תמיד (v. 23). Psalm 74 contains a lament over the ongoing state of the temple. It has a tripartite structure: verses 1–11 a lengthy lament pondering how long the temple will remain defiled and ruined, verses 12–17, a hymnic section in which the actions of Yahweh as king and creator are recounted, and verses 18–23 an appeal to Yahweh to intervene to overturn the disaster.[86]

At the very heart of the poem is a hymnic section in which the powerful deeds of Yahweh accomplished in the distant past are recounted as the basis for an appeal to the character of the deity to alter the present situation. The praise-like character of these verses, along with the repetition of ארץ in verses 12 and 17 and the repeated second person direct address to the deity with a sixfold use of אתה in verses 13–17, distinguish this section as a unit within the lament. After marking the shift from complaint to a hymnic confession of trust by the use of ואלהים (v. 12),[87] verses 13–15 portray Yahweh's sovereign acts in creation and in the establishment and fixation of cosmic time and order in verses 16–17. A break in the repetition of אתה at verse 16 demarcates a division between the myth of Yahweh as creator and a tradition about the origin of time and the cosmos.[88] Conjoined, the two answer the bases for the complaint of verses 1–11 about the desolate state of the temple and how long the present distress will continue.

It is generally understood that the language and imagery of the confession of trust stems from the Canaanite or Mesopotamian myth of the divine battle, with the forces of chaos figured as watery forces and sea-monsters,[89] or from the *Heilsgeschichte* traditions of the

---

[86] J. van der Ploeg, 'Psalm 74 and its Structure', in M. S. H. G. Heerma van Voss et al. (eds.), *Travels in the World of the Old Testament: Studies Presented to Professor M. A. Beek on the Occasion of his 65th Birthday* (Assen: Van Gorcum, 1974), 204–10; G. E. Sharrock, 'Psalm 74: A Literary-Structural Analysis', *Andrews University Seminary Studies* 21 (1983); P. Auffret, 'Essai sur la structure littéraire du psaume 74', *VT* 33 (1983), 129–48; A. G. Hunter, *Psalms* (OTR; London and New York: Routledge, 1999), 154; Cole, *Shape and Message*, 28–36.

[87] J. Day, *God's Conflict with the Dragon and the Sea: Echoes of a Canaanite Myth in the Old Testament* (COP, 35; Cambridge: Cambridge University Press, repr. 1988), 21 n. 55.

[88] J. A. Emerton, ' "Spring and Torrent" in Psalm lxxiv 15', *Congress Volume: Genève 1965* (SVT, 15; Leiden: Brill, 1966), 122–30, argues convincingly against the view that v. 15 should be understood as a reference to the drying up of primordial waters and thus a conclusion to vv. 13–14.

[89] H. Gunkel, *Schöpfung und Chaos in Urzeit und Endzeit: eine religionsgeschichtliche Untersuchung über Gen 1 und Ap Joh 12* (Göttingen: Vandenhoeck & Ruprecht,

Hebrew Bible, particularly the Exodus event and wilderness wanderings,[90] or a combination of the two.[91] It is not within the purview of this thesis to argue for the origin of the imagery; suffice it to say that the language of myth is more persuasive than that of the salvation history of ancient Israel.[92] The description in verses 12–17 makes no appeal to any historical event. Interpreters who find allusions to the Exodus do so by contextualizing the hymnic section and noting language of creation and redemption in verse 2. However, based on the language of verse 2, arguments for an association with the Exodus fail to convince because traditional language is used within a section explicitly concerned with the choice of Zion as the place of divine presence and lacks any reference to the events of the Exodus.[93] There appears to be a myth of primeval origins which existed independently of the story of the Exodus, perhaps even before it, as Gunkel surmised.[94] What is particularly important is that the myth of Yahweh victorious over the forces of the sea serves as the basis for the shift from the lament to the appeal. Because Yahweh acted this way in the past, his involvement is claimed for the future. The hymnic section answers the lament by portraying the rulership of Yahweh established in the battle with chaos almost as divorced from historical time (vv. 12–15). The vanquishing of the sea monsters allowed the first event of creation, that of the establishment of time (v. 16) followed by the ordering of the cosmos (v. 17). The community petitions this Yahweh who established his sovereignty in primordial events.[95]

2nd edn. 1921), 42–5; *idem, Die Psalmen,* 321, 324–5; Buttenwieser, *Psalms,* 614; Oesterley, *Psalms,* ii. 348; Day, *God's Conflict,* 23–5; Seybold, *Psalmen,* 289. Cf. A. Lelièvre, 'YHWH et la mer dans les psaumes', *RHPR* 56 (1976), 256–63.

[90] E. König, *Die Psalmen* (Gütersloh: C. Bertelsmann, 1927), 350–1, 670–1; S. I. L. Norin, *Er spaltete das Meer: die Auszugsüberlieferung in Psalmen und Kult des alten Israel* (CBOT, 9; Lund: Gleerup, 1977), 112–14; Watson, 'The Theme of "Chaos" in the Psalter'.

[91] Most scholars fall within this group; for example, Briggs, *Psalms,* ii. 155–6; Weiser, *Die Psalmen,* ii. 340–1; Kraus, *Psalmen,* ii. 681; Anderson, *Psalms,* ii. 537–47; B. F. Batto, *Slaying the Dragon: Mythmaking in the Biblical Tradition* (Louisville, Ky.: Westminster/John Knox Press, 1992); J. L. Mays, *Psalms* (Interpretation; Louisville, Ky.: John Knox Press, 1994), 245–6; Hunter, *Psalms,* 154.

[92] See the critique by Emerton, ' "Spring and Torrent" ', 30–3; Day, *God's Conflict,* 23.

[93] B. Anderson, *From Creation to New Creation: Old Testament Perspectives* (OBT; Minneapolis, Minn.: Fortress Press, 1994), 83–4.

[94] Gunkel, *Schöpfung und Chaos,* 41–5.

[95] Also, Klein, 'A Theology for Exiles', 133–4.

In Psalm 74 an ancient myth of kingship is combined with an ancient myth of creation so that neither is a theological statement in its own right. The creation and sustenance of the world are a consequence of the rise to divine rule by the deity. In the situation of sixth-century Judah, during a time when the people were suffering under the rulership of an imperial power, the concept of Yahweh's reign takes on greater importance. The community declares that the sovereignty of their deity is not only eternal, but that which was established through conflict with primeval forces. In this way, the kingship of Yahweh is linked first to the great power of the deity and secondly to the continued triumph over the primeval forces. It is only by Yahweh's refusal to wield power that chaos is able to overwhelm the people of God (v. 11). That Yahweh can choose to exercise his might in future on behalf of his people remains a constant source of hope amid the present distress. Secondly, the kingship of Yahweh forged in the midst of battle does not remain a stagnant event in the past, but, rather, it functions to sustain the created order. Thus, creation follows from kingship.[96] The people further believe in the continued and active governance of the deity. The cosmic myth of Yahweh as king and creator responds to the dual concerns of the complaint: the ruination of the temple and other holy places and the time-frame of the disaster.

Historical Tradition: Isaiah 63: 7–64: 11—A Lament over Desolation

It has long been held that Isaiah 63: 7–64: 11, a communal lament found in the final chapters of Isaiah usually associated with the Second Temple period, belongs to national mourning rituals held at the temple after 587.[97] The association of the origin of the psalm with the Templeless period is based on references to the destruction of the temple (63: 18; 64: 10), the suggestion of foreign rule (63: 19),

---

[96] Unlike in Job where creation precedes kingship; cf. Day, *God's Conflict*, 39.
[97] C. Westermann, *Das Buch Jesaja Kapitel 40–66* (ATD, 19; Göttingen: Vandenhoeck & Ruprecht, 1986), 307; Williamson, 'Isaiah 63,7–64,11'. J. Goldenstein, *Das Gebet der Gottesknechte: Jesaja 63,7 – 64,11 im Jesajabuch* (WMANT, 92; Neukirchen-Vluyn: Neukirchener Verlag, 2001), 8–29, deals extensively with the history of interpretation of this lament in his monograph.

the complete devastation of the city of Jerusalem and outlying areas (64: 9), and the inactivity (64: 6, 11) and anger of the deity (64: 4, 8). It is also clear that the singularly positive message of Isaiah 60–2 responds to the complaints raised in this lament.[98] The inclusion of the lament over ruination in 63: 7–64: 11 subsequent to the future blessings predicted in chapters 60–2 is part of a second layer of tradition. In it, the prophet explicates reasons why Yahweh's intervention has not taken place as predicted. In so doing, its use demonstrates that the situation was ongoing in the period of the early return. Though often thought to be similar to other communal laments which originated in the sixth century, such as Psalms 44, 74, 79, 89, and to the book of Lamentations, there are features of this communal lament that set it apart from almost all others.[99] Instead of the threefold structure of lament, confession of trust, and appeal to which the communal laments of the Psalter correspond, Isaiah 63: 7–64: 11 follows a distinctive tripartite pattern of historical retrospect predominantly in the language of praise (63: 7–14), a confession of sin (63: 15–64: 6), and an appeal for salvation (64: 7–11). The historical recital functions as an adapted profession of trust whilst the confession of sin serves as the lament over the present distress. Notably, the elements of lament are included in the confession (63: 18, 19), but they also function to provide additional motivation for the appeal (64: 9–10, 11; cf. Ps. 79: 7, 10–12). This mixture of historical recital, confession of sin, and appeal is found in only two other laments, Psalm 106 and Nehemiah 9.[100]

The historical recital in Isaiah 63: 7–14 functions to some extent as the confession of trust, that is, the reason to believe that Yahweh will act salvifically in the future. The beginning of the recital exhibited the saving deeds of Yahweh revealed by his presence among and saving actions for the people in their affliction in Egypt (vv. 6–9). The recitation concludes with abbreviated references to the Exodus narrative, wilderness wanderings, and entry into the land (vv. 11–14).[101]

---

[98] Westermann, *Jesaja*, 240–1; Smith, *Rhetoric and Redaction*, 44–7.
[99] Westermann, *Jesaja*, 306–7.
[100] Williamson, 'Structure and Historiography in Nehemiah 9'; idem, 'Isaiah 63,7–64,11', 55–8.
[101] On these, see also, J. Muilenburg, 'Isaiah', in *The Interpreter's Bible*, v (New York: Abingdon Press, 1956), 729, 733–5; Williamson, 'Isaiah 63,7–64,11', 56–7.

A reflection on the people's rebellion that resulted in Yahweh's turning against them as a divine warrior (literally, enemy איב; v. 10) interrupts the otherwise positive historical recital. The placement of the statement about the sinful behaviour of the community in the midst of an otherwise positive historical recital suggests that Yahweh as enemy is not the end of the story. Indeed the nature of the deity's intervention in history provides sound evidence that a future beyond the present distress is attainable. Hope in this psalm is not based on myth, but on a history of Yahweh's actions of redemption. It is not the kingship of the deity that forms the basis of belief in divine concern in the future nor his continuing maintenance of creation, but the Exodus event and entry into the land. The grounds for complaint include the destruction of Jerusalem and the temple and the loss of sovereignty over the land. Because the real problem is with the deity who failed to intervene, the poet recalls the historical event that most poignantly exhibited Yahweh's active saving presence in the past. Like the mythological presentation of Yahweh as divine ruler and creator, tradition-history functions to highlight that which is required most by the petitioners.

Combined Traditions

Heretofore, the lament literature associated with the Templeless period provides evidence of a variety of traditional influences and a flexibility in formal elements. What is particularly interesting is that the bases for confessions of trust in Psalm 74 and Isaiah 63: 7–64: 11 stem from mythic and historical traditions independent of each other. In two other examples of laments associated with this period, myth combines with historical recital to relate Yahweh's past actions more specifically to the present distress. The mythological presentation of Yahweh can be associated either with the Davidic covenant as in Psalm 89 or with the Zion traditions[102] as in Psalm 102.

[102] The interpretation advocated here understands Zion as an historical choice made by Yahweh in the past. It is of course based on an almost mythic belief in Yahweh's future intervention on behalf of the city and the Davidic king, but it is, nevertheless, based on what was believed to have been the election of Zion through an historical event, that is, the turning back of Sennacherib in 701.

Mythological Tradition and Covenant: Psalm 89—A Lament for the House of David

Although considered a royal psalm by Gunkel,[103] Psalm 89 if viewed from the perspective of the lament in verses 39–46 represents a communal lament and is thus included by some among the national complaints thought to have arisen on Judah's soil during the Templeless period.[104] In spite of a variety of proposals on the nature of the interplay of various independent poems, hymnic elements (vv. 6–19), a prophetic oracle (vv. 20–38, cf. 2 Sam. 7), and lament (vv. 39–52),[105] recent attempts to regard it as a unity are largely successful.[106] In terms of genre, the three formal elements constituent of other communal laments can be isolated with relative ease: a hymnic recital functioning as a confession of trust (vv. 2–38), lament (vv. 39–46), and appeal (vv. 47–52). Dumortier has shown convincingly that a royal psalm (vv. 2–5, 20–38) and a cosmogonic myth (vv. 6–19), thought to represent two independent poems later joined together, were actually written as a literary unit.[107] Verses 2–38 function as a profession of trust in which Yahweh's battle with the sea has been welded to his covenant with David. Myth and history combine in the psalm to provide a distinctive expression of confidence in Yahweh's future intervention. Whilst the majority of commentators associate it with the military defeat of a king and therefore

---

[103] Gunkel, *Die Psalmen*, 140–71, followed by Kraus, *Die Psalmen*, ii. 202. G. H. Wilson, 'Evidence of Editorial Divisions in the Hebrew Psalter', *VT* 34 (1984), 337–52, supports Gunkel's argument by showing that royal psalms have been placed at the seams of the Psalter. The royal overtones of the psalm feature within a communal lament which expresses concern over the loss of the Davidic king.

[104] J. M. Ward, 'The Literary Form and the Liturgical Background of Psalm lxxxix', *VT* 11 (1961), 321–9.

[105] See the commentaries. Tate, *Psalms 51–100*, 413–18, provides a useful summary of positions.

[106] Recent arguments in favour of the unity of the psalm based on literary criteria include: Ward, 'The Literary Form', 327–8, 335–6; Clifford, 'Psalm 89'; M. H. Floyd, 'Psalm lxxxix: A Prophetic Complaint about the Fulfilment of an Oracle', *VT* 42 (1992); K. M. Heim, 'The (God-)Forsaken King in Psalm 89: A Historical and Intertextual Enquiry', in J. Day (ed.), *King and Messiah in Israel and the Ancient Near East* (JSOTSup, 270; Sheffield: JSOT Press, 1998).

[107] J.-B. Dumortier, 'Un rituel d'intronisation: le Ps lxxxix 2–38', *VT* 22 (1972), followed by Clifford, 'Psalm 89', 40–7.

place its composition sometime in the First Temple period,[108] it is not a battle defeat that causes the distress, but the complete rejection of the Davidic covenant by Yahweh. The removal of the Davidic king from the throne in 598 and 587 by the Babylonians represents the only action in the history of ancient Israel that would have elicited thoughts of Yahweh's absolute abrogation of his promise to David and his descendants.[109] In fact, the Templeless period like no other raised concerns about the actions of the deity. To this time alone can the psalm relate.[110]

The hymnic confession of trust contains two strophes that can be delineated further into stanzas.[111] The introductory verses set off from the hymn of verses 6–38 by a סלה at the end of verse 5[112] and the repetition of forever עולם and for all generations לדר ודור (in vv. 2 and 5) introduce the dual foci of the entire recital: an emphasis on the saving deeds of Yahweh (vv. 2–3 // vv. 6–15) and the covenant with the Davidic line (vv. 4–5 // vv. 16–38). The two strophes of the hymn develop these two emphases:

1. Hymn of praise to and about Yahweh (vv. 6–15)

   a. Celebration in heaven of Yahweh's cosmogonic victory (vv. 6–9)

   b. Cosmogonic victory of Yahweh (vv. 10–15)

2. Hymn extolling Yahweh's interactions with the people and his choice of David (vv. 16–38)

   a. Celebration on earth of Yahweh's cosmogonic victory (vv. 16–19 // 6–9)

   b. Yahweh's choice of David as his earthly regent (vv. 20–8)

---

[108] See the commentaries and Ward, 'The Literary Form', 336–9; Clifford, 'Psalm 89', 46–7. Cf. N. M. Sarna, 'Psalm 89: A Study in Inner Biblical Exegesis', in A. Altmann (ed.), *Biblical and Other Studies* (Cambridge, Mass.: Harvard University Press, 1963), 39–44.

[109] Heim, 'The (God-)Forsaken King in Psalm 89', 298; now, also, J. Day, *The Psalms* (OTG; Sheffield: Sheffield Academic Press, 1990), 105.

[110] T. Veijola, *Verheissung in der Krise: Studien zur Literatur und Theologie der Exilszeit anhand des 89. Psalm* (Suomalaisen Tiedeakatemian toimituksia, 220; Helsinki: Suomalainen Tiedeakatemia, 1982).

[111] In agreement with the insights of Dumortier, 'Un rituel', and Clifford, 'Psalm 89', 40–6.

[112] The other סלה in the psalm does not appear until the end of v. 38.

c. Extension of the Yahwistic promise to descendants of David[113] (vv. 29–38)

The thematic differences between verses 6–15 and 16–38 suggest the division of the hymnic profession of trust into two strophes. Literary clues such as 'happy are' אשרי at the beginning of verse 16, and the almost line-by-line echo in 16–38 of the concepts which appeared in verses 6–15, support this minor separation.[114] Furthermore, the earthly inhabitants in verses 16–19 reiterate the praise of the heavenly host in 6–9 so that the praise of Yahweh for his victory at the beginning of time surrounds the detail of that accomplishment (vv. 10–15).[115] In the first part of the hymn, the cosmogonic myth of Yahweh over the sea is associated with his rule and ordering of creation (vv. 6–9).[116]

It is usually thought that a redactor added a poetic adaptation of the prophetic oracle to David in 2 Samuel 7 (cf. Ps. 132) to the cosmogonic myth detailed above.[117] In contrast to the prophetic oracle of 2 Samuel 7, the promises to David become unconditional in the psalm. Moreover, Dumortier has shown that the governance of Yahweh established through his victory over Rahab (vv. 6–19) is echoed in the royal psalm which focuses on the governance of David and his dynasty established by an everlasting covenant with the supreme ruler, Yahweh (vv. 20–38).[118] Yahweh's defeat of the sea results in the maintenance of world order envisioned as the sea and rivers (v. 26) being entrusted to the care of his viceroy on earth, in this case David, but includes his successors as well (vv. 29–38). As a whole, the cosmogonic myth and the Davidic covenant tradition function within the lament in a similar way to the recital of Yahweh's

---

[113] Dumortier, 'Un rituel', 190–1, followed by Clifford, 'Psalm 89', 45–6, notes that vv. 29–38 form a chiastic pattern.
[114] Dumortier, 'Un rituel'.
[115] Ibid., 179–85, delineates the sections of the poem similarly.
[116] Gunkel, *Schöpfung und Chaos*, 34–5; idem, *Die Psalmen*, 387; Weiser, *Die Psalmen*, ii. 388–9; Kraus, *Psalmen*, ii. 787–8; Day, *God's Conflict*, 26–7. There is no allusion to the Exodus here, contra König, *Die Psalmen*, 485; Norin, *Er spaltete das Meer*, 115; Ahlström, *Psalm 89*, 71; Batto, *Slaying the Dragon*.
[117] Sarna, 'Psalm 89', 29–46; F. M. Cross, *Canaanite Myth and Hebrew Epic* (Cambridge, Mass.: Harvard University Press, 1973), 257–61; Veijola, *Verheissung in der Krise*, 60–9.
[118] Dumortier, 'Un rituel', 185–92, and Clifford, 'Psalm 89', 43–6.

role as ruler and creator in Psalm 74, as a confession of trust. The poet utilizes the myth and the tradition as a means of recalling the past actions of Yahweh as sovereign over the universe and over the people Israel through his regent, the king, in order to ground their petition and to encourage Yahweh to act consistently with his past 'wondrous deeds' in the present lamentable crisis. The issue causing distress in this psalm is the severe abrogation of the covenant by Yahweh. The present is certainly contrary to the promise in verse 29, where Yahweh declares through the poet, 'My steadfast love I will keep for him forever, and my covenant will stand firm for him. I will establish his line forever and his throne as the days of the heavens' (vv. 29–30). In fact, whatever wicked deeds the successors of David commit (vv. 31–3) Yahweh promises never to relinquish his support of the king (vv. 34–8). The eternal nature of the covenant with David punctuates and closes the oracle to him and his successors.

In Psalm 89, the profession of trust exhibits an interesting difference to that of Psalm 74 and Isaiah 63: 7–64: 11 in that it combines myth with historical tradition. In Psalm 74, the confession of trust utilized the battle with the sea to ground the appeal in past actions of Yahweh where he established his kingship and creative power. There the cosmogonic myth simply glorified the power and justice of the deity who rules over the created order. In Isaiah 63: 7–64: 11 it was the historical traditions of Yahweh's abiding presence throughout the Exodus narrative which led even to entry into the land that formed the basis of the belief in the deity's willingness and ability to intervene salvifically at some future stage. In contrast, Psalm 89 utilizes the myth of the kingship of the deity in conjunction with the tradition of the covenant with David and his successors. The reign of the earthly king is seen as divinely sustained and commissioned, but more than that he is Yahweh's viceroy with dominion even over the riotous seas stilled in the divine battle for cosmic sovereignty; 'I will set his hand over the sea and his right hand over the rivers' (v. 26, cf. v. 10). The myth and historical interlude resolve the lament. In the case of Psalm 74, where the issue is the rebuilding of the temple, the myth of Yahweh's victory and creation provides the vehicle to trust in his ability and desire to rectify the situation in the future. In Psalm 89, the lament focuses on the loss of the Davidic king. The mythic power of Yahweh was joined to his promise to David and his descendants to acknowledge that any future resolution of the collapse of the Davidic line belongs resolutely with Yahweh, who established the covenant with David in the first place. Myth and history combine in Psalm 89 to address a specific lament over the loss of the Davidic king.

Mythological Tradition and Zion Theology: Psalm 102—A Lament about the Ruination of Jerusalem

Unlike the psalms previously discussed, Psalm 102 represents the lament of an individual which is clearly seen by the added title (v. 1) and verses 2–12 and 24–5, in which the speaker portrays a situation of great distress likened to an illness.[119] Although Psalm 102 represents the lament of an individual, it deserves some mention in conjunction with the laments of the people in the Templeless period because its background is that of the lamentable state of Zion and its form has been adapted to a communal complaint.[120] In the first place, several references suggest a time period congruent with the other laments surveyed so far—Zion in ruins (v. 15), the oppression of the people (vv. 18, 21), the restoration of Zion by Yahweh projected into the future (v. 17 in prophetic perfect), and the revelation of his glory (vv. 16–17 in prophetic perfects). Secondly, the poet inserted a communal prayer about the restoration of Zion into the lament of a single sufferer in the agony of some unstated illness in vv. 13–23.[121] In its final form, the fate of the sufferer is inseparable from that of Zion. The resumption of the individual appeal after the infixed prayer for Zion highlights the conjoining of the two. Psalm 102 has been adapted to a communal lament through the inclusion of the communal prayer, the plural ending of verse 29, and the appearance of features common to communal laments, that of

[119] Gunkel and Begrich, *Einleitung in die Psalmen*, 215–50; Westermann, *Praise and Lament*, 64–81, on the constituent parts of an individual complaint psalm. On individual laments in general, E. S Gerstenberger, *Der bittende Mensch: Bittritual über Klagelied der Einzelnen im Alten Testament* (WMANT, 51; Neukirchen-Vluyn: Neukirchener Verlag, 1980); Veijola, 'Das Klagegebet'.
[120] Janssen, *Juda in der Exilszeit*, 19–20.
[121] L. C. Allen, *Psalms 101–150* (WBC, 21; Waco, Tex.: Word Books, 1983), 11–13; Seybold, *Psalmen*, 398; E. S. Gerstenberger, *Psalms, Part 2, and Lamentations* (FOTL, 15, Grand Rapids, Mich.: Eerdmans, 2001), 212–13.

lament (vv. 4–12, 24–5), appeal (vv. 2–3), and confession of trust (vv. 13–23, 26–9). The liturgical function of the psalm provides a means to perceive the material as a unity.[122] The shift back and forth between lament and hymn results from the belief that upon invocation, the salvation of God is made present for the worshippers. Its unity, then, can be explained as a consequence of its utilization in the cult. Like Psalm 89, though, the statements professing confidence in Yahweh's ability to act do not exist in isolation from other traditions. They are appended to concepts prevalent in Zion theology. The lament features two topics which are answered in the confessions of trust: (1) an emphasis on time—the life of the speaker ebbs away (vv. 4a, 12, 24–5) and (2) a focus on the results of the illness on the body of the sufferer, that is, its ruination (vv. 4b–11).

Confessions of trust appear in verses 13 and 26, but are appended to wider concepts, a movement already noticeable in Psalm 89 among the communal laments. The statement about the eternal kingship of Yahweh in verse 13 is connected to his purposes of restoration for Zion (vv. 14–23). The lament of the individual extends from verse 2 to verse 26, interrupted by a direct address to Yahweh demarcated by 'But you' ואתה and the subsequent communal prayer for the restoration of Zion which lies in ruins. The placement of the confession of trust after lamentation over what is portrayed as a terminal illness associates the afflictions of the individual directly with the sorry state of the city of Zion. The kingship of the deity is linked with the vindication of the name of Yahweh among the nations and presumably, though not stated outright, his servants who are destitute and imprisoned (vv. 18, 21). Through the divine restoration of Zion, the nations and kingdoms will gather together to serve Yahweh in Jerusalem (v. 23). The psalm connects Second Temple Zion theology, with its emphasis on the in-gathering of the nations, with the revelation of Yahweh's glory, and the vindication of his name through the restoration of Zion.

After the expression of trust in Yahweh as king without mythic overtones and the appended emphasis on the vindication of Zion and Yahweh's servants, the lament resumes in verse 24 broken only by a second confession of trust which emphasizes the creator

---

[122] Weiser, *Die Psalmen*, ii. 431.

deity (v. 26). The idea of Yahweh as an eternal creator is juxtaposed with the ephemeral nature of human life exhibited by the sufferer (vv. 24–5). It is the contrast between all things of the cosmos which will fade and Yahweh that gives the Psalmist hope for 'the children of your servants' (v. 29). The closing hymn (vv. 27–9) appeals to the eternal reign of Yahweh as creator and sustainer of the universe in order to contrast the limited lifespan of the sufferer which is drawing nigh and that of Yahweh which is eternal. The issue for the speaker seems to be that the period of time in which he languished calls into question Yahweh's governance. As long as Jerusalem remains in ruins and the servants remain prisoners, how can it be said that Yahweh reigns? The poet associated the image of the deity as creator and his continued sustenance of the world with the speaker and the speaker's audience. Confidence lies in the perpetual governance of Yahweh established over creation, but also within the sphere of history through the choice of a people special to the deity. The psalmist seeks the restoration of ruined Jerusalem as a means to exhibit the vindication of Yahweh's servants.

The concept of the limited timespan of the life of the speaker contrasted to the timelessness of Yahweh intermingles in verse 25: ' "O my God," I say, "do not take me away at the mid-point of my life, you whose years endure throughout all generations." ' The echoes of a concern with time in various places in the lament (vv. 11, 23, 24a) highlight the desire for the restoration of Zion in verse 14 in which the speaker declares that 'because the time עת has come to favour her, the appointed time מועד has come'.[123] The restoration of Zion affects the servants of the deity who know the name of Yahweh as well as the nations. The prophecy predicts that the most important result of the advent of the deity is the restoration of the city of Jerusalem which vindicates the name of Yahweh among the nations. Further consequences include the awe-inspiring reputation of the deity among the nations who will fear the name of the deity and among all the kings who will tremble at his glory (v. 16), and the kingdoms will be gathered to serve Yahweh (v. 23b). In sharp contrast to the resulting effect of the deity's intervention on other nations, the servants of the deity will recount the event for future

---

[123] כי בא מועד often taken as a gloss or textual variant on the previous עת.

generations (v. 19a), praise him (vv. 19b, 22b), proclaim the name of Yahweh in Zion (v. 22a), be gathered together (v. 23a), and remain and dwell (v. 29a) with their children established in the presence of the deity (v. 29b).

Like other psalms of this period, Psalm 102 laments the destruction of Jerusalem and emphasizes the longevity of suffering. In response to the lament, two confessions of trust about the kingship of Yahweh and the eternal nature of the deity intertwine with historical issues about Zion and time. The themes expanded in this psalm—the timeframe, the distinction between the true servants of the deity and the nations, the coming of the nations to serve Yahweh, and the emphasis on his name and glory—suggest that this psalm combines the themes of Yahweh as creator and king with Second Temple Zion theology and name theology.

CONCLUSIONS

An analysis of some of the laments associated with the Jerusalem temple in the aftermath of 587 reveals that there is great variety not only in the arrangement of the formal elements, but in the traditions regarded to be essential in the presentation of the complaint. The three main formal categories common to all the surveyed communal complaints—the lament, the appeal, and the confession of trust—vary in order between the poems with only Psalm 79 lacking a confession of trust. Psalms 74 and 89, and Isaiah 63: 7–64: 11 contain the simplest version of the three elements. Psalm 74 begins with the lament in verses 1–11 followed by the confession of trust (vv. 12–17) and the appeal (vv. 18–23). The order of the elements in Psalm 89 and Isaiah 63: 7–64: 11, though formulated differently, corresponds, with the first element being a profession of trust in a hymnic recital (Ps. 89: 2–38) or an historical retrospect (Isa. 63: 7–14) followed by the lament (Ps. 89: 39–46) or a confession of sin which corresponds loosely to the complaint of the people (Isa. 63: 15–64: 6) and concludes with an appeal (Ps. 89: 47–52; Isa. 64: 7–11). Psalm 102 shows a very complex mixture of the elements because an individual lament has been adapted to a communal concern, but the three elements are apparent in the appeal (vv. 2–3), a lament (vv. 4–12, 24–5), and a confession of trust (vv. 13–23, 26–9). In Psalms 74 and 89, and Isaiah 63: 7–64: 11, the lament and confession of trust appear before the appeal whilst Psalm 102 begins with the appeal followed by the co-mingling of the lament and profession of confidence in the character of Yahweh. With regard to the order of the formal criteria, then, the communal laments associated with rituals at the temple in the sixth century exhibit a marked degree of flexibility.

A similar variety occurs in the types of traditions which function to provide a basis for the belief in the future intervention of the deity. The analysis here confirms those of Clifford and Broyles, who argued that the confessions of trust correspond specifically to the disastrous events which necessitate correction.[124] In his concern with the appeal section of the lament: Broyles, for example, finds the appearance of two primary traditions operative in communal laments: covenant theology and Zion theology. In his view, an appeal to covenant traditions results in the depiction of Yahweh as an aggressor. In contrast, when a poet utilizes elements of Zion theology the lament centres on the anger or neglect of the deity. Each appeal responds directly to the type of complaint being made.

A similar type of association has been seen to operate in the confessions of trust as evidenced in Table 3.1 (see p. 168).

The above study has found that the cosmological myth of kingship and creation devoid of historical overtones appeared in Psalm 74 whilst the Exodus historical tradition and settlement of the land are utilized in Isaiah 63: 7–64: 11. Although Psalm 79 contains no separate confession of trust, it includes concepts associated with the election of the people. In a more complex way, myth is combined with history in Psalm 89 where the poet conceived of Yahweh as the cosmological ruler who chooses and sustains an earthly regent. Psalm 102 reflects a similar perspective as there Yahweh's kingship is associated with Zion, but the psalmist interestingly correlates Yahweh's role as creator to the prolonged suffering of an individual. The recollection of Yahweh's actions in the realm of myth or history, in addition to seeking renewed divine assistance, relate specifically to the unpleasant, even lamentable, experiences of the petitioners. When the

---

[124] Clifford, 'Psalm 89'; Broyles, *The Conflict of Faith and Experience*.

Table 3.1

	Lament/complaint	Confession of trust	Yahweh's role (based on Broyles)
Psalm 74	destruction of temple	creation myth: Yahweh versus forces of chaos	Yahweh withdraws support/inactive
	prolonged distress	Yahweh creates time and cosmic order	
Psalm 79	destruction of the temple	none: Zion tradition of election is implied	Yahweh is angry
Psalm 89	loss of Davidide and abrogation of Davidic covenant	cosmic myth joined to Davidic promise	Yahweh active as an aggressor
Psalm 102	Zion in ruins	Yahweh as king connected to the restoration of Jerusalem	passive Yahweh who has hidden his face
	longevity of the distress	Yahweh as creator linked to the timelessness of the deity	
Isaiah 63: 7–64: 11	destruction of Jerusalem and temple, subjugation by enemies	historical traditions: Exodus and the inheritance of the land	Yahweh is angry and silent

destruction of the temple is lamented, the myth of Yahweh as king rises to the fore (Ps. 74), but when the issue is loss of sovereignty over the land, the historical traditions of the Exodus and settlement are used (Isa. 63: 7–64: 11). Combinations of motifs such as the cosmological myth and the Davidic covenant occur with complaints over the loss of the earthly king (Ps. 89) whilst the hope for restoration and security in the land yields the association of Yahweh as king and creator with the events of the present distress (Ps. 102). In a similar vein, the appeal to Yahweh from the perspective of election ideology suggests that the issue is that world events have placed the special relationship between the deity and the people in doubt (Ps. 79). The hymnic recitation of the saving activities of Yahweh in myth and the history of the world and in the history of the people contrasts starkly with the detailed presentation of the crisis. In highlighting various facets of Yahweh's interaction in the cosmos and the world, the

Conceptions of Judah, II: Yahwistic Worship 169

positive assessment of the deity in the confessions of trust recalls the past to Yahweh as a means of encouraging him to act thus in the present.

The results of this analysis demonstrate further that there is too great a variety of traditions invoked to determine a specific location for the provenance of the laments without a clear understanding of the type of thought that would be central to a population remaining in Judah. Indeed, delineated according to the characteristic form elements as above, the theological underpinnings suggest in certain cases an alignment with what is known about *Golah* thought. The combination of the cosmogonic myth and the historical traditions of the Exodus is a well-known feature of *Golah* literature, but the attribution of literature to a Judahite locale based on the lack of its appearance is not tenable. Klein's short study of kingship in laments of the period is laudable in its attempt to discern patterns of thought applicable to both communities, but unfortunately he applies the flawed logic that kingship divorced from the Exodus indicates a setting other than Babylon. Certain themes in Psalm 102, for instance, are more consistent with that of the *Golah* or even the prophetic literature of the early Second Temple period.[125] It is apparent from this survey of literature associated with the Jerusalemite temple that a better understanding of ideas reflective of the community in the land is a necessary precursor to differentiating liturgy and literature of this period with any degree of certainty.

In addition, reconstructions of Yahwistic practice in Templeless Judah are made on the basis of very little that can be attributed to the inhabitants of the land themselves. The belief that certain laments arose from Templeless Judah reflects to a large extent a conception of the period made by modern interpreters (albeit on the basis of long-standing traditions like the Septuagint). Although there is good reason to believe in the participation in Yahwistic worship

---

[125] Certain expressions in Ps. 102 fit well with *Golah* thought: the distinction between the true servants of the deity and the nations, the coming of the nations to provide service to the deity, and the emphasis on the name and glory of Yahweh. Otherwise, certain statements are consistent with literature of the late Templeless period such as that about the coming of the favourable and appointed time (v. 14). Haggai and Zechariah 1–8 evoke concern for time in conjunction with the reconstruction of the second temple whilst Isaiah 60–2 contains the belief in the contribution of the nations to the new Jerusalem.

by the inhabitants in the homeland—either through sporadic and spontaneous worship at the ruins of the Jerusalem temple or through regular ritual at a sanctuary in Bethel—there is no direct confirmation of its existence. Attempts to isolate Yahwistic liturgy and praxis in Judah deserve praise because an understanding of Judahite Yahwistic belief cannot be found in literature produced by the exiles. However, a clearer understanding of Judahite reflection still requires attention. The final chapter examines the liturgical literature most commonly associated with Templeless Judah, namely, Lamentations, in order to establish some criteria for isolating additional literature from this setting.

4

The Voice of the Land: Lamentations

INTRODUCTION

In the light of the varieties of expression in liturgical literature attributed to worship at the temple site in Judah in post-587 Jerusalem, a consideration of the poems most likely from this setting deserves attention in its own right. Hence this chapter focuses on Lamentations in order to elucidate themes and motifs pertinent to the experience in Judah. It is hoped that such a study will isolate concepts consistent with the thought of the inhabitants of the land in order to provide some sense of what else could be attributable there. If amid the rhetoric we can find traces of a community adapting to its circumstances, it is possible to ascertain responses to the disaster consistent with Yahwistic belief that actually occurred in Judah.

Other than a desire to hear the Judahites' theological reflection in its own right divorced from the polemical perspective of their brethren in Babylon, there are two important reasons—one having to do with modern interpretation whilst the other remains firmly in the thought of the period itself—to consider this issue. In the first place, modern interpreters argue that in the early Persian period a rupture emerged between two distinct societal groups, the people who had remained in the land during the Templeless period and the returnees from Babylon. Although the actual catalyst for the schism varies between interpreters, the most frequent attribution of conflict stems from disagreements over theological interpretation.[1] In fact,

---

[1] P. D. Hanson, *The Dawn of Apocalyptic* (Philadelphia, Pa.: Fortress, Press, 1975); A. Rofé, 'Isaiah 66: 1–4: Judean Sects in the Persian Period as Viewed by Trito-Isaiah', in A. Kort and S. Morschauer (eds.), *Biblical and Related Studies Presented to Samuel Iwry*

in reconstructions that accept a conflict model in the early Second Temple period, the sanctuary tends to be the locus of competition between the population that remained in the land and the repatriated exiles.[2] However, no analysis proceeds with a clear understanding of the thought of the Judahites during the Babylonian period. Surely, before arguments for the development of animosity between two groups can be made with any certainty, the thought of both ought to be taken into consideration. Since the concern of this thesis is with Jeremiah's so-called 'poor of the land', a natural focus is on the perspective of this community.

Moreover, in literature associated with the *Golah* community, the issue of worship comes to the fore, not only through the disparagement of other deities as has been noted already, but also in conjunction with questions about the availability of Yahweh's presence to the exiles and through literature that reflects the background of worship. Ezekiel 11: 16 speaks of Yahweh's presence among the exiles in the terminology of a sanctuary for a short time or a little sanctuary מקדש מעט which has sparked a great deal of discussion about whether the origin of synagogues belongs to this period.[3] The mobility of Yahweh's spirit and its availability to the exiles in Babylon answers the lament raised in Psalm 137 (which may not stem from this period, but surely reflects on it): How can it be possible to worship the deity

---

(Winona Lake, Ind.: Eisenbrauns, 1985), 205–17; M. Smith, *Palestinian Parties and Politics that Shaped the Old Testament* (London: SCM Press, 2nd edn. 1987), 75–95; J. Blenkinsopp, 'A Jewish Sect of the Persian Period', *CBQ* 52 (1990), 5–20; B. Schramm, *The Opponents of Third Isaiah: Reconstructing the Cultic History of the Restoration* (JSOTSup, 193; Sheffield: Sheffield Academic Press, 1995); J. Kessler, 'Reconstructing Haggai's Jerusalem: Demographic and Sociological Considerations and the Search for an Adequate Methodological Point of Departure', in L. L. Grabbe and R. D. Haak (eds.), *'Every City shall be Forsaken': Urbanism and Prophecy in ancient Israel and the Near East* (JSOTSup, 330; Sheffield: Sheffield Academic Press, 2001), 137–58. Cf. J. A. Middlemas, 'Divine Reversal and the Role of the Temple in Trito-Isaiah', in J. Day (ed.), *Temple Worship in Biblical Israel: Proceedings of the Oxford Old Testament Seminar* (JSOTSup, 422; London and New York: T & T Clark International, 2005), 164–87.

[2] P. R. Bedford, *Temple Restoration in Early Achaemenid Judah* (JSJSup, 65; Leiden: Brill, 2001); Kessler, 'Reconstructing Haggai's Jerusalem'.

[3] The מקדש מעט was already understood in the Targum as a reference to synagogues. A. Sperber (ed.), *The Bible in Aramaic: The Latter Prophets according to Targum Jonathan* (Leiden: Brill, 1992), 283. On the meaning of מקדש מעט, see P. M. Joyce, 'Dislocation and Adaptation in the Exilic Age and After', in J. Barton and D. J. Reimer (eds.), *After the Exile: Essays in Honour of Rex Mason* (Macon, Ga.: Mercer University Press, 1996), 45–58.

when on foreign soil? Ezekiel assures a community languishing in a foreign land that Yahweh's presence is among them.[4] In a slightly different way, the Deuteronomistic History provides what appears to be a liturgical recital. It exhibits a cyclical structure of sin, punishment, and redemption that resembles closely an extended confession of faith.[5] In the case of the History, the abjectly depressing end in which Jehoiachin is released from prison, but still in captivity,[6] begs the question of the possibility of the future intervention of the deity in a miraculous way.[7] The Deuteronomistic History ends with the removal of the possibility of human initiative, but the historical recital leaves open the probability of a new divine act of salvation. Moreover, Deutero-Isaiah is thought to contain laments transformed into oracles of salvation which originated in worship. Literature commonly thought to stem from the sixth century BCE contains a significant amount of reflection on issues that relate to the worship practices of ancient Israel. Furthermore, it hints that the exiles in Babylon observed worship practices for Yahweh. Since Ezekiel, the Deuteronomistic History, and Deutero-Isaiah probably exhibit the views of the community in exile, one pauses to wonder about the homeland. Is there any liturgy that can be posited to the inhabitants of the land?

Because worship practices formed a constituent part of both ancient and modern thought on the events of the sixth century, it would be helpful to understand more clearly what happened in the minds and hearts of the people left in Judah. The probability of the sporadic use of the ruins of the temple and more regular cultic rituals

[4] P. Joyce, *Divine Initiative and Human Response in Ezekiel* (JSOTSup, 51; Sheffield: JSOT Press, 1989); J. F. Kutsko, *Between Heaven and Earth: Divine Presence and Absence in the Book of Ezekiel* (BJS, 7; Winona Lake, Ind.: Eisenbrauns, 2000).

[5] H. W. Wolff, 'Das Kerygma des deuteronomistischen Geschichtswerkes', ZAW 73 (1961), 171–85, ET 'The Kerygma of the Deuteronomic Historical Work', in W. Brueggemann and H. W. Wolff (eds.), *The Vitality of Old Testament Traditions* (Atlanta, Ga.: John Knox Press, 1978), 83–100; P. R. Ackroyd, *Exile and Restoration: A Study of Hebrew Thought of the Sixth Century BC* (London: SCM Press, repr. 1994), 77–83.

[6] M. Noth, *Überlieferungsgeschichtliche Studien: Die sammelnden und bearbeitenden Geschichtswerke im Alten Testament* (Schriften der königsberger Gelehrten Gesellschaft, 18; Tübingen: Max Niemeyer, 3rd edn. 1967).

[7] G. von Rad, 'Die deuteronomistische Geschichtstheologie in den Königsbüchern', in *Gesammelte Studien zum Alten Testament* (TB, 8; Munich: Kaiser, 1958), 189–204, ET 'The Deuteronomic Theology of History in I and II Kings', in *The Problem of the Hexateuch and Other Essays* (Edinburgh: Oliver & Boyd, 1966), 281–307.

at a sanctuary in Bethel has already been discussed in conjunction with an argument for the continuation of ritual observance in the homeland. Because laments thought to stem from national ceremonies in that setting exhibit a wide variety of expressions and do not correspond with each other in terms of thought, it is difficult to associate them with Judah. Widespread, almost unanimous agreement, a remarkable feat in modern interpretation, holds that the biblical book of Lamentations stems from the land of Judah after the events of 587. It is hoped that an examination of the poems contained therein will enable a better understanding of the thought of the land as a means to hear more clearly the voice of the Judahites as well as to formulate a series of themes that would be pertinent to them. Unfortunately, space prevents the use of the model advocated here being applied to literature elsewhere associated with Templeless Judah, but such a study deserves attention in the future.

LAMENTATIONS

The book of Lamentations is composed of what are thought to have been five independent poems that reflect on the situation of the destruction of 587, especially that which took place in and around Jerusalem. Poems 1, 2, 3, and 4 are written as alphabetic acrostics whilst the number of verses in the fifth chapter corresponds to the number of consonants in the Hebrew alphabet. General discussions of the book have moved beyond questions of authorship[8] and its relationship to or dependence on Mesopotamian laments over the

---

[8] A conservative list of commentaries includes H.-J. Kraus, *Klagelieder (Threni)* (BKAT, 20; Neukirchen-Vluyn: Neukirchener Verlag, 3rd edn. 1968); W. Rudolph, *Das Buch Ruth—Das Hohe Lied—Die Klagelieder* (KAT 17; Güttersloh: Gerd Mohn, 1962); T. J. Meek, 'The Book of Lamentations', in *The Interpreter's Bible*, vi (New York: Abingdon Press, 1968), 3–38; R. Gordis, *The Song of Songs and Lamentations: A Study, Modern Translation and Commentary* (Texts and Studies of the Jewish Theological Seminary of America, 20; New York: KTAV Publishing House, 3rd edn. 1974); D. R. Hillers, *Lamentations* (AB; New York: Doubleday, 2nd rev. edn. 1992); I. Provan, *Lamentations* (NCBC; London: Marshall Pickering, 1991); J. Renkema, *Lamentations* (HCOT; Leuven: Peeters, 1998).

destruction of cities⁹ to the theology of the book¹⁰ or its relevance for the modern day.¹¹ Discussions in previous work which conceived of the period as the 'Exile' have naturally included the book of Lamentations.¹² For instance, Klein's overview of literature of the 'Exilic period' begins his examination with a consideration of Yahweh as king and enemy in Lamentations.¹³ In his analysis, he makes three important points that in many ways pre-empted future discussions of the book, but deserve further examination. The first compares the thought of Lamentations and Deutero-Isaiah, of which he says: 'In certain respects his limited outlook towards the future forms an important foil to the more exuberant message of Second Isaiah at the other end of the Exile. Zion's frequent complaint that there is no one to comfort her (Lam. 1: 2, 9, 16, 17, 21) differs dramatically from

⁹ T. F. McDaniel, 'The Alleged Sumerian Influence upon Lamentations', *VT* 18 (1968), 198–209; W. C. Gwaltney, 'The Biblical Book of Lamentations in the Context of Near Eastern Lament Literature', in W. W. Hallo, J. C. Moyer, and L. G. Perdue (eds.), *Scripture in Context*, ii: *More Essays on the Comparative Method* (Winona Lake, Ind.: Eisenbrauns, 1983), 191–211; P. W. Ferris, Jr, *The Genre of Communal Lament in the Bible and Ancient Near East* (SBLDS, 127; Atlanta, Ga.: Scholars Press, 1984), 167–74; F. W. Dobbs-Allsopp, *Weep, O Daughter of Zion: A Study of the City-Lament Genre in the Hebrew Bible* (BO, 44; Rome: Editrice Pontificio Istituto Biblico, 1993).

¹⁰ N. K. Gottwald, *Studies in the Book of Lamentation* (SBT, 14; London: SCM Press, rev. edn. 1962); B. Albrektson, *Studies in the Text and Theology of the Book of Lamentations* (Lund: Gleerup, 1963); M. S. Moore, 'Human Suffering in Lamentations', *RB* 83 (1990), 535–6; Renkema, *Lamentations*; J. Hunter, *Faces of a Lamenting City: The Development and Coherence of the Book of Lamentations* (BEATAJ, 39; Frankfurt am Main: Peter Lang, 1996); T. Linafelt, 'Zion's Cause: The Presentation of Pain in the Book of Lamentations', in T. Linafelt (ed.), *Strange Fire: Reading the Bible after the Holocaust* (BS, 71; Sheffield: Sheffield Academic Press, 2000), 267–79; idem, *Surviving Lamentations: Catastrophe, Lament, and Protest in the Afterlife of a Biblical Book* (Chicago, Ill.: University of Chicago Press, 2000).

¹¹ P. Joyce, 'Sitting Loose to History: Reading the Book of Lamentations without Primary Reference to its Original Historical Setting', in E. Ball (ed.), *In Search of True Wisdom: Essays in OT Interpretation in Honour of Ronald E. Clements* (JSOTSup, 300; Sheffield: Sheffield Academic Press, 1999), 246–62; T. Linafelt, 'The Impossibility of Mourning: Lamentations after the Holocaust', in T. Linafelt and T. K. Beal (eds.), *God in the Fray: A Tribute to Walter Brueggemann* (Minneapolis, Minn.: Fortress Press, 1998), 279–89; Linafelt, *Surviving Lamentations*; K. M. O'Connor, *Lamentations and the Tears of the World* (Maryknoll, NY: Orbis, 2002); N. C. Lee, *The Singers of Lamentations: Cities Under Siege, From Ur to Jerusalem to Sarajevo* (BIS, 60; Leiden: Brill, 2002).

¹² C. W. Miller, 'The Book of Lamentations in Recent Research', *Currents in Biblical Research* 1 (2002), 9–29, provides a useful survey of research on Lamentations.

¹³ R. Klein, *Israel in Exile: A Theological Interpretation* (OBT; Philadelphia, Pa.: Fortress Press, 1979; repr. Mifflintown, Pa.: Sigler Press, 2000), 9–22.

the opening words of Second Isaiah: "Comfort, comfort my people" (Isa. 40: 1).'[14] Klein's brief comparison actually prefigured discussions on the relationship between Lamentations and Deutero-Isaiah in recent times. That Deutero-Isaiah responds to the laments of the Judahite population has been discussed elsewhere,[15] but the distinctive point of view of Lamentations needs to be more fully explored.

A second point raised by Klein has also been elaborated in recent years. Almost as a side note, he states that 'Zion is urged in 2: 19 to cry to Yahweh amidst her tears: "Look, Yahweh, and consider whom you have treated so" (2: 20).'[16] The fact that Zion is urged to speak in chapter 2 has been explored to some extent with regard to her assuming a posture of protest in response to the anguish that afflicts the community.[17] Moreover, it has implications for the understanding of the collection as a whole as literature of exclamation and vociferous complaint, not only lament.[18] The third point Klein picks up bears on the usefulness or purposefulness of the laments in the collection: 'The crying of Zion and the poet must be seen not only as expression of grief, as emotional catharsis—though they surely are that. They are also designed to attract God's attention to Zion's plight.'[19] This third point suggests that there is more to the book of Lamentations than mourning. The literature functions to entice Yahweh to return in a salvific way to the people in the land of

---

[14] Klein, *Israel in Exile*, 13–14.

[15] Gottwald, *Studies*, 44–6; C. Westerman, *Die Klagelieder: Forschungsgeschichte und Auslegung* (Neukirchen-Vluyn: Neukirchener Verlag, 1990), 95–6, ET *Lamentations: Issues and Interpretations* (Edinburgh: T & T Clark, 1994), 104–5; C. A. Newsom, 'Response to Norman K. Gottwald, "Social Class and Ideology in Isaiah 40–55" ', *Semeia* 59 (1992), 73–8; P. T. Willey, *Remember the Former Things: The Recollection of Previous Texts in Second Isaiah* (SBLDS, 161; Atlanta, Ga.: Scholars Press, 1997); B. D. Sommer, *A Prophet Reads Scripture: Allusion in Isaiah 40–66* (Contraversions; Stanford, Calif.: Stanford University Press, 1998), 127–30; Linafelt, *Surviving Lamentations*, 62–79; K. M. O'Connor, ' "Speak Tenderly to Jerusalem": Second Isaiah's Reception and Use of Daughter Zion', *Princeton Seminary Bulletin* 20/3 (1999), 281–94, and idem, *Lamentations and the Tears of the World* (Maryknoll, NY: Orbis Books, 2002).

[16] Klein, *Israel in Exile*, 16.

[17] Linafelt, 'Zion's Cause', and *Surviving Lamentations*.

[18] G. Brunet, *Les Lamentations contre Jérémie: Réinterpretation des quatre premières Lamentations* (Paris: Presses universitaires de France, 1968); H. J. Boecker, *Die Klagelieder* (ZBK, 21; Zurich: Evangelische Verlag, 1985).

[19] Klein, *Israel in Exile*, 16.

Judah. This, too, has been the basis of recent studies,[20] but should be more strongly emphasized in view of the situation in the land.

In some respects, the insights of Klein regarding the book of Lamentations included themes that have become increasingly important in interpretations of the collection over recent years. In comparison with literature from the Babylonian community, the book of Lamentations reveals a distinctive theological expression that is voiced in a different way, through protest, and which seeks through its distinctive prayer to encourage the deity to return. In his brief analysis of Lamentations, Klein moves past the points he raised in conjunction with divergent expressions of the book to focus on the 'resolution of grief' in hopeful passages, a move in which he is matched by most interpreters of the text.[21] The three points, however, deserve further consideration because of the significant amount of interest the Templeless period and the early Second Temple period garner in current research. The conditions of the land in the aftermath of 587 created a situation in which a community struggled to function and rebuild while at the same time witnessing the effects of the surrounding devastation. As difficult as life in the land might have been, a significant portion of the people remained in Judah and their experiences shaped their liturgy, just as the literature of the Babylonian exiles was shaped by their context in Babylon. As the distinctive thought of the population in the homeland is the concern here, the historical background of the collection and a brief overview of the poems provide an introduction to a consideration of theological interpretation that arose in Judahite lament literature.

PROVENANCE

The five poems of Lamentations are most commonly dated to Templeless Judah because they appear to represent eyewitness reactions to the events of 587 and because of their unified focus on the ongoing

---

[20] e.g. Westerman, *Die Klagelieder = Lamentations*.
[21] Klein, *Israel in Exile*, 13–18. T. Linafelt, 'Surviving Lamentations', *HBT* 17 (1995), 45–61, and *Surviving Lamentations*, 1–18, highlights the concentration in scholarship on sources of hope in Lamentations as a strategy for the survival of painful imagery and language.

tragedy in the city of Jerusalem.[22] Few have followed the wary view of Provan that the ambiguous nature of the historical allusions disallows any precision in dating[23] or the more radical arguments advanced in favour of a Maccabean date.[24] However, both positions caution the interpreter to appreciate more fully the stereotypical and formulaic nature of Lamentations as a liturgical and literary enterprise that cannot be associated with any specific historical event with ease. A way around the impasse is to consider the outlook of the material in conjunction with other corroborating evidence, such as historical references, linguistic data, and tradition. There is widespread unanimity regarding the placement of Lamentations in postwar Jerusalem.

As a whole the focus of the poems fits well with the period in Judah following the Babylonian destruction of 587 to before the reconstruction of the temple in 515. The association with the population in the land in the Templeless period tends to issue in the first place from the concrete historical portrait of the book: the temple is destroyed, enemies have invaded the sanctuary, and the human toll is tremendous—people have died or suffer from illness, starvation, or are subjugated as vassals. At its background, Lamentations has the fall of Jerusalem and the atrocities that accompanied a lengthy siege and war.[25] Thematically, the poems fit more appropriately in Judah than without. The focus on suffering that is unmatched anywhere in the Hebrew Bible indicates a closeness to the events as does its pessimistic outlook. The graphic portrayal of the suffering of the inhabitants of the city which distinguishes the biblical Lamentations from its ANE counterparts likewise suggests a closeness to the events.[26] Moreover, the collection ends on a note of uncertainty which surely

---

[22] A review of recent scholarship in conjunction with historical questions is provided by F. W. Dobbs-Allsopp, 'Linguistic Evidence for the Date of Lamentations', *JANES* 26 (1998), 2–11.

[23] I. Provan, 'Reading Texts against an Historical Background—Lamentations 1', *SJOT* 1 (1990), 130–43, and *idem*, *Lamentations* (NCB; London: Marshall Pickering, 1991), 11–19.

[24] S. Lachs, 'The Date of Lamentations', *JQR* 57 (1968), 46–56.

[25] E. Janssen, *Juda in der Exilszeit: Ein Beitrag zur Frage der Entstehung des Judentums* (Göttingen: Vandenhoeck & Ruprecht, 1956), 9–12; Hillers, *Lamentations*, 3–6, 9–10.

[26] Gwaltney, 'The Biblical Book of Lamentations', 191–211.

places it before the optimism which accompanied the rise of Cyrus some time after 550 as reflected in the *Golah* literature. In support of a provenance before 550 is the fact that Deutero-Isaiah appears to know about and respond to laments in the book.[27]

In addition to historical references that suggest a placement in the sixth century BCE, an especially heavy concentration on the city of Jerusalem and Judah suggests it originated in Judah. More epithets for the city and the nation are found in the poems of Lamentations than anywhere elsewhere in the Hebrew Bible: בת ציון 'Daughter Zion' (1: 6; 2: 1, 4, 8, 10, 13, 18; 4: 22), בתולה בת ציון 'Virgin Daughter Zion' (2: 13), בת יהודה 'Daughter Judah' (1: 15; 2: 2, 5), בתולה בת יהודה 'Virgin Daughter Judah' (1: 15), בת ירושלם 'Daughter Jerusalem' (2: 13, 15), and בת עמי 'Daughter of my people' (2: 11; 3: 48; 4: 3, 6, 10). Moreover, the poet captures the drama of the disaster by representing the city of Jerusalem as a woman (1: 1) who even speaks in her own voice (1: 9c, 11c, 12–22; 2: 20–2).[28] The poet even discusses the distress of the inhabitants in chapter 1 with reference to the city personified; *her* priests, *her* maidens, *et al.*[29] An analysis of the motif of the land in the poems by Helberg confirms this almost myopic focus on Jerusalem.[30] His study shows that there are relatively few references to other areas devastated by the enemies. The plight of Jerusalem is shared, albeit minimally by Judah (2: 2, 5; 5: 2, 11) and includes a few glimpses of people deported from the land (1: 3, 5, 18; implicitly: 1: 6, 7; 2: 9, 14; 4: 16, 22).[31] When the exile is mentioned the issue is never the loss of the land, but rather, that deportation is just one consequence of a wider disaster. The very perspective of the poems situates them in Judah because of its concern with the ongoing dire present in Jerusalem.

---

[27] Westermann, *Die Klagelieder*, 95–6 = *Lamentations*, 104–5; Renkema, *Lamentations*, 54–7; A. Berlin, *Lamentations* (OTL; Louisville, Ky.: Westminster/John Knox Press, 2002), 33–5.

[28] W. F. Lanahan, 'The Speaking Voice in the Book of Lamentations', *JBL* 93 (1974), 41–9, and B. B. Kaiser, 'Poet as "Female Impersonator": The Image of Daughter Zion as Speaker in Biblical Poems of Suffering', *JR* 67 (1987), 174–82.

[29] F. W. Dobbs-Allsopp, *Lamentations* (Interpretation; Louisville, Ky.: John Knox Press, 2002), 62.

[30] J. L. Helberg, 'Land in the Book of Lamentations', *ZAW* 102 (1990), 372–85.

[31] Helberg, 'Land', 372–3.

Because an appeal to general outlook and historical references alone does not suffice to position the composition of the poems in the sixth century BCE, Dobbs-Allsopp considers other aspects such as the language and genre of the collection as well as the evidence of later tradition.[32] In the first place, ancient witnesses such as the Septuagint, Vulgate, Peshitta, Targum, and rabbinic sources associated Lamentations with the events of 587. Equally important is the ascription of the laments to the prophet Jeremiah that dates back at least to the Septuagint. Tradition is supported to some degree by linguistic evidence. In an analysis of the linguistic features of the poems, Dobbs-Allsopp reveals that the language utilized in the writing of Lamentations lies transitionally between Standard Biblical Hebrew of the monarchic period and Late Biblical Hebrew of the Second Temple period. The language of Lamentations fits well with the sixth century BCE.

In addition, the genre of the biblical Lamentations is very similar to that of a wide variety of laments generally categorized as Mesopotamian City Laments that were used to mourn the loss of cities and temples in the ANE. Just as its ANE counterparts responded to the crisis of the destruction of a city and/or its temple, the biblical poems are likely to have responded to such a catastrophe. In the light of the similarities between biblical Lamentations and the Mesopotamian laments, it is striking that the former lacks a resolution like that often found in the latter. Mesopotamian City Laments were recited upon the completion of a restoration project and tended to end on a festal note which celebrated the return of the deity. Since the biblical Lamentations end without a clear resolution, they probably do not have the same *Sitz im Leben* as their ANE counterparts. A smaller class of Mesopotamian laments known as *balags* and *eršemmas* were recited at the beginning of the construction of a temple to entreat the deity's blessing and thus, in contrast to the Mesopotamian City Laments, they do not tend to have a happy ending. Instead, they maintain a sustained focus on the present ruined state of the temple.[33] The biblical Lamentations is again like and unlike these. Although similar to the *balags* and *eršemmas* with respect to the

---

[32] Dobbs-Allsopp, 'Linguistic Evidence', 3–11.
[33] Edelman, 'The "Empty Land" as a Motif in City Laments', in G. Brooke and T. Romer (eds.) (forthcoming).

lack of a redemptive conclusion, the biblical Lamentations, nevertheless, remains distinct from them because it considers the ongoing suffering of the inhabitants more often and more persistently than the state of the temple.[34] Again, the provenance of the poems should be found at a time other than during temple construction. In spite of being of a genre akin to the Mesopotamian City Laments, Dobbs-Allsopp has shown that Lamentations draws also from the language of prophetic oracles of the Hebrew Bible. The poems found therein, therefore, represent a native Judahite genre and relate more appropriately to services of public mourning rituals that commemorated the catastrophic events of 587.

Although it is generally agreed that as a whole the collection fits well with the period following 587, the order of the poems in terms of composition varies among interpreters.[35] Furthermore, certain poems are thought to stem from time periods outside of the accepted dates of the Templeless period. For instance, Rudolph regards the failure of chapter 1 to refer directly to the actual destruction of the temple as an indicator that it belongs to just after the events of 597, not 587.[36] Alternatively, chapters 3[37] and 5[38] are dated later than the sixth century. However, the majority of commentators posit all five poems to the period following the disaster of 587 and before the period of the return c.539 or at least by the time of the rebuilt temple in 515.[39] It is difficult to provide an exact chronological sequence of

[34] Linafelt, *Surviving Lamentations*, 49–61.

[35] Westermann, *Die Klagelieder*, 56–7, = *Lamentations*, 54–5, provides a convenient summary of opinions on the order of the poems.

[36] W. Rudolph, *Die Klagelieder* (KAT, 17/3; Gütersloh: Gerd Mohn, 2nd edn. 1962), 193, 209–10. A persuasive rebuttal of his view is provided by Janssen, *Juda in der Exilszeit*, 10–12.

[37] Westermann, *Die Klagelieder*, 65–70, 95, 137–60, = *Lamentations*, 66–72, 105, 160–93.

[38] Janssen, *Juda in der Exilszeit*, 10–12, places the fifth chapter during the time of the rebuilding the temple in the early Second Temple period because there appears to be a distance between the events of 587 and the communal lament. Against his view, the references to the city do not necessarily indicate a time long past as the situation appears to be continuing in the present (vv. 1–18) and the historical background places it within the same situation as the other four chapters.

[39] A notable exception is O. Kaiser, *Klagelieder* (ATD, 16; Göttingen: Vandenhoeck & Ruprecht, 1981), 293–396, who in his detailed analysis of the poems ascribed them to different periods between the fifth and fourth centuries BCE in an order not reflected in the final form of the book.

the poems although the final form of the book with its concern over whether or not Yahweh will act salvifically for his people suggests that all five poems were put together before the end of the Templeless period. It is outside the purview of this book to order the poems according to the date of their composition.[40] Even if Lamentations 1 should be taken to refer to events following 597 and not 587, a theory which has many merits, the continuation of public rituals during the Templeless period raises the possibility that all the poems were used liturgically during that time. More importantly, it is the underlying themes of the poems that deserve our attention.

Though the date of the material fits well with the era following the disaster of 587, further dissent centres on whether Judah or Babylon provided the setting for the composition of the poems. Gwaltney, for example, uses the commonality between the biblical Lamentations and those of Mesopotamia in order to argue for a Babylonian provenance.[41] In his reckoning, the exiles encountered the form of lament for the destruction of a city in Mesopotamia. However, the poems share a significant amount of thematic and formulaic motifs with such biblical literature as the communal laments of the Psalter[42] and the prophetic oracles against foreign nations.[43] In his comparison of the biblical Lamentations and Mesopotamian laments, Dobbs-Allsopp established a distinctive genre of lamentation common to the traditions of the Hebrew Bible.[44] Furthermore, the fact that the forms of Mesopotamian laments existed from the second millennium BCE to the beginning of the Common Era provides some confidence in the belief that a milieu of mourning literature with common motifs, language, and themes could be tapped at many times and places to express national grief. It is likely that Lamentations drew from a stock

---

[40] With Hillers, *Lamentations*, 10, I agree that the attempts to determine the chronological order of the poems are not persuasive. The collection of individual poems belongs as a unit to the sixth century BCE. Elsewhere, I have argued that the present order of the collection may reflect a later attempt to give a meaningful overall shape to the book, see J. A. Middlemas, 'The Violent Storm in Lamentations', *JSOT* 29 (2004), 81–97.

[41] Gwaltney, 'The Biblical Book of Lamentations', 208.

[42] Westermann, *Klagelieder*, 60–1, 89–90, 97, = *Lamentations*, 95–8, 58–61, 106.

[43] McDaniel, 'The Alleged Sumerian Influence'.

[44] Dobbs-Allsopp, *Weep, O Daughter of Zion*.

of common phrases and concepts in its expression of communal mourning.⁴⁵

For a number of reasons, the poems of the Hebrew Lamentations correspond well to the Judahite population in post-war Jerusalem. There is one notable exception. It has long been recognized that chapter 3 differs in form and content from the other poems. In terms of form, the third chapter shifts oddly between an individual complaint of a suffering solitary figure introduced by 'I am the man' אני הגבר (vv. 1–21), a didactic hopeful interlude (vv. 22–39), a communal confession in the first person plural (vv. 40–7), and a conclusion by a suffering individual (vv. 48–66). The acrostic is different as well in that the Hebrew consonants introduce three lines apiece producing an impressive total of 66 verses. In addition to containing different formal features, the third chapter exhibits less concern for the plight of the community and a marked shift away from a focus on the city of Jerusalem.⁴⁶ Like nowhere else in Lamentations, chapter 3 contains a sustained hopeful interlude akin to wisdom literature in verses 19–39 which serves purposes of a didactic nature.⁴⁷ The paraenetic section is distinguished in two ways from the rest of the poems: through the portrait of the deity as divine saviour rather than as divine warrior and by the inclusion of a paradigmatic figure whose message is the redemptive nature of suffering like that more commonly associated with the suffering servant of Deutero-Isaiah.⁴⁸ Taken together, these factors support Westermann's contention that the third poem derives from a different hand from the rest of the material.⁴⁹ This does not necessarily suggest a different time period. Not only is the poem found in the centre of a collection attributable to the period after 587 but

---

⁴⁵ Ferris, *The Genre of Communal Lament*, 174.
⁴⁶ Hillers, *Lamentations*, 120.
⁴⁷ Westermann, *Klagelieder*, 68–9, = *Lamentations*, 70; F. W. Dobbs-Allsopp, 'Tragedy, Tradition, and Theology in the Book of Lamentations', *JSOT* 74 (1997), 29–60.
⁴⁸ A more complete analysis of this section especially with a concern to demonstrate that it represents an exilic corrective to the response to suffering found elsewhere in Lamentations can be found in J. A. Middlemas, 'Did Second Isaiah Write Lamentations 3?', in an unpublished paper given at the International Organization for the Study of the Old Testament Conference, Leiden, 2004 (forthcoming), and at the SBL Annual Meeting, San Antonio, Texas, November 2004.
⁴⁹ Westermann, *Klagelieder*, 65–71, = *Lamentations*, 66–73.

before 550,[50] the fact that the hope of the central verses is eclipsed by suffering sets these verses well within the outlook of the whole.[51] The third chapter with its odd admixture of forms and its central optimistic vision seems to be from a different thought milieu from the rest of the material and will not be considered in conjunction with chapters 1, 2, 4, and 5.

The events of 587 that catapulted Judah into the nations and resulted in systemic collapse in the homeland make it almost unique among the diverse invasions and sackings that occurred throughout the history of Judah. The compatibility of the images and themes found in the biblical Lamentations with post-war Jerusalem and Judah provide support for its origin in this time period. In particular, Lamentations 1, 2, 4, and 5 belong to the Judahites left in the land. It is the contention of this book that these poems can be used as a means to indicate features consistent with a theological response from the inhabitants of the land. Following an overview of these chapters, five motifs distinctive to the Judahite population will be examined.

OVERVIEW

This overview organizes the material of Lamentations according to four foci that link the thought of the poems. These foci are intrinsic to the collection of Lamentations, but do not serve as the motifs distinctive to the book. Rather they enable us to summarize the message of Lamentations in order for such a study to take place.

Even a cursory glimpse at the poems of Lamentations confirms that the images of past and present violence feature strongly. Lamentations represents a hotchpotch of formal elements thrown together to elicit the literary effect of the chaos that is picked up in the teeming images of tragedy in the individual poems. As such, the chapters resist organization. Images veritably tumble over each other with no recognizable ordering principle. Nevertheless, it is possible

---

[50] Kraus, *Klagelieder*, 11.
[51] Provan, *Lamentations*, 20–5; Linafelt, 'Zion's Cause'.

to order the material thematically. Hunter, for example, provided a helpful rubric with which to approach Lamentations systematically.[52] In his view, the first eleven verses of chapter 1 define the types of concepts developed and expanded elsewhere in the material. Following his line of enquiry, a close analysis of 1: 1–11 reveals that four of the important themes isolated by Hunter actually appear succinctly as interjections into the surrounding material. The interruptions of the material are particularly striking because according to a close analysis of Lamentations by Johnson, chapters 1, 2, and 4 each have a 'fact half' in which events are described and an 'interpretive half' in which implications of the description are drawn out.[53] In this scheme, chapter 1 contains a sustained narration of the events in an objective report in verses 1–11. The account of disaster almost exactly coincides with Johnson's 'fact half', except that the pattern is broken by two interpretative statements (1: 5b, 8a) and two statements of direct address to the deity (1: 9c, 11c) that disrupt the narrative. Interestingly, verses 1–11 also conform most closely with the funeral song except for these four disruptions in which elements of the lament genre infiltrate.[54] The appearance of four statements distinguished from the material in which they are found—the interjection of reflection in an otherwise third-person eyewitness report and the interruption of elements of complaint into a funeral dirge—suggest their importance. Indeed, they function paradigmatically to indicate the themes that recur in all the poems of the book and provide a helpful rubric with which to introduce this widely divergent collection.

In an otherwise introductory report of the situation at hand in chapter 1, two statements reflect on the disaster and attribute the current situation to the deity and to egregious sin (vv. 5b, 8a). The poet begins with a description of the city whose present contrasts sharply with its past. Although, at one time, the city was 'full[55] of

[52] Hunter, *Faces of a Lamenting City*.
[53] B. Johnson, 'Form and Message in Lamentations', *ZAW* 97 (1987), 58–73.
[54] Linafelt, *Surviving Lamentations*, 37–9.
[55] 1: 1a MT אֵיכָה יָשְׁבָה בָדָד הָעִיר רַבָּתִי עָם 'How lonely sits the city (once) full of people.' T. F. McDaniel, 'Philological Studies in Lamentations I & II', *Bib* 49 (1968), 27–53, 199–220, suggests that רבתי is the counterpart to the masc. substantive רב 'chief' and is an honorific title 'mistress of the people' akin to those given to Ugaritic goddesses who were addressed as *rbt*, cf. Isa. 47: 1–5. Hunter, *Faces of a Lamenting*

people', 'mistress among the nations', and 'princess of the provinces', it now 'sits alone like a widow and has become a slave'. Disguised as the eyewitness, the poet fleshes out the description by depicting further the distress of the city and aligning it with that of its inhabitants (vv. 1–5a). The section closes in verse 5b with an explanation for the startling transformation: Yahweh has done this! The dire present is the result of divine agency; 'Because Yahweh has caused her grief on account of the multitude of her sins.' Immediately after this sudden interjection, the poet continues his litany of suffering. Every member of society from children to adult nobles and leaders has been taken into exile (vv. 5c–6) or slaughtered (v. 7b). Zion, again depicted alone, ponders her suffering and her homeless ones (v. 7a). At this point, the narrator interjects a second time to interpret the reason for the change. In verse 8a, he focuses exclusively on Jerusalem's culpability, her great sin. He explains that 'Jerusalem has sinned extraordinarily, therefore she has become an object of scorn.'[56] Thereafter, the description returns to concentrate on the present distress and highlights the desecration of the sanctuary (v. 10) and famine of the people (v. 11). In what largely corresponds in form to a funeral dirge, that is, a song that laments the death of an individual, the poet mourns the figurative death of Jerusalem's past glory.

Just as two interpretations intrude into the description of the present distress and provide two themes that unite the collection—Yahweh's agency and human rebellion—Lady Jerusalem makes two

---

City, 94–5, however, notes against him that רבתי as 'full' is more consistent with usage in the Hebrew Bible. So also Rudolph, *Klagelieder*, 206; Hillers, *Lamentations*, 64–5; Provan, *Lamentations*, 35. The fivefold emphasis in chapter 1 on the phrase 'there is no-one to comfort [Jerusalem]' (1: 2, 9, 16, 17, 21) supports the traditional translation as 'full' by its concern for a solitary and isolated Jerusalem.

[56] MT לְנִידָה The noun is a *hapax legomenon* and is of uncertain meaning. Scholars tend to favour one of two interpretations: (1) with LXX, T, Arabic (and 4QLam^a lnwd 'to wander') read as a noun from the middle weak root נוד which according to *BDB*, 626, can mean any number of things including 'move to and fro, wander, flutter, and show grief'. It is often taken in the sense of shaking the head or nodding in mockery, so Kraus, *Klagelieder*, 29; Meek, 'Lamentations', 10; Gordis, *Lamentations*, 155; Hillers, *Lamentations*, 70; Provan, *Lamentations*, 44, or (2) with Aq, Symm, P read as an alternative spelling of נִדָּה from נדד 'impurity' implying an unclean/menstruous woman, so Rudolph, *Klagelieder*, 206; Kaiser, 'Poet as "Female Impersonator" ', 125; Renkema, *Lamentations*, 133–4.

statements in the midst of the third person address that also function paradigmatically. In verse 9c she appeals directly to Yahweh to consider the exaltation of her enemies: 'See my affliction, O Yahweh, because the enemy has made himself great.' With a second intrusion Lady Jerusalem urges the deity to consider her humiliation: 'See, Yahweh, and consider for I have become worthless' (v. 11c). Twice Zion addresses the deity directly in language familiar from laments of the Psalter. Because Zion is not dead, she interrupts the funeral song of the narrator and complains directly to the deity. The cries of Lady Jerusalem in 9c and 11c delineate two additional ideas that are found in all the poems of the collection: the exaltation of the enemy and the humiliated state of the city.[57] In spite of the tumultuous presentation of a variety of lamentable circumstances, the cohesion of the collection is made possible through the four themes which oddly intercede in verses 1–11—Yahweh's volition, human responsibility, frenetic foes, and humiliated Zion.

Although Jerusalem briefly interrupted the account of the eyewitness in 1: 1–11, her voice concludes the poem (vv. 12–22). In her first-person response to the tragic events depicted by the poet in verses 1–11, Lady Zion provides the first clear indication of how the themes of the intentionality of the deity, sin, triumph of the enemies, and public disgrace will be developed and elucidated in the rest of the poems.[58] At the beginning of her speech, she calls to passers-by to witness her suffering (v. 12) and affirms that the ultimate responsibility for the tragedy and her pain, in particular, belongs with the deity 'who has caused her to suffer on the day of his burning anger'[59].

---

[57] Hunter, *Faces of a Lamenting City*, 146, listed 8 themes developed throughout the book, but there is some overlap between them suggesting the four motifs listed here. Klein, *Israel in Exile*, 9–11, discusses an overview of the book according to the four criteria of disaster: (1) scorn of the enemy, (2) anguish of the elect, (3) scope of the destruction, and (4) famine and siege. The four isolated here with the exception of the emphasis on sin correspond to Westermann's three constituent elements of a Lament: Yahweh, the lamenter, and the enemy. Cf. C. Westermann, 'Struktur und Geschichte der Klage im Alten Testament', *ZAW* 66 (1954), 44–80, and *idem*, 'The Role of the Lament in the Theology of the Old Testament', *Int* 28 (1974), 20–38.

[58] Linafelt, *Surviving Lamentations*, 35–61, provides one of the most powerful studies of Lady Zion's speech here and in ch. 2.

[59] Yahweh's 'day of burning anger' forms part of the motifs of prophetic oracles of judgement; cf. Isa. 13: 9, 13; Jer. 4: 8, 26; 25: 37–8; Hos. 11: 9; Nah. 1: 6; Zeph. 2: 2. Jerusalem acknowledges that the foretold judgement of the Lord has been brought

In associating her present distress with Yahweh, Lady Jerusalem is more outspoken in her accusation against the deity than the narrator. From her perspective, Yahweh has acted like a violent abuser, a destroyer, a hunter, and an abandoner (vv. 13–17). In fact, instead of calling an assembly to vindicate her, Jerusalem declares that Yahweh 'threshed my young men' (v. 15b). An independent witness, most likely the poet of verses 1–11, confirms Lady Jerusalem's accusation and states, 'As in a winepress, Adonai treads upon the virgin daughter Judah' (v. 15c). As well as having been an active aggressor, the deity abandoned Lady Jerusalem whose claim that a comforter is far away from her (v. 16) is echoed by the eyewitness (v. 17a). Finally, Yahweh as aggressor and abandoner is connected explicitly to the enemies who 'commanded concerning Jacob "his enemies shall surround him" ' (v. 17b). Like the eyewitness who spoke in v. 17b, Jerusalem connects the actions of the enemies with divine judgement: 'All my enemies have heard of my trouble, they exult that you, yourself, have done this' (v. 21b), and 'Adonai has given me into the hands of those whom I could not withstand' (v. 14c).

Because Yahweh's actions against the people and the city are interwoven with the actions of adversaries, it is clear that the enemy serves as the instrument through which Yahweh punished his people. Not surprisingly, Lady Jerusalem finds no consolation in the divine origin of the enemy's behaviour. She is convinced that earthly foes will prevail 'because[60] the enemy is mighty' (v. 16c). Indeed, there is no safe haven for the people because in the street they die by the sword and in the house they perish from hunger or disease (v. 20c). Already in the first part of the chapter, the eyewitness has testified to the havoc wreaked by the enemies in Jerusalem (vv. 3c, 5ac, 6c, 7bc, 10). The enemies prosper as ruler (v. 5a), they are likened to pursuers who hem the people in as they try to escape (v. 3c), press their leaders into exile (v. 6c), wantonly slaughter (v. 7b), find pleasure in the humiliation of Zion (v. 7c), and greedily take the nation's valuables while defiling the sanctuary with their

---

about in Judah. Traditionally, the 'day of Yahweh' suggests the ultimate victory of God over injustice and oppression. Cf. Gottwald, *Studies*, 72–7; Renkema *Lamentations*, 157–9.

[60] Reading causal *ky* rather than emphatic.

presence (v. 10).⁶¹ Even former allies have become foes (vv. 2c, 8b, 17b, 19a). From every corner, Jerusalem is beset by an adversary. Unlike the narrator, Lady Jerusalem does not expand upon any specific deeds of the enemy. Instead her concern lies with Yahweh's appointment of human agents to carry out divine wrath (v. 21b). The atrocities they commit lead ultimately to her cry for vengeance (vv. 21c–22).⁶²

Lady Jerusalem acknowledges responsibility for the fate that has come upon her in her declaration: 'Righteous is Yahweh for I rebelled against his word' (v. 18a). The term צדיק 'righteous' stems from language of the courtroom. An accused utilizes this term to profess acceptance of a verdict. In this case, personified Zion states that Yahweh is right and accepts her collapse as punishment for sin.⁶³ This brief statement is both an acknowledgement of Yahweh's justice and an expression of the conviction of the fairness of the deity.⁶⁴ Lady Jerusalem's statement in verse 18 draws on a previous comment by the narrator in which he attributed the ultimate source of the present trouble to 'the severity of her sins'⁶⁵ (v. 5b cf. v. 8a). The primary concern, however, is that her people are dying or have been taken

---

⁶¹ The affinity of the imagery of the enemy's entrance into the temple and seizure of booty with that of rape has been noted frequently by commentators.

⁶² 1: 21c הֵבֵאתָ MT 'you have brought'. Hillers, *Lamentations*, 78, 91, and Gordis, *Lamentations*, 160, regard the verb as a precative perfect expressing a wish or request. P translates as an imperative which is followed by some, Kraus, *Klagelieder*, 29; Rudolph, *Klagelieder*, 208; Westermann, *Klagelieder*, 102. The context makes the past tense 'you have brought' unlikely, contra Albrektson, *Lamentations*, 83–4; Meek, 'Lamentations', 15; Provan, *Lamentations*, 56; Renkema, *Lamentations*, 195–7. There is some dispute over the translation of this passage. It centres on whether or not 21c refers to the judgement of the enemies or the judgement of Israel that has already come about. Since the judgement of Israel is ongoing, as is clearly shown through the agony that the poet and Lady Jerusalem express, I suggest that all of v. 21c refers to future judgement rather than just וְיִהְיוּ כָמוֹנִי. As such it introduces the same theme as in v. 22. The future judgement of the enemies is a central motif that reappears throughout the rest of the book.

⁶³ G. von Rad, 'Gerichtsdoxologie', in *Gesammelte Studien zum Alten Testament*, ii (Munich: Kaiser, 1973), 245–54; F. Crüsemann, 'Jahwes Gerechtigkeit (צדק/צדקה) im alten Testament', *ET* 36 (1976), 427–50.

⁶⁴ Renkema, *Lamentations*, 179–81, emphasizes the nature of צדק as severe punishment, appealing to 2 Chr. 12: 6; Isa. 10: 22; Ezra 9: 15; Dan. 9: 14 while at the same time suggesting a salvific dimension as in Pss. 31: 2; 116: 5; 145: 17.

⁶⁵ פשע 'rebellion, transgression' originally derived from political life as a common term for revolt against an overlord (2 Kgs. 1: 1; 3: 5, etc.); Hillers, *Lamentations*, 84. It is also used in texts depicting Israel going after other gods.

away and that she is in great pain. After the exhortation to Yahweh to destroy her enemies, she moans that she is failing 'for my groans are many and my heart is faint' (v. 22). Ultimately, at least in the eyes of Zion, salvation comes when the enemies are vanquished. She does not deny her culpability, but declares, finally, that it is too much to bear. Her entire existence and naturally that of her inhabitants lie in the balance.

The final theme expanded by Lady Jerusalem in chapter 1 is that of her humiliation. Although the eyewitness has already remarked on her collapse, stating for example that she has come down to a lowly state (v. 9b), she is an object of scorn (v. 8a), naked (v. 8b), unable to even look upon herself (v. 8c), ritually impure (v. 9a) and alone (v. 9, cf. vv. 1, 2), Lady Jerusalem, too, considers the degradation of her present situation. She speaks of herself as a ruin (v. 13c) who is unwell (vv. 13c, 21c), as ritually impure[66] (v. 17c), and without comfort (vv. 16b, 17a, 21a). Her present state is truly ignominious. However, as with the theme of responsibility for the disaster, she places less emphasis on her fall than on Yahweh's abuse and on the chosen instrument, the enemy. Perhaps coinciding with her inability to look at herself (v. 8), Lady Jerusalem mentions some of the distressful events highlighted by the eyewitness, but fails to elaborate on them. The present is simply too much to bear.

The four motifs interjected into the material in 1: 1–11 which reappeared in striking combinations in Jerusalem's speech recur throughout poems 2, 4, and 5, but are developed in new and startling ways. For instance, the primary focus in chapter 2 is on the enemy. The ultimate foe is Yahweh. Where historical enemies appear, they function primarily as objects of the mighty purposes of Yahweh (2: 7, 17, 22a), but also as protagonists who jibe or mock Jerusalem in her collapse. The culpability of Yahweh again comes to the foreground, but it is elaborated in verses 1–9. Replete with images of Yahweh as a violent warrior deity who terrorizes, the poet names him an adversary thrice (vv. 4a, 5a). In Zion's speech at the close of the poem, she attributes the destruction of her people to Yahweh and says, 'On the

---

[66] This does not have to imply menstruous as many commentators understand, esp. Kaiser, 'Poet as "Female Impersonator"', 174–6. It could be a reference to corpse contamination as suggested by Linafelt, *Surviving Lamentations*, 157 n. 59.

day of your anger, you killed, you slaughtered without sparing,' and elaborates, 'There is no-one who escaped or survived on the day of Yahweh's anger' (v. 22b). Through the emphasis on the destructive power of Yahweh which was revealed on the day of his anger (vv. 1, 2b, 3, 4c, 6c, 17), the poet radically presents human foes as the divine agents of destruction (vv. 3b, 7ab, 17c, 22a). Bitter still is the fact that the deity withdrew from saving Israel (v. 3b), rejected his sanctuary (v. 7a), handed over Jerusalem's very walls to the enemy (v. 7b), exalted them (v. 17c), almost as if summoning them to participate in a feast day (v. 22a). The association of Yahweh with human agents is reinforced by the threefold use of בלע in conjunction with both the actions of Yahweh and the enemies in verse 16b. The poet depicts the adversaries acting on their own initiative elsewhere at verses 7c, 15–16, 22c. Saturated with the violence perpetrated against Jerusalem and its inhabitants, chapter 2 pays particular attention to Yahweh's volition.

The other two themes of the sin and humiliation of Jerusalem also appear in this chapter, even though the main emphasis is on what the deity has done. In contrast to chapter 1 in which transgression was accepted as a reason for the disaster, there is no acknowledgement of sin here. Instead, the narrator states only once that 'Your prophets have seen visions for you that were vain and false;[67] they have not made known your iniquity in order to reverse your judgement,[68] but have seen vain and misleading[69] oracles for you' (v. 14). The implication is that poor prophetic advice resulted in the fall of the city. Instead of repenting from sin, the inhabitants rested secure in the belief that the city was impenetrable to attack.

---

[67] תפל MT lit. 'whitewashed'. The sense is that like whitewash, it concealed the true situation. It is figuratively used of false prophecy in Ezek. 13: 10, 11, 14, 15, contra Renkema, *Lamentations*, 110, who notes the use of tasteless food in Job 6: 6 and favours this understanding here.

[68] MT K שביתך Q שבותך. Literally, 'restore your fortunes'. The Qere is more consistent with the expression as it appears elsewhere. J. M. Bracke, 'šûb šᵉbût: A Reappraisal', *ZAW* 97 (1985), 233–44.

[69] מדוחים This Hiphil plural participle is a *hapax legomenon*. It is thought to be either from נדה 'to thrust, banish' hence 'a thing to lead aside, entice' (so P and T), followed by Gottwald, *Studies*, 11; Kraus, *Klagelieder*, 47; Albrektson, 'Lamentations', 112; Meek, 'Lamentations', 20; Renkema, *Lamentations*, 288; or 'banishment' (as LXX), followed by Rudolph, *Klagelieder*, 220. In a context in which prophetic words are spoken about as being false, 'misleading' makes more sense.

The theme of the 'worthlessness' of Jerusalem appears more often in this chapter, however. From the first verse, the lowly state of Zion is emphasized: 'Adonai has cast the glory of Israel down from the heavens to the earth' (v. 1b). Having suffered divinely ordained humiliation, Jerusalem is further disgraced by the enemies who raise a shout in the 'house of the Lord' as though it were a feast day (v. 7c), clap their hands in mockery (v. 15a), hiss and shake their heads (v. 15b), jeeringly open their mouths wide (v. 16a), grind their teeth[70] (v. 16b), and figuratively wring their hands in glee as they observe: 'surely, this is the day for which we have been waiting, we have discovered it and we see it!' (v. 16c). More disturbing still is that they recognize that this was once the city that was called 'perfect in beauty' and 'joy of all the land' (v. 15c).[71] Even the narrator comments on the dreadful present recognizing that 'your brokenness is as great as the sea, who can heal you?' (v. 13c). The great reversal of Jerusalem and the fact that even Yahweh has become a pursuer results in the disgrace and humiliation of the city.

Chapter 4 is made up of a series of observations on the physical suffering that afflicts all members of the population. The violent hunting images of Yahweh are not present here. At one point alone the poet depicts the Lord as an aggressor where he comments that Yahweh himself scatters[72] them[73] and no longer looks on them (v. 16a). In the fourth poem, Yahweh is the absentee overlord and the leaders of the community have been scorned by him. Verse 11 attributes the explanation for the change in behaviour to the fact that the judgement day of Yahweh has occurred: 'Yahweh has accomplished his fury, he has poured out his burning anger; He kindled a fire in Zion and it consumed her foundations.' The destruction

[70] Usually of anger Ps. 112: 10; mockery 35: 16; menace or threat 37: 12.

[71] Gottwald, *Studies*, 57–8, used of choice cities; Albrektson, *Lamentations*, 224–5.

[72] חלקם MT Piel pf 3ms חלק (I) 'to scatter', as in Gen. 49: 7. LXX, Syr., and some Heb. MSS point as the noun with mpl suffix 'their portion'. Hillers takes from חלק (II) 'to destroy', which has cognates in Akk., Ug., Eth. There is another difficulty with 'the face of Yahweh' as it is always subject to a plural verb. Thus, Meek, 'Lamentations', 33–4, understands the word to be the noun and translates, 'The face of those whose portion was in Yahweh he no longer regards.' However, because חלק is parallel with יסף it suggests that it is a verb, so also, Rudolph, *Klagelieder*, 249; Albrektson, *Lamentations*, 191; Renkema, *Lamentations*, 542–3.

[73] The uncertain third masculine plural object 'them' refers either back to the priests and prophets of v. 13 or to the priests and elders of the same line.

wrought by the deity on the city, its buildings, and its temple has occurred. The prophecies of doom have been fulfilled even though Jerusalem was believed to be impenetrable to enemy attack (v. 12).

The fact that the image of the foe and the enemy advancing upon the city and entering through the gates of Jerusalem in verse 12 follows immediately upon Yahweh's destruction of the city in verse 11 suggests strongly that divine judgement was fulfilled through the actions of the enemy. Elsewhere the poet depicts the human foes as hunters and pursuers in verses 18–20. Moreover, the relentless pursuit of the adversaries led to the capture of the king whom the poet nostalgically terms 'the breath of our nostrils, Yahweh's anointed' and recalls that of him it was said, 'in his shadow we will live among the nations' (4: 20). Even the king has been ensnared in their traps. These images, fast and fleeting, result not in an outpouring of grief, but in the cry for retribution. In verses 21–2, the poet exultantly declares to Edom with terminology that implies the surety of the prediction 'to you also shall the cup pass',[74] 'you will get drunk and strip yourself bare',[75] and 'He pays attention to your iniquity, O daughter of Edom, he will uncover your sins.' Divine wrath spent in the collapse of Jerusalem is prophesied to Edom, the only named enemy in Lamentations.

The concept of the humiliation and worthlessness of Jerusalem and its inhabitants which immediately opens the chapter continues unabated throughout it. In verses 1–2, the children of Zion are likened to gold that has lost its shine, precious stones scattered at every street corner, and although once like gold, they are now only shards of a potter. Those once precious and valuable are now worthless. The reversal continues to define every segment of society. Even those who ate delicacies and were dressed in fine clothing starve. Pictured as vagrants they rummage through rubbish heaps searching for food (v. 5). The men of high rank who were more pure than snow, more dazzling than milk (v. 7), are now only wasted images of their past selves with their form darker than blackness and their skin

---

[74] Jer. 25: 21; 49: 12 explicitly state that Edom must drink the cup of Yahweh's judgement, cf. Isa. 34: 1–17; 63: 1–6.

[75] Nakedness reflects shame and disgrace as with Daughter Zion in 1: 8. Cf. Gen. 3: 9; 9: 20–7; Isa. 3: 17; 20: 4; Ezek. 16: 7–8. It is especially used with personified cities such as Nineveh in Nah. 3: 5–6, Jerusalem in Jer. 13: 26, and Babylon in Jer. 47: 3.

shrivelled upon their bones (v. 8). Even the priests wear bloodstained clothing (v. 14) and are avoided as unclean (v. 15). A wide spectrum of society from the youngest to the oldest, from the poorest to the richest, suffers in a city under judgement.

The reversal of fortunes in this chapter is attributed to the sins of the people. In verse 6, the poet announces that surely 'the sin of the daughter of my people is greater than the sin of Sodom which was overthrown in a moment'.[76] With such a marked paucity of references to sin, its appearance in verse 6 along with the inclusion of Sodom emphasizes its importance and its association with the present distress. Although also the object of divine wrath, Sodom in Genesis 19 was overturned in an instant and its inhabitants did not suffer a constant trial of starvation. Because of the contrasting fates of the two, the poet concludes that the sin of Jerusalem must be greater than that of Sodom. Sin occurs once more in a context that associates it with the enemy's triumphant march through the gates of the city (vv. 11–12). These events have taken place 'on account of the sins of her prophets, the iniquities of her priests, the ones who shed the blood of the righteous in her midst' (v. 13). Societal leaders are to blame. Although the allusion to 'those who shed the blood of the righteous' can represent the people (Jer. 7: 6; Ezek. 33: 25; Ps. 106: 38–9), it is more likely that the reference includes political rulers (2 Kgs. 21: 16; Jer. 22: 17; Ezek. 22: 6, 27) along with the indictment of the priests and prophets.[77] Just as every member of society suffers from the effects of famine, every group in society—the people (v. 6), priests and prophets (v. 13), and rulers (v. 13)—are culpable for their contribution to the nation's sin and its subsequent collapse.

The communal lament in chapter 5 provides a summary of the various themes of the other poems. With each verse having only one line, the form of this last lament suggests that the people are calling out in their last breath in a gasp that fades away under duress.[78] The

---

[76] Gottwald, *Studies*, 65–66, notes that the destruction of Sodom provided a measuring rod with which all subsequent sin was compared. It was particularly noted for its suddenness, violence, and finality. Sodom becomes one of the stock images synonymous with divine judgement for sin.

[77] Hillers, *Lamentations*, 149.

[78] W. H. Shea, 'The *qinah* Structure of the Book of Lamentations', *Bib* 60 (1979), 103–7.

four themes which recur in each of the previous poems also occur here, but as before, the emphasis placed on each one is different. The complaint about the enemies, for instance, occupies lengthy sections (vv. 2–6, 8–15) compared to the other themes and it is tied inextricably to humiliation. In verse 1, the community calls out to Yahweh to consider their situation. In so doing, they echo Lady Jerusalem (cf. 1: 11c; 2: 20) with their plea, 'Look and see our reproach.'[79] Afterwards follows a litany of the deeds of the foe, which concludes: 'our heart has become faint', 'our eyes grow dark', and 'Mount Zion lies desolate and jackals prowl' (vv. 17–18). The complete ruination of the city and its inhabitants resulted from enemy intrusion and subjugation (vv. 2–6, 8–15). The promised land of milk and honey has been handed over to invaders who have left children without fathers and women without husbands, who charge for the barest necessities like water and wood, and who harass the inhabitants (vv. 2–6). With greater intensity, verses 8–15 depict the people as 'slaves' (v. 8) subjugated to the enemy who harry them even as they search for food (v. 9), rape women (v. 11), hang up princes,[80] disrespect the elders (v. 12), and force the young men and boys to do the simplest labour of grinding grain and gathering wood (v. 13).

It is not that the people felt themselves blameless, but the complete exaltation of their enemies was difficult to bear. In two points they acknowledge their sin. In the first, they attribute their current distress to the behaviour of their predecessors and complain, 'Our fathers sinned, they are no more; We, ourselves, bear the burden of their iniquities' (v. 7). The noun for father אב can indicate either the leaders of the community or ancestors.[81] With either, the

---

[79] הביט MT 'He has looked.' The Qere reads הַבִּיטָה. Read with Q based on parallelism of these two verbs elsewhere 1: 11; 2: 20.

[80] בידם Kraus, Klagelieder, 89–90, renders 'hung up by their hands' and understands the treatment as a type of execution in which the victim was impaled or crucified. Meek, 'Lamentations', 37; Hillers, Lamentations, 158; Renkema, Lamentations, 610–11, understand the ב of agency, 'at their hands', and understand that it refers back to the conquerors of 5: 8. Provan, Lamentations, 131, suggests that death is not necessarily implied, rather, the concern could be with humiliation or intimidation.

[81] As Gottwald, Studies, 67–8, shows, there is evidence for the application of the use of אב to rulers, priests, prophets, and noblemen, as in Gen. 45: 8; Judg. 17: 10; 18: 19; 1 Sam. 24: 11; 2 Kgs. 2: 12; 3: 13; 6: 21; 13: 14; 2 Chr. 2: 2. He also entertains the translation of 'ancestors'.

responsibility for the present distress is placed elsewhere. However, the community acknowledges that their guilt is their own in v. 16: 'Woe to us for we have sinned.' Although the present distress was attributed to their own actions, the emphasis of the lament, lying as it does on the outrageous behaviour of the enemies, thereby implies that the judgement far outweighed the sin committed.

The final prayer to Yahweh provides the ultimate acknowledgement that the deity has brought this suffering and that it is only through divine action that there will be relief (vv. 19–22). In the moment of greatest despair, the community echoes an age-old belief in their deity as eternal king: 'You, Yahweh, sit enthroned forever, your throne is from generation to generation' (v. 19).[82] Unfortunately, according to the people, it is exactly this deity who has brought about the present circumstances through anger and rejection. The final section of the prayer struggles with a question regarding a restored future (vv. 20–2). The final word of a people who have experienced torture, abuse, starvation, oppression, and exile is one of uncertainty. Even their age old belief in Yahweh enthroned in the heavens for eternity does not prevent them from expressing their distress at having been forsaken, perhaps even forever. The book of Lamentations offers no easy solutions and it provides no helpful theological clichés; rather, it ends with speculation and concern. In the midst of their distress so graphically presented, a communal appeal is made to Yahweh to intervene, but ultimately a question mark remains on whether or not divine resolution will come to pass.

What becomes abundantly clear in this survey of Lamentations 1, 2, 4, and 5 is that in spite of the lack of organization of the images and expressions of the poems, four themes recur throughout. The themes of the responsibility of Yahweh, the present distress of the lamenter, the exaltation of the enemies, and the sinfulness of the people enable a convenient introduction to the material. Nevertheless, the four poems betray a myriad of images that do not flow together logically or for the sake of a single argument—in many respects like a grieving

---

[82] Albrektson, *Lamentations*, 227–8, appeals to Pss. 9: 8, 12; 48: 2; 99: 2, etc., and understands this statement as 'an expression of the understanding of Yahweh's kingship which was current in the cultic traditions of Jerusalem, and was there linked to the idea of Zion as the abode of God'.

process.[83] In the aftermath of the disasters of the early part of the sixth century the nation grieves. What is distinctive about their mourning remains to be seen.

THE DISTINCTIVE CONTRIBUTION OF LAMENTATIONS

The four themes which run throughout the poems of Lamentations provided a means to introduce the material, but they do not indicate features distinctive to the Judahite population in and of themselves. In fact, at least three of them—the lamenter, Yahweh, and the enemy— are common elements of laments of the Psalter.[84] Sin, the other organizing rubric, functions in *Golah* literature of the period to pinpoint one of the reasons for the disaster. Thus, the intention to define concepts consistent with the Judahite population in post-war Judah comes about through a closer analysis of the language of Lamentations. Together the four organizing elements—the intentionality of Yahweh, the adversaries, the humiliation and worthlessness of the city and its inhabitants, and the culpability of the people—point to at least one emphasis featured in Judahite literature, that of the graphic depiction of situations of distress that continue to afflict members of the community. Human suffering is one feature that has been commented upon in recent years as intrinsic to Lamentations.[85] As a distinctive feature of the literature of Templeless Judah, it will be discussed in conjunction with other concepts featured in the collection, such as the lack of an expressed confidence in future hope, the deconstruction of the confession of sin, the vocalization of pain, and the formfulness of grief. The analysis advocated here benefits from the elucidation of concepts consistent with Judahite interpretation which will hopefully inform, if not enable, future endeavours to isolate literature from Templeless Judah.

---

[83] Joyce, 'Lamentations and the Grief Process', *BibInt* 1/3 (1993), 304–20; Reimer, 'Good Grief?'

[84] Westermann, 'Struktur und Geschichte'.

[85] Gwaltney, 'Lamentations', 208; Moore, 'Human Suffering'; Dobbs-Allsopp, 'Tragedy'; Linafelt, 'Zion's Cause'.

Human Suffering

The theology of the collection has received a great deal of attention spurred on, not a little bit, by the influential works of Gottwald and Albrektson.[86] Gottwald was one of the first to attempt to understand the underlying theology of the eclectic group of poems.[87] He determined that the main problem with which the book of Lamentations grappled was the failure of the Deuteronomic view to provide a meaningful explanation for Yahweh's violent actions in history against his own people. How could the efforts of a people so earnest in reform come to naught? In his critique of Gottwald, Albrektson rightly points out that the responsibility of the deity for the actions of 598 and 587 does not sit uncomfortably with Deuteronomic theology.[88] In fact, the exact opposite is true as the ideology presupposed by the Deuteronomic viewpoint is one in which righteous behaviour is rewarded whilst unrighteous behaviour or covenant infidelity is punished by preordained divine judgement. Since Lamentations has several passages that take into account the sinfulness of the people (1: 5, 8, 18; 2: 14; 4: 6, 13; 5: 7, 16), however ambiguously defined in the book, Albrektson is correct in his assessment that the people attribute the disaster in part to the consequences of their own actions. According to Albrektson, the poems reveal a marked dependence on the blessings and curses of Deuteronomy 28. In so doing, Lamentations confirms that Israel did not obey the stipulations set out therein that ensured life and prosperity in the land. The problem with which the poems wrestled in his view, then, stems from the conceptualization of Jerusalem and the temple in Zion theology. In contrast to claims about the centrality and inviolability of Zion, the city fell. Although Albrektson is surely correct in this assessment of the influence of Zion theology on the poems, the allusions to Deuteronomy 28 explain the disaster on the basis of covenant infractions. Because utilization of Deuteronomic theology and traditions about the esteemed state of Zion undergird the collection, Lamentations does

---

[86] Moore, 'Human Suffering', 534–9; Provan, *Lamentations*, 20–5; Hunter, *Faces of a Lamenting City*, 73–84. Westermann, *Klagelieder*, 32–81, = *Lamentations*, 24–108, provides a history of interpretation of Lamentations.

[87] Gottwald, *Studies*.

[88] Albrektson, *Lamentations*, 214–39.

not in actual fact grapple with either. They serve merely to inform its composition.

The focus of the poems is on the inordinate amount of suffering that met the fall of the city. In his review of Gottwald and Albrektson, Moore raised to prominence what has been considered a secondary theme in the literature, that is, the issue of the graphic portrayal of pain.[89] The theme of human suffering is interwoven throughout each chapter. Myriad images that vividly portray the devastating effects of war on every member of society function alongside the personification of the city to enliven the tragedy.[90] Moore's analysis shows how each chapter of the book of Lamentations is concerned with the 'horrifying scope of human suffering which [the poet] had witnessed with his own eyes when Jerusalem fell'.[91] The poet used a variety of means to emphasize the human aspect of the tragedy such as the use of the motif of the reversal of fortune, the horrific depiction of famine, the city figured as a heart-broken woman, and the role of the enemies.

One of the stylistic means by which the poet reinforced the dire present was through the use of the 'reversal of fortunes' theme. The reversal of fortune has its origin in the funeral dirge and was used by mourners to highlight the past glory of the deceased.[92] In Lamentations this concept functions as a strategy to maintain a focus on the present distressful situation experienced daily by the inhabitants of the city. The influence of the funeral dirge on the book of Lamentations is apparent in statements about the past glory of Jerusalem's inhabitants (e.g. 4: 5, 7) and through laments over the dire present (e.g. 1: 1, 19–20; 2: 11, 21; 4: 5). The application of dirge elements in conjunction with the city *and* its inhabitants indicates how keenly the sense of agony was felt. The fundamental difference between

---

[89] Moore, 'Human Suffering', 534–55.
[90] Ibid., 546–8, provides a useful chart of the references.
[91] Ibid., 554.
[92] H. Jahnow, *Das hebräische Leichenlied im Rahmen der Völkerdichtung* (BZAW, 36; Giessen: A. Töpelmann, 1923), 124–62. According to Jahnow the main elements of the dirge that appear in Lamentations are the use of איכה, comparisons between the former glory and present distress, the description of misery, and the derision of the enemies. In this Jahnow is followed by Gottwald, *Studies*, 33–7, 54–60; Linafelt, *Surviving Lamentations*, 35–8; Lee, *The Singers of Lamentations*, 33–7. Westermann, *Klagelieder*, 96–8, = *Lamentations*, 105–8, attributes them to the communal lament.

Lamentations and the funeral lament is that the theme of the reversal of fortune functions in the book of Lamentations to highlight the present distress by mourning not the dead primarily, but the destruction wreaked in Jerusalem.[93] The present circumstances are particularly ignominious. The glorious city of the past has been destroyed and its people languish, defeated and humiliated (1: 1, 6; 2: 1, 2, 3, 15; 4: 1, 2, 5, 7–8, 10, 13–14, 15, 20; 5: 2, 14–16). The ruins of the city are especially troublesome. Passers-by wag their heads and hiss whilst denigrating the present sorry state of the city with their sarcastic question: 'Is this the city which was called the perfection of beauty, the joy of all the earth?' (2: 15).

The poet shifts back and forth between considerations of the city and the people. The motif of the famine exhibits the human side of the tragedy in a poignant way. In contrast to the blessings of a physical nature having to do with security and the productivity of the land predicted in Deuteronomy 28, the poet depicts the exact opposite for post-587 Jerusalem. Instead of blessing, the community languishes under the fulfilment of Yahweh's covenant curses and starves. Some of the most horrific scenes in the collection appear in conjunction with the poet's use of the famine to depict the human tragedy that surrounds him. Grisly imagery captures the physical toll of the disaster by linguistically painting skin shrivelled and blackened and mothers eating their children. Time and again, the poet graphically portrays the effects of Yahweh's abandonment without resolving or alleviating the distress. The use of the motif of reversal of fortunes thus contributes to the sense of suffering evoked through explicit statements about the personified city and the people.

More than any other book, Lamentations contains metaphorical epithets ('daughter of GN' and 'maiden daughter of GN') for Israel.[94] These epithets function to associate the present distress with Jerusalem, but more importantly, they figure the city as a woman.[95] Properly understood, the personification of the city as a grief-stricken woman heightens the sense of distress and registers pain in

---

[93] Gottwald, *Studies*, 52–62; Linafelt, *Surviving Lamentations*, 37–8.

[94] Following Hillers, *Lamentations*, 30–1; Moore, 'Human Suffering', 546. The metaphorical epithets occur 20 times in Lamentations, but only roughly 45 times elsewhere in the HB with the second largest amount of 16 featuring in Jeremiah.

[95] On the personification of the city, see also Dobbs-Allsopp, *Weep, O Daughter of Zion*, 75–90; Kaiser, 'Poet as "Female Impersonator" '; K. M. Heim, 'The Personifica-

a less abstract way.[96] The use of Jerusalem the woman, widowed and abandoned, certainly could function to evoke empathy within the community that receives the text and utilizes it in worship,[97] but more than that, the personal nature of the tragedy serves as a strategy to evoke the compassion and empathy of the deity. As a woman without a husband or children, Lady Jerusalem is the equivalent of one of the weakest members of society in ancient Israel (1: 1). As an eyewitness reporter, the poet depicts her as heart-broken, in absolute anguish: tears stream down her cheeks (1: 2a), she groans and turns her face away (1: 8c), and stretches out her hands for comfort (1: 17a). Yet, within the boundaries of the text, the fivefold repetition of the lack of a comforter (1: 2, 9, 16, 17, 21) highlights the isolation of the city personified as a woman. In her own voice, she relates her distress in provocative detail (1: 12–22; 2: 20–2). The image of Lady Zion grasping her middle (1: 20ab) and weeping ceaselessly (1: 16a) painfully wondering aloud, 'Is there any pain like my pain?'(1: 12b) lingers. Through personification the poet accomplishes the masterful feat of urging the listener or reader, indeed Yahweh himself, to feel with Lady Zion the anguish of her distress. No longer a rote metaphor, the city grieves as a woman who has lost everything and the language of her despair urges all who hear her embittered cry to share in her sorrow.

Along with the eyewitness narrator and the city personified as a woman, two other characters feature in the poems, Yahweh and the enemies. In contrast to what Dobbs-Allsopp regards as one prevalent feature in the Mesopotamian laments—that is, the voice of the deity entreating for or responding to the lament over the ruination of the city and its temple—the deity of Israel does not speak.[98] Nevertheless, Yahweh functions as a character in Lamentations because he features in depictions of the suffering as the aggressor *par excellence*. As noted already, historical enemies appear in the poems as well, but

---

tion of Jerusalem and the Drama of Her Bereavement in Lamentations', in R. S. Hess and G. J. Wenham (eds.), *Zion, City of Our God* (Grand Rapids, Mich.: Eerdmans, 1999), 129–69; Dobbs-Allsopp, *Lamentations*, 50–3.

[96] Hillers, *Lamentations*, 17; Lanahan, 'The Speaking Voice', 43–5; Kaiser, 'Poet as "Female Impersonator" ', 175.

[97] A. Mintz, 'The Rhetoric of Lamentations and the Representation of Catastrophe', *Prooftexts* 2 (1982), 2–3.

[98] Dobbs-Allsopp, 'Tragedy', 44–5; already implied in Lanahan, 'The Speaking Voice', 49.

their actions are associated with the intentions of the deity. The clearest confirmation of the enemies acting on behalf of Yahweh occurs in 1: 17b: 'Yahweh has commanded concerning Jacob "his enemies shall surround him" ', and 2: 7b, 'He has delivered up the walls of her strongholds into the hand of the enemy' (cf. 1: 5ab, 14c; 2: 17, 22; 4: 11–12). The third-person narrator hints at the agency of adversaries within Yahweh's plan of retribution in 1: 5ab, but it is not until Lady Jerusalem attributes her degradation directly to Yahweh (1: 12c–15) that the eyewitness describes Yahweh as foe (2: 1–9). These depictions implicate Yahweh in the present distress.[99] In the second chapter, which emphasizes so forcefully the trope of Yahweh as an enemy, the poet nowhere highlights the sin of Zion.[100] The painful present is not equal to the crime committed. The sense of the injustice of Yahweh's aggression against his own people is magnified by his choice of foreign foes who contribute to past, present, and even future, suffering. With their own deity against them, how could there be any relief? The motif posits the origin of suffering to Yahweh himself. It is human suffering on a divine scale.

The human tragedy of Lamentations arises literarily through a variety of means at the poet's disposal. The explicit portrayal of scenes of starvation, disease, death, and deportation functions within the literary artistry that interweaves the theme of reversal of fortunes. The tragedy strikes a more personal and desperate note through the personification of the city as a woman in the throes of despair. Finally, Yahweh as divine warrior fighting against his own people completes the sense of suffering by showing that there was no escape as long as affliction was divinely ordained. One of the distinctive features of Lamentations is its focus on the human aspect of the tragedy. Rather than explaining or rationalizing the disaster, the people in Judah lamented it and agonized over it. One of the key features of Lamentations is a presentation of pain.

Lack of Confidence in Future Hope

In addition to the obvious foregrounding of the suffering of the city and its inhabitants, the biblical Lamentations struggles with

---

[99] Dobbs-Allsopp, 'Tragedy', 38.   [100] Linafelt, 'Zion's Cause', 279.

uncertainty. This is particularly apparent in Renkema's analysis of the theology of the collection.[101] Building on the theological interpretations of Gottwald and Albrektson, Renkema, too, notes the contribution of Deuteronomic interpretation and the Zion traditions to the poems. In his analysis, though, he recognizes that the authors of Lamentations accepted the events of 587 as punishment for sin, but remained unsure about the exact nature of their transgression. This vague, almost ambiguous, recognition of transgression creates a tension in the book which remains unresolved. According to Renkema, the authors are unable to move beyond the present situation to resolution without a clear understanding of the nature of sin. In his view, the book rests on a fulcrum of doubt in which any hope is countered by uncertainty regarding a future different from the present. Renkema's contribution to discussions about the theology of Lamentations brings to the fore the issue of the lack of confidence in future hope that is a significant feature of the collection. However, Renkema's insights are more pertinent to the *expression* or *vocalization* of future hope. It will be shown later that in spite of the expressed uncertainty and concomitant silence surrounding future possibilities, the form of the collection conveys a sense of hope.

One of the more prominent examples of the doubt of the collection occurs in the last poem. Westermann recognizes that chapter 5 is one of the purest examples of a communal lament in the Hebrew Bible;[102] nevertheless, it has two distinct developments that set it apart from other like complaints. In the first place, it has a lengthy section of complaint (vv. 1–18), which places greater stress on the present misery of the people than in any other communal lament found in the Hebrew Bible.[103] Secondly, whilst other complaints of the people include a section outlining reasons for belief in the willingness and ability of the deity to act on their behalf thought of as a 'certainty of hearing', chapter 5 concludes with a unique form-critical category characterized more appropriately as 'the uncertainty of a hearing'. In the fifth poem, a lengthy series of pastiches of tragedy

---

[101] J. Renkema, *'Misschien is er hoop...': De theologische vooronderstellingen van het boek Klaagliederen* (Franeker: Wever, 1983) and more recently in his commentary, *Lamentations*.
[102] Westermann, *Lamentations*, 211, 219–20.
[103] Provan, *Lamentations*, 23.

lead into a brief petition to the deity (vv. 19–22) which includes only a faltering confession of trust in verse 19. Even there, the emphasis is not on the steadfast governance of the deity so much as on the uncertainty of the possibility of future divine intervention on behalf of the community in crisis. The communal lament of the collection picks up one of the main emphases of the book and appropriately concludes on a note of uncertainty (vv. 20–2).

20 למה לנצח תשכחנו תעזבנו לארך ימים:
21 השיבנו יהוה אליך ונשוב חדש ימינו
כקדם: 22 כי אם־מאס מאסתנו קצפת
עלינו עד־מאד:

Why do you forget us forever, abandon us for so long? Return us to you, Yahweh, that we may return. Renew our days as of old, unless you have utterly rejected us and are wroth with us forever.

v. 21 ונשוב MT 'so that we may return'. The *Qere* points as a cohortative. Following an impv. the simple conjunction + impf. has the sense of 'so that, in order that', thus, the sense is not altered.

v. 22 The translation of כי אם is disputed. It occurs over 150 times, but is never followed by an infinitive absolute + perfect as here. A summary of views is available in Hillers, *Lamentations*, 160–1, and R. Gordis, 'The Conclusion of the Book of Lamentations', *JBL* 93 (1974), 289–93. A close analogy is כי אם + abs. + impf. which is frequently rendered 'if...' of the protasis (Exod. 22: 22; Deut. 11: 22; Josh. 23: 12; 1 Sam. 20: 9, etc.), but once as the apodosis (Exod. 23: 22). Linafelt, *Surviving Lamentations*, 58–61, and idem, 'The Refusal of a Conclusion in the Book of Lamentations', *JBL* 120 (2001), 340–3, translates the line as a protasis without an apodosis and leaves an ellipsis. However, a conditional rendering is not found with a perfect construction. Most frequently, with a perfect it means 'unless' (Gen. 32: 27; Lev. 22: 6; 2 Kgs. 4: 24; Isa. 55: 10, 11; Amos 3: 7; Ruth 3: 18; Esther 2: 14). Quite often it represents 'but' (Gen. 40: 14; 2 Kgs. 23: 9; Isa. 65: 6; Jer. 37: 10; Ezek. 12: 33; Lam. 3: 32), and less frequently, 'even, surely' (2 Sam. 5: 6; 2 Kgs. 5: 20; Jer. 51: 14), 'then' (1 Sam. 25: 34), and 'that' (Gen. 47: 18). With Rudolph, *Klagelieder*, 258, who is followed by the NRSV, I prefer 'unless'. Though Albrektson, *Studies*, 205–7, notes that the translation 'unless' follows a negative, once it does not (Isa. 55: 10). Fittingly, the verse closes the collection on a note of uncertainty.

The final lament picks up the doubt of the preceding chapters and closes on a note of despair. The people are left wondering if there is a future for them and if their deity will restore them by entering salvifically in their midst.

As Provan notes, Lamentations does not leave us with hope, but with doubt.[104] This is particularly clear in the final note of the collection, but it is apparent elsewhere in texts where statements of hope are undermined. Two statements of hope are eclipsed by the tragedy that surrounds them. According to many interpreters the clearest statement of hope in the collection is located at the final verse of the fourth poem—significantly in the final verse of the last poem that has an acrostic structure.[105] The fourth chapter maintains an almost myopic focus on the extent of human suffering, both economic and social, as has been noted already. In chapter 4, the impersonal eyewitness returns, but provides only a series of observations on the human aspect of the tragedy which culminates in the desperate attempt of the people to flee from the city and the capture of the king (vv. 18–20).[106] There are no interjections in the first person and Lady Zion no longer speaks as in chapters 1 and 2. The poem closes with an oracle against Edom in which is sandwiched what appears to be a statement absolving the sins of Jerusalem (vv. 21–2):

22 תם־עונך בת־ציון לא יוסיף להגלותך
פקד עונך בת־אדום גלה על־חטאתיך:

Your iniquity will be completed, O daughter of Zion, you will no longer be exiled; He will punish your iniquity, O daughter of Edom, he will uncover your sins.

There is some uncertainty regarding how to translate the perfect verbs in the verse. As the continuation of an imprecation begun in v. 21, the most likely rendering is future, understanding the verbs as precative perfects whose

---

[104] Provan, *Lamentations*, 22–3.
[105] Kraus, *Klagelieder*, 73, 83–4; Rudolph, *Klagelieder*, 249; Hillers, *Lamentations*, 152–3; Provan, *Lamentations*, 123; Dobbs-Allsopp, *Lamentations*, 138; Berlin, *Lamentations*, 114. Westermann, *Lamentations*, 206; E. S. Gerstenberger, *Psalms*, pt. 2 and Lamentations (FOTL, 15; Grand Rapids, Mich.: Eerdmans, 2001), 500, liken it to Deutero-Isaiah.
[106] Lanahan, 'The Speaking Voice', regards the eyewitness as a different persona from the eyewitness of chs. 1–2 and characterizes him as a bourgeois who highlights the social and economic impact of the disaster. Interestingly, the narrator is more detached than encountered heretofore. He could actually be the same figure, but with a different shift in focus. See the commentaries.

accomplishment is assured. Most commentators understand תם as a reference to past or present time ('is or has been accomplished'). Because it is in parallel with the imperfect יוסיף whose translation is not in doubt and continues the wish of v. 21, a future sense is to be understood. A case for the appearance of precative perfects in the HB with particular reference to Lamentations has been made by I. W. Provan, 'Past, Present and Future in Lamentations III 52–66: The Case for a Precative Perfect Re-examined', *VT* 41 (1991), 164–75.

Because most interpreters render the perfect of verse 22a in the past, they understand it to be a reference to the completion of the period of judgement. Almost unanimous opinion views it, therefore, as the clearest example of hope in the book.

Against this widespread agreement, Renkema argues that there is absolutely no evidence that the punishment is at an end.[107] His understanding rests on three insights: (1) the preceding poems conclude with statements of misery and chapter 5 resumes a description of the ongoing nature of affliction of chapter 4; (2) continuing distress is understood to refer to contemporary experience and, thus, tends to be rendered in the present tense in all five poems; and (3) in his view תמם connotes more appropriately the total execution of something rather than its completion. In Renkema's analysis, then, verse 22a reveals the complete execution of Yahweh's judgement for sin, rather than its conclusion. In his attempt to maintain an emphasis on the distress, Renkema is correct in that a precative rendering of the verbs is more in keeping with verses 21–2. Within its immediate context, the completion of Zion's punishment is sandwiched between statements about the future judgement of Edom. Moreover, the lament of chapter 5 clearly shows that the punishment has not ended. Of all communal laments, Lamentations 5 has the most persistent focus on the complaint and devotes very little attention to a confession of trust (v. 19 only) or even to a petition for future intervention (v. 21). The future vindication of Zion will occur when retribution is meted out against the enemies who had participated in and mocked at the collapse of Judah, in this case, Edom. A future sense, then, is more in keeping with the imprecations against Edom and with the collection as a whole. A turnaround in

---

[107] Renkema, *Lamentations*, 564–6.

Zion's present is predicated upon the just meting out of retribution against the enemies. Since the hope of 4: 22 is projected into an uncertain future, the context undermines its force.

Although chapter 5 ends on a hesitant note, it contains a statement of hope based on the character of Yahweh:

19 אתה יהוה לעולם תשב
כסאך לדר ודור:

You, yourself, Yahweh, sit (enthroned) forever. Your throne is from generation to generation.

The people affirm that Yahweh is sovereign and that his reign is timeless. Klein, for example, viewed 5: 19 as the most poignant declaration of hope in the whole collection.[108] The source of hope, however, fades in comparison to the wider focus of chapter 5 on relentless tragedy. The lament veritably tumbles over itself with detailed descriptions of the current undesirable situation. It outlines the loss of sovereignty over the land, the pressures of imperial governance, the complete disgrace of all members of society and ends with the sorry picture of Mount Zion among whose ruins packs of jackals prowl (vv. 1–18). The appeal by a people who believe themselves to have been forgotten, forsaken, and possibly rejected eclipses this brief statement of trust (vv. 20–2). The belief in a future restored by the deity rests on the eternal kingship of Yahweh, but there is no avowal of confidence at the close of the lament. Instead it ends with a question mark which ponders the possibility that Yahweh has chosen to reject his people forever (v. 22). The eternal kingship of Yahweh is never in doubt, only whether or not the deity will choose to enter into a covenant relationship with this people again.

Moreover, the attestation of Yahweh's eternal rule follows the only mention of Mount Zion in the poem, which cannot be a coincidence. In verse 18 the temple is a ruin, desolate and the home of jackals. Elsewhere the temple is referred to rarely, only six times (1: 10; 2: 1, 4, 6, 7, 20) where it is the object of Yahweh's destructive behaviour. In 2: 4, Yahweh 'poured out his wrath' against the temple alluded to by the 'tent of Daughter Zion',[109] and in 2: 6, Yahweh perpetrated violence

---

[108] Klein, *Israel in Exile*, 17.
[109] 2: 4 אהל בת יציון 'the tent of Daughter Zion'. Renkema, *Lamentations*, 234, summarizes the two common understandings of this expression: (1) Jerusalem as a

against 'his booth' and destroyed the place of his appointed time, but the deity also rejected it and its altar in 2: 7. Once elsewhere the temple mount comes into focus, but there, too, it has been destroyed. In 2: 1b, Yahweh has cast down the 'splendour of Israel', which should probably be understood as a reference to the temple mount which was thought to have extended into heaven (Ps. 48: 2–3).[110] The extent of Yahweh's fury includes even the 'the stool of his feet' הדם רגליו a veiled allusion to the temple itself.[111] The reference to הדם רגליו evokes thoughts of the temple as the place from which the deity engaged in human affairs, thereby providing an allusion to the relevance of the kingship of Yahweh to the present distress. The loss of the temple corresponds to the loss of the presence of the deity. If

dwelling place and (2) the temple. He concludes that the referent is to the city which included the temple, which could be the case. Lady Zion speaks of the slaughter of priests and prophets in the sanctuary (2: 20) and people in the streets (2: 21). There is some disagreement over the division of the verse. If taken with 2: 4c, as here, it more naturally alludes to the temple. As Renkema acknowledges, the temple is not infrequently referred to as an אהל in the Psalms (Pss. 15: 1; 27: 5; 61: 5; 78: 60). There is a significant degree of overlap between the language of Lamentations and the Psalms. An allusion is consistent with the poetic aversion to using an explicit term for the temple when Yahweh is the one who destroys it. Elsewhere, for example, the poet employs מקדש in relation to the invasion of the nations (1: 10), as the recipient of the deity's scorn (2: 7), and as the location of the slaughter of the priests and prophets (2: 20).

[110] 2: 1b תפארת ישראל 'the splendour of Israel' is sometimes taken to refer to the temple, but is more properly understood as the temple mount, so Weiser, *Klagelieder* (ATD, 16; Göttingen: Vandenhoeck & Ruprecht, 1958), 62, followed by Renkema, *Lamentations*, 217–18.

[111] Most exegetes favour the temple. The expression הדם רגליו occurs four times elsewhere. It is the ark of the covenant (1 Chr. 28: 2), the temple (Pss. 99: 5, cf. v. 9 with the exact phrase, but the substitution of לחר קדשו for הדם רגליו; 132: 7 // משכנות), and the earth (Isa. 66: 1). The order of the depiction of the images in 2:1 clarifies the referent. At the beginning of a chapter which focuses on the capricious actions of the deity against his own people, the poet highlights the city, the temple mount, and the temple to expose the extent of the disaster. This verse exhibits a clear narrowing of the recipient of the deity's anger from the entire city in v. 1a to Mount Zion in v. 1b, which in ancient thought was considered to stretch into the heavens and could be thrown down from the heavens, to refer even more narrowly to the temple in v. 1c. Read this way, the conceptual progression from the city to Mount Zion to the temple itself creates a type of merism which includes in the destruction the entire social, political, and religious structures of ancient Judah. Additional support for this reading is provided by literature contemporary to Lamentations where the temple is referred to in a similar way as מקום כפות רגלי 'the place of the soles of my feet' (Ezek. 43: 7) and מקום רגלי 'the place of my feet' (Isa. 60: 13).

Yahweh is king, from whence shall he rule? The dirge mourns the figurative death of the temple in 2: 1, but more importantly, it contextualizes the statement of trust in 5: 19 which raises a query about the possibility of the deity's governance. Just as the verses after it (vv. 20–2) highlight concerns about whether or not Yahweh will choose to be the king of this people, the ruination of the temple in 5: 18 with the concomitant allusion to its destruction in 2: 1 reinforces the query. Doubt surrounds the present and future reign of the deity, not as a question of Yahweh's sovereignty, but as a question of practicality and volition.

The events of 598 and 587 were understood to be part of the righteous intervention of the deity who responded to the repeated failure of covenant fidelity with the day proposed long ago and predicted by the prophets. Lamentations considered the disaster of 587, especially the destruction of the temple thought in some traditions to be inviolable, to be part and parcel of the day of divine anger. Even though rationalized and understood through the interpretative lenses of prophecy, the suffering of the people in the aftermath of war remained inexplicable. The description of Yahweh as enemy in the second and fourth chapters (2: 4–5; 4: 11, 16) questions the justice of Yahweh. The deity is actually conceived of as an enemy three times in 2: 4–5[112] and implied as such by Lady Jerusalem in 2: 22. Had the deity acted capriciously after all?

An appeal to Yahweh as king rises to the foreground in a situation in which there is no earthly ruler. The theological contribution of the book of Lamentations is diverse. In contrast to the predominantly hopeful accounts of an exultant return like that predicted by Deutero-Isaiah or the belief in the ability of Yahweh to change the hearts of his people as found in Ezekiel, the book of Lamentations, because of its setting among a war-torn and war-weary people, testifies to the very human experience of despair. Moreover, it provides a type of response to the concern about the end of suffering by basing its belief solely in the character of Yahweh as a righteous king. The collection of laments deconstructs positive statements even whilst affirming the sovereignty of Yahweh. The tragedy of

---

[112] Dobbs-Allsopp, *Lamentations*, 83–4.

Lamentations lies in the very fact that belief about if, how, or when the deity will choose to exercise that rule remains uncertain.

It was already noted that in contrast to Mesopotamian laments, the biblical Lamentations has no response from the deity. One further distinction highlights the uncertainty evoked by the tragedy. The Mesopotamian laments serve as more than expressions of grief. True, they mourn the destruction of the city and the temple, but they almost always resolve the tension of the state of distress. Indeed, Dobbs-Allsopp shows that they end not as tragedies, but as comedies in the modern literary sense of the word in that the god returns and a banquet is held in celebration.[113] In the biblical Lamentations there is no happy ending—Yahweh does not return, he does not even speak. Uncertainty surrounds every statement of hope. In fact it encompasses the book. A further astute observation by Dobbs-Allsopp is that the opening verse 1: 1 and the last verse 5: 22 frame the collection of poems with the theme of abandonment by the deity.[114] Instead of celebrating the return of Yahweh at the end of Lamentations, the community languishes, despondent that their deity has not returned and shows no signs of doing so in the future. Together the lack of hope for divine restoration and explicit formulations of a future different from the present highlight uncertainty as a prominent distinguishing feature of the book and of Judahite reflection.

Sin

An additional theme significant in its development in Lamentations has to do with the concept of sin. Indeed, the presence of transgression in the poems provided one of the principles which allowed for an organized rendering of the collection. In terms of sin, Gottwald's study of the theology of Lamentations disclosed that two types appear: the sin of the people and the sin of the leaders.[115] Moreover, Gottwald provides a list of the language used for a variety of transgressions and concludes with an almost perplexed statement regarding their vague depictions in the text. No specific indictments appear

---

[113] Dobbs-Allsopp, 'Tragedy', 32–4.   [114] Ibid., 33–4.
[115] Gottwald, *Studies*, 69–70.

other than one that accuses the prophets and priests of shedding blood (4: 13). Although ambiguously dealt with in the collection, the analyses of Albrektson and Renkema regard the nation's sin as a contributing factor in the devastation of 587. Hunter takes this argument even further by arguing that the reality and the confession of sin feature as one of two main foci of the collection.[116] In his view the consequences of the people's sin were acknowledged in Lamentations by the repetition of the motif of transgression: 'These poets fully understood the relationship between sinning and punishment and also, the relationship between confession and restoration.'[117] His analysis implies that the book of Lamentations functions as a lengthy confession of sin meant to entreat Yahweh's goodwill. However, more recent interpretations which acknowledge the role played by human pain in the collection tend to stress that the suffering entailed far exceeded any transgression committed. Against Hunter, then, current research reveals the downplaying of sin.[118] In Provan's estimation, for instance, the concept of sin and its acknowledgement contribute to the collection of poems, but without anywhere evidencing a wholehearted confession.[119]

With a slightly different understanding, Dobbs-Allsopp, in his consideration of the biblical Lamentations against the backdrop of tragedy and the Mesopotamian laments, shows that in the mind of the poet the sin of Judah was not equal to the amount of the suffering experienced.[120] According to Dobbs-Allsopp, three aspects of the description of sin downplay its significance: (1) sin is referred to relatively infrequently when compared to images of suffering, (2) there is a noticeable lack of specificity when references are made, and (3) some of the confessions of sin are intentionally undermined contextually, e.g. 1: 18; cf. 1: 15. He concludes that 'There is genuine acknowledgment of sin in Lamentations, but that is not the whole story, or even the most important part of the story.'[121] By concentrating on the figure of Zion personified, Linafelt, similarly, notes the

---

[116] Hunter, *Faces of a Lamenting City*, 143–7.   [117] Ibid., 144.
[118] Provan, *Lamentations*, 20–5; Linafelt, 'Zion's Cause', 273–9.
[119] Provan, *Lamentations*, 23.
[120] Dobbs-Allsopp, 'Tragedy', 36–9, and *idem*, *Lamentations*, 60–2.
[121] Dobbs-Allsopp, 'Tragedy', 37. Cf. *idem*, *Weep, O Daughter of Zion*, 54–5.

shift away from sin to the expression of the extent of human pain. In his view, whilst Zion never claimed to be innocent in 1: 18–22, the emphasis of her speech is not on her guilt, but her agony. In chapter 2, the shift away from the importance of sin becomes clearer because there is no confession to detract from the sustained focus on Yahweh as divine warrior.[122] Although the concept of transgression united the poems, the fact that it is downplayed, even deconstructed, in the book highlights another distinctive feature of Lamentations.

A consideration of the passages that speak of sin[123] confirms the conclusions of Dobbs-Allsopp and Linafelt, but highlights additional concepts worthy of comment. The first is that of the occurrences of sin, the most frequent appearance is in chapter 1 (vv. 5, 8, 14, 18, 22) with the second most frequent in chapter 4 (vv. 6, 13, of Edom 22). In terms of sheer numbers, sin is far outnumbered by scenes of violence, terror, and woe in the text. Chapters 2 and 5 address the issue of rebellion quite rarely, once and twice, respectively (2: 14; 5: 7, 16). There are three statements about it that explicitly implicate the leaders of the community (2: 14; 4: 13; 5: 7). The only pure confession of sin is located in the communal lament in 5: 16—'Woe to us for we have sinned'—toward the conclusion of the litany of misery (vv. 1–18)—where arguably the form necessitated its inclusion. Other texts surely acknowledge sin outright (1: 8–9, 14–15; 5: 16) and even the greatness of it (4: 6), but Lamentations repeatedly attests the perspective that the punishment far outweighed the crime.

As such, the poems do not function as theodicy, but almost as a lengthy accusation against the deity, perhaps '*theo-diabole*'. The portrait of Yahweh as an aggressor actively pursuing and destroying his own people combines with the shift in emphasis away from sin. Significantly, chapter 2, which maintains an almost univocal focus on the destructive power of the deity, from his actions and those committed by human agents, contains only one statement about misconduct. There it resulted from the failure of the prophets to make the people aware of their transgression (v. 14). In their positioning of suffering in the spotlight, the poems of Lamentations

---

[122] Linafelt, *Surviving Lamentations*, 46–9.
[123] The two texts about uncleanness טמאה probably do not refer to sin in their contexts and will not be considered here (1: 9; 4: 15).

downplay the theme of sin in favour of an emphasis on the people's distress. Through the image of Yahweh as a divine warrior the poet further discloses that the deity is complicit in the present state of affairs.

In addition, Dobbs-Allsopp's analysis revealed that the context undermines the impact of sin in certain cases. Two of the texts he highlights in this regard (1: 5, 18) are particularly worthy of note. Dobbs-Allsopp argues that the force of the confession is softened by contrasting blatant statements of transgression with images of pain and exile. Actually, both verses are 'softened' by references to deportation. It is conceivable that in the light of the application of sin elsewhere to specific members of the community, such as the prophets of 2: 14, the priests and prophets of 4: 13, and the leaders of 5: 7, the blame for trespass is laid on the exiles in 1: 5, 18.[124] The first acknowledgement of sin in the collection occurs in 1: 5, whose thought continues to verse 6.

> 5 היו צריה לראש איביה שלו
> כי־יהוה הוגה על רב־פשעיה
> עולליה הלכו שבי לפני־צר:
> 6 ויצא מן־בת־ציון כל־הדרה
> היו שריה כאילים לא־מצאו מרעה
> וילכו בלא־כח לפני רודף:

Her adversaries have become 'her masters', her enemies are at ease, because Yahweh has caused her suffering on account of the multitude of her sins; Her children go into captivity before the adversary. All her splendour has gone from the Daughter of Zion. Her princes have become like harts who cannot find a pasture. They have walked with no strength before the pursuer.

v. 6 כל־הדרה MT 'all her splendour/glory'. The exact meaning of the phrase is in dispute. Renkema, *Lamentations*, 122–3, thinks of the temple, others believe that it refers to the temple treasures, such as Westermann, *Klagelieder*, 101 n. 7a, 111–12 = *Lamentations*, 112 n. 7a, 127); Berlin, *Lamentations*, 53; while Hillers, *Lamentations*, 85, suggests the glory may be a referent back to the children who have gone into captivity in v. 5c. But, in the context of the deportation of the nobles who feature in 1: 6bc, it is more likely that it reflects on the nobles who have gone into captivity.

---

[124] H. G. M. Williamson, 'Laments at the Destroyed Temple', *BRev* 4/4 (1990), 12–17, 44.

The suffering that Yahweh caused in v. 5b resulted from a multitude of sins. More importantly, the ascription of the sin is contained within a unit that maintains a consistent focus on deportation. Helberg has noted the rarity of any consideration of captivity in Lamentations, so the present references to children, leaders, and princes being pursued into exile is, therefore, significant. It is arguable that the sin of Jerusalem in this case is being directly associated with the exiles. They have sinned, therefore they suffer by being removed from the land. A similar thought appears in 1: 18. The rebellion of which Lady Zion speaks is directly related to the exile of her maidens and young men. In two instances, a case can be made for the direct link between transgression and the fate of the population deported by the Babylonians.

The association of the exiles with the nation's sin is in keeping with the perception Ezekiel gives of the inhabitants of Judah. Ezekiel utilized the religio-historical situation of Judah to proclaim judgement on the inhabitants of the land. Twice his condemnation of them is bolstered by examples of the type of thought considered by him to be blasphemous that took place among the population in Judah after 587. Before the destruction of the temple, Ezekiel during the lengthy temple vision of chapters 8–11 assaults the belief prevalent among the inhabitants of the land that occurred after the first Babylonian incursion and, indeed, the first deportation of a segment of the population (Ezek. 11: 14–21). The Judahites consider the judgement of Yahweh to have been accomplished in the events of 598 and regard their continued existence in the land as a form of blessing. According to Ezekiel, they even believed that the land was given to them as an inheritance. Speaking of the deportees they exclaim, 'They have gone far away from Yahweh, *to us* the land is given as a possession' (Ezek. 11: 15).[125] The prophet quotes the claim of the Judahites in order: (1) to proclaim the finality of their judgement, (2) to predict the return of the exiles with which will come the purification of the land of its idols (vv. 17–21), and (3) to further expand on the abandonment of the city by the presence of Yahweh. The scene actually closes with the

---

[125] Ezek. 11: 15 רַחֲקוּ MT qal imperative 'Go far away'. In the context of past actions, the qal perfect pointing makes better sense and is followed by many commentators.

removal of the glory of Yahweh from the temple and its relocation to the outskirts of the city (vv. 22–3). Further, within this passage the presence of Yahweh is made available to the exiles in Babylon as a little sanctuary (v. 16). It is within this narrative that the emptiness of the claim of the inhabitants of the land becomes glaringly obvious. In verse 15, they attribute the deportation of 598 to sinful behaviour and exclaim that the land has become theirs to possess. After the destruction of the temple, Ezekiel more adamantly refutes a similar claim in 33: 23–9.

In an attempt to delineate attitudes formed by the events of 587 with regard to an understanding of the concept of Israel, Japhet focuses on these two texts as indicative of the thought of the people of the land from this period.[126] Ezekiel 11: 15 and 33: 25 function in the Templeless period to claim that the identity of Israel lies with those who remained in Judah. But, the statements regarding the exiles reveal more than a claim about rightful inheritance and possession. As Japhet argues there is a theological component that underlies the Judahite view. In her view, Ezekiel 11: 15 echoes and fulfils Isaiah 6: 11–13, which posits a remnant, a 'stump', which will survive the disaster. The second text that highlights the claim of the inhabitants in Ezekiel 33: 23–9 takes the conception of inheritance further by applying the promises given to Abraham to those who remained in the land. In claiming their right to possess the land, the Judahites distinguish between themselves as the righteous remnant and the deported population in Babylon which has been judged for sin and removed far from Yahweh. Naturally, Ezekiel condemns this line of thinking. He counters their thought by: (1) associating the population in the land with future judgement for grave sins and (2) showing that the presence of Yahweh, repulsed by their foul deeds, has, in fact, abandoned his holy temple and city, and has moved to be present with the exiles in Babylon. For our purposes, what is particularly striking in Japhet's analysis is the theological basis for the Judahites' assertion. An association is made between the sin of the nation and the punishment of deportation. The exiles counter this

---

[126] S. Japhet, 'People and Land in the Restoration Period', in G. Strecker (ed.), *Das Land Israel in biblischer Zeit: Jerusalem Symposium 1981* (GTA, 25; Göttingen: Vandenhoeck & Ruprecht, 1983), 106–8.

claim by forcefully attributing the nation's downfall to the continued worship of deities other than or in addition to Yahweh in the homeland. Furthermore, literature of the *Golah* displays the concern to lay claim to the concept of the righteous remnant. Distinctively, the Judahites take the opposite view to the exiles with regard to the designation of the righteous remnant and in certain texts undermine the acknowledgement, even the extent, of sin.

One indication of the thought of the community in the land in the light of the disasters of 598 and 587 is the prevalent belief in the innocence and even vindication of the people in the homeland. This line of thought, which is distinct from that of the community in exile, provides one clue in the attempt to isolate literature from this population. The downplaying of sin elsewhere, the vague references to sinfulness, its attribution to other members of society, and a literary softening of the impact of the attribution of sin all contribute to a significant difference in Judahite literature of the period, that is, the devaluation of aberrant behaviour. Because of the lesser emphasis on sinfulness, the great historical recitals of a history of sin so common to literature of the Babylonian exiles (e.g. Ezek. 20) would not be expected in theological reflection in the homeland. A downplaying of the significance of transgression would be more likely.

Emphasis on the Vocalization of Pain

An additional emphasis distinctive to Lamentations is on the declaration of suffering—in other words the need to cry out to Yahweh. In chapters 1 and 2 an anonymous eyewitness narrator and the city of Jerusalem speak about the tragedy that has befallen the city. The eyewitness described the reversal of fortunes of the city in 1: 1–11b. Lady Jerusalem speaks in verse 12 and continues until the end of the chapter (v. 22). Before her lengthy speech she twice interrupts the narrator at verses 9c and 11c almost as if she cannot keep silent in the face of so much pain. In her interjections, Lady Jerusalem insists that Yahweh look and take note of her distress. Zion's response to the litany of description is to cry out to the deity. Her voice then drowns out that of the narrator and closes the chapter with a focus on Yahweh as the causative force behind her ignoble fate. Subsequently, the narrator accepts Zion's designation of Yahweh as an aggressor and shifts his focus in chapter 2 to include images of the hostile actions of Yahweh as divine warrior in verses 1–9.

There are two important differences between chapters 1 and 2 that are telling. The first is that in the second chapter the voice of the narrator continues uninterrupted until 2: 19. In addition, the otherwise impersonal reporter interrupts the recital of the events to speak in the first person of his despair. The second poem is characterized by a marked contrast between the violent, raucous actions of the deity and the utterly silent response of the people whose quiet is broken only by the weak cries of children for food (verses 11b–12).[127] The extent of the human toll of the disaster, especially the fainting children who whimper for food, forces the eyewitness to break off his report and disclose his own personal reactions to the disaster—his eyes weep, his stomach churns, and his bile is poured on the ground (verse 11). Aware of Lady Zion's depression and withdrawal which parallels that of the elders and the maidens of verse 10, he turns to her for the first time in an attempt to proffer comfort (v. 13) perhaps as in an organized mourning ritual.[128] What he says is only that which echoes her sorrows (vv. 14–17). Her fate is grim: the divine plan has been executed.

Significantly, after recounting Lady Jerusalem's brokenness, the narrator urges, even commands her to speak out. In contrast to the first poem in which she appeared eager to speak, even interrupting the narrator to halt the impersonal descriptions of disaster in order to call out directly to Yahweh, she is reluctant to voice her pain in chapter 2, as if bowed down from grief. In response to her silence, the narrator coaxes her to address Yahweh in verses 18–19:

18 צעק לבם אל אדני
חומת בת ציון הורידי כנחל דמעה יומם
ולילה אל־תתני פוגת לך אל־תדם
בת־עינך:
19 קומי רני בליל לראש אשמרות
שפכי כמים לבך נכח פני אדני

---

[127] Lanahan, 'The Speaking Voice', 47.
[128] X. H. T Pham, *Mourning in the Ancient Near East and the Hebrew Bible* (JSOTSup, 302; Sheffield: Sheffield Academic Press, 1999).

שְׂאִי אֵלָיו כַּפַּיִךְ עַל־נֶפֶשׁ עוֹלָלָיִךְ
הָעֲטוּפִים בְּרָעָב בְּרֹאשׁ כָּל־חוּצוֹת:

Let your heart cry out to Adonai, O wall of Daughter Zion; Let tears stream down like a wadi day and night; Do not let yourself rest, do not still the pupil of your eye. Arise, cry out in the night as the watch begins; Pour out your heart like water before the presence of Adonai; Lift up your hands to him for the lives of your children.

v. 18a צָעַק לִבָּם MT 'Their heart cried out' though supported by the versions has no referent. Provan, *Lamentations*, 75–6, regards the subject as the inhabitants of Jerusalem whilst Renkema, *Lamentations*, 307–11, envisions an anticipatory allusion to the children of 19b. The repetition of imperatives is instructive here; שפכי, רני, קומי, אל תדם, אל־תתני, הורידי. Because of the repetitive imperatives used to address Lady Zion throughout vv. 18–19, many commentators emend the text here to either צעקי לך following Bickell or צעקי לבך following Ewald, as do Rudolph, *Klagelieder*, 220 n. 18a; Albrektson, *Lamentations*, 116–18; Hillers, *Lamentations*, 101; Westermann, *Klagelieder*, 126, = *Lamentations*, 146. Gordis, *Lamentations*, 166–8, accepts an imperative here, but alters to צקי 'pour out'. His intuition is correct, but there is no need to alter the root of the verb. The final *mem* on לב is explained more likely as reflecting the common error between מ and כ in palaeo-Hebrew rather than as an enclitic *mem*, contra Hillers, *Lamentations*, 111, or as an adverbial *mem*, contra McDaniel, 'Philological Studies', 203–4.

v. 18a חומת בת ציון MT 'wall of Daughter Zion'. The odd phrase is supported by the versions. If considered a vocative, 'O wall', it appears either to understand that the wall represents Zion as a whole or to be a reference to the wall itself. In conjunction with Mesopotamian laments over the destruction of cities where inanimate objects are used figuratively to express the breadth of the disaster, Dobbs-Allsopp, *Weep, O Daughter of Zion*, 34–5, 89–90, and *idem*, *Lamentations*, 98; Berlin, *Lamentations*, 74–5, regard it as illustrative of the disaster. Gottwald, *Lamentations*, 101, emends incorrectly to נחמת the niphal fem. ptc. 'O remorseful Daughter Zion'.

At the insistence of the narrator, Lady Jerusalem speaks. She describes the fate of the inhabitants of the city as well as her own. She closes in verse 22 accusing Yahweh of instigating their disaster. She says 'You invited my enemies[129] from all around as if for the day of a festival; and on the day of the anger of Yahweh no-one escaped or survived;

---

[129] 2: 22a מְגוּרַי מִסָּבִיב literally 'my terrors from all around'. Taken from מגור 'terror' and found in Jeremiah as מגור מסביב 'terror from every side' (Jer. 6: 25; 20: 3, 10; 46: 5; 49: 29). This is a common translation, see Kraus, *Klagelieder*, 37; Albrektson, *Lamentations*, 124–5; Meek, 'Lamentations', 22. Alternatively, Rudolph,

those whom I bore and reared my enemy has destroyed.' Interestingly, Lady Jerusalem begins by speaking of enemies in the plural and ends with 'enemy' in the singular. The text could be ambiguous at this point as singular איב can represent a collective, but it is more likely the case that the singular adversary represents the deity, especially since this chapter highlights the actions of Yahweh as an aggressor (vv. 1–9) who is labelled repeatedly as איב in 2: 4–5.

One of the most sensitive studies on the figure of Zion in Lamentations is that of Linafelt, who concentrates on the importance of Zion's posture of protest in chapter 2. In his view, interpretations of Lamentations have been overshadowed by attempts to tone down the acute agony of the book in favour of a hope-centred message.[130] In particular, Linafelt regards the figure of Zion as an alternative model to the individual sufferer of chapter 3 who advocates silent submission and patience in the face of a painful present. Additionally, the presentation of pain advocated by the eyewitness and the personified city provides a foil to the suffering servant of Deutero-Isaiah. In the case of Jerusalem, the claim is never made that pain has a redemptive function. Instead, all four poems attributable to Templeless Judah verbalize the tragic reality of human suffering. When Zion can no longer speak, the impersonal eyewitness returns in chapter 4, but the description of the disaster takes on a human element that is not sustained at such length heretofore. Finally, the communal lament of chapter 5 positions the suffering in an explicit context of prayer. At the beginning of their lament (5: 1), the community resumes Zion's muted voice in an almost verbatim quotation of her plea to the deity (1: 11c; 2: 20a, cf. ראה 1: 9c, 20a) and to passers-by (1: 12b, cf. ראה 1: 18b). Though the voice of Zion faded, her cause was renewed by the

---

Klagelieder, 221 n. 22a, points מְגוֹרְרָי as a *polel* participle and translates, 'those who terrify me', followed by Hillers, *Lamentations*, 102, who views מְגוֹרָי as a contracted form appealing to GKC 72cc and understands 'attackers' based on Job 18: 19; cf. McDaniel, 'Philological Studies', 42–4. It refers to the enemies.

[130] Linafelt, 'Zion's Cause', 268–73, and *idem*, *Surviving Lamentations*, 43–9. Among others, hope-centred analyses include Gottwald, *Studies*, 96–9, 105–11; Hillers, *Lamentations*, 5–6, 119–23; Mintz, 'Rhetoric'; R. Brandscheidt, *Gotteszorn und Menschenleid: Die Gerichtsklage des leidenden Gerechten in Klgl 3* (Trier: Paulinus-Verlag, 1983), 20–235, 344–52; Johnson, 'Form and Message', 65–8; J. Krašovec, 'The Source of Hope in the Book of Lamentations', *VT* 42 (1992), 223–33; R. B. Salters, *Jonah and Lamentations* (OTG; Sheffield: Sheffield Academic Press, 1994), 117.

other voices of the book that graphically portray the distress and pityingly plead for divine intervention.

Chapters 1 and 2, through the voices of the eyewitness and Lady Jerusalem, provide an alternative to the silent submission advocated in chapter 3. Moreover, the concern to evoke the compassion of the deity does not fade away like the voice of Lady Jerusalem burdened by despair, but becomes more urgent. The emphasis on vocalizing the pain suggests that in the mind of some it was right and proper to bring suffering before Yahweh in worship and to protest the existence, even the extent, of that suffering. That the eyewitness urges Zion to speak is noted by many, but its implications for understanding a distinctive Judahite response to the disaster have been commented upon only rarely. The emphasis on grieving, even on shouting out the pain, shows that the Judahite community did not advocate silent submission in the light of the catastrophe of 587.

The Formulation of Grief

Heretofore we have considered the types of motifs significant to the homeland as revealed by the language of suffering. It is also the case that the form and setting of the poems signify something distinctive about Judahite interpretation. The form in which the poems were written encapsulates and binds the tumultuous literary litany of tragedy. Even more significantly, it moves it past the mere exclamation of grief by placing every grievance with Yahweh through worship. By its form and *Sitz im Leben*, Lamentations situates a painful present in the context of future orientation. In so doing, the collection intrinsically moves towards a hopeful future that is not explicitly expressed in the laments themselves.

Already, especially in conjunction with the Psalter, the form-critical considerations of Westermann[131] and Gerstenberger,[132]

[131] e.g. Westermann, 'Struktur und Geschichte'; *idem, Das Loben Gottes in den Psalmen* (Göttingen: Vandenhoeck & Ruprecht, 4th edn. 1968), ET *The Praise of God in the Psalms* (Richmond, Va.: John Knox Press, 1965); *idem, Praise and Lament in the Psalms* (Atlanta, Ga.: John Knox Press, 1981); *idem*, 'The Role of the Lament in the Theology of the Old Testament', *Int* 28 (1974), 20–38; *idem, Klagelieder = Lamentations*.
[132] E. Gerstenberger, 'Der Klagende Mensch', in H. W. Wolff (ed.), *Probleme biblischer Theologie: Gerhard von Rad zum 70. Geburstag* (Munich: Kaiser, 1971), 64–72, is particularly instrumental in the analysis of individual laments.

followed by Brueggemann,[133] stress the form of the lament and its relation to function. In terms of form, invariably the communal laments of the Psalter move through and past elements of complaint to conclude with a transition to praise or a confession of trust (but see Ps. 88). To use Brueggemann's terminology there is a 'formfulness' to grief that allows for the legitimate expression of disorientation and the embrace of reorientation. The form of complaint songs, then, whilst appealing to Yahweh, nevertheless ends with the confident hope that the address has been successful in enlisting the support of the deity. The choice of the form itself represents a type of protest.[134] The inclusion of elements of the lament genre in a stylized way such as complaint and even accusation verging on indictment move the mourner through a situation of despair to a positive transformation.

In terms of form-critical categories, Lamentations contrasts sharply, however, with the complaints of the Psalter, even with the so-called national laments with which it is most closely aligned because its poems vacillate between the inclusion of the language of the funeral dirge along with that of the communal lament through which it achieves no comfortable resolution. Actually, chapters 1, 2, and 4 exhibit the combination of the formulaic elements of the communal lament and the funeral dirge whilst the fifth chapter represents one of the purest forms of the communal lament in the Hebrew Bible.[135] The actual ascription of the different elements of complaint and funeral song to Lam. 1, 2, and 4 varies between interpreters with Jahnow arguing for a greater amount of dirge elements and Westermann for that of lament.[136] In distinction, Lee

---

[133] W. Brueggemann, 'Psalms in the Life of Faith: A Suggested Typology of Function', *JSOT* 17 (1980), 3–32; *idem*, 'From Hurt to Joy, From Death to Life', *Int* 28 (1974), 3–19; *idem*, 'The Formfulness of Grief', *Int* 31 (1977), 263–75; *idem*, 'The Costly Loss of Lament', *JSOT* 36 (1986), 57–71. All articles are reprinted in W. Brueggemann, *The Psalms and the Life of Faith* (Minneapolis, Minn.: Fortress Press, 1995).

[134] Acknowledged to some extent by Westermann, 'The Role of the Lament', 30, cf. *idem*, *Klagelieder*, 86–7 = *Lamentations*, 91–3: 'Insofar as the absurd is laid before God, the lament of the nation contains a dimension of protest.'

[135] H. Gunkel, and J. Begrich, *Einleitung in die Psalmen: Die Gattungen der religiösen Lyrik Israels* (Göttingen: Vandenhoeck & Ruprecht, 1933), 136, were the first to associate the form of poems 1, 2, and 4 with the dirge.

[136] Jahnow, *Das hebräische Leichenlied*, 124–62; cf. Westermann, *Klagelieder*, 15–20 = *Lamentations*, 1–9.

holds the two together and comes up with a new form which she terms the communal dirge.¹³⁷ Perhaps the best analysis is that of Linafelt, who shows that although the two forms intertwine, the form gradually beginning to predominate is that of the communal lament.¹³⁸ Linafelt's analysis is confirmed by the form of the fifth poem, which is only a communal lament. Even though the elements of complaint and funeral song exist in a dialectical relationship, chapters 1, 2, and 4 exhibit a gradual lessening of the dirge elements in favour of the lament formulae so that the dirge-laden chapter 1 gives way in the end to the communal complaint of chapter 5.

The form of the expression of Jerusalem's grief conveys meaning. The funeral song is characterized by third-person speech about the death of a loved one and tends to be backward-looking, but could be used according to Jahnow as a form of accusation against a perpetrator of violence, an oft-overlooked use carefully noted by Lee.¹³⁹ Through its struggle against the present distress, the communal lament directs second-person speech to the deity and asserts confidence in the transformation to restoration. Linafelt discusses the two forms in conjunction with survival literature and notes that the dirge can be characterized by a tragic reversal and the lament by a saving reversal. Until the final chapter of Lamentations, though, the hope for a salvific future is bound by reflections on the ignoble collapse of the city and its dire consequences for the present state of the community so poignantly expressed through the language of the funeral song. A shift in Lamentations towards the use of the complaint of the people alone reveals a turn from the contemplation of death to the embrace of life. By the *form*, although not the message, of the final chapter, the structure of Lamentations turns ever so slightly towards a belief in future hope.

The language of grief in Judah corresponds to that of Mesopotamian lament literature. Although this has been the source of enlightening scholarly endeavours, the implications of that have seldom been brought to bear on a discussion of the interplay between the language and the function of the biblical Lamentations. The

---

¹³⁷ Lee, *The Singers of Lamentations*, 1–46.
¹³⁸ Linafelt, *Surviving Lamentations*, 75; cf. Lee, *The Singers of Lamentations*, 37.
¹³⁹ Jahnow, *Das hebräische Leichenlied*, 88; Lee, *The Singers of Lamentations*, 33–7.

Mesopotamian laments used hyperbole and exaggeration, even seemingly inaccurate depictions with respect to the extent of damage, to encourage the deity to return to the city and to the temple with blessing so that reconstruction and restoration might take place under divine aegis.[140] The function of the laments to encourage the return of the deity is just as significant as that which was lamented. In his assessment of the literary character of Lamentations, Provan found that one predominant feature is its hyperbolic language.[141] Of course, the implication of that awareness in his view suggests that Lamentations cannot be dated to a particular time period with any precision.

The language of hyperbole and exaggeration could function within the biblical Lamentations in a similar way to that of its Mesopotamian counterparts. Dobbs-Allsopp revealed how the instruction to Lady Zion to cry out to Yahweh resonates with Mesopotamian laments which function to gain the attention and compassion of the deity.[142] Furthermore, in the ancient world as evidenced by Mesopotamian literature the destruction of a city could only take place after it had been abandoned by its deity or after the withdrawal of divine support.[143] The Mesopotamian laments served to entreat the deity to return to the city and the temple usually during a period of reconstruction, and consequently they end with a feast celebrating divine return and the restoration of the temple. With its lament over the destruction of the city, its temple, and the disasters that accompanied it, the various speaking voices of Lamentations seek divine resolution to their predicament. As in the Mesopotamian laments, hyperbolic and exaggerated language function as a means to spur the deity to action. The present is dire, but the graphic, even horrific, portrayal of destruction and physical suffering explores the limits of language in the attempt to motivate Yahweh to do something, anything! If the language of Lamentations is uncertain, its similarity to the genre of city laments indicates that in form it is hopeful. After all,

---

[140] An introduction to Mesopotamian laments is in J. Krecher, 'Klagelied', in D. O. Edzard (ed.), *Reallexikon der Assyriologie und Vorderasiatischen Archäologie*, vi (Berlin: de Gruyter, 1980–3), 1–6; W. W. Hallo, 'Lamentations and Prayers in Sumer and Akkad', in J. M. Sasson (ed.), *Civilizations of the Ancient Near East*, iii (London and New York: Simon & Schuster, 1995), 1871–81.

[141] Provan, *Lamentations*, 6.
[142] Dobbs-Allsopp, *Weep, O Daughter of Zion*, 34–5.
[143] Ibid., 45–51.

in crying out the people affirm their belief that Yahweh will hear. In so doing, they express hope that the deity will act salvifically.

Ultimately, Lamentations positions the suffering of a community in the very heart of Yahweh and uses the avenue of worship to achieve that end. Brueggemann's insights in this regard are telling. In an exploration of the relationship between form and function of various genres of the Psalms, he speaks of lament psalms as purveyors of a hermeneutic of dislocation.[144] The people's complaint advances the abominable and unacceptable present to the deity, suspicious of a future hope, but claiming it nonetheless. There are two important events that coincide with this declaration of pain that are important especially in the context of the book of Lamentations. Brueggemann speaks at one point of the need to express the agony:

> But to first speak the words to the disoriented and then to have the disoriented actually speak the words can be a new recognition and embrace of the actual situation which would rather be denied... The 'language event' of the lament thus permits movement beyond *naivete* and acceptance of one's actual situation *critically*.[145]

In this regard, the vocalization of pain allows for it to be confronted and eventually dealt with. In Lamentations the impersonal eyewitness ceased his descriptive narration in order to speak directly to Lady Jerusalem and she responded. In so doing, the miserable conditions were acknowledged in a more personal way. Lamentations agonizes over the distress, but vocally accepts its presence. That the pain is not only visualized and remembered in an objective report, but vocalized, even in liturgy, communicates the distress directly to the deity.

Secondly, Brueggemann notes that 'songs also function to evoke and form new realities that did not exist'. In conjunction with this, he highlights that the Psalmic exclamation that 'Yahweh is king' is not mere description, but invokes the deity to kingship. In his words, 'It calls him to throne.'[146] A similar declaration about the governance of Yahweh is affirmed in 5: 19. In Lamentations, though, the statement about Yahweh's kingship arises after a serious perusal of complaint

---

[144] Brueggemann, 'Psalms and the Life of Faith', 12–14.
[145] Ibid., 18.   [146] Ibid., 18.

and before a conclusion that evokes uncertainty rather than surety. The community hopes for the sure and unfettered governance of Yahweh in the midst of its troubles. The present has not been transformed, but the appearance of this exclamation suggests that it shall be. However, two points urge us to be cautious in situating the community in a future-orientated outlook. First, other than this passage, few passages in Lamentations correspond to what can be thought of as a confession of trust. An eagerness to find a source of hope among the collage of suffering and despair finds many commentators gravitating toward the only passage of sustained hope in the book, 3: 22–9. Unfortunately, these verses belong to a different thought milieu than the rest of the material. Outside these hopeful verses swirl a relentless array of images highlighting the continued dire circumstances of the people. Secondly, in spite of the appearance of a claim about the kingship of the deity, it arises as a necessary element of the form of the final chapter. That it is eclipsed by a question once it is spoken downplays its force. Though the community appears to express confidence in Yahweh, it has already been seen that there is no clear, unequivocal vocalization of hope in the collection. Nevertheless, the inclusion of a confession of trust at all communicates the desire of the people for a restored future in a kind of hope for hope.

Through the form of Lamentations, its odd combination of genres—the communal dirge, communal lament, and city lament—the poet of Lamentations turns an otherwise desperate situation into a vision for the future. In spite of the language of human suffering so prevalent throughout the poems, the formation of its grief binds it to a fundamental belief in restoration. The hope indicated by the form is further reinforced by the setting in worship. By positioning loss and pain in worship, the Judahites claimed the validity of communicating their present experience and their refusal to explain it away through serious theological formulations. Their grief mattered to them. Because they formulated it in prayer, they believed ultimately that it mattered to their deity. Through Lamentations the community in Judah, in sharp contrast to that in Babylon, neither formulated any grand future vision of hope nor explicitly expressed belief in the coming intervention of the deity in a restorative way. Instead, amazingly, a sense of hope in future possibilities arises from the *form* of their grief. The formfulness of their grief, as a mix of dirge and lament that moves to a pure communal lament, suggests that in spite of their pessimism, they believed fundamentally that in the setting of worship, their present could be transformed. The fact that they could not express that hope more clearly than in the forms that they used to bind the images of a painful present attests to how keenly felt were their circumstances. Nevertheless, in spite of their inability to state outright belief in future hope, the form of their grief conveys it.

CONCLUSIONS

In the biblical Lamentations, five distinctive features pertinent to the community in the land came to the fore: an emphasis on human suffering, the lack of statements of confidence in future hope, a de-emphasis on the instrumentality of sin, the need to verbalize the raw emotions of grief, and the formulation of painful protest. These motifs could assist in the association of other literature, particularly that of the lament genre, to a setting in Judah. The utilization of any of these elements in conjunction with a land-centric viewpoint would suggest a Judahite provenance.

The distinctiveness of Lamentations is apparent not only by the language of despair that suffuses its poetry, but by its form and setting. The form, for example, contributed to a sense of the tension with which the Judahite population grappled. Were they dead or was there hope? That the collection ends with a communal lament suggests that Judah journeyed through an expression of their pain towards a belief in a restored future different from their past and present. In expressing their agony and present distress, the community sought throughout to evoke the compassion of the deity. By setting their grief in the context of worship, the Judahites insisted that ultimately their lot lay with Yahweh. Interestingly, their laments do not praise Yahweh. The equivalent of an explicit confession of trust was included only at 5: 19 as an element of the communal lament. Instead, Lamentations insists on exhibiting the disaster as divinely ordained and sustained. Theirs was not the resoundingly joyful message of Deutero-Isaiah or the hope for restoration and resurrection of Ezekiel. Their hope was tried in the fire of ruination, but though Lady Zion's voice died away, the community picked up her lament and placed her and their agony in the very heart of the deity through worship.

What becomes immediately apparent is that the language of Lamentations is the language of current affliction. When there is hope, either through the move to communal lament or through the use of the genre of city lament, even in its *Sitz im Leben* of worship, the poetry of the book envisions nothing like the imaginative future events found in *Golah* literature. Deutero-Isaiah conceptualizes the return to Zion as a new Exodus, even more spectacular than the former one from Egypt, whilst Ezekiel pictures a restored temple of inconceivable proportions. In contrast, the Judahite population wrestles with tragedy in the midst of the fray and prays fervently for release. Bearing the brunt of subjugation and misery, the Judahites do not simply accept their lot. Instead, they vocalize it. Although the recent past and the mournful present bear down on them and banish all thoughts of a future other than the present, they protest. Even when the voice of the personified city falls silent as she is cowed beneath the weight of tragedy, an aloof narrator abandons his impartiality. With the acceptance of his own agonized response to the terrible and horrific events unfolding around him, the eyewitness urges Lady Jerusalem, commands her even, to speak out. Moreover, when her voice finally fails, the communal voice echoes her plea. Faced with human suffering on a divine scale, mournful Judah does not metaphorically sit in an ash heap and ruminate, but shouts of loss and limitation. The formation of the protest of pain and its setting in worship is just as significant as that which has been said. In spite of everything, the people in Judah prayed to their God. Through doing so, they provided hints as to what types of themes would have been pertinent to themselves post-587.

The previous chapter demonstrated that there have been a variety of perceptions about the literature from Judah after the collapse of Jerusalem without any clear grounds for attribution to that setting. It is hoped that the present study contributes in a significant way to an understanding of the distinctive thought of the homeland. More importantly, the criteria delineated here provide a necessary prerequisite and indeed the catalyst for future analysis of literature often associated with Templeless Judah. In a follow-up study, I propose to reconsider the laments commonly associated with worship at the temple site along with Noth's provocative suggestion of the origin of the Deuteronomistic History in Templeless Judah. The present study has provided a benchmark of sorts with which to raise awareness of theological reflection particular to the homeland.

Conclusion

At the outset of the present study it was asserted that the period in Judah subsequent to the Babylonian destruction of Jerusalem in 587 marked an era considered to be of fundamental significance to the historical, social, and theological development of ancient Israel. It was particularly during this time that conceptualizations of the state, community, and religion were reassessed and reformulated. Because the Templeless period was perceived by the Hebrew Bible and modern scholarship to have been so foundational, it behoves the current generation to be more aware of the situation in Judah. Several recent studies have pointed to the possibility of creative literary activity in the homeland. Yet, clear parameters for understanding themes consistent with Judahite thought have until now not been clearly elucidated. Important work on the *Golah* literature and its relationship to the setting in Babylonia have raised to prominence the influence reality exerts on literary formulation. The further efforts to add to our knowledge of Judah during this epoch by various interpreters have likewise raised to the foreground the need for more clarity. One necessary precursor to a study of the literature from Judah, then, was the implementation of a reconstruction of the social situation in the land.

In the first chapter, the biblical history of Judah in the Templeless period was supplemented with the evidence of material culture available from excavations and surveys and the impact of Babylonian rule on conquered states in order to construct a backdrop for the development of theological literature in the homeland. Biblical historiography provided an entry point to the discussion of post-587 Judah. The little information available from the biblical narrative depicts the homeland devastated by attack, settled by only the poor people of the land, farmed by vinedressers and ploughmen, and in serious need of political and religious leadership. No other details are forthcoming in the literature beyond this relatively incomplete and bleak picture. In spite of the fact that the historiographical portrait contains a gap for the era under question, certain textual clues elsewhere provided reasons to believe that Judah contained a relatively secure infrastructure. The likelihood of the continuation of political authority under the aegis of governors, although only hinted at in the biblical material, provided one reason to believe there was a measure of stability for the inhabitants of the land. In all probability, political leaders existed alongside religious personnel. The presence of a scribal class who rallied around the prophet Jeremiah and who documented the events of Gedaliah's short rule further indicates that literary activity could continue in the homeland. Finally, although Judah returned to normal activities before the murder of Gedaliah, it is conceivable that certain members of society, namely the עם הארץ, exerted their authority to institute stability after his untimely death.

Other sources of information about the period, such as those from the archaeological record and an understanding of the Babylonian empire, confirm to some extent the mixed portrait of the Hebrew Bible. In particular, the archaeological record vividly represents the extent and ferocity of the Babylonian campaign. Jerusalem and the south were especially hard hit. At the same time the material culture of the Benjamin region, in particular, reveals continuity with the monarchic period. The locus of community life shifted north in the Templeless period, to Mizpah, the newly established administrative centre, and its environs. Furthermore, the material evidence indicates not only the existence of a relatively sizeable population in Judah, but also, judging from the remains of wine vats and silos for grain storage, a degree of sustenance, even prosperity, that was achieved therein. Finally, Babylonian interaction in Judah and the western periphery represents destruction and renewal. Although there are no extant records for the fall of Jerusalem in 587 outside of the biblical literature, the archaeological evidence of Jerusalem and the Philistine cities supports the biblical suggestion of devastation and destruction. However, it is likely that the Babylonians instituted a change in policy in the western periphery and operated a provincial system. As a province Judah would have had a degree of security which enabled conditions to improve after the disaster. The existence of imperial authority in the region is especially provocative in light of what appears to have been the establishment of Mizpah as an administrative centre *before* the actual fall of Jerusalem and Gedaliah's appointment as governor. The biblical portrait, the archaeological data, and knowledge of Babylonian imperial ruling strategies enable a probable reconstruction of the social and historical situation of Templeless Judah. Despite devastation and severe disruption, certain clues indicate the restoration of activity that would be normative for an agricultural society and the existence of a stable infrastructure within which cultic ritual continued along with the generation of religious literature.[1]

Because ancient Israel maintained copious literature that is theological in nature and the *Golah* community invested much energy in the reflection on worship, it was important to consider how the situation in the homeland impacted theological conceptions of reality. The second and third chapters, therefore, considered religious thought of the period. It was clear from both that conceptions of theological belief attributed to Templeless Judah tended to come from perceptions not necessarily of the population in the homeland. In Chapter 2, for instance, it was shown that a great deal of literature from the Templeless period focused on the ongoing worship of deities either in distinction or in addition to Yahweh. In conjunction with that discussion, it was noted that except for the material evidence afforded by the Judaean Pillar Figurines, the attestation of these practices did not stem from sixth-century Judah and tended to serve a greater theological agenda. The attribution to the homeland of the continuation of aberrant worship practices functioned ideologically to deny categorically the community therein a place in the divinely ordained and sustained future Jerusalem. In their literature, the *Golah* placed their Judahite brethren under the continued judgement of Yahweh. In so doing, they superimposed an understanding of religious life in the land that may or may not have had a basis in reality.

In a similar way, Chapter 3 showed that although there is good reason to believe in the participation in Yahwistic worship by the inhabitants in the homeland—either through sporadic and spontaneous worship at the ruins of the Jerusalem temple or through regular ritual at a sanctuary in Bethel—there is no direct confirmation of its existence. Moreover, the lament literature attributed to this *Sitz im*

---

[1] J. Blenkinsopp, 'The Age of the Exile', in J. Barton (ed.), *The Biblical World*, i (London and New York: Routledge, 2002), 426, reaches similar conclusions.

Leben tends to show no clear indication of provenance. In fact, of the laments surveyed which included only a portion of the liturgical literature thought to stem from Templeless Judah, the outlook and traditions are much too various to associate strictly with the homeland. Indeed, Psalms 74, 79, 89, and 102, and Isaiah 63: 7–64: 11 find their basis in diverse traditions which included Zion theology, election ideology, Ezekiel's emphasis on the vindication of the divine name, cosmogonic mythological traditions, salvation history, and covenant, or combinations of any of the above. With such a wide variety of influences, the attempt to attribute laments to Judah without an understanding of what might be typical of Judahite thought is precarious at best. Moreover, the ascription of laments to worship at the temple represents another outside conception—in this instance from modern scholarship.

In the first three chapters, then, we surveyed much of what is thought about the homeland from the evidence of an historical and an ideological nature without actually contemplating the Judahite response to the events of 587 and their circumstances. Chapter 4 turned, therefore, to Lamentations, which is most widely regarded as stemming from Templeless Judah. The book of Lamentations was used typologically in order to isolate prominent concepts. From an analysis of poems 1, 2, 4, and 5 the themes distinctive to the Judahite situation emerge: (1) the concentration on the extent of unalleviated human suffering, (2) the explicit assertion of uncertainty in future possibilities, (3) a deconstruction of the efficacy of human sin, (4) the need to witness to pain through the vocalization of grief especially within worship, and (5) the forming of grief in such a way as to limit it and evoke a future orientation. The delineation of these themes creates a type of measuring rod with which to approach other material thought to stem from Judah. Especially if these ideas can be found in conjunction with a land-centric viewpoint that perceives the exile as just one consequence of a wider disaster, they should enable the association of additional literature to Templeless Judah. These parameters can be used, therefore, to reconsider various literature thought to belong to sixth-century Judah, including some already surveyed in this book such as the laments at the temple, but also the Deuteronomistic History, which may stem in part from Templeless Judah like the final form of Jeremiah.

The title, *The Troubles of Templeless Judah*, encapsulates the dual foci of this thesis. On the one hand, there is great difficulty in approaching this time period—sources are incomplete and their use is disputed—a lamentable situation indeed. Moreover, other sources of information for Judah exhibit an ideological stance not in keeping with a perception from the homeland itself. The troubles of Templeless Judah, then, suggests the need: (1) to assimilate as much data as possible across a variety of fields and through a diversity of sources in order to capture roughly the situation in the land and (2) to ascertain thought consistent with a Judahite perspective of the inhabitants in the homeland in the sixth century BCE. On the other hand, 'troubles' alludes to the type of literature which was surveyed in relation to Judah as a means to assess a typically Judahite response. The book of Lamentations is no easy read, instead it mourns and laments past and ongoing suffering. The voice of the land represents a community that agonized over its troubles. In so doing, the laments attributable to Templeless Judah provide a means to ascertain other literature with a similar provenance.

Though often not taken into consideration as a means to approach the literature of the sixth century, the short studies of Klein, Williamson, and Helberg are instrumental in having raised awareness of the distinctiveness of Judahite thought. In the first place, Klein attempted to show how the idea of kingship varied between Judahite literature and that of the *Golah* group.[2] Secondly, Williamson noted a separate class of laments united by the similar form of an historical recital conjoined to a confession of sin in Nehemiah 9, Isaiah 63: 7–64: 11, and Psalm 106.[3] In an analysis of them, he defended arguments that thematically these historical laments fit well with a perspective from the inhabitants in the land following the catastrophe of 587. Finally, Helberg in his analysis of the use of the motif of the land in Lamentations found that the focus of the collection

---

[2] R. W. Klein, 'A Theology for Exiles: The Kingship of Yahweh', *Dialog* 17 (1978), 128–34.
[3] H. G. M. Williamson, 'Structure and Historiography in Nehemiah 9', *Proceedings of the Ninth World Congress of Jewish Studies* (Jerusalem: Magnes Press, 1985), 117–31; idem, 'Isaiah 63,7–64,11: Exilic Lament or Post-Exilic Protest?' *ZAW* 102 (1990), 48–58; idem, 'Laments at the Destroyed Temple', *BRev* 4/4 (1990), 12–17, 44.

remains almost univocally on Judah.[4] When the exile is referred to, it is mentioned as just one consequence of a series of disasters. All three studies reveal features consistent with Judahite reflection on the catastrophic events of the early part of the sixth century. To a large degree, this study confirms the conclusions reached by Klein, Williamson, and Helberg. More importantly, having understood theological reflection to be linked to community life, it sets out themes consistent with Judahite conceptions of reality in conjunction with its socio-historical situation.

One of the significant features of Templeless Judah in its community and literature is that it exhibits continuity with monarchic Judah rather than a break. This continuity is attested by the material evidence which urges us to posit a break between Iron Age II and III at the end of the sixth century rather than at its beginning. Continuity in religious thought urges a similar conception of the period. In contrast to the *Golah* group in Babylon who reformulated their traditions in light of the circumstances of deportation and resettlement in a foreign country, the inhabitants of the land thought less about their situation. Instead, they mourned it. In many respects, then, the understanding of the 'exilic age' as a real watershed in the history, literature, and theology of ancient Israel is only applicable when viewed from the perspective of the *Golah*. Templeless Judah represents continuity rather than change.

There are several ways this study impacts future research on that of ancient Israel and the Hebrew Bible. In the first place, it provides a current analysis and synthesis of the situation in Judah which contributes a much-needed study of the homeland in the period traditionally, and hopefully now anachronistically, known as 'the exile'. Moreover, current discussions regarding the return and reconstructions of community life in the early Second Temple period have a resource with which to understand the population that remained in the land. Secondly, it urges us to reconsider our terminology for this period and, indeed, even our perception of it. The 'exilic age' as a title not only fails to account for the various Judahite populations that existed after the collapse of Jerusalem, it overshadows the *continuity* that defined the situation in the homeland. The alternative expres-

---

[4] J. L. Helberg, 'Land in the Book of Lamentations', ZAW 102 (1990), 372–85.

sion, 'the Templeless period', is more in keeping with the recognition of the diversity of populations and their conceptions of reality. Finally, the delineation of themes consistent with a Judahite perspective urges the reappraisal of literature from the period. Studies of the laments associated with worship at the temple following the catastrophe of 587, and even the Deuteronomistic History, deserve further attention in light of the conclusions reached here. Like Lady Jerusalem who tenaciously refused to accept the narrative mourning of her death, the various speaking voices in Lamentations persistently and ceaselessly proclaimed their misery. In spite of the fact that their testimony to defeat was overshadowed by *Golah* interpretation in the Hebrew Bible and in modern scholarship, their distinctive perspective survives.

Bibliography

ABERBACH, D., *Imperialism and Biblical Prophecy, 750–500 BCE* (London: Routledge, 1993).
ACKERMAN, S., 'A MARZĒAḤ in Ezekiel 8:7–13?', *HTR* 82 (1989), 267–81.
—— *Under Every Green Tree: Popular Religion in Sixth-Century Judah* (HSM, 46; Atlanta: Scholars Press, repr. 2001).
—— "And the Women Knead Dough": The Worship of the Queen of Heaven in Sixth-Century Judah', in Day, *Gender and Difference in Ancient Israel*, 109–24.
ACKROYD, P. R., 'The Book of Haggai and Zechariah I–VIII', *JJS* 3 (1952), 151–7.
—— 'Criteria for the Maccabean Dating of Old Testament Literature', *VT* 3 (1953), 113–32.z
—— *Exile and Restoration: A Study of Hebrew Thought of the Sixth Century BC* (London: SCM Press, repr. 1994).
—— 'Goddesses, Women and Jezebel', in Cameron and Kuhrt, *Images of Women in Antiquity*, 245–59.
—— 'Historians and Prophets,' *SEÅ* 33 (1968), 18–54.
—— 'The History of Israel in the Exilic and Post-Exilic Periods', in Anderson, *Tradition and Interpretation*, 320–50.
—— *Israel under Babylon and Persia* (NCBOT, 4; Oxford: Oxford University Press, 1970).
—— 'The Jewish Community in Palestine in the Persian Period', in *CHJ*, i. 130–61.
—— 'Studies in the Book of Haggai', *JJS* 2 (1951), 163–76.
—— 'Studies in the Book of Haggai (Continued from Vol. II—No. 4)', *JJS* 3 (1952), 1–13.
—— 'The Temple Vessels: A Continuity Theme', in *Studies in the Religion of Ancient Israel* (SVT, 23; Leiden: Brill, 1972), 166–81.
—— *Studies in the Religious Tradition of the Old Testament* (London: SCM Press, 1987).
AHLSTRÖM, G. W., *The History of Ancient Palestine* (Minneapolis: Fortress Press, 2nd edn. 1994).
—— *Psalm 89: eine Liturgie aus dem Ritual des Leidenden Königs* (Lund: Gleerup, 1959).

ALBERTZ, R., *Die Exilszeit* (BE, 7; Stuttgart: W. Kohlhammer, 2002); ET *Israel in Exile: The History and Literature of the Sixth Century B.C.E.* (Studies in Biblical Literature; Atlanta: Scholars Press, 2003).

—— 'Die Exilszeit als Ernstfall für eine historische Rekonstruktion ohne biblische Texte: Die neubabylonischen Königsinschriften als "Primarquellen" ', in Grabbe, *Leading Captivity Captive*, 22–39.

—— *Persönliche Frömmigkeit und offizielle Religion: Religionsinterner Pluralismus in Israel und Babylon* (CTM, 9; Stuttgart: Calwer, 1978).

—— *Religionsgeschichte Israels in alttestamentlicher Zeit* (ATD, 8; Göttingen: Vandenhoeck & Ruprecht, 1992); ET *A History of Israelite Religion in the Old Testament Period*, vols. i–ii (London: SCM Press, 1994).

ALBREKTSON, B., *Studies in the Text and Theology of the Book of Lamentations* (STL, 21; Lund: Gleerup, 1963).

ALBRIGHT, W. F., 'Bethel in Iron II', *AASOR* 39 (1968), 36–7.

—— 'King Jehoiachin in Exile', *BA* 5 (1942), 49–55.

ALLEN, L. C., *Psalms 101–150* (WBC, 21; Waco: Word Books, 1983).

ALLEN, N., 'The Identity of the Jerusalem Priesthood During the Exile', *HeyJ* 23 (1982), 259–69.

ALT, A., 'Die Rolle Samarias bei der Entstehung des Judentums', in *Festschrift Otto Procksch zum 60. Geburtstag* (Leipzig: A. Deihert and J. C. Hinrichs, 1934), 5–28.

—— *Kleine Schriften zur Geschichte des Volkes Israel*, ii (Munich: C. H. Beck, 1953).

ALTMANN, A. (ed.), *Biblical and Other Studies* (ST, 1; Cambridge, Mass.: Harvard University Press, 1963).

AMIRAN, R., 'A Note on the "Gibeon Jar" ', *PEQ* 110 (1975), 129–32.

'AMR, A.-J., 'Ten Human Clay Figurines from Jerusalem', *Levant* 20 (1988), 185–96.

ANDERSON, A. A., *Psalms*, 2 vols. (NCB; London: Oliphants, 1972).

ANDERSON, B., *From Creation to New Creation: Old Testament Perspectives* (OBT; Minneapolis: Fortress Press, 1994).

ANDERSON, G. A., *A Time to Mourn, a Time to Dance: The Expression of Grief and Joy in Israelite Religion* (University Park: Pennsylvania State University Press, 1991).

—— (ed.), *Tradition and Interpretation: Essays by Members of the Society for Old Testament Study* (Oxford: Clarendon Press, 1979).

ANDREWS, D. K., 'Yahweh and the God of the Heavens', in McCullough, *The Seed of Wisdom*, 45–57.

APPLEGATE, J., 'Jeremiah and the Seventy Years in the Hebrew Bible: Inner-Biblical Reflections on the Prophet and His Prophecy', in Curtis and Römer, *The Book of Jeremiah and its Reception*, 91–110.

ARNOLD, P. M., *Gibeah: The Search for a Biblical City* (JSOTSup, 79; Sheffield: JSOT Press, 1990).

AUFFRET, P., 'Essai sur la structure littéraire du psaume 74', *VT* 33 (1983), 129–48.

AVI-YONAH, M. (ed.), *Encyclopedia of Archaeological Excavations in the Holy Land*, vol. iii (Englewood Cliffs: Prentice-Hall, 1975).

AVIGAD, N., *Bullae and Seals from a Post-Exilic Judean Archive* (Qedem, 4; Jerusalem: Institute of Archaeology, 1976), 1–36.

—— 'Two Hebrew Inscriptions on Wine Jars', *IEJ* 22 (1972), 1–9.

BALL, E. (ed.), *In Search of True Wisdom: Essays in OT Interpretation in Honour of Ronald E. Clements* (JSOTSup, 300; Sheffield: Sheffield Academic Press, 1999).

BARKAY, G., 'The Iron Age IIIb—The Sixth Century BCE', in Ben-Tor, *The Archaeology of Ancient Israel*, 302–73.

—— *Ketef Hinnom: A Treasure Facing Jerusalem's Walls* (Jerusalem: Israel Museum, 1986).

—— 'The Redefining of Archaeological Periods: Does the Date 588/586 B.C.E. Indeed Mark the End of Iron Age Culture?', in Biran and Aviram, *Biblical Archaeology Today*, 106–9.

BARSTAD, H. M., 'After the "Myth of the Empty Land": Major Challenges in the Study of Neo-Babylonian Judah', in Lipschits and Blenkinsopp, *Judah and the Judeans*, 3–20.

—— *The Babylonian Captivity of the Book of Isaiah: 'Exilic' Judah and the Provenance of Isaiah 40–55* (ISK; Oslo: Novus, 1997).

—— *The Myth of the Empty Land: A Study in the History and Archaeology of Judah during the 'Exilic' Period* (SO, 28; Oslo: Scandinavian University Press, 1996).

—— 'On the History and Archaeology of Judah During the Exilic Period', *OLP* 19 (1988), 25–36.

—— 'On the so-called Babylonian Literary Influence in Second Isaiah', *SJOT* 2 (1987), 90–110.

—— 'The Strange Fear of the Bible: Some Reflections on the "Bibliophobia" in Recent Ancient Israelite Historiography', in Grabbe, *Leading Captivity Captive*, 120–7.

—— *A Way in the Wilderness: The 'Second Exodus' in the Message of Second Isaiah* (JSSM, 12; Manchester: University of Manchester Press, 1989).

BARTHÉLEMY, D. (ed.), *Critique textuelle de l'Ancien Testament*, iii: *Ezéchiel, Daniel et les 12 prophètes* (OBO, 50/3; Göttingen: Vandenhoeck & Ruprecht, 1992).

BARTLETT, J. R., 'Edom and the Fall of Jerusalem, 587 B.C.', *PEQ* 114 (1982), 13–24.

—— 'Edomites and Idumaeans', *PEQ* 131 (1999), 102–14.
BARTON, J. (ed.), *The Biblical World*, i (London and New York: Routledge, 2002).
—— 'Wellhausen's Prolegomena to the History of Israel: Influence and Effects', in Smith-Christopher, *Text and Experience*, 316–29.
BARTON, J. and REIMER, D. J. (eds.), *After the Exile: Essays in Honour of Rex Mason* (Macon: Mercer University Press, 1996).
BATTO, B. F., *Slaying the Dragon: Mythmaking in the Biblical Tradition* (Louisville: Westminster/John Knox Press, 1992).
BECKING, B., 'Continuity and Discontinuity after the Exile: Some Introductory Remarks', in Becking and Korpel, *The Crisis of Israelite Religion*, 1–8.
—— 'Ezra's Re-enactment of the Exile', in Grabbe, *Leading Captivity Captive*, 40–61.
—— 'Inscribed Seals as Evidence for Biblical Israel? Jeremiah 40.7–41.15 par exemple', in Grabbe, *Can a 'History of Israel' be Written?*, 64–84.
BECKING, B. and DIJKSTRA, M. (eds.), *On Reading Prophetic Texts: Gender Specific and Related Studies in Memory of Fokkelien van Dijk-Hemmes* (BIS, 18; Leiden: Brill, 1996).
BECKING, B. and KORPEL, M. C. A. (eds.), *The Crisis of Israelite Religion: Transformation of Religious Tradition in Exilic and Post-Exilic Times* (OTS, 42; Leiden: Brill, 1999).
BEDFORD, P. R., *Temple Restoration in Early Achaemenid Judah* (JSJSup, 65; Leiden: Brill, 2001).
BEN-TOR, A. (ed.), *The Archaeology of Ancient Israel* (New Haven: Yale University Press, 1992).
BERGER, P. R., 'Der Kyros-Zylinder mit dem Zusatzfragment BIN II Nr. 32 und die akkadischen Personennamen im Danielbuch', *ZA* 64 (1975), 192–234.
BERLIN, A., *Lamentations* (OTL; Louisville: Westminster/John Knox Press, 2002).
BERQUIST, J. L., *Judaism in Persia's Shadow: A Social and Historical Approach* (Minneapolis: Fortress Press, 1995).
BERTHOLET, A., *Das Buch Hesekiel* (KHAT, 12; Freiburg: J. C. B. Mohr (Paul Siebeck), 1897).
BEUKEN, W. A. M., *Haggai-Sacharja 1–8: Studien zur Überlieferungsgeschichte der frühnachexilischen Prophetie* (Assen: Van Gorcum, 1967).
—— 'Isaiah 56.9–57.13: An Example of the Isaianic Legacy of Trito-Isaiah', in van Henten *et al.*, *Tradition and Re-Interpretation in Jewish and Early Christian Literature*, 48–64.
BIANCHI, F., 'Zerobabel re di Giuda', *Henoch* 13 (1991), 133–56.
—— 'Le rôle de Zerobabel et de la dynastie davidique en Judée du VIe siècle au IIe siècle av. J.-C.', *Transeuphratène* 7 (1994), 153–65.

BICKERMAN, E. J., 'The Babylonian Captivity', in *CHJ*, i. 342–58.
—— 'En marge de l'Écriture, I: Le comput des années de règne des Achéménides (Néh. i, 2; ii, 1 et Thuc., viii, 58)', *RB* 88 (1981), 19–23.
BINGER, T., *Asherah: Goddesses in Ugaritic, Israel and the Old Testament* (JSOTSup, 232; Sheffield: Sheffield Academic Press, 1997).
BIRAN, A. (ed.), *Temples and High Places in Biblical Times: Proceedings of the Colloquium in Honor of the Centennial of Hebrew Union College Jewish Institute of Religion, Jerusalem, 14–16 March 1977* (Jerusalem: Nelson Glueck School of Biblical Archaeology, 1981).
BIRAN, A. and AVIRAM, J. (eds.), *Biblical Archaeology Today: Proceedings of the Second International Congress on Biblical Archaeology* (Jerusalem: Israel Exploration Society, 1993).
BLENKINSOPP, J., 'The Age of the Exile', in J. Barton (ed.), *The Biblical World*, i (London and New York: Routledge, 2002), 416–39.
—— 'Bethel in the Neo-Babylonian Period', in Lipschits and Blenkinsopp, *Judah and the Judeans*, 93–107.
—— 'The Bible, Archaeology and Politics; or The Empty Land Revisited', *JSOT* 27 (2002), 169–87.
—— *A History of Prophecy in Israel: From the Settlement in the Land to the Hellenistic Period* (London: SPCK, 1984).
—— 'A Jewish Sect of the Persian Period', *CBQ* 52 (1990), 5–20.
—— 'The Judaean Priesthood during the Neo-Babylonian and Achaemenid Periods: A Hypothetical Reconstruction', *CBQ* 60 (1998), 25–43.
—— 'The Mission of Udjahorresnet and those of Ezra and Nehemiah', *JBL* 106 (1987), 409–21.
—— 'There Was No Gap', *BAR* 28/3 (2002), 36–8, 59.
BLOCH-SMITH, E., 'Death in the Life of Israel', in Gittlen, *Sacred Time, Sacred Place*, 139–43.
—— *Judahite Burial Practices and Beliefs about the Dead* (JSOTSup, 123; Sheffield: Sheffield Academic Press, 1992).
BOARDMAN, J. *et al.* (eds.), *The Cambridge Ancient History* (Cambridge: Cambridge University Press, 2nd edn. 1991).
BODA, M. J., *Praying the Tradition: The Origin and Use of Tradition in Nehemiah 9* (BZAW, 277; Berlin: de Gruyter, 1999).
BOECKER, H. J., *Die Klagelieder* (ZBK, 21; Zurich: Evangelische Verlag, 1985).
BONNARD, P. E., *Le Second Isaïe, son disciple et leurs éditeurs: Isaïe 40–66* (EB; Paris: J. Gabalda, 1972).
BONNER, L., *The Stories of Elijah and Elisha as Polemics Against Baal Worship* (POS, 6; Leiden: Brill, 1968).
BRACKE, J. M., 'šûb šᵉbût: A Reappraisal', *ZAW* 97 (1985), 233–44.

BRANDSCHEIDT, R., *Gotteszorn und Menschenleid: Die Gerichtsklage des leidenden Gerechten in Klgl 3* (TTS, 41; Trier: Paulinus-Verlag, 1983).
BRIANT, P., *Histoire de l'Empire perse de Cyrus à Alexandre* (Paris: Fayard, 1996).
BRIGGS, C. A., *A Critical and Exegetical Commentary on the Book of Psalms*, 2 vols. (ICC; Edinburgh: T&T Clark, repr. 1951).
BRIGHT, J., *A History of Israel* (London: SCM Press, 3rd edn. 1986).
—— *Jeremiah* (AB; Garden City, NY: Doubleday, 1965).
BROSHI, M., 'Nasbeh, Tell en-', in *EAEHL*, 912–18.
BROWNLEE, W., 'The Aftermath of the Fall of Judah According to Ezekiel', *JBL* 89 (1970), 393–404.
BROYLES, C. C., *The Conflict of Faith and Experience in the Psalms: A Form-Critical and Theological Study* (JSOTSup, 52; Sheffield: JSOT Press, 1989).
BRUEGGEMANN, W., 'The Costly Loss of Lament', *JSOT* 36 (1986), 57–71.
—— 'The Formfulness of Grief', *Int* 31 (1977), 263–75.
—— 'From Hurt to Joy, From Death to Life', *Int* 28 (1974), 3–19.
—— *Old Testament Theology: Essays on Structure, Theme, and Text* (Minneapolis: Fortress Press, 1992).
—— 'Psalms in the Life of Faith: A Suggested Typology of Function', *JSOT* 17 (1980), 3–32.
—— *The Psalms and the Life of Faith* (Minneapolis: Fortress Press, 1974).
—— 'A Shattered Transcendence? Exile and Restoration', in Kraftchick and Ollenburger, *Biblical Theology*, 169–82.
—— *Theology of the Old Testament: Testimony, Dispute, Advocacy* (Minneapolis: Fortress Press, 1997).
BRUEGGEMANN, W. and WOLFF, H. W. (eds.), *The Vitality of Old Testament Traditions* (Atlanta: John Knox Press, 1978).
BRUNET, G., *Les Lamentations contre Jérémie: Réinterpretation des quatre premières Lamentations* (BEHS, 75: Paris: Presses universitaires de France, 1968).
BURNS, J. B., 'Female Pillar Figurines of the Iron Age: A Study in Text and Artifact', *AUSS* 36 (1998), 23–49.
BUTTENWEISER, M., *The Psalms* (Chicago: University of Chicago Press, 1938).
BUTTRICK, G. A., *et al.* (eds.), *Interpreter's Bible* (New York: Abingdon, 1952–6).
CAMERON, A. and KUHRT, A. (eds.), *Images of Women in Antiquity* (London: Routledge, rev. edn. 1993).
CARDASCIA, G., *Les archives des Murasu, une famille d'hommes d'affaires babyloniens à l'époque perse (455–403 Av. J-C)* (Paris: Imprimerie Nationale, 1951).

CARROLL, R. P., 'Clio and Canons: In Search of a Cultural Poetics of the Hebrew Bible', *BibInt* 5 (1997), 300–23.
—— 'Exile! What Exile? Deportation and the Discourses of Diaspora', in Grabbe, *Leading Captivity Captive*, 62–79.
—— 'Israel, History of (Post-Monarchic Period)', in *ABD* iii. 567–76.
—— *Jeremiah: A Commentary* (OTL; London: SCM Press, 1986).
—— 'The Myth of the Empty Land', in Jobling and Pippin, *Ideological Criticism of Biblical Texts*, 79–93.
CARTER, C. E., *The Emergence of Yehud in the Persian Period: A Social and Demographic Study* (JSOTSup, 294; Sheffield: Sheffield Academic Press, 1999).
—— 'Ideology and Archaeology in the Neo-Babylonian Period: Excavating Text and Tell', in Lipschits and Blenkinsopp, *Judah and the Judeans*, 301–22.
—— 'The Province of Yehud in the Post-Exilic Period: Soundings in Site Distribution and Demography', in Eskenazi and Richards, *Second Temple Studies*, ii. 106–45.
CHILDS, B. S., *Introduction to the Old Testament as Scripture* (Philadelphia: Fortress Press, 1979).
CHISHOLM, R. B., 'The Polemic against Baalism in Israel's Early History and Literature', *BS* 150 (1994), 267–83.
CLARKE, A. D. and WINTER, B. W. (eds.), *One God, One Lord in a World of Religious Pluralism* (Cambridge: Tyndale House, 1991).
CLEMENTS, R. E., *God and Temple* (Oxford: Basil Blackwell, 1965).
—— (ed.), *The World of Ancient Israel: Sociological, Anthropological, and Political Perspectives* (Cambridge: Cambridge University Press, 1989).
CLIFFORD, R. J., *The Cosmic Mountain in Canaan and the Old Testament* (HSM, 4; Cambridge, Mass.: Harvard University Press, 1972).
—— 'The Function of the Idol Passages in Second Isaiah', *CBQ* 42 (1980), 450–64.
—— 'Psalm 89: A Lament over the Davidic Ruler's Continued Failure', *HTR* 73 (1980), 35–47.
COGAN, M., 'Cyrus Cylinder', in Hallo, *The Context of Scripture*, ii. 314–16.
—— *Imperialism and Religion: Assyria, Judah, and Israel in the Eighth and Seventh Centuries B.C.* (Missoula: Scholars Press, 1974).
—— 'Judah under Assyrian Hegemony: A Re-examination of *Imperialism and Religion*', *JBL* 112 (1993), 403–14.
COGAN, M. and EPH'AL, I. (eds.), *Ah, Assyria...: Studies in Assyrian History and Ancient Near Eastern Historiography presented to Hayim Tadmor* (SH, 33; Jerusalem: Magnes Press, 1991).
COGGINS, R. J., 'Do We Still Need Deutero-Isaiah?', *JSOT* 81 (1998), 77–92.

—— 'The Exile: History and Ideology', *ExpT* 110 (1999), 389–93.
—— 'The Origins of the Jewish Diaspora', in Clements, *The World of Ancient Israel*, 163–81.
COHEN, A., *The Psalms* (Soncino Book of the Bible; London: Soncino Press, 1960).
COLE, R. L., The *Shape and Message of Book III (Psalms 73–89)* (JSOTSup, 307; Sheffield: Sheffield Academic Press, 2000).
COLLINS, J. J. and FLINT, P. W. (eds.), *The Book of Daniel: Composition and Reception*, 2 vols. (SVT, 93; Leiden: Brill, 2001).
COOGAN, M. D., 'Life in the Diaspora: Jews at Nippur in the Fifth Century B.C.', *BA* 37 (1974), 6–12.
—— *West Semitic Personal Names in the Murashu Documents* (HSM, 7; Missoula: Scholars Press, 1976).
COOK, J. M., *The Persian Empire* (London: J. M. Dent & Sons, 1983).
—— 'The Rise of the Achaemenids and the Establishment of their Empire', in Gershevitch, *Cambridge History of Iran*, ii. 213–14.
COWLEY, A., *Aramaic Papyri of the Fifth Century B.C.* (Oxford: Clarendon Press, 1923).
CRAIGIE, P. C., *Psalms 1–50* (WBC, 19; Waco: Word Books, 1983).
CROSS, F. M., *Canaanite Myth and Hebrew Epic: Essays in the History of the Religion of Israel* (Cambridge, Mass.: Harvard University Press, 1973).
—— 'Reconstruction of the Judean Restoration', *JBL* 94 (1975), 4–18.
CRÜSEMANN, F., 'Jahwes Gerechtigkeit (צדק/צדקה) im alten Testament', *ET* 36 (1976), 427–50.
CURTIS, A. H. W. and RÖMER, T. (eds.), *The Book of Jeremiah and its Reception* (BETL, 128; Leuven: Leuven University Press, 1997).
DAHOOD, M., 'Textual Problems in Isaia', *CBQ* 22 (1960), 400–9.
DALLEY, S., 'Occasions and Opportunities, 1, To the Persian Conquest', in Dalley *et al., The Legacy of Mesopotamia*, 9–33.
—— 'Occasions and Opportunities, 2, Persian, Greek, and Parthian Overlords', in Dalley *et al., The Legacy of Mesopotamia*, 35–9.
—— 'The Transition from Neo-Assyrians to Neo-Babylonians: Break or Continuity?', *EI* 27 (2003), 25*–28*.
DALLEY, S., *et al., The Legacy of Mesopotamia* (Oxford: Oxford University Press, 1998).
DANDAMAEV, M. A., *A Political History of the Achaemenid Empire* (Leiden: Brill, 1989).
DANDAMAEV, M. A. and LUKONIN, V. G., *The Culture and Social Institutions of Ancient Iran* (Cambridge: Cambridge University Press, 1989).
DANDAMAYEV, M., 'Achaemenid Babylon', in Diakonoff, *Ancient Mesopotamia*, 296–311.

DAVIES, P. R., 'Exile? What Exile? Whose Exile?', in Grabbe, *Leading Captivity Captive*, 128–38.

—— *In Search of 'Ancient Israel'* (JSOTSup, 148; Sheffield: Sheffield Academic Press, 2nd edn. 1995).

—— (ed.), *Second Temple Studies*, i: *Persian Period* (JSOTSup, 117; Sheffield: JSOT Press, 1991).

—— 'The Society of Biblical Israel', in Eskenazi and Richards, *Second Temple Studies*, ii. 22–33.

DAVIES, W. D. and FINKELSTEIN, L. (eds.), *Cambridge History of Judaism*, i: *Introduction: The Persian Period* (Cambridge: Cambridge University Press, 1984).

DAY, J., 'Asherah in the Hebrew Bible and Northwest Semitic Literature', *JBL* 105 (1986), 385–408.

—— 'The Destruction of the Shiloh Sanctuary and Jeremiah VII 12, 14', in Emerton, *Studies in the Historical Books of the Old Testament*, 87–94.

—— *God's Conflict with the Dragon and the Sea: Echoes of a Canaanite Myth in the Old Testament* (COP, 35; Cambridge: Cambridge University Press, repr. 1988).

—— (ed.), *King and Messiah in Israel and the Ancient Near East: Proceedings of the Oxford Old Testament Seminar* (JSOTSup, 270; Sheffield: JSOT Press, 1998).

—— *Molech: A God of Human Sacrifice in the Old Testament* (COP, 41; Cambridge: Cambridge University Press, 1989).

—— *The Psalms* (OTG; Sheffield: Sheffield Academic Press, 1990).

—— 'The Religion of Israel', in Mayes, *Text in Context*, 428–53.

—— *Yahweh and the Gods and Goddesses of Canaan* (JSOTSup, 265; Sheffield: Sheffield Academic Press, 2000).

DAY, P. L. (ed.), *Gender and Difference in Ancient Israel* (Minneapolis: Fortress Press, 1989).

DEVER, W. G., 'Asherah, Consort of Yahweh? New Evidence from Kuntillet 'Ajrud', *BASOR* 255 (1984), 21–37.

—— *What Did the Biblical Writers Know and When Did They Know It?: What Archaeology Can Tell Us about the Reality of Ancient Israel* (Grand Rapids: Eerdmans, 2001).

DIAKONOFF, I. M. (ed.), *Ancient Mesopotamia: Socio-Economic History: A Collection of Studies by Soviet Scholars* (Moscow: Nauka Publishing House, 1969).

DIETRICH, M. and LORETZ, O. (eds.), *Ugarit: Ein ostmediterranes Kulturzentrum im Alten Orient*, I, *Ugarit und seine altorientalische Umwelt* (Abhandlungen zur Literatur Alt-Syrien-Palestinas, 7; Münster: Ugaritverlag, 1995).

DIETRICH, W. and KLOPFENSTEIN, M. A. (eds.), *Ein Gott allein? JHWH-Verehrung und biblischer Monotheismus im Kontext der israelitischen und altorientalischen Religionsgeschichte* (OBO, 139; Freiburg: Universitätsverlag, 1994).

DIJKSTRA, M., 'El, YHWH and their Asherah: On Continuity and Discontinuity in Canaanite and Ancient Israelite Religion', in Dietrich and Loretz, *Ugarit*, 43–73.

—— 'Goddess, Gods, Men and Women in Ezekiel 8', in Becking and Dijkstra, *On Reading Prophetic Texts*, 83–144.

DOBBS-ALLSOPP, F. W., *Lamentations* (Interpretation; Louisville: John Knox Press, 2002).

—— 'Linguistic Evidence for the Date of Lamentations', *JANES* 26 (1998), 1–35.

—— 'Tragedy, Tradition, and Theology in the Book of Lamentations', *JSOT* 74 (1997), 29–60.

—— *Weep, O Daughter of Zion: A Study of the City-Lament Genre in the Hebrew Bible* (BO, 44; Rome: Editrice Pontificio Istituto Biblico, 1993).

DONNER, H. and RÖLLIG, W., *Kanaanäische und aramäische Inschriften*, i (Wiesbaden: Harrassowitz, repr. 1966).

DRIVER, G. R., 'Difficult Words in the Hebrew Prophets', in Rowley, *Studies in Old Testament Prophecy*, 58–9.

DUHM, B., *Das Buch Jesaja* (HAT; Göttingen: Vandenhoeck & Ruprecht, 4th edn. 1922).

DUMORTIER, J.-B., ' Un rituel d'intronisation: le Ps lxxxix 2–38', *VT* 22 (1972), 176–96.

EAKIN, F. E., 'Yahwism and Baalism before the Exile', *JBL* 84 (1965), 407–14.

EATON, J. H., *Kingship and the Psalms* (BS, 3; Sheffield: JSOT Press, 1976, 2nd edn. 1986).

EDELMAN, D. V., 'The "Empty Land" as a Motif in City Laments', in G. Brooke and T. Romer (eds.) (forthcoming).

—— (ed.), *The Fabric of History: Text, Artifact and Israel's Past* (JSOTSup, 127; Sheffield: Sheffield Academic Press, 1991).

—— 'Gibeon and the Gibeonites Revisited', in Lipschits and Blenkinsopp, *Judah and the Judeans*, 153–67.

—— (ed.), *The Triumph of Elohim: From Yahwisms to Judaisms* (CBET, 13; Kampen: Kok Pharos, 1995).

EDWARDS, O., 'The Year of Jerusalem's Destruction', *ZAW* 104 (1992), 101–6.

EDZARD, D. O. (ed.), *Reallexikon der Assyriologie und Vorderasiatischen Archäologie*, vi (Berlin: de Gruyter, 1980–3).

EICHRODT, W., *Der Prophet Hesekiel Kapital 1–18* (ATD, 22; Göttingen: Vandenhoeck & Ruprecht, 1959).

EISSFELDT, O., *Molk als Opferbegriff im Punischen und Hebräischen und das Ende des Gottes Moloch* (Halle: Max Niemeyer Verlag, 1935).
ELAT, M., 'Phoenician Overland Trade within the Mesopotamian Empires', in Cogan and Eph'al, *Ah, Assyria...*, 21–35.
EMERTON, J. A. (ed.), *Congress Volume: Edinburgh 1974* (SVT, 28; Leiden: Brill, 1975).
—— (ed.), *Congress Volume: Salamanca 1983* (SVT, 36; Leiden: Brill, 1985).
—— (ed.), *Congress Volume: Cambridge 1995* (SVT, 66; Leiden: Brill, 1997).
—— 'New Light on Israelite Religion: The Implications of the Inscriptions from Kuntillet 'Ajrud', *ZAW* 94 (1982), 2–20.
—— ' "Spring and Torrent" in Psalm lxxiv 15', *Congress Volume: Genève 1965* (SVT, 15; Leiden: Brill, 1966), 122–33.
—— (ed.), *Studies in the Historical Books of the Old Testament* (SVT, 30; Leiden: Brill, 1979).
—— ' "Yahweh and his Asherah": The Goddess or Her Symbol?', *VT* 49 (1999), 315–37.
EPH'AL, I., 'Syria–Palestine under Achaemenid Rule', in Boardman *et al.*, *The Cambridge Ancient History*, iv. 139–56.
ESHEL, H., 'The Late Iron Age Cemetery of Gibeon', *IEJ* 37 (1987), 1–17.
ESKENAZI, T. C. and RICHARDS, K. H. (eds.), *Second Temple Studies*, ii: *Temple and Community in the Persian Period* (JSOTSup, 175; Sheffield: JSOT Press, 1994).
EYNIKEL, E., *The Reform of King Josiah and the Composition of the Deuteronomistic History* (OTS, 33; Leiden: Brill, 1996).
FAUST, A., 'Judah in the Sixth Century B.C.E.: A Rural Perspective', *PEQ* 135 (2003), 37–53.
FENSHAM, F. C., 'A Few Observations on the Polarisation Between Yahweh and Baal in 1 Kings 17–19', *ZAW* 92 (1980), 227–36.
FERRIS, P. W., *The Genre of Communal Lament in the Bible and Ancient Near East* (SBLDS; Atlanta: Scholars Press, 1992).
FINKELSTEIN, I. and SILBERMAN, N. A., *The Bible Unearthed: Archaeology's New Vision of Ancient Israel and the Origin of its Sacred Texts* (New York and London: Simon & Schuster, 2001).
FITZGERALD, A., 'The Mythological Background for the Presentation of Jerusalem as Queen and False Worship as Adultery in the OT', *CBQ* 34 (1972), 404–16.
FITZMYER, J. A., *A Wandering Aramean: Collected Aramaic Essays* (SBLMS, 25; Missoula: Scholars Press, 1979).
FLOYD, M. H., 'Psalm lxxxix: A Prophetic Complaint about the Fulfilment of an Oracle', *VT* 42 (1992), 442–57.

FORRER, E., *Die Provinzeinteilung des Assyrischen Reiches* (Leipzig: Hinrichs, 1920).
FOSTER, R. S., *The Restoration of Israel: A Study in Exile and Return* (London: Darton, Longman & Todd, 1970).
FREEDMAN, D. N., *et al.* (eds.), *The Anchor Bible Dictionary*, 6 vols. (New York: Doubleday, 1992).
FREVEL, C., *Aschera und der Ausschließlichkeitsanspruch YHWHs: Beiträge zu literarischen, religionsgeschichtlichen und ikonographischen Aspekten der Ascheradiskussion* (BBB, 94/1–2; Weinheim: Beltz Athenäum, 1995).
FRIEDMAN, R. E., *The Exile and Biblical Narrative: The Formation of the Deuteronomistic and Priestly Works*, 2 vols. (HSM, 22; Chico: Scholars Press, 1981).
FRIES, S. A., 'Parallele zwischen den Klageliedern Cap. IV und V und der Maccabäerzeit', *ZAW* 13 (1893), 110–24.
FRYE, R. N., *The History of Ancient Iran* (HAW, 3/7; Munich: Beck, 1984).
GADD, C. J., 'The Harran Inscriptions of Nabonidus', *AS* 8 (1958), 35–92.
—— 'The Second Lamentation of Ur', in Thomas and McHardy, *Hebrew and Semitic Studies*, 59–71.
AL-GAILANI WERR, L., *et al.* (eds.), *Of Pots and Plans: Papers on the Archaeology and History of Mesopotamia and Syria presented to David Oates in Honour of his 75th Birthday* (London: Nabu, 2002).
GALIL, G., 'The Babylonian Calendar and the Chronology of the Last Kings of Judah', *Bib* 72 (1991), 367–78.
—— *The Chronology of the Last Kings of Israel and Judah* (SHANE, 9; Leiden: Brill, 1996).
GARBINI, G., *History and Ideology in Ancient Israel* (London: SCM Press, 1988).
GARELLI, P., 'The Achievement of Tiglath-pileser III: Novelty or Continuity', in Cogan and Eph'al, *Ah, Assyria...*, 46–51.
GARNSEY, P. D. A. and WHITTAKER, C. R. (eds.), *Imperialism in the Ancient World*, ii (Cambridge: Cambridge University Press, 1978).
GASTER, T. H., 'Ezekiel and the Mysteries', *JBL* 60 (1941), 289–310.
GEBRANDT, G. E., *Kingship According to the Deuteronomistic History* (SBLDS, 87; Atlanta: Scholars Press, 1986).
GELSTON, A., 'A Note on Psalm LXXIV 8', *VT* 34 (1984), 82–7.
GERSHEVITCH, I. (ed.), *Cambridge History of Iran*, ii (Cambridge: Cambridge University Press, 1985).
GERSTENBERGER, E. S., *Der bittende Mensch: Bittritual über Klagelied der Einzelnen im Alten Testament* (WMANT, 51; Neukirchen-Vluyn: Neukirchener Verlag, 1980).
—— 'Der Klagende Mensch', in Wolff, *Probleme biblische Theologie*, 64–72.

GERSTENBERGER, E. S., *Psalms*, pt. 2, and Lamentations (FOTL, 15, Grand Rapids: Eerdmans, 2001).

GIESEBRECHT, F., *Das Buch Jeremia* (Göttingen: Vandenhoeck & Ruprecht, 2nd edn. 1907).

GIESELMANN, B., 'Die sogenannte josianische Reform in der gegenwärtigen Forschung', *ZAW* 106 (1994), 223–42.

GINSBERG, H. L., 'An Aramaic Contemporary of the Lachish Letters', *BASOR* 111 (1948), 24–7.

GITTLEN, B. M. (ed.), *Sacred Time, Sacred Place: Archaeology and the Religion of Israel* (Winona Lake: Eisenbrauns, 2002).

GLASSNER, J.-J., *Chroniques mésopotamiennes* (La Roue à Livres; Paris: Les Belles Lettres, 1993).

GOLDENSTEIN, J., *Das Gebet der Gottesknechte: Jesaja 63,7–64,11 im Jesajabuch* (WMANT, 92; Neukirchen-Vluyn: Neukirchener Verlag, 2001).

GOODISON, L. and MORRIS, C. (eds.), *Ancient Goddesses: The Myths and the Evidence* (London: British Museum Press, 1998).

GORDIS, R., 'The Conclusion of the Book of Lamentations', *JBL* 93 (1974), 289–93.

—— *The Song of Songs and Lamentations: A Study, Modern Translation and Commentary* (Texts and Studies of the Jewish Theological Seminary of America, 20; New York: KTAV, 3rd edn. 1974).

GORDON, R. P., 'Aleph Apologeticum', *JQR* NS 69 (1978–9), 112–16.

GOTTWALD, N. K., *Studies in the Book of Lamentation* (SBT, 14; London: SCM Press, rev. edn. 1962).

GRABBE, L. L. (ed.), *Can a 'History of Israel' be Written?* (JSOTSup, 245; Sheffield: Sheffield Academic Press, 1997).

—— *Ezra-Nehemiah* (OTR; London: Routledge, 1998).

—— 'Are Historians of Ancient Palestine Fellow Creatures—or Different Animals?', in Grabbe, *Leading Captivity Captive*, 19–36.

—— 'Israel's Historical Reality after the Exile', in Becking and Korpel, *The Crisis of Israelite Religion*, 9–32.

—— *Judaism from Cyrus to Hadrian* (Minneapolis: Fortress Press, 1992; London: SCM Press, 1994).

—— (ed.), *Leading Captivity Captive: 'The Exile' as History and Ideology* (JSOTSup, 278 and ESHM, 2; Sheffield: Sheffield Academic Press, 1998).

—— 'Reflections on the Discussion', in Grabbe, *Leading Captivity Captive*, 146–56.

GRABBE, L. L. and HAAK, R. D. (eds.), *'Every City shall be Forsaken': Urbanism and Prophecy in Ancient Israel and the Near East* (JSOTSup, 330; Sheffield: Sheffield Academic Press, 2001).

GRAHAM, J. N., 'Palestine during the Period of the Exile 586–539 B.C. (MA thesis, University of Wales, 1977).
—— ' "Vinedressers and Plowmen": 2 Kings 25:12 and Jeremiah 52:16', *BA* 47 (1984), 55–8.
GRAYSON, A. K., *Assyrian and Babylonian Chronicles* (TCS, 5; Locust Valley: J. J. Augustin, 1975).
GREENBERG, M., 'The Design and Themes of Ezekiel's Program of Restoration', *Int* 38 (1984), 181–208.
—— *Ezekiel 1–20* (AB; New York: Doubleday, 1983).
GREENFIELD, J. C., 'The Prepositions B...TAHAT...in Jes 57:5', *ZAW* 73 (1961), 226–8.
GROß, W. (ed.), *Jeremia und die deuteronomistische Bewegung* (BBB, 98; Weinheim: Beltz Athenäum, 1995).
GROSSBERG, D., *Centripetal and Centrifugal Structures in Biblical Poetry* (SBLMS, 39; Atlanta: Scholars Press, 1989).
GUNKEL, H., *Die Psalmen* (HAT, 2; Göttingen: Vandenhoeck & Ruprecht, 4th edn. 1925–6).
—— *The Psalms: A Form-Critical Introduction* (BS, 19; Philadelphia: Fortress Press, 1967).
—— *Schöpfung und Chaos in Urzeit und Endzeit: eine religionsgeschichtliche Untersuchung über Gen 1 und Ap Joh 12* (Göttingen: Vandenhoeck & Ruprecht, 2nd edn. 1921).
GUNKEL, H. and BEGRICH, J., *Einleitung in die Psalmen: Die Gattungen der religiösen Lyrik Israels* (Göttingen: Vandenhoeck & Ruprecht, 1933).
GURNEY, O. R., 'Tammuz Reconsidered: Some Recent Developments', *JSS* 12 (1962), 150–60.
GWALTNEY, W. C., 'The Biblical Book of Lamentations in the Context of Near Eastern Lament Literature', in Hallo, Moyer, and Perdue, *Scripture in Context*, ii. 191–211.
HABEL, N. C., *Yahweh Versus Baal: A Conflict of Religious Cultures* (Concordia Theological Seminary, 6; New York: Bookman Associates, 1964).
HADLEY, J. M., 'Chasing Shadows? The Quest for the Historical Goddess', in Emerton, *Congress Volume: Cambridge 1995*, 169–84.
—— *The Cult of Asherah in Ancient Israel and Judah: Evidence for a Hebrew Goddess* (COP, 57; Cambridge: Cambridge University Press, 2000).
—— 'The Fertility of the Flock? The De-Personalization of Astarte in the Old Testament', in Becking and Dijkstra, *On Reading Prophetic Texts*, 115–33.
—— 'The Khirbet el-Qôm Inscription', *VT* 37 (1987), 50–62.
—— 'Who Is She? The Identity of the Queen of Heaven' (forthcoming).

HAHN, J. (ed.), *Zerstörungen des Jerusalemer Tempels: Geschehen-Wahrnehmung-Bewaltigung* (Wissenschaftliche Untersuchungen zum NT, 147; Tübingen: Mohr Siebeck, 2002).

HALLO, W. W. (ed.), *The Context of Scripture*, i: *Canonical Compositions from the Biblical World* (Leiden: Brill, 1997).

—— (ed.), *The Context of Scripture*, ii: *Monumental Inscriptions from the Biblical World* (Leiden: Brill, 2000).

—— 'Lamentations and Prayers in Sumer and Akkad', in J. M. Sasson (ed.), *Civilizations of the Ancient Near East*, iii (London and New York: Simon & Schuster International, 1995), 1871–81.

HALLO, W. W., MOYER, J. C., and PERDUE, L. G. (eds.), *Scripture in Context*, ii: *More Essays on the Comparative Method* (Winona Lake: Eisenbrauns, 1983).

HALPERN, B., 'Erasing History: The Minimalist Assault on Ancient Israel', *BRev* 11/6 (1995), 26–35, 47.

—— 'A Historiographic Commentary on Ezra 1–6: Achronological Narrative and Dual Chronology in Israelite Historiography', in Propp *et al.*, *The Hebrew Bible and Its Interpreters*, 81–142.

HALPERN, B. and LEVENSON, J. D. (eds.), *Traditions in Transformation: Turning Points in Biblical Faith* (Winona Lake: Eisenbrauns, 1981).

HANSON, P. D., *The Dawn of Apocalyptic* (Philadelphia: Fortress Press, 1975).

HARAN, M., 'Temples and Cultic Open Areas as Reflected in the Bible', in Biran, *Temples and High Places in Biblical Times*, 31–7.

—— *Temples and Temple Service in Ancient Israel: An Inquiry into the Character of Cult Phenomena and the Historical Setting of the Priestly School* (Oxford: Clarendon Press, 1978).

HARDMEIER, C., *Prophetie im Streit vor dem Untergang Judas: Erzahlkommunikative Studien zur Entstehungssituation der Jesaja- und Jeremiaerzahlungen in II Reg 18–20 und Jer 37–40* (BZAW, 187; Berlin: de Gruyter, 1990).

HARTMANN, B., *et al.* (eds.), *Hebräische Wortforschung: Festschrift zum 80. Geburtstag von Walter Baumgartner* (SVT, 16; Leiden: Brill, 1967).

HAYES, J. H. and MILLER, J. M. (eds.), *Israelite and Judaean History* (OTL; London: SCM Press, repr. 1990).

HEIDER, G. C., *The Cult of Molek: A Reassessment* (JSOTSup, 43; Sheffield: JSOT Press, 1985).

HEIM, K. M., 'The (God-)Forsaken King in Psalm 89: A Historical and Intertextual Enquiry', in Day, *King and Messiah*, 296–322.

—— 'The Personification of Jerusalem and the Drama of Her Bereavement in Lamentations', in Hess and Wenham, *Zion, City of Our God*, 129–69.

HELBERG, J. L., 'Land in the Book of Lamentations', *ZAW* 102 (1990), 372–85.

HERRMANN, S., *A History of Israel in Old Testament Times* (London: SCM Press, 1975).
HERTZBERG, H. W., 'Mizpa', *ZAW* 47 (1929), 161–96.
HESS, R. S., 'Yahweh and His Asherah? Epigraphic Evidence for Religious Pluralism in Old Testament Times', in Clarke and Winter, *One God, One Lord in a World of Religious Pluralism*, 5–33.
HESS, R. S. and WENHAM, G. J. (eds.), *Zion, City of Our God* (Grand Rapids: Eerdmans, 1999).
HILLERS, D. R., *Lamentations* (AB; New York: Doubleday, 2nd rev. edn. 1992).
HOERTH, A. J., *Archaeology and the Old Testament* (Grand Rapids: Baker Books, 1998).
HOFFMAN, Y., 'The Fasts in the Book of Zechariah and the Fashioning of National Remembrance', in Lipschits and Blenkinsopp, *Judah and the Judeans*, 169–218.
HOGLUND, K. G., 'The Achaemenid Context', in Davies, *Second Temple Studies*, i. 54–72.
—— *Achaemenid Imperial Administration in Syria-Palestine and the Missions of Ezra and Nehemiah* (SBLDS, 125; Atlanta: Scholars Press, 1992).
HOLLADAY, W. L., *Jeremiah*, ii (Hermeneia; Minneapolis: Fortress Press, 1989).
—— 'On Every High Hill and Under Every Green Tree', *VT* 11 (1961), 170–6.
HOPKINS, W., *The Elephantine Papyri in English: Three Millennia of Cross-Cultural Continuity and Change* (DMOA, 22; Leiden: Brill, 1996).
HORSLEY, R. A., 'Empire, Temple and Community—but no Bourgeoisie! A Response to Blenkinsopp and Petersen', in Davies, *Second Temple Studies*, i. 163–74.
HOUSTON, W., *Purity and Monotheism: Clean and Unclean Animals in Biblical Laws* (JSOTSup, 140; Sheffield: Sheffield Academic Press, 1993).
HUGHES, J., *Secrets of the Times: Myth and History in Biblical Chronology* (JSOTSup, 66; Sheffield: JSOT Press, 1990).
HUNTER, A., *Psalms* (OTR; London and New York: Routledge, 1999).
HUNTER, J., *Faces of a Lamenting City: The Development and Coherence of the Book of Lamentations* (BEATAJ, 39; Frankfurt am Main: Peter Lang, 1996).
IRWIN, W. H., ' "The Smooth Stones of the Wady?" Isaiah 57.6', *CBQ* 29 (1967), 31–40.
JACKSON, J. J., 'Style in Isaiah 28 and a Drinking Bout of the Gods (RS 24.258)', in Jackson and Kessler, *Rhetorical Criticism*, 85–98.
JACKSON, J. J. and KESSLER, M. (eds), *Rhetorical Criticism: Essays in Honor of James Muilenburg* (PTMS, 1; Pittsburgh: Pickwick, 1974).
JACOBSEN, T., 'Toward the Image of Tammuz', *HR* 1 (1962), 189–213.

JACOBSEN, T., *Toward the Image of Tammuz and Other Essays on Mesopotamian History and Culture* (HSS, 21; Cambridge, Mass.: Harvard University Press, 1970).

JAHNOW, H., *Das hebräische Leichenlied im Rahmen der Völkerdichtung* (BZAW, 36; Giessen: A. Töpelmann, 1923).

JAMIESON-DRAKE, D. W., *Scribes and Schools in Monarchic Judah: A Socio-Archaeological Approach* (JSOTSup, 109; Sheffield: Almond, 1991).

JANSSEN, E., *Juda in der Exilszeit: Ein Beitrag zur Entstehung des Judentums* (Göttingen: Vandenhoeck & Ruprecht, 1956).

JANZEN, G. J., 'Double Readings in the Text of Jeremiah', *HTR* 60 (1967), 433–47.

JAPHET, S., 'Exile and Restoration in the Book of Chronicles', in Becking and Korpel, *The Crisis of Israelite Religion*, 33–44.

—— ' "History" and "Literature" in the Persian Periods: The Restoration of the Temple', in Cogan and Eph'al, *Ah, Assyria...*, 174–88.

—— *The Ideology of the Book of Chronicles and its Place in Biblical Thought* (BEATAJ, 9; Frankfurt: Lang, 2nd rev. edn. 1997).

—— 'People and the Land in the Restoration Period', in Strecker, *Das Land Israel in biblischer Zeit*, 103–25.

—— 'Periodization Between History and Ideology: The Neo-Babylonian Period in Biblical Historiography', in Lipschits and Blenkinsopp, *Judah and the Judeans*, 75–89.

—— 'Sheshbazzar and Zerubbabel: Against the Background of the Historical and Religious Tendencies of Ezra-Nehemiah', *ZAW* 94 (1982), 66–98, and *ZAW* 95 (1983), 218–29.

JOANNÈS, F., 'Une visite du gouverneur d'Arpad', *NABU* (1994), 21–2.

JOANNÈS, F. and LEMAIRE, A., 'Trois tablettes cunéiformes à onomastique ouestsémitique (collection Sh. Moussaieff) (Pls. I–II)', *Transeuphratène* 17 (1996), 17–34.

JOBLING, D. and PIPPIN, T. (eds.), *Ideological Criticism of Biblical Texts* = *Semeia*, 59 (1992).

JOHNS, J. P., 'The Worship of Tammuz', *JBL* 36 (1917), 100–11.

JOHNSON, A. R., *Sacral Kingship in Ancient Israel* (Cardiff: University of Wales Press, 2nd edn. 1967).

JOHNSON, B., 'Form and Message in Lamentations', *ZAW* 97 (1987), 58–73.

JONES, D., 'The Cessation of Sacrifice after the Destruction of the Temple in 586 B.C.', *JTS* NS 14 (1963), 12–31.

JOYCE, P. M., 'Dislocation and Adaptation in the Exilic Age and After', in Barton and Reimer, *After the Exile*, 45–58.

—— *Divine Initiative and Human Response in Ezekiel* (JSOTSup, 51; Sheffield: JSOT Press, 1989).

—— 'Sitting Loose to History: Reading the Book of Lamentations without Primary Reference to its Original Historical Setting', in Ball, *In Search of True Wisdom*, 246–62.

JUDGE, H. G., 'Aaron, Zadok and Abiathar', *JTS* NS 7 (1956), 70–4.

KAISER, B. B., 'Poet as "Female Impersonator": The Image of Daughter Zion as Speaker in Biblical Poems of Suffering', *JR* 67 (1987), 164–82.

KAISER, O., *Klagelieder* (ATD, 16; Göttingen: Vandenhoeck & Ruprecht, 1981).

KAPELRUD, A. S., *Baal in the Ras Shamra Texts* (Copenhagen: Gad, 1952).

KARRER, C., *Ringen um die Verfassung Judas: Eine Studie zu den theologisch-politischen Vorstellungen im Esra–Nehemia-Buch* (BZAW, 308; Berlin: de Gruyter, 2001).

KAUFMANN, Y., *The Babylonian Captivity and Deutero-Isaiah* (History of the Religion of Israel, 4; New York: Union of American Hebrew Congregations, 1970), 68–87.

—— *The Religion of Israel: From its Beginnings to the Babylonian Exile* (New York: Schocken Books, abridged edn. 1972).

KEEL, O., *Goddesses and Trees, New Moon and Yahweh: Ancient Near Eastern Art and the Hebrew Bible* (JSOTSup, 261; Sheffield: Sheffield Academic Press, 1998).

KEEL, O. and UEHLINGER, C., *Göttinnen, Götter, und Gottessymbole: Neue Erkenntnisse zur Religionsgeschichte Kanaans und Israels aufgrund bislang unerschlossener ikonographischer Quellen* (QD, 134; Freiburg: Herder, 1992); ET *Gods, Goddesses, and Images of God in Ancient Israel* (Minneapolis, Minn.: Fortress Press, 1998).

—— 'Jahwe und die Sonnengottheit von Jerusalem', in Dietrich and Klopfenstein, *Ein Gott Allein?*, 269–303.

KELSO, J. L., 'Bethel', in *NEAEHL*, i. 191–4.

KEMP, B. J., 'Imperialism and Empire in New Kingdom Egypt', in Garnsey and Whittaker, *Imperialism in the Ancient World*, ii. 7–57.

KENNEDY, C. A., 'Isaiah 57:5–6: Tombs in the Rocks', *BASOR* 275 (1989), 47–52.

KESSLER, J., *The Book of Haggai: Prophecy and Society in Early Persian Yehud* (SVT, 91; Leiden: Brill, 2002).

—— 'Reconstructing Haggai's Jerusalem: Demographic and Sociological Considerations and the Search for an Adequate Methodological Point of Departure', in Grabbe and Haak, *'Every City shall be Forsaken'*, 137–58.

KESSLER, M., 'Jeremiah Chapters 26–45 Reconsidered', *JNES* 27 (1968), 81–8.

KLEIN, J., 'Lamentation over the Destruction of Sumer and Ur', in Hallo, *The Context of Scripture*, i. 535–9.

KLEIN, R. W., *Ezekiel: The Prophet and His Message* (Studies on Personalities in the Old Testament; Columbia: University of South Carolina Press, 1988).

KLEIN, R. W., *Israel in Exile: A Theological Interpretation* (OBT; Philadelphia: Fortress Press, 1979; repr. Mifflintown, Pa.: Sigler Press, 2000).

—— 'A Theology for Exiles: The Kingship of Yahweh', *Dialog* 17 (1978), 128–34.

KLETTER, R., *The Judean Pillar-Figurines and the Archaeology of Asherah* (British Archaeological Reports, International Series, 636; Oxford: Tempus Reparatum, 1996).

KNIBB, M. A., 'The Exile in the Literature of the Intertestamental Period', *HeyJ* 17 (1976), 253–72.

KNOPPERS, G., *Two Nations under God: The Deuteronomistic History of Solomon and the Dual Monarchies*, 2 vols. (HSM, 52; Atlanta: Scholars Press, 1993).

KNOPPERS, G. N. and McCONVILLE, J. G. (eds.), *Reconsidering Israel and Judah: Recent Studies on the Deuteronomistic History* (SBTS; Winona Lake: Eisenbrauns, 2000).

KOCH, K., 'Aschera als Himmelskönigin in Jerusalem', *UF* 20 (1988), 97–120.

—— *Das Buch Daniel* (EF, 144; Darmstadt: Wissenschaftliche Buchgesellschaft, 1980).

—— 'Haggais unreines Volk', *ZAW* 79 (1967), 52–66.

KOENEN, K., *Ethik und Eschatologie im Tritojesajabuch: Eine literarkritische und redaktionsgeschichtliche Studie* (WMANT, 62; Neukirchen-Vluyn: Neukirchener Verlag, 1990).

KORT, A. and MORSCHAUER, S. (eds.), *Biblical and Related Studies Presented to Samuel Iwry* (Winona Lake: Eisenbrauns, 1985).

KOTTSIEPER, I., VAN OORSCHOT, J., RÖMHELD, D. and WAHL, H. M., (eds.), *'Wer ist wie du, Herr, unter den Göttern?': Studien zur Theologie und Religionsgeschichte Israels* (Göttingen: Vandenhoeck & Ruprecht, 1994).

KRAFTCHICK, S. and OLLENBURGER. B. (eds.), *Biblical Theology: Problems and Prospects* (Nashville: Abingdon Press, 1995).

KRAMER, S. N., 'Lamentation over the Destruction of Nippur: A Preliminary Report', *EI* 9 (1969), 89–93.

—— 'Lamentation over the Destruction of Sumer and Ur', in *ANET*[3], 611–19.

—— 'Lamentations over the Destruction of Ur', in *ANET*[3], 455–63.

KRAŠOVEC, J., 'The Source of Hope in the Book of Lamentations', *VT* 42 (1992), 223–33.

KRAUS, H.-J., *Gottesdienst in Israel: Grundriß einer Geschichte des alttestamentlichen Gottesdienstes* (Munich: Chr. Kaiser, 1962); ET *Worship in Ancient Israel: A Cultic History of the Old Testament* (Oxford: Blackwell, 1966).

—— *Die Psalmen*, 2 vols. (BKAT, 15; Neukirchen-Vluyn: Neukirchener Verlag, 3rd edn. 1966).

—— *Klagelieder (Threni)* (BK, 20; Neukirchen-Vluyn: Neukirchener Verlag, 1959, 3rd edn. 1968).

KRECHER, J., 'Klagelied', in Edzard, *Reallexikon der Assyriologie*, vi. 1–6.

KREISSIG, H., *Die sozialökonomische Situation in Juda zur Achämenidenzeit* (Schriften zur Geschichte und Kultur des alten Orients, 7; Berlin: Akademi, 1973).

KUHNE, H., 'Thoughts about Assyria after 612 BC', in al-Gailani Werr *et al.*, *Of Pots and Plans*, 171–5.

KUHRT, A., *The Ancient Near East c.3000–330 B.C.*, ii (Routledge History of the Ancient World; London: Routledge, 1995).

—— 'The Cyrus Cylinder and Achaemenid Imperial Policy', *JSOT* 25 (1983), 83–97.

KUTSKO, J. F., *Between Heaven and Earth: Divine Presence and Absence in the Book of Ezekiel* (BJS, 7; Winona Lake: Eisenbrauns, 2000).

LACHS, S., 'The Date of Lamentations', *JQR* 57 (1968), 46–56.

LANAHAN, W. F., 'The Speaking Voice in the Book of Lamentations', *JBL* 93 (1974), 41–9.

LANGDON, S., *Tammuz and Ishtar* (Oxford: Clarendon Press, 1914).

LAPERROUSAZ, E.-M., 'Jérusalem à l'époque perse (étendu et statut)', *Transeuphratène* 1 (1989), 55–65.

LAPERROUSAZ, E.-M. and LEMAIRE, A. (eds.), *La Palestine à l'époque perse: Etudes annexes de la Bible de Jérusalem* (Paris: Cerf, 1994).

LAPP, N. L. (ed.), *The Third Campaign at Tell el-Fûl: The Excavations of 1964*, *AASOR* 45 (1981).

—— 'Fûl, Tell el-', in *NEAEHL*, ii. 444–8.

LAPP, P. W., 'Tell el-Fûl', *BA* 28 (1965), 2–10.

LARSEN, M. T. (ed.), *Power and Propaganda: A Symposium on Ancient Empires* (Mesopotamia, 7; Copenhagen: Akademisck, 1979).

LEE, N. C., *The Singers of Lamentations: Cities Under Siege, From Ur to Jerusalem to Sarajevo* (BIS, 60; Leiden, Brill, 2002).

LELIÈVRE, A., 'YHWH et la mer dans les psaumes', *RHPR* 56 (1976), 253–75.

—— 'Histoire et administration de la Palestine à l'époque perse', in Laperrousaz and Lemaire, *La Palestine à l'époque perse*, 11–53.

—— 'Les inscriptions de Khirbet el-Qôm et l'Ashérah de Yhwh', *RB* 84 (1977), 595–608.

—— 'Review of N. Avigad, Bullae and Seals from a Post-Exilic Archive', *Syria* 54 (1977), 129–31.

—— 'Who or What was Yahweh's Asherah: New Inscriptions Reopen the Debate about the Meaning of Asherah', *BAR* 10 (1984), 42–51.

—— 'Zerobabel et la Judée à la lumière de l'épigraphie (fin du VIe s. av. J.-C.)', *RB* 103 (1996), 48–57.

LEMCHE, N. P., *Die Vorgeschichte Israels: Von den Anfängen bis zum Ausgang des 13. Jahrhunderts v. Chr* (BE, 1; Stuttgart: Kohlhammer, 1996); ET *Prelude to Israel's Past: Background and Beginnings of Israelite History and Identity* (Peabody: Hendrickson, 1998).

LEVENSON, J. D., *The Death and Resurrection of the Beloved Son: The Transformation of Child Sacrifice in Judaism and Christianity* (New Haven: Yale University Press, 1993).

—— 'From Temple to Synagogue: 1 Kings 8', in Halpern and Levenson, *Traditions in Transformation*, 143–66.

—— *Theology of the Program of Restoration of Ezekiel 40–48* (HSM, 10; Cambridge, Mass.: Harvard University Press, 1976).

LEVINE, B., 'Ritual as Symbol: Modes of Sacrifice in Israelite Religion', in Gittlen, *Sacred Time, Sacred Place*, 125–35.

LEWIS, T. J., *Cults of the Dead in Ancient Israel and Ugarit* (HSM, 39; Atlanta: Scholars Press, 1989).

—— 'How Far Can the Texts Take Us', in Gittlen, *Sacred Time, Sacred Place*, 186–217.

LINAFELT, T., 'The Impossibility of Mourning: Lamentations after the Holocaust', in Linafelt and Beal, *God in the Fray*, 279–89.

—— 'The Refusal of a Conclusion in the Book of Lamentations', *JBL* 120 (2001), 340–3.

—— 'Surviving Lamentations', *HBT* 17 (1995), 45–61.

—— *Surviving Lamentations: Catastrophe, Lament, and Protest in the Afterlife of a Biblical Book* (Chicago: University of Chicago Press, 2000).

—— (ed.), *Strange Fire: Reading the Bible after the Holocaust* (BS, 71; Sheffield: Sheffield Academic Press, 2000).

—— 'Zion's Cause: The Presentation of Pain in the Book of Lamentations', in Linafelt, *Strange Fire*, 267–79.

LINAFELT, T. and BEAL, T. K. (eds.), *God in the Fray: A Tribute to Walter Brueggemann* (Minneapolis: Fortress Press, 1998).

LIPIŃSKI, E., 'The Goddess Atirat in Ancient Arabia, in Babylon and in Ugarit', *OLP* 3 (1972), 101–19.

—— *La liturgie pénitentielle dans la Bible* (LD, 52; Paris: Editions du Cerf, 1969).

—— *La royauté de Yahwé dans la poésie et la culte de l'ancien Israel* (Koninklije Vlaamse Academiae voor Wetenschappen Letteren en Schone Kunsten van Belgie, 27/55; Brussels: Paleis der Academiën, 1965).

—— 'The Syro-Palestinian Iconography of Woman and Goddess', *IEJ* 36 (1986), 87–96.

LIPSCHITS, O., 'Demographic Changes in Judah between the Seventh and the Fifth Centuries B.C.E.', in Lipschits and Blenkinsopp, *Judah and the Judeans*, 323–76.

—— 'The History of the Benjamin Region under Babylonian Rule', *TA* 26 (1999), 155–90.

—— 'Judah, Jerusalem and the Temple 586–539 B.C.', *Transeuphratène* 22 (2001), 129–42.

—— 'Nebuchadrezzar's Policy in "Ḥattu-Land" and the Fate of the Kingdom of Judah', *UF* 30 (1998), 467–87.

—— 'The Rural Settlement of Judah in the Sixth Century B.C.E.: A rejoinder', *PEQ* 136/2 (2004), 99–107.

LIPSCHITS, O. and BLENKINSOPP, J., (eds.), *Judah and the Judeans in the Neo-Babylonian Period* (Winona Lake: Eisenbrauns, 2003).

LIVERANI, M. (ed.), *Neo Assyrian Geography* (QGS, 5; Rome: Università di Roma, 1995).

LLOYD, A. B., 'The Inscription of Udjahorresnet: A Collaborator's Testament', *JEA* 66 (1986), 166–80.

LONG, V. P. (ed.), *Israel's Past in Present Research: Essays on Ancient Israelite Historiography* (SBTS, 7; Winona Lake: Eisenbrauns, 1999).

LONGMAN, T., 'The Adad-Guppi Autobiography', in Hallo, *The Context of Scripture*, i, 477–8.

LOWERY, R. H., *The Reforming Kings: Cult and Society in First Temple Judah* (JSOTSup, 120; Sheffield: JSOT Press, 1991).

LUTZKY, H. C., 'On "the Image of Jealousy" (Ezekiel VIII 3, 5)', *VT* 46 (1996), 121–4.

MAASS, F., 'Tritojesaja', in Maass, *Das ferne und nahe Wort*, 153–63.

—— (ed.), *Das ferne und nahe Wort: Festschrift Leonhard Rost zur Vollendung seines 70. Lebensjahres am 30. November 1966 gewidmet* (BZAW, 105; Berlin: de Gruyter, 1967).

MACHINIST, P., 'Palestine, Administration of (Assyro-Babylonian)', in *ABD*, v. 76–7.

MACY, H. and ANDERSON, P. (eds.), *Truth's Bright Embrace: Essays and Poems in Honor of A. O. Roberts* (Newberg: George Fox University Press, 1996).

MAGEN, Y. and FINKELSTEIN, I. (eds.), *Archaeological Survey of the Hill Country of Benjamin* (Jerusalem: Israel Antiquities Authority, 1993) (Hebrew).

MAIER, C. and DÖRRFUß, E. M., ' "Um mit ihnen zu sitzen, zu essen und zu trinken" Am 6,7; Jer 16, 5 und die Bedeutung von $marze^ah$', *ZAW* 111 (1999), 45–57.

MAIER, W. A., *'Ašerah: Extrabiblical Evidence* (HSM, 37; Atlanta: Scholars Press, 1986).

MALAMAT, A., 'Caught Between the Great Powers: Judah Chooses a Side... and Loses', *BAR* 25/4 (1999), 34–41.

—— 'The Last Kings of Judah and the Fall of Jerusalem', *IEJ* 18 (1968), 137–56.

—— 'The Last Wars of the Kingdom of Judah', *JNES* 9 (1950), 218–27.

—— 'A New Record of Nebuchadrezzar's Palestinian Campaigns', *IEJ* 6 (1956), 246–56.

—— 'The Twilight of Judah: In the Egyptian and Babylonian Maelstrom', in Emerton, *Congress Volume: Edinburgh 1974*, 123–45.

MARGALIT, B., 'The Meaning and Significance of Asherah', *VT* 40 (1990), 264–97.

MASON, R., 'The Purpose of the "Editorial Framework" of the Book of Haggai', *VT* 27 (1977), 413–21.

—— *Preaching the Tradition: Homily and Hermeneutics after the Exile* (Cambridge: Cambridge University Press, 1990).

MAY, H. G., 'The Departure of the Glory of Yahweh', *JBL* 56 (1937), 309–21.

—— 'Some Aspects of Solar Worship at Jerusalem', *ZAW* 55 (1937), 269–81.

MAYES, A. D. H., *Text in Context: Essays by Members of the Society for Old Testament Study* (Oxford: Oxford University Press, 2000).

MAYS, J. L., *Psalms* (Interpretation; Louisville: John Knox Press, 1994).

MCCARTER, P. K., 'Khirbet el-Qom', in Hallo, *The Context of Scripture*, ii. 179–80.

—— 'Kuntillet 'Ajrud', in Hallo, *The Context of Scripture*, ii. 171–2.

MCCONVILLE, J. G., 'Faces of Exile in Old Testament Historiography', in Barton and Reimer, *After the Exile*, 27–44.

MCCOWN, C. C., *Tell en-Nasbeh*, i: *Archaeological and Historical Results* (New Haven: AASOR, 1947).

MCCULLOUGH, W. S., 'A Re-Examination of Isaiah 56–66', *JBL* 67 (1948), 27–36.

—— (ed.), *The Seed of Wisdom: Essays in Honour of T. J. Meek* (Toronto: University of Toronto Press, 1964).

MCDANIEL, T. F., 'The Alleged Sumerian Influence upon Lamentations', *VT* 18 (1968), 198–209.

—— 'Philological Studies in Lamentations I & II', *Bib* 49 (1968), 27–53, 199–220.

MCEVENUE, S., 'The Political Structure in Judah from Cyrus to Nehemiah', *CBQ* 43 (1981), 353–64.

MCKANE, W., 'Worship of the Queen of Heaven (Jer 44)', in Kottsieper *et al.*, '*Wer ist wie du, Herr, unter den Göttern?*', 318–24.

McKay, J. W., *Religion in Judah under the Assyrians 732–609 BC* (SBT 2/26; London: SCM Press, 1976).
McLaughlin, J. L., *The marzēaḥ in the Prophetic Literature: References and Allusions in Light of the Extra-Biblical Evidence* (SVT, 86; Leiden: Brill, 2001).
—— 'The *marzeaḥ* at Ugarit: A Textual and Contextual Study', *UF* 23 (1991), 265–81.
McNutt, P., *Reconstructing the Society of Ancient Israel* (LAI; London: SPCK, 1999).
Meek, T. J., 'Aaronites and Zadokites', *AJSL* 45 (1929), 149–66.
—— 'The Book of Lamentations', in *IB*, vi. 3–38.
Meshel, Z., 'Did Yahweh Have a Consort? The New Religious Inscriptions from Sinai', *BAR* 5/2 (1979), 24–34.
—— 'Kuntillet 'Ajrûd: An Israelite Site from the Monarchical Period on the Sinai Border', *Qadmoniot* 9 (1976), 118–24.
Mettinger, T. N. D., *The Dethronement of Sabaoth: Studies in the Shem and Kabod Theologies* (CBOT, 18; Lund: Gleerup, 1982).
—— *The Riddle of Resurrection: 'Dying and Rising Gods' in the Ancient Near East* (CBOT, 50; Stockholm: Almquist & Wiksell International, 2001).
Meyers, C. L. and Meyers, E. M., *Haggai, Zechariah 1–8* (AB; New York: Doubleday, 1987).
Meyers, E. M., 'The Shelomith Seal and the Judaean Restoration, Some Additional Considerations', *EI* 18 (1985), 31–8.
Middlemas, J. A., 'Did Second Isaiah Write Lamentations 3?' (forthcoming).
—— 'Divine Reversal and the Role of the Temple in Trito-Isaiah', in J. Day (ed.), *Temple and Worship in Biblical Israel: Proceedings of the Oxford Old Testament Seminar* (JSOTSup, 422; London and New York: T & T Clark International, 2005), 164–87.
—— 'The Violent Storm in Lamentations', *JSOT* 29 (2004), 81–97.
Milik, J. T., 'Les papyrus araméens d'Hermoupolis et les cultes syro-phéniciens en Egypte perse', *Biblica* 48 (1967), 556–64.
Milevski, J., 'Settlement Patterns in Northern Judah During the Achaemenid Period', *BAIAS* 15 (1996–7), 7–29.
Millard, A. R., 'Review of *A Primer of Old Testament Archaeology*', *PEQ* 95 (1963), 137–41.
Miller, C. W., 'The Book of Lamentations in Recent Research', *Currents in Biblical Research* 1 (2002), 9–29.
Miller, J. M., 'Is it Possible to Write a History of Israel without Relying on the Hebrew Bible?', in Edelman, *The Fabric of History*, 93–102.
Miller, J. M. and Hayes, J. H., *A History of Ancient Israel and Judah* (London: SCM Press, 1986).

MILLER, P. D., HANSON, P. D., and MCBRIDE, S. D. (eds.), *Ancient Israelite Religion: Essays in Honor of Frank Moore Cross* (Philadelphia: Fortress Press, 1987).
MINTZ, A., 'The Rhetoric of Lamentations and the Representation of Catastrophe', *Prooftexts* 2 (1982), 1–17.
MITCHELL, H. G., SMITH, J. M. P., and BEWER, J. A., *A Critical and Exegetical Commentary on Haggai, Zechariah, Malachi and Jonah* (ICC; Edinburgh: T&T Clark, 1912).
MITCHELL, T. C., 'The Babylonian Exile and the Restoration of the Jews in Palestine (586–c.500 B.C.)', in Boardman *et al.*, *The Cambridge Ancient History*, III/2. 410–60.
MOORE, M. S., 'Human Suffering in Lamentations', *RB* 83 (1990), 539–43.
MOOREY, R., 'Terracotta Imagery in Israel and Judah under the Divided Monarchy (c.925–586 B.C.)', Schweich Lectures, 14 November 2001.
MOORTGAT, A., *Tammuz: Der Unsterblichkeitsglaube in der altorientalischen Bildkunst* (Berlin: de Gruyter, 1949).
MORGENSTERN, J., 'Jerusalem—485 B.C.', *HUCA* 27 (1956), 101–79.
MOWINCKEL, S., *The Psalms in Israel's Worship*, 2 vols. (Sheffield: JSOT Press, repr. 1992).
MUILENBURG, J., 'Isaiah', in *IB*, v. 199–773.
MURTONEN, A., 'Third Isaiah—Yes or No?', *Abr Nahrain* 19 (1980), 20–42.
NA'AMAN, N., 'Province System and Settlement Pattern in Southern Syria and Palestine in the Neo-Assyrian Period', in Liverani, *Neo Assyrian Geography*, 114–15.
—— 'Royal Vassals or Governors? On the Status of Sheshbazzar and Zerubbabel in the Persian Empire', *Henoch* 22 (2000), 35–44.
NA'AMAN, N. and FINKELSTEIN, I. (eds.), *From Nomadism to Monarchy: Archaeological and Historical Aspects of Early Israel* (Jerusalem: Israel Exploration Society, 1994).
NAVEH, J., 'Graffiti and Dedications', *BASOR* 235 (1979), 27–30.
NELSON, R. D., *The Double Redaction of the Deuteronomistic History* (JSOTSup, 18; Sheffield: JSOT Press, 1981).
NEWSOM, C. A., 'Response to Norman K. Gottwald, "Social Class and Ideology in Isaiah 40–55" ', *Semeia* 59 (1992), 73–8.
NEWSOME, J. D., *By the Waters of Babylon: An Introduction to the History and Theology of Exile* (Edinburgh: T&T Clark, 1979).
NICHOLSON, E. W., *Preaching to the Exiles: A Study in the Prose Tradition in the Book of Jeremiah* (Oxford: Blackwell, 1970), 127–33.
NIEHR, H., *Der höchste Gott* (BZAW, 190; Berlin: de Gruyter, 1990).
—— 'In Search of YHWH's Cult Statue in the First Temple', in van der Toorn, *The Image and the Book*, 73–95.

—— 'Religio-Historical Aspects of the "Early Post Exilic" Period', in Becking and Korpel, *The Crisis of Israelite Religion*, 228–44.

NIHAN, C., 'Trois cultes en Ésaïe 57,3–13 et leur signification dans le contexte religieux de la Judée à l'époque perse', *Transeuphratène* 22 (2001), 143–67.

NORIN, S. I. L., *Er spaltete das Meer: die Auszugsuberlieferung in Psalmen und Kult des alten Israel* (CBOT, 9; Lund: Gleerup, 1977).

NORTH, F. S., 'Aaron's Rise in Prestige', *ZAW* 66 (1954), 191–9.

NOTH, M., *Gesammelte Studien zum Alten Testament* (Theologische Bücherei, 6; Munich: Chr. Kaiser, 1960); ET *The Laws of the Pentateuch and Other Essays* (Edinburgh: Oliver & Boyd, 1966).

—— *Geschichte Israels* (Göttingen: Vandenhoeck & Ruprecht, 2nd edn. 1954); ET *The History of Israel* (London: SCM Press, 2nd edn. 1983).

—— *Überlieferungsgeschichtliche Studien: Die sammelnden und bearbeitenden Geschichtswerke im Alten Testament* (Schriften der königsberger Gelehrten Gesellschaft, 18; Tübingen: Max Niemeyer, 3rd edn. 1967); ET *The Deuteronomistic History* (JSOTSup, 15; Sheffield: JSOT Press, 1981).

O'BRIEN, J. M. and HORTON, F. L. (eds.), *The Yahweh/Baal Confrontation and Other Studies in Biblical Literature and Archaeology* (Studies in the Bible and Early Christianity, 35; Lewiston: Mellen Biblical Press, 1995).

O'CONNELL, R. H., *Concentricity and Continuity: The Literary Structure of Isaiah* (JSOTSup, 188; Sheffield: Sheffield Academic Press, 1994).

O'CONNOR, K. M., 'Do Not Trim a Word: The Contribution of Chapter 26 to the Book of Jeremiah', *CBQ* 51 (1989), 617–30.

—— *Lamentations and the Tears of the World* (Maryknoll: Orbis, 2002).

OATES, J., *Babylon* (Ancient People and Places, 94; London: Thames & Hudson, rev. edn. 1986).

ODED, B., 'Judah and the Exile', in Hayes and Miller, *Israelite and Judaean History*, 435–88.

—— *Mass Deportations and Deportees in the Neo-Assyrian Empire* (Wiesbaden: Reichert, 1979).

ODELL, M. S., 'What was the Image of Jealousy in Ezekiel 8?', in L. L. Grabbe (ed.) (forthcoming).

OESTERLEY, W. O. E., *Psalms*, 2 vols. (London: SPCK, 1939).

OFER, A., 'The Judean Hill Country: From Nomadism to a National Monarchy', in Na'aman and Finkelstein, *From Nomadism to Monarchy*, 92–121.

OLYAN, S. M., *Asherah and the Cult of Yahweh in Israel* (Atlanta: Scholars Press, 1988).

—— 'Some Observations Concerning the Identity of the Queen of Heaven', *UF* 19 (1987), 161–74.

OTZEN, B., 'Israel Under the Assyrians', in Larsen, *Power and Propaganda*, 251–61.

PARDEE, D., 'Marziḥu, Kispu and the Ugaritic Funerary Cult: A Minimalist View', in Wyatt et al., Ugarit, Religion and Culture, 273–87.

PATAI, R., 'The Goddess Asherah', JNES 24 (1965), 37–52.

—— The Hebrew Goddess (Detroit: Wayne State University Press, 3rd edn. 1990).

PATRICH, J. and ARUBAS, B., 'A Juglet Containing Balsam Oil (?) from a Cave Near Qumran', IEJ 39 (1989), 43–59.

PAURITSCH, K., Die neue Gemeinde: Gott sammelt Ausgestossene und Arme (Jesaja 56–66): Die Botschaft des Tritojesaia-Buches literatur-, form-, gattungskritisch und redaktionsgeschichtliche untersucht (AnBib, 47; Rome: Biblical Institute Press, 1971).

PELI, P. (ed.), Proceedings of the Fifth World Congress of Jewish Studies (Jerusalem: World Union of Jewish Studies, 1969).

PETERSEN, D. L., Haggai–Zechariah 1–8 (OTL; Philadelphia: Westminster, 1984).

PHAM, X. H. T., Mourning in the Ancient Near East and the Hebrew Bible (JSOTSup, 302; Sheffield: Sheffield Academic Press, 1999).

POHLMANN, K. F., Studien zum Jeremiabuch: Ein Beitrag zur Frage nach die Enstehung des Jeremiabuches (FRLANT, 118; Göttingen: Vandenhoeck & Ruprecht, 1978).

POLAN, G. J., In the Ways of Justice Toward Salvation: A Rhetorical Analysis of Isaiah 56–59 (AUS, 13, and TR, 13; New York: Peter Lang, 1986).

PORTEN, B., Archives from Elephantine: The Life of an Ancient Jewish Military Colony (Berkeley: University of California Press, 1968).

—— The Elephantine Papyri in English: Three Millennia of Cross-Cultural Continuity and Change (DMOA, 22; Leiden: Brill, 1996).

—— 'The Identity of King Adon', BA 44 (1981), 36–52.

—— 'The Jews in Egypt', in CHJ, i. 372–400.

PORTEN, B. and YARDENI, A., Textbook of Aramaic Documents from Ancient Egypt: Texts and Studies for Students, i: Letters (Hebrew University Department of the History of the Jewish People; Winona Lake: Eisenbrauns, 1986).

PRITCHARD, J. B. (ed.), Ancient Near Eastern Texts Relating to the Old Testament (Princeton: Princeton University Press, 3rd edn. 1969).

—— 'El Jîb', in NEAEHL, ii. 511–14.

—— Hebrew Inscriptions and Stamps from Gibeon (Museum Monographs; Philadelphia: University of Philadelphia, 1959).

—— Palestinian Figurines in Relation to Certain Goddesses Known through Literature (AOS, 24; New Haven: American Oriental Society, 1943).

PROPP, W. H., HALPERN, B., and FREEDMAN, D. N. (eds.), The Hebrew Bible and Its Interpreters (BJS, 1; Winona Lake: Eisenbrauns, 1990).

PROVAN, I., Lamentations (NCB; London: Marshall Pickering, 1991).

—— 'Past, Present and Future in Lamentations III 52–66: The Case for a Precative Perfect Re-examined', *VT* 41 (1991), 164–75.

—— 'Reading Texts against an Historical Background: Lamentations 1', *SJOT* 1 (1990), 130–43.

DE PURY, A., RÖMER, T. and MACCHI, J.-D. (eds.), *Israel Constructs its History: Deuteronomistic Historiography in Recent Research* (JSOTSup, 306; Sheffield: Sheffield Academic Press, 2000).

VON RAD, G., 'Gerichtsdoxologie', in *Gesammelte Studien zum Alten Testament*, ii (TB, 8; Munich: Chr. Kaiser, 1973), 245–54.

—— *Gesammelte Studien zum Alten Testament* (TB, 8; Munich: Chr. Kaiser, 1958); ET *The Problem of the Hexateuch and Other Essays* (Edinburgh: Oliver & Boyd, 1966).

RADNER, K., *Die neuassyrischen Texte aus Tall ŠĒḤ ḤAMAD* (Berlin: Dietrich Reimer, 2002).

RAHMANI, L. Y., 'Ancient Jerusalem's Funerary Customs and Tombs. Part One', *BA* 44 (1981), 171–7.

RAITT, R., *A Theology of Exile: Judgment/Deliverance in Jeremiah and Ezekiel* (Philadelphia: Fortress Press, 1977).

REED, W. L., *The Asherah in the Old Testament* (Fort Worth: Texas Christian University Press, 1949).

REIMER, D. J., 'Good Grief? A Psychological Reading of Lamentations', *ZAW* 114 (2002), 542–59.

RENKEMA, J., *Klaagliederen* (Kampen: Kok, 1993); ET *Lamentations* (HCOT; Leuven: Peeters, 1998).

—— '*Misschien is er hoop*...': *De theologische vooronderstellingen van het boek Klaagliederen* (Franeker: Wever, 1983).

RENZ, T., *The Rhetorical Function of the Book of Ezekiel* (SVT, 76; Leiden: Brill, 1999).

ROFÉ, A., 'Isaiah 66: 1–4: Judean Sects in the Persian Period as Viewed by Trito-Isaiah', in Kort and Morschauer, *Biblical and Related Studies*, 205–17.

RÖLLIG, W., 'Deportation und Integration: Das Schicksal von Fremden im assyrischen und babylonischen Staat', in Schuster, *Die Begegnung mit dem Fremden*, 109–12.

ROSE, W. H., *Zemah and Zerubbabel: Messianic Expectations in the Early Postexilic Period* (JSOTSup, 304; Sheffield: Sheffield Academic Press, 2000).

ROUX, G., *Ancient Iraq* (London: Penguin, 3rd edn. 1992).

ROWLEY, H. H., *The Servant of the Lord and Other Essays on the Old Testament* (Oxford: Blackwell, 2nd edn. 1965).

—— (ed.), *Studies in Old Testament Prophecy Presented to Prof. Theodore H. Robinson by the Society for Old Testament Study on his Sixty-Fifth Birthday, August 9th, 1946* (Edinburgh: T & T Clark, 1957).

ROWLEY, H. H., *The Servant of the Lord and Other Essays on the Old Testament* (Oxford: Blackwell, 2nd edn. 1965).

RUDOLPH, W., *Jeremia* (HAT, 12; Tübingen: JCB Mohr (Paul Siebeck), 3rd edn. 1968).

—— *Das Buch Ruth—Das Hohe Lied—Die Klagelieder* (KAT, 17; Güttersloh: Gerd Mohn, 1962).

SACK, R. H., 'Nebuchadnezzar II and the Old Testament: History versus Ideology', in Lipschits and Blenkinsopp, *Judah and the Judeans*, 221–33.

SAGGS, H. W. F., *The Greatness that was Babylon: A Survey of the Ancient Civilization of the Tigris-Euphrates Valley* (London: Sidgwick & Jackson, rev. and updated 1988).

—— *The Might that was Assyria* (London: Sidgwick & Jackson, 1984).

SALTERS, R. B., *Jonah and Lamentations* (OTG; Sheffield: Sheffield Academic Press, 1994).

SARNA, N. M., 'Psalm xix and Northeast Sun-God Literature', *Fourth World Congress of Jewish Studies*, Papers 1 (Jerusalem: World Union of Jewish Studies, 1967), 171–5.

—— 'Psalm 89: A Study in Inner Biblical Exegesis', in Altmann, *Biblical and Other Studies*, 29–46.

SCHAPER, J., *Priester und Leviten im achämenidischen Juda: Studien zur Kult- und Sozialgeschichte Israels in persischer Zeit* (FAT, 31; Tübingen: Mohr Siebeck, 2000).

SCHAUDIG, H., *Die Inschriften Nabonids von Babylon und Kyros' des Großen samt den in ihrem Umfeld entstandenen Tendenzschriften* (AOAT, 256; Münster: Ugarit-Verlag, 2001).

SCHMIDT, B. B., *Israel's Beneficent Dead: Ancestor Cult and Necromancy in Ancient Israelite Religion and Tradition* (FAT, 11; Tübingen: Mohr (Paul Siebeck), 1994).

SCHMIDT, H., *Die Psalmen* (Tübingen: Mohr (Paul Siebeck), 1934).

SCHNIEDEWIND, W. M., 'Are We His People or Not? Biblical Interpretation during Crisis', *Bib* 76 (1995), 540–50.

SCHOORS, A., *I am God your Saviour: A Form-Critical Study of the Main Genres in Is. XL–LV* (SVT, 24; Leiden: Brill, 1973).

SCHRAMM, B., *The Opponents of Third Isaiah: Reconstructing the Cultic History of the Restoration* (JSOTSup, 193; Sheffield: Sheffield Academic Press, 1995).

SCHUSTER, M. (ed.), *Die Begegnung mit dem Fremden: Wertungen und Wirkungen in Hochkulturen vom Altertum bis zur Gegenwart* (CR, 4; Stuttgart-Leipzig: Teubner, 1996).

SCOTT, J. M. (ed.), *Exile: Old Testament, Jewish, and Christian Conceptions* (JSJSup, 56; Leiden: Brill, 1997).

SEITZ, C. R., 'The Crisis of Interpretation over the Meaning and Purpose of the Exile', *VT* 35 (1985), 78–97.

—— 'The Divine Council: Temporal Transition and New Prophecy in the Book of Isaiah', *JBL* 109 (1990), 229–47.

—— *Theology in Conflict: Reactions to the Exile in the Book of Jeremiah* (BZAW, 176; Berlin: de Gruyter, 1989).

—— *Zion's Final Destiny: The Development of the Book of Isaiah: A Reassessment of Isaiah 36–39* (Minneapolis: Fortress Press, 1991).

SEKINE, S., *Die Tritojesajanische Sammlung (Jes 56–66) redaktionsgeschichtlich untersucht* (BZAW, 175; Berlin: de Gruyter, 1989).

SEYBOLD, K., *Die Psalmen* (HAT, 1/15; Tübingen: Mohr (Paul Siebeck), 1996).

SHARROCK, G. E., 'Psalm 74: A Literary-Structural Analysis', *AUSS* 21 (1983), 211–23.

SHEA, W. H., 'The *qinah* Structure of the Book of Lamentations', *Bib* 60 (1979), 103–7.

SINCLAIR, L. A., 'Bethel Pottery of the Sixth Century B.C.', *AASOR* 39 (1968), 70–6.

SMART, J. D., *History and Theology in Second Isaiah: A Commentary on Isaiah 35, 40–66* (London: Epworth, 1967).

SMITH, D. L., *The Religion of the Landless: The Social Context of the Babylonian Exile* (Bloomington: Meyer Stone Books, 1989).

SMITH, Mark S., 'The Death of "Dying and Rising Gods" in the Biblical World: An Update with Special Reference to Baal in the Baal Cycle', SJOT 12/2 (1998), 257–313.

—— 'The Near Eastern Background of Solar Language for Yahweh', *JBL* 109 (1990), 29–39.

—— *Psalms: The Divine Journey* (Mahwah: Paulist Press, 1987).

—— *The Early History of God: Yahweh and the Other Deities in Ancient Israel* (Grand Rapids: Eerdmans, 2nd edn. 2002).

—— 'God Male and Female in the Old Testament: Yahweh and his "Asherah" ', *TS* 48 (1987), 333–40.

—— ' "Seeing God" in the Psalms: The Background to the Beatific Vision in the Hebrew Bible', *CBQ* 50 (1988), 171–83.

SMITH, Morton, 'Jewish Religious Life in the Persian Period', in *CHJ*, i. 219–78.

—— 'A Note on Burning Babies', *JAOS* 95 (1975), 477–9.

—— 'Helios in Palestine', *EI* 16 (1982), 199*–214*.

—— *Palestinian Parties and Politics that Shaped the Old Testament* (London: SCM Press, 2nd edn. 1987).

—— 'The Veracity of Ezekiel, the Sins of Manasseh, and Jeremiah 44:18', *ZAW* 87 (1975), 11–16.

SMITH, P. A., *Rhetoric and Redaction in Trito-Isaiah: The Structure, Growth and Authorship of Isaiah 56–66* (SVT, 62; Leiden: Brill, 1995).

SMITH, S., *Isaiah XL–LV: Literary Criticism and History* (Schweich Lectures; London: Oxford University Press, 1944).

SMITH-CHRISTOPHER, D. L., *A Biblical Theology of Exile* (OBT; Minneapolis: Fortress Press, 2002).

—— 'Reassessing the Historical and Sociological Impact of the Babylonian Exile (597/587–539 BCE)', in Scott, *Exile*, 7–36.

—— 'Resistance in a "Culture of Permission"', in Macy and Anderson, *Truth's Bright Embrace*, 15–38.

—— (ed.), *Text and Experience: Toward a Cultural Exegesis of the Bible* (BS, 35; Sheffield: Sheffield Academic Press, 1995).

SOGGIN, J. A., 'Child Sacrifice and Cult of the Dead in the Old Testament', in *Old Testament and Oriental Studies* (BO, 29; Rome: Biblical Institute Press, 1975), 84–7.

—— *Old Testament and Oriental Studies* (BO, 29; Rome: Biblical Institute Press, 1975).

—— *Storia d'Israele: Dalle Origini a Bar Kochbà* (BCR, 44; Brescia: Paideia, 1984); ET *A History of Israel: From the Beginnings to the Bar Kochba Revolt AD 135* (London, SCM Press, 3rd edn. 1999).

SOMMER, B. D., *A Prophet Reads Scripture: Allusion in Isaiah 40–66* (Contraversions; Stanford: Stanford University Press, 1998).

SPALINGER, A., 'Assurbanipal and Egypt: A Source Study', *JAOS* 94 (1974), 316–28.

—— 'Egypt and Babylonia: A Survey (*c.*620 B.C.–550 B.C.)', *SAK* 5 (1977), 221–44.

—— 'Psammetichus, King of Egypt I', *JARCE* 13 (1976), 133–47.

—— 'Psammetichus, King of Egypt II', *JARCE* 15 (1978), 49–57.

SPERBER, A. (ed.), *The Bible in Aramaic: The Latter Prophets according to Targum Jonathan*, iv (Leiden: Brill, 1992).

STAGER, L. E., 'Ashkelon and the Archaeology of Destruction: Kislev 604 B.C.E.', *EI* 25 (1996), 61*–74*.

—— 'The Firstfruits of Civilization', in J. N. Tubb (ed.), *Palestine in the Bronze and Iron Ages: Papers in Honour of Olga Tufnell* (IAOP, 11; London: Institute of Archaeology, 1985), 172–87.

—— 'The Fury of Babylon: The Archaeology of Destruction', *BAR* 22/1 (1996), 56–69, 76–7.

STAGER, L. E. and Wolff, S. R., 'Child Sacrifice at Carthage: Religious Rite or Population Control?', *BAR* 10/1 (1984), 31–51.

STÄHLI, P., *Solare Elemente im Jahwegaluben des Alten Testaments* (OBO, 66; Göttingen: Vandenhoeck & Ruprecht, 1985).

STARRAKOPOULOU, F., *King Manasseh and Child Sacrifice: Biblical Distortions of Historical Realities* (BZAW, 338; Berlin and New York: Walter de Gruyter, 2004).

STECK, O. H., 'Beobachtungen zur Anlage von Jes 65–66', *BN* 38/39 (1987), 103–16.

—— 'Beobachtungen zu Jesaja 56–59', *BZ* 31 (1987), 228–46.

—— 'Zion als Gelände und Gestalt: Überlegungen zur Wahrnehmung Jerusalems als Stadt und Frau im Alten Testament', *ZTK* 86 (1989), 261–81.

STERN, E., *Archaeology in the Land of the Bible*, ii: *The Assyrian, Babylonian and Persian Periods 732–332 B.C.E.* (New York: Doubleday, 2001).

—— 'The Babylonian Gap', *BAR* 26/6 (2000), 45–51, 76.

—— 'The Babylonian Gap: The Archaeological Reality', *JSOT* 28 (2004), 273–7.

—— *Material Culture of the Land of the Bible in the Persian Period, 538–332 B.C.* (Jerusalem: Israel Exploration Society, 1982).

—— 'The Persian Empire and the Political and Social History of Palestine and the Persian Period', in *CHJ*, i. 70–81.

—— 'Yes There Was', *BAR* 28/3 (2002), 39, 55.

STERN, E., et al. (eds.), *New Encyclopedia of Archaeological Excavations in the Holy Land* (New York: Simon & Schuster, 1993).

STOLPER, M. W., *Entrepreneurs and Empire: The Murašû Archive, the Murašû Firm, and Persian Rule in Babylonia* (Uitgaven van het Nederlands Historisch-Archaeologisch Instituut te Istanbul, 54; Istanbul: Nederlands Historisch-Archaeologisch Instituut, 1985).

—— 'Mesopotamia, 482–330 B.C.', in Boardman *et al.* (eds.), *Cambridge Ancient History*, 2nd edn., vol. vi, 1994, pp. 234–60.

STRECKER, G. (ed.), *Das Land Israel in biblischer Zeit: Jerusalem Symposium 1981* (GTA, 25; Göttingen: Vandenhoeck & Ruprecht, 1983).

SWEENEY, M. A., *Isaiah 1–4 and the Post-Exilic Understanding of the Isaianic Tradition* (BZAW, 171; Berlin: de Gruyter, 1988).

—— *King Josiah of Judah: The Lost Messiah of Israel* (Oxford: Oxford University Press, 2001).

TADMOR, H. and WEINFELD, M. (eds.), *History, Historiography and Interpretation: Studies in Biblical and Cuneiform Literature* (Jerusalem: Magnes Press, repr. 1984).

TATE, M. E., *Psalms 51–100* (WBC, 20: Dallas: Word Books, 1990).

TAYLOR, J. E., 'The Asherah, the Menorah and the Sacred Tree', *JSOT* 66 (1995), 29–54.

TAYLOR, J. G., *Yahweh and the Sun: Biblical and Archaeological Evidence for Sun Worship in Ancient Israel* (JSOTSup, 111; Sheffield: JSOT Press, 1993).

THIEL, W., *Die deuteronomistische Redaktion von Jeremia 26–45: mit einer Gesamtbeurteilung der deuteronomistischen Redaktion des Buches Jeremia* (WMANT, 52; Düsseldorf: Neukirchner Verlag, 1981).

THOMAS, D. W., 'The Sixth Century B.C.: A Creative Epoch in the History of Israel', *JSS* 6 (1961), 33–46.

—— 'Some Observations on the Hebrew Word רַעֲנָן', in Hartmann *et al.*, *Hebräische Wortforschung*, 387–97.

THOMAS, D. W. and MCHARDY, W. D. (eds.), *Hebrew and Semitic Studies Presented to Godfrey Rolles Driver* (Oxford: Clarendon Press, 1963).

THOMPSON, T. L., *The Bible in History: How Writers Create a Past* (Pimlico, 425; London: Pimlico, repr. 2000).

TIGAY, J. H., 'Israelite Religion: The Onomastic and Epigraphic Evidence', in Miller *et al.*, *Ancient Israelite Religion*, 157–94.

—— *You Shall Have No Other Gods: Israelite Religion in the Light of Hebrew Inscriptions* (HSS, 31; Atlanta: Scholars Press, 1986).

TINNEY, S., *The Nippur Lament: Royal Rhetoric and Divine Legitimation in the Region of Isme-Dagan of Isin (1953–1935 B.C.)* (Occasional Publications of the Samuel Noah Kramar Fund, 16; Philadelphia: Samuel Noah Kramer Fund, 1996).

TOLLINGTON, J. E., *Tradition and Innovation in Haggai and Zechariah 1–8* (JSOTSup, 150; Sheffield: JSOT Press, 1993).

TOOMBS, L. E., 'When Religions Collide: The Yahweh/Baal Confrontation', in O'Brien and Horton, *The Yahweh/Baal Confrontation*, 13–46.

TORREY, C. C., *The Chronicler's History of Israel: Chronicles–Ezra–Nehemia Restored to its Original Form* (Port Washington: Kennikat, repr. 1973).

—— *The Composition and Historical Value of Ezra–Nehemiah* (BZAW, 2; Giessen: J. Ricker, 1896).

—— *Ezra Studies* (Chicago: University of Chicago Press, 1910).

—— *Pseudo-Ezekiel and the Original Prophecy* (New Haven: Yale University Press, 1930).

—— *The Second Isaiah* (LBS; New York: Charles Scribner's Sons, 1928).

TOV, E., 'L'incidence de la critique textuelle sur la critique littéraire dans le livre Jérémie', *RB* 79 (1972), 189–99.

TUBB, J. N. (ed.), *Palestine in the Bronze and Iron Ages: Papers in Honour of Olga Tufnell* (Institute of Archaeology Occasional Publication, 11; London: Institute of Archaeology, 1985).

UEHLINGER, C., 'Die Frau im Efa (Sach 5, 5–11): eine Programmvision von der Abschiebung der Göttin', *Bibel und Kirche* 49 (1994), 93–103.

—— '*Figurative Policy*, Propaganda und Prophetie', in Emerton, *Congress Volume: Cambridge 1995*, 297–349.

—— 'Gab es eine joshijanische Kultreform?', in Groβ, *Jeremia und die deuteronomistische Bewegung*, 57–89.

VANDERHOOFT, D. S., 'Babylonian Strategies of Imperial Control in the West: Royal Practice and Rhetoric', in Lipschits and Blenkinsopp, *Judah and the Judeans*, 235–62.

—— *The Neo-Babylonian Empire and Babylon in the Latter Prophets* (HSM, 59; Atlanta: Scholars Press, 1999).

VAN DER PLOEG, J., 'Psalm 74 and its Structure', in van Voss *et al.*, *Travels in the World of the Old Testament*, 204–10.

VAN DER SPEK, R. J., 'Did Cyrus the Great Introduce a New Policy towards Subdued Nations? Cyrus in Assyrian Perspective', *Persica* 10 (1982), 278–83.

VAN DER TOORN, K., 'Anat-Yahu, some Other Deities, and the Jews of Elephantine', *Numen* 39 (1992), 80–101.

—— 'Goddesses in Early Israelite Religion', in Goodison and Morris, *Ancient Goddesses*, 83–97.

—— (ed.), *The Image and the Book: Iconic Cults, Aniconism and the Rise of the Book Religion in Israel and the Ancient Near East* (CBET, 21; Leuven: Uitgeverij Peeters, 1997).

—— 'Israelite Figurines: A View from the Text', in Gittlen, *Sacred Time, Sacred Place*, 45–62.

VAN HENTEN, J. W., *et al.* (eds.), *Tradition and Re-Interpretation in Jewish and Early Christian Literature: Essays in Honor of Jürgen C. H. Lebram* (Studia Post-Biblica, 36; Leiden: Brill, 1986).

VAN KEULEN, P. S. F., *Manasseh through the Eyes of the Deuteronomists: The Manasseh Account (2 Kings 21: 1–18) and the Final Chapters of the Deuteronomistic History* (OTS, 38; Leiden: Brill, 1996).

VAN VOSS, M. S. H. G. Heerma, TEN CATE, J. H., and VAN UCHELEN, N. A. (eds.), *Travels in the World of the Old Testament: Studies Presented to Professor M. A. Beek on the Occasion of his 65th Birthday* (Assen: Van Gorcum, 1974).

VAN ZIJL, P. J., *Baal: A Study of Texts in Connexion with Baal in Ugaritic Epics* (AOAT; Neukirchen-Vluyn: Neukirchener Verlag, 1972).

DE VAUX, R., *Bible et Orient* (Paris: Editions du Cerf, 1967).

VEIJOLA, T., 'Das Klagegebet in Literatur und Leben der Exilsgeneration am Beispiel einiger Prosatexte', in Emerton, *Congress Volume: Salamanca 1983*, 286–307.

—— *Verheissung in der Krise: Studien zur Literatur und Theologie der Exilszeit anhand des 89. Psalm* (Suomalaisen Tiedeakatemian toimituksia, 220; Helsinki: Suomalainen Tiedeakatemia, 1982).

VERMEYLEN, J., *Du Prophète Isaïe à l'apocalyptique: Isaïe I–XXXV, miroir d'un demi-millénaire d'expérience religieuse en Israël*, 2 vols. (EB; Paris: J. Gabalda, 1977–8).

VRIEZEN, K. J. H., 'Cakes and Figurines: Related Women's Cultic Offerings in Ancient Israel', in Becking and Dijkstra, *On Reading Prophetic Texts*, 251–63.

WARD, J. M., 'The Literary Form and the Liturgical Background of Psalm lxxxix', *VT* 11 (1961), 321–9.

WATSON, R. S., 'The Theme of "Chaos" in the Psalter: A Reassessment' (D.Phil. thesis, University of Oxford, 2001).

WEBER, B., 'Zur Datierung der Asaph Psalms 74 und 79', *Bib* 81 (2000), 521–32.

WEBSTER, E. C., 'The Rhetoric of Isaiah 63–65', *JSOT* 47 (1990), 89–102.

WEIDNER, E. F., 'Jojachin, König von Juda, in Babylonischien Keilinschrifttexten', in *Mélanges Syriens offerts à Monsieur R. Dussaud*, ii (Bibliothèque Archéologique et Historique, 30; Paris: Geuthner, 1939), 923–35.

WEINBERG, J., *The Citizen-Temple Community* (JSOTSup, 151; Sheffield: Sheffield Academic Press, 1992).

WEINBERG, S. S., 'Post-Exilic Palestine: An Archaeological Report', *Proceedings of the Israel Academy of Sciences and Humanities* (Jerusalem: Israel Academy of Sciences and Humanities, 1969–70).

WEINFELD, M., 'Burning Babies in Ancient Israel', *UF* 10 (1979), 411–13.

—— 'The Molech Cult in Israel and its Background', in P. Peli (ed.), *Proceedings of the Fifth World Congress of Jewish Studies* (Jerusalem: World Union of Jewish Studies, 1969), 37–61 (Hebrew), 227–8 (English summary).

—— *Social Justice in Ancient Israel and in the Ancient Near East* (Publications of the Perry Foundation for Biblical Research in the Hebrew University of Jerusalem; Jerusalem: Magnes Press, 1995).

—— 'The Worship of Molech and of the Queen of Heaven and its Background', *UF* 4 (1972), 133–54.

WEISE, M., 'Jesaja 57.5f', *ZAW* 72 (1960), 25–32.

WEISER, A., *Die Psalmen*, 2 vols. (ATD, 15; Göttingen: Vandenhoeck & Ruprecht, 1950).

WEISSBACH, F. H. (ed.), *Babylonischen Miscellen* (WVDOG, 4; Leipzig: Hinrichs, 1903).

WELLHAUSEN, J., *Prolegomena zur Geschichte Israels* (Berlin: de Gruyter, 6th edn. 1927).

WERNBERG-MØLLER, P., 'Two Notes', *VT* 8 (1958), 307–8.

WESTERMANN, C., *Das Buch Jesaja: Kapital 40–66* (ATD, 19; Göttingen: Vandenhoeck & Ruprecht, repr. 1986).

—— *Lob und Klage in den Psalmen: 5. erweiterte Auflage von 'Das Loben Gottes in den Psalmen?'* (Göttingen: Vandenhoeck & Ruprecht, 1977); ET *Praise and Lament in the Psalms* (Atlanta: John Knox Press, 1981).

—— *Das Loben Gottes in den Psalmen* (Göttingen: Vandenhoeck & Ruprecht, 4th edn. 1968); ET *The Praise of God in the Psalms* (Richmond: John Knox Press, 1965).

—— *Die Klagelieder: Forschungsgeschichte und Auslegung* (Neukirchen-Vluyn: Neukirchener Verlag, 1990); ET *Lamentations: Issues and Interpretations* (Edinburgh: T & T Clark, 1994).

—— 'The Role of the Lament in the Theology of the Old Testament', *Int* 28 (1974), 20–38.

—— 'Struktur und Geschichte der Klage im Alten Testament', *ZAW* 66 (1954), 44–80.

WHITLEY, C. F., *The Exilic Age* (London: Longmans, Green & Co., 1957).

WHITELAM, K. W., *The Invention of Ancient Israel: The Silencing of Palestinian History* (London: Routledge, 1996).

WIDENGREN, G., 'The Persian Period', in *CHJ*, i. 489–538.

WIGGINS, S. A., *A Reassessment of 'Asherah': A Study According to the Textual Sources of the First Two Millennia B.C.E.* (AOAT, 235; Neukirchen-Vluyn: Neukirchener Verlag, 1993).

WILLEY, P. T., *Remember the Former Things: The Recollection of Previous Texts in Second Isaiah* (SBLDS, 161; Atlanta: Scholars Press, 1997).

WILLI, T., *Juda–Jehud–Israel: Studien zum Selbstverständnis des Judentums in persischer Zeit* (FAT, 12; Tübingen: Mohr (Paul Siebeck), 1995).

WILLIAMSON, H. G. M., *The Book Called Isaiah: Deutero-Isaiah's Role in Composition and Redaction* (Oxford: Clarendon Press, 1994).

—— 'The Composition of Ezra i–vi', *JTS* NS 34 (1983), 1–30.

—— *Ezra, Nehemiah* (WBC, 16; Waco: Word Books, 1985).

—— 'The Governors of Judah under the Persians', *TynB* 39 (1988), 59–82.

—— 'Isaiah 63,7–64,11. Exilic Lament or Post-Exilic Protest?', *ZAW* 102 (1990), 48–58.

—— 'Laments at the Destroyed Temple', *BRev* 4/4 (1990), 12–17, 44.

—— 'Structure and Historiography in Nehemiah 9', *Proceedings of the Ninth World Congress of Jewish Studies* (Jerusalem: Magnes Press, 1985), 117–31.

WILSON, G. H., 'Evidence of Editorial Divisions in the Hebrew Psalter', *VT* 34 (1984), 337–52.

WISEHÖFER, J., *Das antike Persien von 550 v. Chr. bis 650 n. Chr.* (Zurich: Artemis & Winkler, 1993), 71–88.

WOLFF, H. W., 'Das Kerygma des deuteronomistischen Geschichtswerkes', *ZAW* 73 (1961), 171–85; ET 'The Kerygma of the Deuteronomic Histor-

ical Work', in Brueggemann and Wolff, *The Vitality of Old Testament Traditions*, 83–100.
—— (ed.), *Probleme biblischer Theologie: Gerhard von Rad zum 70. Geburtstag* (Munich: Chr. Kaiser, 1971).
WYATT, N., WATSON, W. G. E. and LLOYD, J. B. (eds.), *Ugarit, Religion and Culture: Proceedings of the International Colloquium on Ugarit, Religion and Culture: Edinburgh, July 1994: Essays Presented in Honour of Professor John C. L. Gibson* (UBL, 12; Münster: Ugarit-Verlag, 1996).
YADIN, Y., *The Art of Warfare in Biblical Lands in the Light of Archaeological Discovery* (London: Weidenfeld & Nicolson, 1963).
YAMAUCHI, E. M., 'Additional Notes on Tammuz', *JSS* 11 (1966), 10–15.
—— 'Tammuz and the Bible', *JBL* 84 (1965), 283–90.
ZADOK, R., *The Jews in Babylonia during the Chaldean and Achaemenid Periods* (Haifa: University of Haifa Press, 1979).
ZEVIT, Z., 'The Khirbet el-Qôm Inscription Mentioning a Goddess', *BASOR* 255 (1984), 39–47.
ZIMMERLI, W., *Ezechiel 1–24* (BKAT, 13; Neukirchen-Vluyn: Neukirchener Verlag, repr. 1969, 1979).
ZORN, J. R., 'Mesopotamian-Style Ceramic "Bathtub" Coffins from Tell en-Nasbeh', *TA* 20 (1993), 216–24.
—— 'Mizpah: Newly Discovered Stratum Reveals Judah's Other Capital', *BAR* 23/5 (1997), 29–38, 66.
—— 'Nasbeh, Tell en-', in *NEAEHL*, iii. 1098–1102.
—— 'Tell en-Nasbeh and the Problem of the Material Culture of the Sixth Century', in Lipschits and Blenkinsopp, *Judah and the Judeans*, 413–47.
ZORN, J., YELLIN, J., and HAYES, J., 'The m(w)sh Stamp Impressions and the Neo-Babylonian Period', *IEJ* 44 (1994), 161–83.

Index of Biblical References

Genesis
3: 9	193 n. 75
4: 1	91 n. 64
9: 20–7	193 n. 75
14: 19	91 n. 64
14: 22	91 n. 64
19	194
32: 27	204
39: 4	63 n. 144
39: 5	63 n. 144
40: 14	204
45: 8	195 n. 81
47: 18	204
49: 7	192 n. 72

Exodus
22: 22	204
23: 14–16	125
23: 19	126
34: 13	86 n. 36
34: 23	125
34: 26	126

Leviticus
11	112
17–26	76
18: 21	105
20: 2–5	105, 142–3
20: 3	142–3
22: 6	204
26: 1	111
26: 34–5	8

Numbers
23: 21	90 n. 57
33: 52	111

Deuteronomy
4: 17–18	110
4: 23–4	92
7: 5	86 n. 36
8: 19	94 n. 75
8: 20	94 n. 75
9: 4	94 n. 75
9: 5	94 n. 75
11: 22	204
12: 3	86 n. 36
12: 31	105
16: 13–17	125
16: 21	86 n. 36
18: 10	99, 105
18: 14	99
25: 2	94 n. 75
28	198, 200
32: 6	91 n. 64

Joshua
6: 26	126
16: 1	142
23: 12	204

Judges
1: 22	135
2: 13	86 n. 37, 95 n. 78
3: 7	86 n. 36, 88 n. 47
3: 31	86 n. 38
5: 6	86 n. 38
6	88
6: 25	86 n. 36, 95 n. 77
6: 26	86 n. 36, 95 n. 77
6: 28	86 n. 36, 95 n. 77
6: 30	86 n. 36, 95 n. 77
10: 6	86 n. 37, 95 n. 78

Judges (cont.)

11	105
17: 10	195 n. 81
18: 19	195 n. 81
20–1	134
20: 18	135 n. 39
20: 26	135 n. 39
20: 31	135 n. 39
21: 2	135 n. 39

1 Samuel

1: 24	126, 131
3: 15	126, 131
7: 3	86 n. 37, 95 n. 78
7: 4	86 n. 37, 95 n. 78
7: 5–6	134
7: 9–10	134
10: 17	134
12: 10	86 n. 37, 95 n. 78
12: 12	90 n. 57
13: 2	142
20: 9	204
24: 11	195 n. 81
25: 34	204
31: 10	86 n. 37, 95 n. 78

2 Samuel

5: 6	204
12: 20	126, 131

1 Kings

8	145
8: 33–4	145
8: 35–6	145
8: 37–45	145
8: 44–51	133
8: 46–50	145
11: 5	86 n. 37, 95 n. 78
11: 28	63 n. 144
11: 33	86 n. 37, 95 n. 78
14: 15	86 n. 36
14: 23	86 n. 36
15: 13	86 n. 36, 88 n. 47, 95 n. 77
16: 33	86 n. 36, 95 n. 77
18: 19	86 n. 36, 88 n. 47, 95 n. 77

2 Kings

1: 1	189 n. 65
2: 2	135 n. 39
2: 12	195 n. 81
2: 23	135 n. 39
3: 5	189 n. 65
3: 13	195 n. 81
3: 27	105
4: 24	204
5: 20	204
6: 21	195 n. 81
10: 29	135 n. 39
11: 13–20	35
13: 6	86 n. 36, 88
13: 14	195 n. 81
13: 18	95 n. 77
14: 19–22	35
16: 34	75 n. 10
17: 10	86 n. 36
17: 16	86 n. 36
17: 17	105
18: 4	86 n. 36, 95 n. 77
21: 1–9	75 n. 10, 106
21: 3	86 n. 36, 116
21: 5	116
21: 6	99
21: 7	86 n. 36, 88 n. 47, 92, 95 n. 77
21: 16	194
21: 24	35
23: 4	86 n. 36, 88 n. 47, 95 n. 77, 116, 135 n. 39
23: 5	116

23: 6	86 n. 36, 93, 95 n. 77	1: 29	100
23: 7	86 n. 36, 88 n. 47, 95 n. 77	2: 2	140
		2: 11	140
		2: 12	140
23: 9	204	2: 13	140
23: 10	105, 108	2: 14	140
23: 11	116	2: 15	140
23: 13	86 n. 37, 95 n. 78	2: 17	140
23: 14	86 n. 36	3: 17	193 n. 75
23: 15	86 n. 36	6: 1	138
23: 30	35	6: 5	90 n. 57
23: 31–6	51	6: 11–13	215
24: 1	52 n. 97	9: 17	94 n. 75
24: 2	29	10: 22	189 n. 64
24: 8–9	75 n. 10	13: 9	187 n. 59
24: 10–11	29	13: 13	187 n. 59
24: 12–17	29	17: 8	86 n. 36
24: 14	8, 29, 35 n. 25	17: 10–11	115
24: 17	29	20: 4	193 n. 75
24: 20	29	22: 16	141
25: 1	30, 128	27: 9	86 n. 36
25: 3	128	28: 7–8	113
25: 6–7	30	33: 10	138
25: 8	30, 128	33: 22	90 n. 57
25: 9	131, 132	34: 1–17	193 n. 74
25: 11	8, 30	40–55	77
25: 12	8, 30, 58	40: 1	176
25: 13	131, 132	40: 9	137–8
25: 14–15	132	41: 21	90 n. 57
25: 18–21	123	44: 28	27
25: 21	8, 30	45: 1	27
25: 22	63 n. 144, 67	47	137–8, 139
25: 23	31, 34, 63 n. 144	47: 1–5	185 n. 55
25: 24–25	67	49: 22	138
25: 24	67	55: 10	204
25: 25	31, 128	55: 11	204
25: 26	8, 31	56–66	75
25: 27–30	31	56: 1–8	104
		56: 5	104
Isaiah		56: 9–57: 21	78
1: 21	137–38	56: 9–57: 13	139

Index of Biblical References

Isaiah (*cont.*)
56: 9–57: 2	78	63: 15–64: 6	166
57	76, 95	64: 7–11	166
57: 3–13	74, 78, 79, 80, 91 n. 61, 98, 104, 117, 139, 140, 142–3	64: 9	139
		65–66: 17	79, 80
		65–66	79, 80
		65	76
57: 3–4	79, 98–9, 139	65: 1–7	74, 79, 117
57: 3	78, 137	65: 1–5	118
57: 5–6	98, 99–102, 104, 137, 142–3	65: 3–4	74, 79
		65: 3	80, 83, 91, 95, 109, 118, 119
57: 5	100, 102	65: 4	80, 118–19
57: 6–13	138, 139	65: 6–7	118
57: 6	79, 100, 101–2	65: 6	204
57: 7–10	98, 102–3, 141, 142–3	65: 7	79, 80, 109
		65: 8–10	117
57: 7–8	138	65: 11–12	117
57: 7	79, 136–42	65: 11	74, 79, 117, 139
57: 8	104, 141	65: 13–16	117
57: 9	79, 103, 104	66: 1	208 n. 111
57: 11–13	98	66: 3–4	79
57: 11	139	66: 3	74, 80
57: 13	78, 79, 102, 104, 105, 138, 139, 141	66: 7–8	139
		66: 10–13	139
		66: 17	74, 79, 80, 109, 119
57: 14–21	78		
57: 15	138		
59: 20	139	**Jeremiah**	
60–62	77, 169 n. 125	1: 1	86 n. 38
60: 13	208 n. 111	1: 16	109
60: 14	139	1: 18	35 n. 25
61: 3	139	2: 8	106
62: 1	139	2: 23	97, 106
62: 3	139	3: 8	99
62: 11	139	3: 9	99
62: 12	139	3: 24	97, 105, 108–9
63: 1–6	193 n. 74	4: 8	187 n. 59
63: 6	7 n. 13	4: 26	187 n. 59
63: 7–64: 11	80, 145–6, 149, 156–8, 166–8, 232, 233	5: 7	99
		6: 25	218 n. 129
		7:–8: 3	75

Index of Biblical References

7	74, 76, 87, 96	25: 21	193 n. 74
7: 1–15	83	25: 37–8	187 n. 59
7: 2	131	26: 2	131
7: 6	109, 194	26: 6	132 n. 26
7: 9	106, 108, 109	26: 7	131
7: 14	132 n. 26	26: 9	132 n. 27
7: 16–20	83	26: 10	131
7: 17–18	84	27–28	29
7: 18	84, 87, 94 n. 76	27: 16	131
7: 30	75	27: 18	131
7: 31	97, 105, 106–7, 108	27: 21	131
		28: 1	131
8: 2	117	28: 3	131
9: 2	99	28: 5	131
9: 13	106	28: 6	131
9: 14	106	29: 5	9
11: 10	109	29: 23	99
11: 12	109	29: 26	131
11: 13	106, 108, 109	32: 29	108
11: 17	106, 108	32: 34	75
12: 16	106	32: 35	97, 105, 106, 107–8
13: 10	109		
13: 26	193 n. 75	33: 11	131
16: 5	113	34: 7	30, 42
16: 11	109	34: 19	35 n. 25
17: 2	86 n. 36	35: 2	131
17: 26	131	35: 4	131
18: 15	109	35: 5	131
19: 4	109	35: 11	29
19: 5	97, 105, 106, 107–8	35: 15	109
19: 13	109, 117	36: 6	131
19: 14	131	36: 8	131
19: 15	97	36: 10	131
20: 1	131	37–44	33
20: 2	131	37: 2	35 n. 25
20: 3	218 n. 129	37: 10	204
20: 10	218 n. 129	37: 11–15	33
22: 17	194	37: 13	33
23: 3	9	38: 14	131
23: 13	106	38: 18	33
23: 27	106	39: 1	128
25: 6	109	39: 5–7	30

Index of Biblical References

Jeremiah (cont.)

39: 10	58
39: 14	33
40: 5	30 n. 15, 34, 63 n. 144
40: 6	31, 34
40: 7	30 n. 7, 34, 63 n. 144
40: 10	31, 67
40: 11	4, 9, 63 n. 144
40: 11–12	34
40: 12	9, 31, 67
40: 13	31
40: 14–15	31
40: 15	31
41	4, 124, 130
41: 1–3	128
41: 1–2	31
41: 1	31
41: 2	63 n. 144
41: 3	31, 67
41: 5	125–6, 130, 131–2, 134
41: 10	31
41: 12	67
41: 16	67
41: 17–18	126
41: 17	67
41: 18	31, 63 n. 144
42: 10–12	9
42: 15	9
43: 3	34
43: 4–7	126
44	74, 76, 87, 96
44: 1–30	84
44: 3	84–5
44: 5	84–5
44: 7	85
44: 8	85
44: 11–14	85
44: 15–19	83, 85
44: 17	75, 87
44: 18	93
44: 20–3	85
44: 21	35 n. 25, 75, 87
44: 24–5	85
44: 25	83
46: 2	52 n. 92
46: 5	218 n. 129
47: 3	193 n. 75
49: 12	193 n. 74
49: 29	218 n. 129
51: 14	204
51: 51	131
52: 4	30
52: 9–11	30
52: 13	131, 132
52: 17	131, 132
52: 16	30, 58
52: 18–19	132
52: 20	131
52: 24–7	123
52: 27	8, 30
52: 28	29
52: 29	30
52: 31–4	31

Ezekiel

5: 6	94 n. 75
5: 11	110
5: 13	91 n. 64
6	109
7: 20	110
8–11	93
8	74, 75, 76, 96, 109
8: 3	83, 91, 91–2
8: 5	83, 91, 91–2
8: 7–13	110–14
8: 9–12	110
8: 9	110, 111
8: 10	110–11
8: 11	111

8: 12	111	22: 9	113
8: 13	110	22: 27	194
8: 14	114–15	23	102, 109
8: 16–18	115–17	23: 25	91 n. 64
8: 16	115, 116	23: 37	97, 99, 102 n. 96
11: 14–21	214	23: 39	99, 105
11: 15	214–15	23: 45	99
11: 16	172, 215	33: 12	94 n. 75
11: 17–21	214	33: 19	94 n. 75
11: 17	9	33: 21–7	58
11: 18	110	33: 23–9	215
11: 21	111	33: 24	9
11: 22–3	214–15	33: 25	194, 215
12: 33	204	37: 23	111
13: 10	191 n. 67	39: 17–20	113
13: 11	191 n. 67	40–48	73, 76
13: 14	191 n. 67	43: 7	208 n. 111
13: 15	191 n. 67		
14	109	**Hosea**	
16	102, 109	4: 16–19	113
16: 7–8	193 n. 75	11: 9	187 n. 59
16: 20	97, 102	12: 5	135 n. 39
16: 21	97, 102, 105		
16: 32	99	**Joel**	
16: 36	97, 102 n. 96, 105	2: 17	116
16: 38	91 n. 64, 99		
16: 42	91 n. 64	**Amos**	
18	109	3: 7	204
18: 6	113	4: 4	135 n. 39
18: 11	113	4: 11	113
18: 15	113	6: 7	113
18: 20	94 n. 75		
18: 27	94 n. 75	**Micah**	
20	109, 216	2: 12	9
20: 7	111	5: 13 (ET 14)	86 n. 36
20: 8	111		
20: 26	97, 105	**Nahum**	
20: 30–1	111	1: 6	187 n. 59
20: 31	97, 105	3: 5–6	193 n. 75
22	109		
22: 6	194	**Zephaniah**	
		2: 2	187 n. 59

Index of Biblical References

Haggai

1–2	76, 123, 169 n. 125
1: 1	37, 63
1: 14	37, 63
2: 2	37, 63
2: 10–14	130
2: 21	37, 63
2: 23	63

Zechariah

1–8	73–4, 76, 123, 126–7, 130, 135–6, 169 n. 125
1: 1	94
1: 7	94
1: 12	128 n. 17
4: 9–10	63
5: 1–11	74, 83, 91
5: 5–11	93, 96
5: 6–11	94
5: 6	94
5: 8	94
5: 11	94
7–8	124, 126
7: 1–6	127
7: 1	94, 127
7: 2	134–6, 142
7: 3	127–30
7: 5	127–30
8: 19	127, 128–30
8: 20–3	127 n. 12, 136

Malachi

1: 14	94 n. 75
3: 15	94 n. 75
3: 19	94 n. 75

Job

6: 6	191 n. 67

Psalms

9: 8	196 n. 82
9: 12	196 n. 82
10: 16	90 n. 57
15: 1	208 n. 109
24: 8	90 n. 57
24: 10	90 n. 57
27: 5	208 n. 109
29: 10	90 n. 57
31: 2	189 n. 64
35: 16	192 n. 70
37: 12	192 n. 70
44	145–6
47: 3	90 n. 57
48: 2–3	208
48: 2	196 n. 82
61: 5	208 n. 109
69	150 n. 76
74	145–6, 148, 149, 150, 152–6, 166–8, 232
74: 1–11	153–4, 166
74: 2	91 n. 64
74: 12–17	154–5, 166
74: 18–23	166
78: 60	141, 208 n. 109
79	128 n. 17, 145–6, 149, 150–2, 166–8, 232
79: 1–5	150
79: 6–13	150
80	150 n. 76
83	150 n. 76
84: 3	90 n. 57
89	145–6, 148 n. 70, 149, 159–63, 166–8, 232
89: 2–38	166
89: 39–46	166
89: 47–52	166
93: 1	90 n. 57

Index of Biblical References

95: 3	90 n. 57	1: 1–11	185–7, 216
96: 10	90 n. 57	1: 1–5	186
97: 1	90 n. 57	1: 1	123, 179, 190, 199, 200, 201, 210
98: 6	90 n. 57		
99: 1	90 n. 57	1: 2	175, 186 n. 55, 189, 190, 201
99: 2	196 n. 82		
99: 5	208 n. 111	1: 3	79, 188
99: 9	208 n. 111	1: 4	123, 133, 153 n. 84
102	145–6, 149, 163–6, 166–8, 169 n. 125, 232	1: 5–6	186, 213–14
		1: 5	179, 185–6, 188, 189, 198, 202, 212, 213
102: 2–3	167		
102: 4–12	167	1: 6	179, 188, 200, 213
102: 13–23	167	1: 7	179, 186, 188
102: 24–5	167	1: 8–9	212
102: 26–9	167	1: 8	185–6, 189, 190, 193 n. 75, 198, 201, 212
106	145–6, 233		
106: 37–8	105		
106: 38–9	194	1: 9	175, 179, 185, 186 n. 55, 187, 190, 201, 212 n. 123, 216, 219
106: 41	145 n. 58		
106: 46	145 n. 58		
106: 47	145 n. 58		
109	150 n. 76		
112: 10	192 n. 70	1: 10	186, 188–9, 207, 208 n. 109
116: 5	189 n. 64		
132: 7	208 n. 111	1: 11	179, 185, 186, 187, 195, 216, 219
137	150, 152, 172		
139: 13	91 n. 64	1: 12–22	179, 187, 201, 216
142	150 n. 76	1: 12–15	202
145: 17	189 n. 64	1: 12	187, 201, 219
		1: 13–17	188
Proverbs		1: 13	190
11: 5	94 n. 75	1: 14–15	212
13: 6	94 n. 75	1: 14	188, 202, 212
		1: 15	153 n. 84, 179, 188, 211
Ruth			
3: 18	204	1: 16	175, 186 n. 55, 188, 190, 201
Lamentations		1: 17	175, 186 n. 55, 188, 189, 190, 201, 202
1–5	145		
1	185–90, 221–2, 232		

Lamentations (*cont.*)
1: 18–22	212
1: 18	179, 189, 198, 211, 212, 213, 214, 219
1: 19–20	199
1: 19	189
1: 20	188, 201, 219
1: 21–22	189
1: 21	175, 186 n. 55, 188, 189, 190, 201
1: 22	190, 212
2	190–2, 212, 221–2, 232
2: 1–9	190, 202, 216–17, 219
2: 1	179, 191, 192, 200, 207, 208–9
2: 2	179, 191, 200
2: 3	191, 200
2: 4–5	209, 219
2: 4	179, 190, 191, 207, 208 n. 109
2: 5	179, 190
2: 6	123, 133, 153 n. 84, 191, 207–8
2: 7	123, 133, 153 n. 84, 190, 191, 192, 202, 207–8, 208 n. 109
2: 8	179
2: 9	179
2: 10	179, 217
2: 11–12	217
2: 11	179, 199, 217
2: 13	179, 192, 217
2: 14–17	217
2: 14	179, 191, 198, 212, 213
2: 15–16	191
2: 15	179, 192, 200
2: 16	191, 192
2: 17	190, 191, 202
2: 18–19	217–18
2: 18	179, 218
2: 19	176, 217
2: 20–2	179, 201
2: 20	123, 132, 176, 195, 207, 208 n. 109, 219
2: 21	199, 208 n. 109
2: 22	153 n. 84, 190, 191, 202, 209, 218–19
3	181, 183–4
3: 1–21	183
3: 19–39	183
3: 22–9	225
3: 22–39	183
3: 32	204
3: 40–7	183
3: 48–66	183
3: 48	179
4	192–4, 221–2, 232
4: 1–2	193
4: 1	200
4: 2	200
4: 3	179
4: 5	193, 199, 200
4: 6	179, 194, 198, 212
4: 7–8	200
4: 7	193, 199
4: 8	193–4
4: 10	179, 200
4: 11–12	194, 202
4: 11	192, 193, 209
4: 12	193
4: 13–14	200
4: 13	194, 198, 211, 212, 213
4: 14	194
4: 15	194, 200, 212 n. 123

Index of Biblical References

4: 16	179, 192, 209	2: 64	43, 44
4: 18–20	193, 205	3: 1–6	133
4: 20	193, 200	3: 3	94 n. 76, 133
4: 21–2	193, 205–6	4: 2	133, 144
4: 22	179, 205–7, 212	5: 3	37 n. 34
5	181, 194–6, 203–5, 221–2, 232	5: 6	37 n. 34
		5: 14	37
5: 1–18	203, 207, 212	6: 3	133
5: 1	195, 219	6: 6	37 n. 34
5: 2–6	195	6: 13	37 n. 34
5: 2	179	9: 15	189 n. 64
5: 7	195–6, 198, 212, 213		
		Nehemiah	
5: 8–15	195	3: 7	47
5: 8	195	5: 14–16	64
5: 9	195	7	44
5: 11	179, 195	7: 66	43, 44
5: 12	34 n. 22, 195	9	145–6, 233
5: 13	195	10: 19	86 n. 38
5: 14–16	200		
5: 16	196, 198, 212	**1 Chronicles**	
5: 17–18	195	7: 8	86 n. 38
5: 18	207, 209	8: 24	86 n. 38
5: 19–22	196, 203–4	28: 2	208 n. 111
5: 19	196, 204, 205, 207, 209, 224–5, 226	**2 Chronicles**	
		2: 2	195 n. 81
5: 20–2	196, 204, 207, 209	12: 6	189 n. 64
5: 21	204, 205	14: 2 (ET 3)	86 n. 36
5: 22	204, 207, 210	15: 16	86 n. 36, 88 n. 47
		17: 6	86 n. 36
Esther		19: 3	86 n. 36
2: 14	204	24: 18	86 n. 36
		31: 1	86 n. 36
Daniel		33: 3	86 n. 36
1–12	27–8	33: 6	99
4: 34	90	33: 7	92
9: 14	189 n. 64	33: 15	92
11: 37	115	33: 19	86 n. 36
		34: 3	86 n. 36
Ezra		34: 4	86 n. 36
1–6	25, 31	34: 7	86 n. 36
1: 2	90	36: 20–1	8, 13
1: 8	63–4		
2	44		

Subject Index

Adad-Guppi (mother of Nabonidus) 57, 124
Ahab 106
Ammon 4, 31, 34
Anat 86, 86 n. 38
Anat-Bethel 89
Anat-Yahu 89
Arvad 56
Ashdod 45, 56, 64, 66
Asherah 83, 86, 86 n. 36, 88, 89–90, 91, 92, 95, 99, 109
Ashkelon 45, 64
Ashratum 90
Ashtoret(roth) 86, 86 n. 37, 95
Assyria 48, 49–51, 66
Athirat 89–90
Azekah 30
Azor 41

Baal 95, 106–9, 115
Babylon(ia) 48, 51–2, 60, 61, 64, 67
  Judahite community in 4, 32, 129; see also *Golah*
  personification of 138, 139, 193 n. 75
Babylonian Chronicles 29 n. 10, 29 n. 11, 52, 54
  fifth Chronicle 57
  sixth Chronicle 65
  references to 29 n. 10, 52 n. 92, 52 n. 96, 52 n. 97, 53 n. 98
Babylonian gap, discussions of 38–9
Benjamin, region of 39 n. 39, 40–1, 42, 45, 46, 47, 70, 134, 144 n. 53

bêt marzēaḥ 112–13
Beth-Shemesh 40, 41
Bethel 41, 45, 46, 134, 134–5, 136, 231
  temple 131, 133–44
Bethlehem 42
biblical historiography 24–6
  gap therein 31–3
Byblos 56

Cambyses 68–9
Carchemish 52
child sacrifice 97–105, 106–9, 142–3
communal laments 144–7, 166–9, 197, 221
conceptions of idolatry, *see* idolatry, conceptions of
conceptions of worship, *see* worship, conceptions of
Court Calendar prism 56–57, 60, 64
covenant theology 167–8
cult of the dead 103–4, 118–19
Cyrus 2, 5, 15, 27, 29, 68–9, 123

Darius I 54, 69
Davidic covenant 2, 159–63
deportation 4, 20, 32
Deuteronomic ideology 152, 198, 203
Deuteronomistic History 11–12, 228, 232
disaster, religious response to 70–1, 72–3, 74

Subject Index

divine kingship 148, 155–6, 164, 196, 207–9, 224
Dur-Katlimmu 66

Ebabbar temple tablets 62–3
Edom 34, 193, 205–6
Egypt 48, 51–2, 62, 64, 66, 67, 68
  Judahite community in 4, 32, 84, 88–9, 129
Ekron 64
election 151–2, 232
Elephantine, temple 88–9, 124
Elijah 106
En-Gedi 40, 41
Etemenanki cylinder 60, 62–3, 64
exile 1–3
  reactions to 14, 72–4, 122–4, 234
  terminology for 4–5, 10–11
  see also Babylon(ia): Judahite community in; Egypt: Judahite community in
Ezekiel, depictions of Judahites remaining in Judah 214–16

fasts 127–9, 145
funeral dirge 185, 187, 199–200, 221–2
funerary inscription of Adad-Guppi (mother of Nabonidus) 57

Gad 110, 117
Gaza 56, 66
Gedaliah 25, 30–1, 32, 34, 35, 36, 37, 45, 60, 63, 68, 69, 70, 122–3, 126, 128, 129, 230
Gibeah (Tell el-Fûl) 41, 46
Gibeon (El-Jîb) 41, 46
Golah 6–7, 9–10, 16–17, 22, 44, 71, 73, 76, 81, 120–1, 145 n. 58, 148, 169, 227, 231, 233–5

heterodox religious practices:
  Deuteronomistic History 73
  Deutero-Isaiah 73
  Trito-Isaiah 74–80, 96, 98
  Jeremiah 73, 75–6
  Ezekiel 73, 75–6
  Zechariah 1–8 73–4
historical laments 148–9
historical reconstruction
  use of laments 26
  use of prophecy 26–7
history and myth combined, use in Psalms 158, 161–3, 164–6, 167–8, 232
Horvat Zimri (Pizgat Ze'ev 'D') 41
House of Yahweh 125–6, 130, 131, 134

idol worship 110, 110–14, 119–20
idolatry, conceptions of:
  Deuteronomistic History 73
  Deutero-Isaiah 73, 120
  Trito-Isaiah 74, 77, 96, 98
  Jeremiah 73, 76, 98, 109
  Ezekiel 73, 76, 98, 109, 120
  Zechariah 1–8 73
incubation 118–19
individual lament 163–4
Ishtar 86, 86 n. 39

Jehoahaz 51
Jehoiachin 25, 29, 31, 173
Jehoiakim 51, 52
Jeremiah, final form 15–16, 20–1
Jericho 40
Jerusalem 123, 136, 139–40
  fall of 29–31, 40, 41–2, 46–7, 53
  personification of 99, 102, 137–8, 139, 141, 142, 179, 193 n. 75, 199, 200–1

Jerusalem (cont.)
  temple 123, 124, 130, 131–3, 134, 143, 231
  Temple Mount 137, 138–9, 140, 141–3, 207–9
Jeshua 133
Jezebel 106
Josiah 52, 116
  successors to 75
Josianic reforms 75, 93, 144
Judaean hill country 39 n. 39, 40, 42, 46
Judaean or Judahite Pillar Figurines 81–3, 85, 96, 231
Judah 66, 67, 69–70
  annexation to Samaria 68
  history and archaeology 24–71, 229–31
  Judahites remaining in 214–16, 171, 177
  Neo-Babylonian; *see* Neo-Baylonian Judah
  Templeless period 5-6, 234–5; *for other aspects of the period see specific topics*, e.g., Bethel, Psalms

Khirbet el-Qôm inscription 89
Khirbet el-Ras 41
Khirbet Tubeiqah 46
Kuntillet 'Ajrud inscription 89

Lachish 30, 40
  ostraca 29 n. 12
Lamentations 26, 144–5
  chapter 3 183–4, 220
  composition 181–2; location of 182–3
  date 177–81
  form 220–22, 225–26
  Judahite specific themes 197–228

overview 184–97
laments, *see* communal laments; historical laments; individual lament; Mesopotamian City Laments; Psalms
Lebanon 56, 64
Letter of Adon 51, 55

Manasseh 92, 92–3, 106, 116
Mattaniah-Zedekiah, *see* Zedekiah
Meni 110, 117
Mesopotamian City Laments 26, 125, 174–5, 180–1, 182–3, 201–2, 210, 211, 222–3
Mizpah (Tell en-Nasbeh) 31, 33–4, 41, 42, 45, 47, 53, 66, 67, 68, 123, 134, 136, 144, 230
  temple 131, 134
Moab 4
Molek 101, 103, 104, 105, 143
  conflation with Baal 106–9
mourning:
  public 126–9, 182
  spontaneous observance 125–6
Mozah 41, 46
mulk sacrifice 103 n. 100, 105
myth, use in Psalms 149, 154–6, 158, 167–8, 232
myth and history combined, use in Psalms 158, 161–3, 164–6, 167–8, 232
myth of the empty land 7–10

Nabonidus 57, 58, 59, 61
Nabopolassar 57, 59, 61
Nebuchadnezzar 29, 52, 53, 54, 55–6, 57, 58, 62, 64, 67, 68, 69, 123
necromancy 118–19
Negev 39 n. 39
Nehemiah (as governor) 47

Subject Index

Neo-Babylonian Judah:
  biblical portrait 28–37
  discussion of 17–21, 33–6
  imperial administration of 48–70
  material culture 17–19, 37–48
Neriglissar 65–66
Nineveh 51 n. 85, 60, 61
  personification of 193 n. 75

overland trade 62, 65, 70

'the people of Judah' 35
'the people of the land' 35, 70, 230
Persia 49, 69 n. 166
Philistia 34, 56, 58, 60, 64
  cities 67
Phoenicia 34, 56, 60
popular religion 74, 119
population numbers 20, 42–4
priests 1, 2, 123, 129–30, 133, 144, 211
Psalms:
  communal laments 144–7, 166–9, 197, 221
  individual lament 163–4
  theological motifs 149–66
  use of historical traditions 149, 154–5, 157–8, 167–8, 232
  use of history and myth combined 158, 161–3, 164–6, 167–8, 232
  use of myth 149, 154–6, 158, 167–8, 232

Queen of Heaven 74 n. 6, 75, 83–90, 93, 94 n. 76, 115

Rahab 161
Ramat Rahel 40, 41

Regem Melek 134
religious response to disaster 70–1, 72–3, 74
remnant 8–9, 13

Samaria 68
  personification of 99
Sar-ezer 134
Sargon II 50 n. 84
scribes/scribal class 36, 70, 230
Sennacherib 158 n. 102
Seraiah 123
Shalmenessar V 50 n. 84
Shephelah 40
Sheshbazzar 37, 63–4
Shiloh 131–2, 134, 141
Sidon 56
Sodom 194
statue of jealousy 83, 91–3
Sumerian city laments, *see* Mesopotamian City Laments
sun worship 110, 114–15, 115–17
Syria 61, 62, 65

Tammuz 110, 114
Tekoa 47 n. 73
Tel Batash-Timnah 64
Tell Beit Mirsim 40
Tell Negilah 41
Tell Tubeiqah (Beth Zur) 47 n. 73
temple 124
  Bethel 131, 133–44, 142
  Elephantine 88–9, 124
  Jerusalem 123, 124, 130, 131–3, 134, 143, 231
  Mizpah 131, 134
temple ideology 124–5
theo-diabole 212
Tiglath-pileser III 49–50, 53
Topheth 106–7, 108

trade, overland 62, 65, 70
Tyre 56, 58, 62

Valley of Hinnom 107

Wadi-Brisa inscription 55–6, 64
woman in the Epha 83, 91, 93–5
worship, conceptions of:
   Deuteronomistic History 173
   Deutero-Isaiah 173
   Ezekiel 172–3
   see also Yahwistic worship

Yahweh, House of 125–6, 131, 134
Yahwistic worhip 122–70

Zedekiah (Mattaniah-Zedekiah) 29–30
Zephaniah 123
Zerubbabel 37, 63, 133
Zion theology 1–2, 125, 151–2, 164, 167, 198, 203, 232